A MOST INGENIOUS PARADOX

A MOST INGENIOUS PARADOX

The Art of Gilbert & Sullivan

Gayden Wren

OXFORD

UNIVERSITY PRESS

2001

OXFORD
UNIVERSITY PRESS

Oxford   New York
Athens   Auckland   Bangkok   Bogotá   Buenos Aires   Cape Town
Chennai   Dar es Salaam   Delhi   Florence   Hong Kong   Istanbul   Karachi
Kolkata   Kuala Lumpur   Madrid   Melbourne   Mexico City   Mumbai   Nairobi
Paris   São Paulo   Shanghai   Singapore   Taipei   Tokyo   Toronto   Warsaw

and associated companies in
Berlin   Ibadan

Published by Oxford University Press, Inc.,
198 Madison Avenue, New York, New York 10016

Oxford is a registered trademark of Oxford University Press.

Library of Congress Cataloging-in-Publication Data
Wren, Gayden, 1961–
A most ingenious paradox : the art of Gilbert and Sullivan / Gayden Wren.
p. cm.
Includes bibliographical references and index.
ISBN 0-19-514514-3
1. Gilbert, W. S. (William Schwenck), 1836–1911—Criticism and interpretation.
2. Sullivan, Arthur, Sir, 1842–1900. Operas.   I. Title.
ML410.S95 W76 2001
782.1'2'092—dc21   2001021713

1 3 5 7 9 8 6 4 2

Printed in the United States of America
on acid-free paper

DEDICATION

Many people have contributed to the creation of this book, and it could be argued that there are many others who have made this book what it is, from my family and friends to my theatrical collaborators and many others; without each of them, it would have been different and probably worse.

Nonetheless, this one's for Stephanie M. Muntone, without whose decade-plus of prodding, probing, questioning, and challenging it might well never have been finished at all.

Preface

How to Use This Book

I hope this book will be useful to a wide variety of readers, from hardcore Gilbert & Sullivan aficionados to performers and directors looking for insights into a particular show—not to mention devotees of musical theater, more casual Gilbert & Sullivan fans, and anyone else.

Accordingly, I've attempted to organize the book in such a way that each of these constituencies will be able to find what they're looking for in it.

To begin with, the chapters themselves assume basic familiarity with the story and characters of the opera in question—plot information seemed to be cluttering up the chapters unnecessarily, and I decided it was fair to assume in most cases that a reader wouldn't be reading a chapter about an opera that he or she hadn't seen, heard, or at least read.

However, my first appendix consists of plot summaries of all 14 Gilbert & Sullivan operas; anyone reading a chapter on an unfamiliar opera should start with the appendix so as to have the basic information necessary to make sense of the chapter.

Similar considerations led me to provide a detailed examination of the post-opening revisions of *Ruddigore* in the second appendix, rather than in chapter 12, where it might otherwise belong. Again, it will help to read the appendix before tackling the chapter itself.

On numerous occasions, I discuss Gilbert's use of rhyme schemes in the overall context of his work. Several different formats are conventionally used for such material. I have chosen the A/B format, as being the clearest—if occasionally the most initially intimidating—of the lot.

In this scheme, the final sound in the last syllable of each line is awarded a letter—the first one A, the second B, and so forth. If, however, a line rhymes with a preceding one, the same letter is used.

Thus, the familiar "Twinkle, Twinkle Little Star" would be an AABB song, with "star" rhymes tagged A and "high" rhymes B:

"Twinkle, twinkle, little *star*   (A)
how I wonder what you *are,*   (A)
   Up above the world so *high,*   (B)
   like a diamond in the *sky.*   (B)

On the other hand, "A Wandering Minstrel I" is an ABBA song:

"A wandering minstrel *I,*   (A)
   a thing of shreds and *patches,*   (B)
   of ballads, songs and *snatches,* (B)
and dreamy lulla*by*   (A)

I hope this won't unduly confuse fans of the famous Swedish rock band Abba. . . .

I've put extra effort into making my index detailed and, I hope, helpful to the reader who's primarily interested in a particular show, character, or subject. I hope it will let readers find what they want, whether they're browsing it for useful tidbits or trying to find a passage they read previously.

By the same token, the bibliography includes brief critical appraisals of each work. I've always been annoyed to see a book listed in a bibliography and not know whether the author thinks I should read it—or if, perhaps, he or she found it ghastly and not at all helpful.

Last, in deference to readers who may not read the entire book, I've tried to make each chapter, if not a self-contained entity, at least a coherent unit in its own right. Inevitably, this involves occasionally repeating information, if not word for word at least in its general shape. I've tried to keep this to a minimum, though, and I hope the beginning-to-end reader won't find it unduly annoying.

Garden City, New York   G. W.
June 1999

Acknowledgments

Before we get underway, a few words of thanks are appropriate. There could be hundreds, but in an effort to be concise, I'll group it into three categories:

My first encounters with Gilbert & Sullivan were as an audience member and as a performer, and I still think the operas are best appreciated in performance. As a Gilbert & Sullivan performer and director, my primary homes have been the Gilbert & Sullivan Light Opera Company of Long Island and the Gilbert & Sullivan Players of Oberlin College. My thanks to both groups, and especially to Sally Buckstone, Phil Gellis, Stephen O'Leary, and Raymond J. Osnato on Long Island, and to Christopher P. Ertelt, Suzanne Fatta, Alison Gent, Peter Gibeau, Sara Elizabeth Holliday, Jeffrey C. Mead, Kathy Anne Powell, and Bill Stevens in Oberlin.

The roots of this book lie in a course on Gilbert & Sullivan taught at Oberlin in 1982–83, and many of my ideas originated in comments, questions, or objections raised by my students there. My thanks, especially, to Monica Gfoeller, Vance Lehmkuhl, Paul V. Patanella, and Kara Sherwood.

And, finally, I owe a special note of thanks to those who have read the book's various chapters and protochapters since 1984, offering everything from heartening praise to savage criticism. There may be others I've forgotten, and if so I apologize; but my particular thanks to Sally Ann Denmead, Christopher P. Ertelt, Sara Elizabeth Holliday, Janette Kennedy, Daniel Kravetz, Vance Lehmkuhl, Ralph MacPhail Jr., the late Jerry March, Stephanie M. Muntone, and Raymond J. Osnato. At a late date, Steven Lichtenstein, Louis Silverstein, and Mike Storie provided useful attributional help.

Special thanks are also due to John Wright, a Gilbert & Sullivan fan and book industry professional who gave me a gratis tutorial on the workings of the book business; without his advice and counsel the book might never have seen print. Maribeth Anderson Payne, music editor at Oxford University Press, also deserves a round of applause for shepherding the project from manuscript through completion, as do Ellen Welch and Bob Milks.

The book is much the richer for the various people who helped me acquire the illustrations and the rights to reprint them. Most of all, I am indebted to the staff of The Pierpont Morgan Library in New York: curators Frederic Woodbridge Wilson and Rigby Turner, the endlessly patient staff of the Reading Room and the Photography & Rights department, including Marilyn Palmeri, Despina Coutavas, and Joseph Vehavi.

I am also grateful to A. Ahmed, Victor Bristoll, and The British Library; Ralph MacPhail Jr. and The MacPhail Collection; Cathy Haill and the Theatre Museum of the Victoria & Albert Museum; and Cristina Mancini, Thomas Meissnest, and Universal Pictures. An unexpectedly imposed last-minute fee prevented my using any material from the D'Oyly Carte Archive, but Mary Gilhooly's work is still much appreciated.

Four of today's finest musical-theater artists were kind enough to allow me to quote from their work without fee: I am very grateful to Jerry Bock, Sheldon Harnick, Stephen Schwartz (and Hope Taylor, from his office), and Stephen Sondheim (and David C. Olsen of Warner Bros. Publications).

Contents

A MOST INGENIOUS PARADOX

Introduction

The question is, why?

Any proper book should answer at least one question. This is true of novels and nonfiction in general, but it's especially true of books about other books. They should tell us something we didn't already know—otherwise, why read them? And the easiest way to do that is to answer a question.

In my case, the question is: "What is it with Gilbert & Sullivan?" Or, in longer form, "Why is it that, more than a century after their last collaboration, Gilbert & Sullivan remain a vital part of theatrical life wherever English is spoken?"

That this is so can hardly be denied. I personally know of at least 200 groups that perform exclusively or primarily the works of Gilbert & Sullivan, scattered throughout the United States, Canada, England, Australia, South Africa, even the Caribbean. This is remarkable; only one other body of theatrical works anywhere in the English-speaking world can claim such universal popularity, and that is the plays of Shakespeare.

Further, Gilbert & Sullivan attracts a particular sort of enthusiasm that borders on zealotry. More than 125 years after they first collaborated, the world is full of people who delight in arcane trivia about the men and their works. Besides the performing companies, there are groups of Savoyards who assemble to discuss the operas, publications galore about them, and more.

This is quite astonishing, if you think about it. Gilbert & Sullivan's prime period was in the 1880s, well over a century ago. No other English-language plays from that period are regularly performed, and little more than a handful of novels, songs, or other works are current for anyone but scholars. The 1930s, much closer to us, produced no significant English-language theater works that retain popularity.

Gilbert & Sullivan, on the other hand, are more popular now than they were at their creation. During the 1980s, *The Pirates of Penzance* was a Broadway smash all over again, running for longer than it had originally in London and New York combined, and reaching millions more people. Even works that were relative failures at the time, such as *Princess Ida* and

3

Ruddigore, are acknowledged classics. Movie and television adaptations of the operas have made them accessible to more people on a single night than viewed even *The Mikado* in its entire original run.

What has made these works so astonishingly durable and so lastingly popular? Some people attribute this longevity to Sullivan's music, which is certainly remarkable. Others praise the cleverness of Gilbert's lyrics. Still others cite the team's singular fusion of words and music.

Personally, I don't find any of these explanations persuasive. Listening to operas of the day and later, one can find many composers who shared Sullivan's gift for melody, from Offenbach through Rudolph Friml, many of whom excelled him in orchestration, harmonic ingenuity, and sheer musical originality.

As for Gilbert's lyrics, they are indeed clever. But the Victorians were a clever bunch, and many lyricists from his day and later can match Gilbert for tripping rhythms, intricate rhyming, and the like. And, let's face it, while Gilbert's humor is less dated than that of most of his contemporaries, it has lost some of its zip over the years. On many occasions I've heard an average Neil Simon play draw more laughs than *The Mikado.*

Even the remarkable artistic fusion that marks Gilbert & Sullivan's songs can't account for their success. The same creative symbiosis can be seen in the songs of George and Ira Gershwin or of Richard Rodgers and Lorenz Hart; but despite their being closer to us in time, hence more accessible, the Gershwin and Rodgers & Hart shows have not survived. Their songs have, of course, in concert performances, recordings, and pastiche shows; and if it were merely the simpatico of composer and lyricist that made Gilbert & Sullivan unique, one would expect their works to survive primarily in these forms.

But this is not the case. Unlike most works of George M. Cohan, Irving Berlin, the Gershwins, Jerome Kern, Noel Coward, Ivor Novello, Rodgers & Hart, Cole Porter, and the like, Gilbert & Sullivan opera survives essentially in its original form—as musical theater.

The answer, I think, therefore lies in their works *as theater.* Beneath the surface charm of the Savoy operas, I believe, lies a powerful thematic core that makes their works effective to this day.

Despite the wit of the operas, their thematic substance is generally not comic. In fact, in nearly all of the operas, the most effective points are serious moments as often as funny ones. The operas are at bottom a series of powerful, very human stories whose themes are as universal as their parody and satire are dated, and it is this fact that I think accounts for the operas' longevity. In this book, I hope to explore those themes and present a coherent argument for my premise that these are, for the most part, serious works, not musical comedies but comedies in the Shakespearean sense.

My focus therefore is only incidentally on Gilbert as a lyricist or Sullivan as a composer. I explore these areas, but only to the extent that they reflect on the thematic considerations I regard as central; technical analysis is kept to a minimum.

To a considerable extent, I treat Gilbert & Sullivan as if they were a single playwright, because in certain key areas they are. To read Gilbert's works without Sullivan or to listen to Sullivan's works with other librettists is to see how much each brought to the other's work. Thus, throughout this book, I refer to "Gilbert & Sullivan" when treating them as a collective author and "Gilbert and Sullivan" when referring to them as individuals.

In particular, Sullivan was intimately involved in developing the stories and characterizations of the operas, before a word or a note was set onto a page. Since I hold the stories and characterizations to be the key aspects of the operas, I consider Sullivan to be in certain respects as much their creator as Gilbert. It is no coincidence that the partnership's peak period began when Sullivan became directly involved in shaping the stories or that it ended when he retreated from that field.

Three final notes, on side issues. First, on what one of my readers has called "the intentionality issue." My readings of the operas rely heavily on connections between imagery, characterization, and thematic content. I see the operas as strongly integrated works, with the various elements coming together in a remarkable synthesis.

The question then arises: "Are you saying that Gilbert & Sullivan *meant* to do this?" Noting flower imagery running throughout *Ruddigore*, and specifically relating on several occasions to gender-role questions and matters of morality, am I arguing that Gilbert consciously deploys flower imagery in a concerted effort to write a play about this subject?

Where Gilbert is concerned, my answer is no. His creative process has been meticulously documented, drawing in particular on his plot books, and it seems unlikely that so detail-oriented a man would have failed to sketch out these structures in advance if he had been fully aware of them.

In Sullivan's case, the answer is probably yes. A great admirer of Wagner's leitmotif technique, he clearly intended his mature operas to be more than mere collections of songs. With his exhaustive musical training, it is almost certain that when he reuses a musical theme or harmonic progression, he is doing so specifically to link the song with a previous number.

In a larger sense, however, my answer is: "It doesn't matter," any more than do similar questions about Shakespeare. In both cases, the facts are the same: What's there is there, and it affects audiences in ways that are the same whether the author consciously put it in or did so subconsciously or even if it got there entirely coincidentally. In any event, the richness of Shakespeare is what makes his works endure, and the same is true of Gilbert & Sullivan.

I will try to demonstrate what is there and how it functions, and leave to others the question of how it got there.

Second, I must note that I am a Gilbert & Sullivan director, and my understanding of the operas has arisen, in large part, through my experiences directing the shows.

I hope, however, that the subjective, interpretive art of directing has not crept into my attempt at objective, descriptive analysis. To me, the job of the analyst is to describe the building as we find it, from its foundations to its decorative trim; the job of the director is to furnish the building in order to make it habitable by a particular cast, audience, and so on.

If I have done my job, my directing will be informed by the analytic work that has gone into the book, but none of my elaboration in the directing process will have found its way back into the book.

If I haven't done my job, I'm sure there will be plenty of people to let me know!

Which leaves us with the book, which hopefully will provide an answer to the question raised earlier. Not *the* answer, of course—great works are notoriously hard to definitively explain—but an answer.

Ultimately, of course, the works themselves are the answer—which was my response to an early reader who said, in comment on a chapter, that I had "taken all the fun out of Gilbert & Sullivan."

Nonsense, I said. These would be pretty pallid works if one critic—right, wrong, or otherwise—could knock the fun out of them. The operas are as much fun now as they ever were, and no matter how many people write books about them, they'll stay that way.

My greatest hope, naturally, is that my book will offer people a new way of seeing the operas, both those they know and those they don't—and that they'll take that new way and go to see the operas!

Facing page: FIGURE 1.1. W. S. Gilbert at around 40. Gilbert was a tall man whose scowling brows, massive forehead and commanding demeanor helped enforce the rigorous discipline he demanded as a pioneering stage director. *Source: The Pierpont Morgan Library, Gilbert and Sullivan Collection.*

1

Gilbert before Sullivan

When Gilbert and Sullivan collaborated for the first time in 1871, it was by no means apparent that Gilbert's destiny lay in opera, or in collaboration with Sullivan. There were, however, important signs pointing in that direction.

At 35, Gilbert was widely respected, but he was only one of a number of prominent dramatists of his day. He was, in fact, as well known for his skills as a director—or, as the British called it, a producer or stage manager—as for his writing. And as a writer, though he had scored several substantial hits on the stage, he was still at least as well known as the author of *The Bab Ballads*.

It is thus no surprise that *Thespis* and, most often, the pair's first five collaborations usually were billed as the work of "Sullivan & Gilbert." While Gilbert's temperament and working methods ensured that he would be the dominant personality from the start, in the eyes of the public Sullivan was the bigger name—as indeed the composer customarily was in any operatic collaboration.

William Schwenck Gilbert was born in London on November 18, 1836. His father, William Gilbert, was a former naval surgeon who, after retiring upon receiving a large inheritance, was subsequently to embark on a career as a novelist and essayist.

The future dramatist's early life was marked by a series of tentative career moves—government service, law, journalism. Only at journalism did he achieve any success, most notably in his work for *Fun*, which today is most notable for the *Bab Ballads* but included a stream of short stories, reviews, essays, and incidental pieces. By the late 1860s, however, the *Bab Ballads* had emerged from the (frequently anonymous) mix of *Fun* staples to make Gilbert's name, and had he desired he might easily have continued as a comic journalist for the rest of his life.

He did not so desire, however. By the time Bab made his presence felt, Gilbert was already drawn to the theater. Indeed, a famous anecdote from his youth has him running away from school at age 15 and attempting to gain admission to the company of the famous actor Charles Kean,[1] though it should be noted that most of Gilbert's anecdotes have a smack of the apocryphal about them.

Nevertheless, he was a regular London theatergoer by the early 1860s, both as a reviewer and out of personal interest. He also traveled frequently to France, where he made it his business to hear the operettas of Offenbach, who remained a lifelong favorite.

Gilbert's reviews from this period reveal the already emerging ideas that were to drive his own theatrical career: an emphasis on professionalism in presentation, a dislike of incoherent plots, and a firm conviction that most of the librettists of the day were inept.

In 1867, for example, he reviewed *Cox and Box*, the first operatic work by the young Arthur Sullivan. Writing in *Fun*, he was generally complimentary toward the composer, but took a dimmer view of librettist F. C. Burnand:

"Mr. Sullivan's music is, in many places, of too high a class for the grotesquely absurd plot to which it is wedded," he wrote. "It is very funny, here and there, and grand or graceful when it is not funny; but the grand and the graceful have, we think, too large a share of the honors to themselves."[2]

Gilbert's illustrations for *Fun* and especially those for the *Bab Ballads* also foreshadowed his future path. While the *Ballads* themselves are often cited as forerunners of the Savoy operas, and indeed engendered a number of Savoy plots, the illustrations are more evocative of his theatrical style to come: Painstakingly detailed, with meticulous attention to physical attitude and to details of costume and props—every button just so, hats, gloves, belts, and footwear intricately rendered—they are at once wildly implausible in content and excruciatingly realistic in form, as Gilbert's plays would be in years to come.

From the day he began working at *Fun* in 1861, Gilbert was on the fringes of the theatrical world. In those days, comic journalism had at least one foot on the stage, in the loosely knit comic genre known as burlesque. The most successful comic journalists also wrote burlesques, while the most successful burlesque playwrights also wrote for the comic papers.

Burlesque was not to be confused with legitimate theater. Its extravagant plots, generally parodies of popular operas or plays, were joined with a pathological love of punning to produce an art form that was half performer showcase, half joke collection. Indeed, its sensibility was so close to that of the comic journals that Gilbert occasionally took a rejected burlesque and published it in a comic paper.

The "*Fun* Gang" included many active burlesque writers—the paper's first editor, H. J. Byron, among them—and chances are that some of Gilbert's jokes found their way, uncredited, into burlesques as early as 1861 or 1862. His first play, the short "comedietta" *Uncle Baby*, scored only a modest success in 1863, and it was not until 1866 that his stage career really got underway, with his first staged burlesque, *Dulcamara*. (He had been writing burlesques without success at least since 1860.)

Like such successors as *La Vivandiere* (1868), *The Merry Zingara* (1868), and *Robert the Devil* (1868), *Dulcamara* doesn't seem especially Gilbertian today. All they really show is that Gilbert could parody opera and melodrama as well as his peers and that he could wring out a pun with the best of them.

However questionable their intrinsic merit, though, these plays are important for having established Gilbert's name in theatrical circles and for having intrigued him with the financial rewards of writing for the stage. After 1866, Gilbert would average four or more plays annually for the next five years, culminating in 1871, when *Thespis* would be the last of seven works he would premiere.

More relevant to Gilbert's future were the six musical works he wrote for Thomas German Reed's Royal Gallery of Illustration—*No Cards* (1869), *Ages Ago* (1869), *Our Island Home* (1870), *A Sensation Novel* (1871), *Happy Arcadia* (1873), and *Eyes and No Eyes* (1875). Operettas in miniature (Reed's tiny stage allowed for casts of four or five at most), their relatively sophisticated lyrics show Gilbert beginning to emerge as a lyricist. He had written numerous song lyrics previously, but almost always to preexisting tunes lifted from operatic or other sources; the Reed pieces were the first he had written in his own rhythms and on his own subject matter.

This was to be a key to his future career, because while Gilbert was a master of rhyme and often displayed felicity at lyrical expression, his greatest gift as a lyricist was his rhythmic flair. A boon to every composer who worked with him, it was particularly appreciated by Sullivan.

"Have you noticed what an extraordinary polish there is to his versification?" the composer said in an 1885 interview. "There is never a weak syllable or a halting foot. It is marvelous. He has a wonderful gift, too, of making rhythms, and it bothers me to death sometimes to make corresponding rhythms in music."[3]

In addition to establishing him in a more respectable area of theater— *Ages Ago*, with music by Frederic Clay, was his greatest success to date— the Reed shows also offered Gilbert the chance to write for skilled performers and to see and hear his work performed in close to optimal conditions.

Burlesque performers varied widely in talent—some of its best-loved stars were women whose appeal lay mainly in their lovely legs—and were allowed to mangle the author's work in practically any way they liked, in search of laughs or simply more attention to themselves. Reed's shows were authorially based, however, in the sense that they were performed according to the original script and score and utilized performers (Reed, his wife, and later their son among them) who had the talent and the rehearsal time to do justice to their work.

Finally, as Jane W. Stedman has observed,[4] the Reed shows lacked the elaborate scenery and special effects that were so much a part of burlesque—their narrow stage could accommodate no aquatic ballets, no descents into hellfire, no shipwrecks crashing onto rocks. The play was paramount, if only by default, and the writing was not only allowed but required to be the center of attention.

The Princess (1870) represented an outgrowth of that experience. While musically its setting of new lyrics to old tunes represented a step back,[5] its book was Gilbert's most ambitious to date, a cross between burlesque and more serious drama. Combining groaner puns with more self-consciously poetic speeches, it clearly shows Gilbert stretching himself as a playwright.

(Years later, it would be the source material for Gilbert & Sullivan's *Princess Ida.*)

Stedman, author of the definitive Gilbert biography, dates Gilbert's involvement in directing from the late 1860s, though often other men received credit for his work. Certainly, by the end of 1870 Gilbert's directorial style was well established, and in his authorial contracts he would demand full control of the stage management of nearly all of his future plays.

Gilbert was not a director in the sense the term is used today—an artist whose role is to interpret various authors' work and, with each play, shape the efforts of the various actors, designers, and others into a coherent whole.

Indeed, he doesn't seem to have perceived himself as filling two functions (except when it came time to be paid). To him, directing was a logical extension of authorship, a means of ensuring that recalcitrant producers, actors, or designers didn't ruin his ideas in execution. Once he had sufficient prestige to do so, he never allowed anyone else to direct his plays; but neither did he ever direct anyone else's. There would have been little point in doing so for a director whose entire approach was based on having written the play in question.

As a director, Gilbert's central concerns reflected his authorship. He was famously demanding of his actors when it came to diction—every syllable of his work had to be clearly audible from every seat in the house. He exercised rigorous control over the actors' stage business, rejecting nearly every interpolated "gag" or bit of business that was likely to draw attention to the actor over the material. There was no question that in a Gilbert play, everyone involved was subordinate to the play itself.

As late as *The Gondoliers* (1888), Gilbert still felt that this point needed to be made. In a letter to producer Richard D'Oyly Carte,[6] he complained strongly about Rutland Barrington's introducing "gags" into his role:

> The piece is, I think, quite good enough without the extraneous embellishments suggested by Mr. Barrington's brief fancy. Anyway it must be played *exactly as I wrote it.* I won't have an outside word introduced by anybody. If once a license in this direction is accorded it opens the door to any amount of tomfoolery. . . . I am determined to stamp out the nuisance. It is not enough that the departures are unimportant—there should—and shall—be no departures of any kind whatever.

Gilbert also controlled the production designs of his shows, frequently drawing on his artistic background to create at least the initial sketches for sets and costumes.

Even in his most fanciful plays, realism was the watchword. Gilbert was a disciple of the director/playwright T. W. Robertson (1829–71), whose moral dramas had been distinguished by meticulously realistic presentations, especially in terms of set design and stage business. Whereas previous designers, for example, would put as many chairs into a dining-room scene as there were actors who needed to sit down, Robertson would insist on as many chairs as would realistically be in that dining room, even if some were never actually used.

Gilbert freely acknowledged his debt to Robertson:

Why, he practically invented stage management. It was an unknown art before his time. Formerly, in a conversation scene for instance, you simply brought down two or three chairs from the flat and placed them in a row in the middle of the stage, and the people sat down and talked, and when the conversation was ended the chairs were replaced.

Robertson showed how to give life and variety and nature to the scene, by breaking it up with all sorts of little incidents and delicate by-play. I have been at many of his rehearsals, and learned a great deal from them.[7]

Gilbert's penchant for realism outpaced even Robertson's, if only because Robertson generally wrote "cup-and-saucer plays" utilizing prosaic modern, domestic settings—usually interiors, whereas Gilbert preferred exterior scenes—in which realism was unobtrusive for its very familiarity.

Gilbert, on the other hand, tended to set plays in fantastic settings, historical or otherwise, involving elaborate costumes, fanciful scenery, and an array of unusual weapons, furnishings, accessories, and decorative elements—all of which he insisted be as picture-perfect as his *Bab Ballads* illustrations.

This meticulousness extended to physical movement and the rendering of dialogue. With a strong rhythmic sense of his lines, Gilbert wanted them spoken a certain way, and while he might allow alternative readings if he liked them, he was determined to stamp out any errors of stress or pronunciation. He drilled his actors relentlessly in extended rehearsal periods and outside of rehearsals, coaching them again and again on how a given line should be uttered or how a particular walk or gesture should be performed.

For this reason he increasingly favored young actors, even novices. In his early days he allied himself with certain established actors—Madge and William H. Kendal and Marie Litton among them—whose styles he found compatible with his approach, but in later years he preferred to shape young performers. He said that this was because they had less bad practice to unlearn, but it may also have been because younger, less established performers were more willing to accept his domineering style.

This perfectionism also accounted for Gilbert's mixed reputation in the theatrical trade, where he was viewed simultaneously as a talented innovator and as a martinet extremely difficult to work with. An anonymous reviewer in the 1870s spoke for many when he wrote that Gilbert was personally unpopular, due to "a little want of temper and a great want of tact."[8]

Nevertheless, his work—and the success of that work—helped to bring about a reordering of the theatrical world, with authors and directors gaining power at the expense of producers and, especially, actors. With some justice, Hesketh Pearson could write in 1957: "His influence on stagecraft was so great that he may be called the father of modern play-production."[9]

1870 and 1871 saw Gilbert make the final leap that was to define his stage career. *The Palace of Truth* (1870), the first of his "fairy comedies," established him as a straight dramatist—it has substantial comic elements, of course, but it plays as drama in its own right, as opposed to the knock-about comedies he had previously written. Barely a year later *Pygmalion and Galatea* (1871) scored his greatest hit outside of his collaboration with Sullivan.

Together, these plays—and successors such as *The Wicked World* (1873) and *Sweethearts* (1874)—did for Gilbert on the dramatic stage what the Reed shows had done for him on the musical stage: established that his capabilities extended far beyond the crass commercialism of burlesque, winning him both respectability and artistic credentials.

Though highly dated, many of these plays still have appeal today. They are of a different class entirely from his previous work, and they were essential to the Savoy operas in at least two ways. First, they gave Gilbert confidence in his dramatic skills—allowed him to dare to not be funny, in short. They established him in his eyes, the eyes of the profession, and the eyes of the public as a writer of wide range, one as comfortable with human drama as with farcical humor.

Second, these plays, especially *Pygmalion and Galatea*, gave him a prestige that he had not previously enjoyed, and that would be crucial to an on-going collaboration with so respected a musician as Sullivan. He might not be nearly as eminent in his profession as the composer was in his, but he had demonstrated that he could produce work on a comparable level.

The collaboration with Sullivan would allow him to combine the three strands of his authorial career—clever lyrics, humorous dialogue, and serious drama—with his state-of-the-art stagecraft to create a new context that would ultimately define both men for posterity.

2

Sullivan before Gilbert

When Gilbert and Sullivan collaborated for the first time in 1871, it was by no means apparent that Sullivan's destiny lay in opera, or in collaboration with Gilbert. There were, however, important signs pointing in that direction.

At 29, Sullivan was one of England's most prominent musicians, a respected conductor who was generally considered the nation's best composer as well. But his most popular compositions had been orchestral or choral works. He'd made three attempts at opera, and his only success had been the small-scale *Cox and Box* (1866), a hastily composed, hour-long, three-man work originally meant as a party entertainment.

Thus, while the musical public awaited *Thespis* with interest, there was no sense that Sullivan had found his musical niche or that Gilbert was to be any more important in the composer's career than any of his previous collaborators on songs, oratorios, or operas.

Arthur Sullivan was born in London on May 13, 1842, the son of a lower-middle-class instrumentalist and bandmaster. His musical talent was apparent early; he first earned admission to the prestigious Chapel Royal and then won the first Mendelssohn Scholarship at the Royal Academy of Music, which led to three years of study at the Leipzig Conservatory in Germany.

Sullivan came to Leipzig as a pianist and left it as a conductor. He was never to relinquish this new passion: Throughout his career with Gilbert he would sustain a second career as a conductor, associated most prominently with the Leeds Festival. He was a champion both of new music and of neglected older works during his seven terms as music director of that triennial festival from 1880 to 1898.

It was as a composer, however, that Sullivan first appeared before the English musical public. His incidental music for Shakespeare's *The Tempest*, composed as a student at Leipzig, was performed at London's Crystal Palace in 1862. It was a major success and made the 20-year-old composer famous. He would remain an eminent figure on the English musical scene for the next 38 years.

Sullivan spent the remainder of the 1860s primarily composing orchestral music, while he scrambled to make a living as a conductor, organist, teacher, and choirmaster.

Of his orchestral works, only the "Overtura di Ballo" (1870) is heard today with any frequency. Other major works included his First Symphony (1866) and the overtures "In Memoriam" (1866) and "Marmion" (1867).

From the early 1870s, he largely deserted orchestral works in favor of choral music, which was the easiest route to success for a classical musician. Seven years after his early cantata *Kenilworth* (1864), he presented his first oratorio, *The Prodigal Son* (1871). Its success led to *The Light of the World* (1873), *The Martyr of Antioch* (1880), and *The Golden Legend* (1886).

Sullivan's attraction to the theater had been evident early, however. It was his incidental music for *The Tempest* that won him his fame, and his lifelong attraction to Shakespeare (which had reportedly led him, at 15, to compose an overture for *Timon of Athens* in 1857)[1] would later lead to incidental music for *The Merchant of Venice* (1871), *The Merry Wives of Windsor* (1874), *Henry VIII* (1877), and *Macbeth* (1888). He scored a ballet, *L'Ile Enchantée*, in 1864, and even made a first attempt at writing an opera with *The Sapphire Necklace*, an unfinished opera of 1863–64.

Nor was Sullivan's love of the stage purely musical. By the early 1860s, he was already taking a professional perspective on how musical theater was and should be crafted, aided by a meeting with the great composer Gioachino Rossini, whom he met in 1862. In an 1895 interview with *The Strand* magazine, he said:

> I think that Rossini first inspired me with a love for the stage and things operatic, and this led to my undertaking the duties of organist at the Royal Italian Opera (London) under the conductorship of my friend Sir (then Signior) Michael Costa. At his request I wrote a ballet entitled *L'Ile Enchantée*, and my necessary interviews with the stage employees, dancers and others gave me much insight into the blending of music and stage management, which became very valuable to me as time progressed.[2]

From then on, Sullivan would be increasingly involved in nearly every aspect of the operas he set. While many composers focused simply on the quality of the lyrics and on technical musical questions, Sullivan was a true collaborator. His degree of interest can be judged from an 1887 diary entry, recounting Gilbert's presentation of a proposed new opera (the so-called lozenge plot, which was never set by Sullivan):

> At night Gilbert read me a scenario for proposed new piece. Clear, but I think very weak dramatically; there seems no "go" in it. The 1st Act promises to lead to something, but that something doesn't appear in the 2nd Act, which is the old story over again of whimsical fancies and subtle argument, but it is a "puppet-show," and not human. It is impossible to feel any sympathy with a single person. I don't see my way to setting it in its present form.[3]

Clearly, Sullivan's early interest in the nonmusical aspects of musical theater only grew in ensuing years.

The hour-long *Cox and Box*, with lyrics by the future *Punch* editor F. C. Burnand, was the first practical application of Sullivan's emerging theatrical gift.

Though its immediate successor, the full-length Sullivan/Burnand opera *The Contrabandista* (1867), was a failure, *Cox and Box* was easily Sullivan's most profitable musical venture to date, and he couldn't help but keep an eye open for similar opportunities in the future. The success of *Cox and Box* unquestionably influenced Sullivan's decision to agree to write *Thespis*.

In fact, the two men nearly collaborated the preceding year.[4] Thomas German Reed, whose Royal Gallery of Illustration had been the home of both *Cox and Box* and several early Gilbert operettas (including *Ages Ago* [1869], on whose set Gilbert and Sullivan were reportedly first introduced by composer Frederic Clay), tried to hire Sullivan to set Gilbert's operetta *Our Island Home* (1870). However, the composer's required fee was too high for the thrifty Reed, who ended up setting the piece himself.

From a modern viewpoint *Cox and Box* has many flaws in words and music alike, testifying to the efforts of theatrical novices in both departments. But it remains an engaging work of musical theater and is justly the earliest of Sullivan's works to remain in frequent performance today.

The composer's contributions by far excel the librettist's. The play's generally strong dialogue and amusing theatrical situation (two lodgers unknowingly sharing the same room, misled by a duplicitous landlord) are both taken almost intact from the source play, John Maddison Morton's *Box and Cox* (1847). (In light of Sullivan's later crusade for authorship rights, it is worth noting that, despite his complaints, Morton apparently never received a penny of the proceeds from *Cox and Box*, though he lived until 1891.)

Burnand's lyrics range from the clever to the inane, with a propensity for the strained rhymes common in English burlesque: A typical instance rhymes "Rosherville" with "squash I feel" and "Macintosh I will." Burnand later fancied himself Gilbert's rival as a lyricist, but *Cox and Box* offers little to support such pretensions.

But Sullivan's music displays many of the traits that would characterize his early works with Gilbert. He has a natural talent for melody, producing a beautiful tune even for a lullaby sung to a piece of bacon. Paired with this gift is a willingness to employ rhythmic and harmonic intricacies on a level considerably beyond contemporary theatrical practice, bringing the full range of his extensive training as a composer to bear on ensemble numbers in particular.

Just as important, Sullivan has an innate flair for the dramatic, as well as a musical sense of humor. The best moments of *Cox and Box* pair the two, as in Box's recounting of his own feigned suicide, which builds to a frenzied, melodramatic pitch in splendid mock-operatic fashion, only to cut into bouncy patter at the moment of near-death.

Most noticeably absent from *Cox and Box*, in light of Sullivan's later career, is any genuine emotion. As befits characters in a farce, Cox, Box,

and their retired-officer landlord are essentially puppets, farcical characters who veer from one tack to another without any consistency whatever.
In less than a minute, the two lodgers go from preparing for a duel to
embracing each other as long-lost brothers (based on the fact that neither
has a distinguishing birthmark!).

Still, it can justly be said that the Sullivan of 1871 was closer to the
Sullivan of 1886 (for example) than the Gilbert of 1871 was to his later
level. In both form and content, *Cox and Box* shows that as early as 1866
Sullivan had the makings of a fine operatic composer.

All he needed was time, motivation, and the right collaborator.

3

Thespis

No Gilbert & Sullivan opera is less familiar than *Thespis*, and for good reason. It was their first collaboration, its 80 performances made it their shortest-running work, and, from what we know of it, it is the least effective. To top it off, it comes down to us seriously incomplete.

Gilbert's words have apparently survived intact. (Terence Rees has argued[1] that the libretto as we know it represents a rough draft, but his case is not entirely persuasive, especially given Gilbert's general care to ensure that his work was printed accurately.)[1]

Sullivan's music has been lost, however, except for two numbers: "Little Maid of Arcady," a ballad popular enough to have been issued as sheet music, and the chorus "Climbing Over Rocky Mountain," later transplanted into *The Pirates of Penzance*. (Some of its ballet music has supposedly also been recovered, though I find the attribution a bit questionable.)

Because of this, any commentary on *Thespis* can be only provisional. Even assuming that Gilbert is accurately represented, the lack of the music is a crippling blow. It means that we can never see the "real" *Thespis* staged, which would be essential to fully appreciate what was very much a theatrical work. There have been numerous reconstructed/recomposed versions of *Thespis*, but they can be little more than speculative.

Accordingly, readers should insert "As far as we can tell" every paragraph or so in this chapter. I believe that enough of *Thespis* survives to yield some meaningful insights, but we can't be entirely sure.

Considering *Thespis* in the context of Gilbert & Sullivan opera, the most important point is that it isn't a Gilbert & Sullivan opera.

It is by W. S. Gilbert and Arthur Sullivan, of course, but they approached it much differently from the Savoy operas, and the results were therefore considerably different.

To begin with, *Thespis* wasn't produced by Richard D'Oyly Carte, as all of the subsequent operas would be, nor was it written for a standing company of performers trained in the "Gilbert & Sullivan style." One looks in vain for the "funny little man" role for George Grossmith, the "pompous ass" role for Rutland Barrington, and so on.

Instead, *Thespis* was written for John Hollingshead's Gaiety Theatre, a noted burlesque house that lacked the spit-and-polish professionalism and theatrical integrity that were to be Savoy trademarks. Instead of selecting their own performers, Gilbert & Sullivan were forced to tailor their work to the members of Hollingshead's existing company, which was particularly hard on Sullivan, given that (except for his brother Fred, in the small role of Apollo) these were comedians, not singers.

As Hollingshead himself remarked of the two stars of *Thespis*, "Neither Mr. J. L. Toole nor Miss Nelly Farren could be called 'singers' even in the most elastic English."[2]

As by now he always did, Gilbert directed his own play. But, according to Hollingshead, his demands for precision met considerable opposition from the less-disciplined Gaiety performers. Ultimately, reviewers reported, many of the actors were unprepared on opening night—not surprising, perhaps, given that the authors had only five weeks to write and rehearse the opera, a sharp contrast to the meticulous pace of the Savoy, where six months might easily be spent on the writing alone.

So there is a much different "feel" to *Thespis*, reflecting its unique context. Created under these conditions, even *The Mikado* would have been in many ways unlike Gilbert & Sullivan as we know it.

But *Thespis* is not *The Mikado*. It is the first Gilbert & Sullivan collaboration, and naturally finds them at their least assured. Even more than *The Sorcerer* or *H. M. S. Pinafore, Thespis* is a convention-bound show: The Gilbert and Sullivan who would reshape comic opera are still a decade away. Instead, *Thespis* shows the hands of two young men (35 and 29), still comparative novices to the operatic stage, who regularly fall back on conventional devices at the expense of theatrical imagination.

Nor are the conventions those used in the later operas. Being a Gaiety show, *Thespis* is grounded as much in the thoroughly English traditions of burlesque, extravaganza, and pantomime as in the conventions of European comic opera. The fusion of English burlesque and Offenbachian operetta produces a show whose governing aesthetic isn't what we expect from "Gilbert & Sullivan."

Unlike American burlesque, the black-sheep brother of vaudeville, English burlesque was often suggestive but seldom raunchy—at least where the lines themselves were concerned, though a leering delivery could speak volumes. And instead of the variety-show format used in America, English burlesque generally employed a loose narrative framework.

But it resembled its American cousin in being a showcase for performers, not writers. Actors and actresses drew the audiences, with authors, composers and directors occupying a subordinate role. Scripts and songs were routinely altered by and for performers, with outside material interpolated whenever an actor saw fit.

In the case of *Thespis*, Hollingshead already had under contract several popular comedians, and Gilbert & Sullivan were obliged to tailor their work to these performers. This was particularly true of Sullivan: One critic remarked approvingly that the composer had "not marred the effect by ambitious music"—a remark not heard at the Savoy in later years.[3]

The title role, for example, went to Toole, who according to Sullivan had a musical range of only two notes. We cannot tell what his showpiece song, "I Once Knew a Man Who Discharged a Function," sounded like—but Sullivan presumably denied himself the musical freedom he later took with more accomplished singers. (Toole also appeared in a three-act drama that opened an evening that totaled a bit over five hours long—

clearly, Victorian theatergoers had stronger constitutions than their modern-day descendants!)

Co-star Farren likewise never would have appeared at the Savoy. She apparently compensated for her lack of musical ability with deft comic timing—and with a very attractive pair of legs, which she was accustomed to display in the tights she wore when playing boy's roles. As Mercury, she presumably cut a comely figure but hardly a plausible one.

This is probably even more true of Mlle. Clary, who appeared in the "leading man" role of Sparkeion. The Sparkeion-Nicemis duet, "Here, Far Away from All the World," may seem reminiscent of future tenor-soprano duets such as "Were You Not to Ko-Ko Plighted" or "None Shall Part Us from Each Other," but it unquestionably sounded much different as a duet for two women.

These extraneous considerations affect nearly every aspect of *Thespis*, tainting whatever in it may reflect Gilbert & Sullivan's actual inspirations. For example, the prominence given to the drunkard Tipseion, whose plot importance is extremely minor, is hard to understand until one learns that Tipseion was played by Robert Soutar, who happened to be married to the star, Nelly Farren.

English pantomime is a tradition that continues to the present day. Drawing on Italian commedia del'arte, it is highly stylized, generally beginning with a fairly conventional play in which, at a magical moment, the characters are transformed into the prototypical pantomime characters Harlequin, Columbine, Pantaloon, and so forth. For the remainder of the show, these stock characters interact in the "harlequinade," a loose format allowing for ample improvisatory clowning by the performers.

Thespis is not itself a pantomime—the closest Gilbert & Sullivan came to writing one was *Trial by Jury*, which for many years the D'Oyly Carte Opera Company ended with a segue into a harlequinade. But pantomime is particularly associated with the Christmas season, and *Thespis*, premiering on December 26, reflects its influence.

This is most obvious in the play's use of improvisatory physical comedy. For example, the roles of Preposteros and Stupidas are all but incoherent on the page. One stage direction reads: "STUPIDAS endeavors, in pantomime, to reconcile him. Throughout the scene, PREPOSTEROS shows symptoms of breaking out into a furious passion, and STUPIDAS does all he can to pacify and restrain him."

While hardly helpful in staging the show, this direction reflects the show's theatrical context. Preposteros and Stupidas were played by the Payne brothers, popular comedians who presumably brought to this scene a great deal of "stage business" of their own, more or less extraneous to the story.

Such insertions of elaborate comic byplay were not unusual—Gilbert's short story "Maxwell and I" mentions, in passing, the difficulties two writers have with a comedian who insists on interpolating his trademark "bit," a climb over a wall studded with broken glass.

All of which is to say that *Thespis* was surely not on the stage what it is on the page—not because Gilbert made unrecorded revisions but because traditional practice encouraged ad-libbing and improvisation by the actors (which, of course, Gilbert detested). The occasional references in reviews to lines that don't appear in the published script, especially lines from Toole as Thespis, probably reflect ad-libbing rather than authorial revision.

Pantomime also often featured elaborate theatrical effects of the kind also seen in the theatrical form called extravaganza. Gilbert alludes to this in *Thespis*, when Jupiter hurls a lightning bolt and is answered with a cavalier "Ah, yes, it's very pretty, but we don't want any at present. When we do our Christmas piece, I'll let you know."

Thespis, of course, was a Christmas piece, and is far more theatrically extravagant than any of the later operas, even *The Sorcerer*. The opening chorus of stars is surely intended primarily for picturesque theatrical effect, while the liberal use of the fog machine evokes 1990s Broadway. The "Ballet Divertissement" that closes the opera was presumably on a grand scale, despite having no real dramatic purpose. Throughout, the script's detailing of tableaux and processions reveals a greater interest in stage effect than in theatrical consistency or dramatic power.

Overall, then, *Thespis* offers only the faintest opportunity to see the emerging Gilbert & Sullivan. Even if the music still existed, we would be seeing not their earliest ideas of comic opera but a version of those ideas heavily distorted by the expectations of the Gaiety audience.

In their later careers, Gilbert and Sullivan were both what modern slang would call "control freaks." They took their artistic work seriously and demanded control of every aspect of the production process. Many of their disagreements with each other centered on this need for control.

Their partnership with D'Oyly Carte gave them an unprecedentedly free hand to express their creative ideas. From *The Sorcerer* through *The Grand Duke*, it is fair to treat the operas, for better or worse, as faithful representations of Gilbert & Sullivan's ideas. Other than in compromises with the other, neither man was ever forced to yield his artistic intent because of financial considerations, censorship, opinions of the public, the producer or the performers, or any other reason. As a result, their works represent a purer manifestation of artistic purpose than practically any opera or play before or since.

This was not the case with *Thespis*. In fact, *Thespis* was a worst-case scenario, doubtless a strong incentive for their subsequent insistence on iron control. Thus we must be cautious in looking at *Thespis* for signs of their "state of the art" in 1871. Much of the show probably reflects necessity rather than choice, and much of what seems to be missing might have been there had they enjoyed greater control over the production.

Even so, *Thespis* deserves attention. However distorted, it is our first view of Gilbert & Sullivan, and if it shows little of where they were to go, it at least provides a starting point.

On Sullivan's contributions we can unfortunately say little. One of the surviving numbers, "Little Maid of Arcady," exists only in the 1872 simplified piano-vocal version, whose piano part is so simplistic that it is almost certain that Sullivan did not do the arrangement. What it sounded like in orchestrated form—and sung by a woman playing a man—we can only guess. From what we have, it seems to be an appealing little ballad of no great pretensions.

"Climbing Over Rocky Mountain" is the best sample we have, surviving more or less in Sullivan's own version—in fact, the original manuscript score of *The Pirates of Penzance* (now in the Morgan Library in New York) reveals that the composer literally pasted in the original *Thespis* pages for the early part of the number. The only mystery is the vocal range of the "four voices" who sang the solo verses. At least one was probably male, since the first half of the second verse, allotted to Kate in *Pirates*, lies awkwardly low for a woman.

"Rocky Mountain" is a good example of the early Sullivan's flair for elaborating on a fairly unimaginative lyric, in straight rhymed couplets (except for the introduction, which is in the marginally more inventive AABBCDDEEC). Through a sprightly orchestration, deft harmonies, and melodic liberality—a lesser composer would have set both solo verses to the same tune—Sullivan takes a merely functional lyric and infuses it with lively energy.

Given these two elements, it is intriguing—and eternally frustrating!—to speculate on what the full score sounded like.

Gilbert's contributions are, of course, easier to evaluate. The librettos for both *Thespis* and *Trial by Jury* were created without significant input from Sullivan. Subsequently, the composer would enjoy hands-on involvement not only in lyrics but also in story, characters, and even dialogue. But in the first two operas he essentially set Gilbert's existing words, so the Gilbert of *Thespis* is in some ways "purer" than the later Gilbert.

Thespis is the only Gilbert & Sullivan opera prior to *The Mikado* that is not based, at least in part, on some previous work by Gilbert. Instead, as most young authors do, Gilbert copied the older authors he most admired.

Gilbert had translated some works by Offenbach's librettists, Meilhac and Halevy, and he had also written parody lyrics to Offenbach tunes for *The Princess* (1870) and similar plays. He frequently reviewed the French composer's works for *Fun* and various other journals. (And in reviewing English operettas, he often compared them disparagingly to Offenbach.) He admired Offenbach's shows for their musical inventiveness, humorous situations, and effective theatrical presentation.

What Gilbert didn't like about the Offenbach operettas was their suggestive humor. *Thespis* resembles *La Belle Helene* and *Orpheus in the Underworld* (Gilbert's favorite), in which classical or supernatural figures are used to bring out the fallible ways of mortals. But Offenbach threw his gods into the racy settings of contemporary Paris; Gilbert prefers to focus on the more decorous goings-on up above. Instead of "The Gods Grown Old," *Thespis* might have been subtitled "Meanwhile, Back on Olympus."

Nevertheless, *Thespis* is the most overtly suggestive of Gilbert's libretti. Drawing on both Offenbachian roots and the bawdy tradition of the Gaiety, Gilbert allows the gods some not-too-veiled insinuations as to why they want to visit Earth. Apollo sets out:

> to earth away to join in mortal acts,
>   and gather fresh materials to write on,
> investigate more closely several facts
>   that I for centuries have thrown some light on!

Diana, the moon, is even more explicit:

> I, as the modest moon with crescent bow,
>   have always shown a light to nightly scandal.
> I must say I should like to go below
>   and find out if the game is worth the candle!

Meanwhile, back in Olympus, Daphne urges Thespis to consult *Lempriere's Classical Dictionary*, providing an occasion for a little wink-wink-nudge-nudge, as he reads of the many "marriages" of Apollo:

> *Thespis:* Ha! I didn't know he was *married* to them.
> *Daphne:* (Severely) Sir! This is the Family Edition!
> *Thespis:* Quite so.

These and similar passages might seem tame on modern television, but in the context of Gilbert & Sullivan, in which sexuality is always decorously couched and never a source of humor, they border on being "a joke that's too French."

The plot of *Thespis* is distinctly Offenbachian, which is to say not very Gilbertian. The cosmic scale of events does not suit Gilbert's penchant for human-scale stories examining human-scale questions. In the later operas, even on the rare occasions when supernatural characters are introduced, they exercise their powers to market a love potion, nestle in a nutshell, or compel income-tax fraud, not to bring about the abolition of war, for example, as in *Thespis*.

More characteristically Gilbertian is the material that fills out the Offenbachian frame. Unlike Offenbach's Parisian boulevardiers, Gilbert's primary characters are performers (as in *The Yeomen of the Guard* and *The Grand Duke*). He is much more comfortable with the theatrical scenes than with the cosmic scenes—the early Olympian scenes feel strained, and the final "judgment" scene falls a bit flat (admittedly in large part because of the inappropriately prominent role given Tipseion).

But the theatrical scenes have some pop. Jupiter is funnier getting lessons from Thespis in how to play the role of Jupiter than he is in his own scenes, and the early act 2 scenes in which the actors try to sort out the romantic entanglements of their new roles are the opera's funniest.

The early-second-act scenes also are the ones that most resemble the mature Gilbert & Sullivan. As Pretteia wrestles with a role that requires love scenes with her father and grandfather, or Nicemis (cast as the moon) defends her insistence on spending the night with her husband (cast as the sun), we see some of the "person versus role" conflicts that generate humor in *The Pirates of Penzance* or *Iolanthe.* The stage manager Sillimon, with his meticulous insistence that "The exact connubial relation of the different gods and goddesses is a point on which we must be extremely particular," is a very Gilbertian figure.

Overall the narrative framework of *Thespis,* derived from Offenbach and augmented by the showy excess of extravaganza, works against Gilbert. In the later operas, loose plot structures allow ample room for both thematic development and comic elaboration. The rigid, "high concept" plot structure of *Thespis* doesn't allow for either. In so plot-driven a story, there is little room for even a romantic story line, let alone the multiple stories that provide the thematic power of the Savoy operas.

Thus Gilbert's humor can be found only piecemeal, alternating with other sequences designed to show off the performers, to gratify the burlesque delight in puns (which, admittedly, Gilbert shared), to provide for stage spectacle, and so forth. There is no opportunity for serious character drama, which was to be the linchpin of the mature Gilbert & Sullivan operas.

From a technical point of view, *Thespis* clearly betrays its author's newness to the genre. Its comedy, lyrics, and stagecraft are wildly inconsistent in both quality and style, producing a show that, barring superlative performances, seems as if it would proceed with a great many stops and starts.

The lyrics are particularly inconsistent. Gilbert is already coming up with tripping lines and clever rhymes—"Here's a pretty tale for future Iliads and Odysseys,/mortals are about to personate the gods and goddesses." On the other hand, he slips frequently, often putting accents on the wrong syllable or forcing rhymes—the first verse of the same song rhymes "below" and "clothes."

The songs also lack structural diversity, with nearly every one in couplets, either straight (AABB) or interlocked (ABAB, also called quatrain). More damaging, most are only loosely integrated into the story, with several preceded by variants on "Don't you know the song about . . . ?" Only a few numbers, such as the intriguing "You're Diana, I'm Apollo" quartet (which seems to show a touch of *The Gondoliers'* "In a Contemplative Fashion"), are smoothly integrated in the style of the later operas.

The dialogue is also uneven, mixing vintage Gilbertian lines with others that are labored, meandering, or simply overly wordy. Michael Shawn Stone, in his reconstruction of *Thespis*,[4] cites this wordiness as evidence that the libretto is a rough draft; I don't find this persuasive, since the same is true of Gilbert's plays at this time and even of *The Sorcerer.* I think it's more likely a young author's typical lack of self-judgment; Gilbert eventually became a merciless editor of his own work, but in his early plays he tends to err on the side of excess.

This excess can be seen in a familiar Gilbertian thought—that good wins over evil only on the stage. Preposteros complains that, as the villain, he must be defeated every night, and Thespis replies, "But look here, you know—virtue only triumphs at night from seven to 10—vice gets the better of it during the other 23 hours. Won't that satisfy you?"

It's a clever line, but far wordier and less effective than the Mikado's "It's an unjust world, and virtue is triumphant only in theatrical performances."

The dramatic shape of the opera is, by the standards of the Savoy operas, appalling. Gilbert later became a master of pacing and dramatic flow, but *Thespis* is very weak in these areas—though, again, Gilbert had no control over many aspects of the show.

There is no human drama whatever to *Thespis.* The story has no point (unless it's a simplistic "Stick to your own line" or "It's harder to run the universe than you might think") and no thematic resonance. *Thespis* is straightforward, aiming to get some laughs while providing a showcase for its performers. Both goals were amply realized in later Gilbert & Sullivan operas, but strictly incidentally to a larger artistic purpose. In *Thespis*, they are all there is.

As a Gilbert & Sullivan opera, *Thespis* would be at best mediocre if it could be staged. To judge it by the criteria of the Savoy operas is unfair to *Thespis* and to its creators. They weren't trying to create a Savoy opera, and at this stage of their careers they didn't know how to, either.

The hallmarks of the Savoy operas would be respectful fidelity to the text, a minimum of performers' self-indulgence, and a commitment to dramatic realism. These were and are the essential elements of any effective staging of the operas.

But *Thespis* wouldn't reward this approach. The text is rough and unrealistic, built on the concepts of improvisation, elaboration, and even performers' self-indulgence. Pressing it into the mold of later operas would highlight its shortcomings while suppressing its strengths.

The reverse is also true, of course. A production of *Iolanthe* staged with a devil-may-care approach to its drama, allowing the performers to fiddle with the text at will, would be memorably bad. Such a production would reflect ignorance of what *Iolanthe* is or how it was meant to be done.

Thespis deserves similar consideration. Its reputation as a Gilbert & Sullivan failure is unjustified—it ran for two and a half months, outlasting nearly all the year's Christmas-season plays, and drew many glowing reviews (Sutherland Edwards of *The Musical World* wrote: "In almost all conjunctions of music and words, there is a sacrifice of one to the other; but in *Thespis* . . . [s]ufficient opportunities have been given for music; and the music serves only to adorn the piece").[5] Richard D'Oyly Carte would later propose Christmas revivals of the show in 1875 and in 1895, though neither materialized.

It's natural that *Thespis* seems a failure when viewed in the context of the later operas, as is inevitable today. To a sensibility accustomed to the Savoy operas, *Thespis* is foreign. It must be acknowledged as such and judged accordingly, in the same way that Gilbert's earlier plays or Sullivan's later operas demand assessment on their own terms.

A balanced judgment probably finds *Thespis* a flawed but promising work, deserving both the lavish praise and the sarcastic criticism that various reviewers provided. It surely would never have survived in any form were it not for its creators' subsequent triumphs, but in its own right it has a fair amount to recommend it, and some intriguing foreshadowing of later operas.

If only we could listen to it!

Facing page: FIGURE 4.1. Fred Sullivan as the Learned Judge in *Trial by Jury*. The composer's brother created the roles of the Judge and of Apollo in *Thespis* and was intended to play John Wellington Wells in *The Sorcerer* until his unexpected death provided an opportunity for the young George Grossmith. *Source: The Pierpont Morgan Library, Gilbert and Sullivan Collection.*

4

Trial by Jury

In some ways, *Trial by Jury* is peripheral to the creative development of Gilbert & Sullivan. In spite of some elements in common with their later works, it has many more discontinuities. In terms of their partnership, it is less a road not taken than a side street, a detour from what was to become the central direction of the collaboration.

This is hardly surprising, since it is the last Gilbert & Sullivan work not written as part of an ongoing collaboration. Like *Thespis*, it began as an isolated project for each man. But after *Trial by Jury* notched nearly 300 performances, not only the ambitious Richard D'Oyly Carte but also Sullivan and Gilbert themselves were thinking in terms of a sustained partnership.

This conscious collaboration, of course, created their greatest works. But it also imposed a certain gravity: A collaboration pairing England's leading comic playwright and her most revered composer was expected to be extraordinary, and both men approached it as such. After *Trial by Jury* their operas would be increasingly ambitious, ultimately crafting an entirely new way of combining the serious and the satiric in a musical-theater format.

With *Trial by Jury* the context is wholly different. Composed and rehearsed in only a few weeks, it is a goof, a bit of tomfoolery meant solely to amuse. In expanding his one-page comic poem, first published in *Fun* in 1868, into a stageable-length work (originally intended as a curtain-raiser for the Carl Rosa Opera Company's English premiere of Wagner's *Lohengrin*),[1] Gilbert feels no pressure to earn a place in the theatrical pantheon of the day, any more than Sullivan, in setting it, feels obliged to produce work worthy of England's greatest composer. Both are having fun, writing a skit for its own sake and having a good time doing it.

In short, *Trial by Jury* offers a unique glimpse at Gilbert and at Sullivan before they became "Gilbert & Sullivan," the English institution. Their talent shows through, if not yet their genius, and the result is a work that, while lacking the depth of their mature operas, offers as much sheer fun as anything they ever wrote.

It is easy to list the differences between *Trial by Jury* and the later operas. It has no dialogue, and its characters (except perhaps the gleefully incompetent judge) are two-dimensional stereotypes. Dramatically, it is structured differently from the later works, and is shorter and less ambitious in scope.

But *Trial by Jury* deserves attention in its own right, offering a valuable glimpse at the young Gilbert & Sullivan, just beginning their careers as creators of comic opera.

Of all the contrasts between *Trial by Jury* and its successors, the most obvious is the difference in scope. As early as *Thespis*, Gilbert & Sullivan aimed high. *Thespis* was a "big" show, in two acts, with a large cast, extravagant production numbers, and attempts at social commentary as well as pure entertainment. Its book and, as far as we can tell, its score were ambitious, intended to show the world what these two young men could do. *The Sorcerer*, too, would be a "big" show, a conscious calling-card heralding what they and Carte hoped would be a new era of comic opera. In the early operas especially, Gilbert & Sullivan often reveal ambitions that outstrip their abilities. Their comic operas seem more opera than comic—we sense them trying too hard to be "big," resulting in numbers that sag under the weight of rhetorical excess in both words and music.

Trial by Jury is the antithesis of such ambition, a single-scene show with a small cast and music that, while sophisticated, is largely accessible and easily sung. It has no grand artistic scheme, no attempt to make its characters and situations "believable." It is pure fun. And thus it remains the most enjoyable of the early shows: Where *Thespis* or *The Sorcerer* aim high and fall a bit short, *Trial by Jury* aims low and scores a bull's-eye.

The key to its success is its lack of pretension. Its songs are short, averaging less than two minutes in length (by *The Mikado* in 1885, that average would double), and are purely comic. The authors never linger on anything long enough either to give it real depth or to risk being overbearing.

This is especially true of Gilbert's words. Sullivan's music has at least parodic scope, and is certainly more musically challenging than most comparable contemporary works. Even today, numbers such as "A Nice Dilemma" or "I Love Him, I Love Him" test performers and conductors alike.

But Gilbert's lyrics are the simplest he ever wrote for Sullivan. In both form and content, they reflect the show's origin as a one-page poem. Of *Trial by Jury's* 23 pieces—15 songs and eight connecting recitatives—a full 20 are written in four-line, double-couplet form. Of these, 13 are in interlocked couplets (ABAB) and seven in straight couplets (AABB).

In later years, far less frequent use of such couplet structures drew complaints from Sullivan. In *Trial by Jury*, however, he cheerfully plays with the one structure he is given: Again and again, he takes a short lyric and elaborates it into a longer number—"Hark the Hour of 10" or "A Nice Dilemma"—or writes different vocal lines for each verse, as in the Usher's "Now, Jurymen, Hear My Advice." The result is a surprising variety of sparkling tunes.

The content of the lyrics is as simple as their form. Even given its unfamiliar setting—films and television shows may have left a modern audience modestly familiar with English criminal law, but the civil law remains largely unknown—*Trial by Jury* remains accessible in large part because its lyrics are so straightforward. What the characters are getting at is always immediately clear.

In his "serious" works, Gilbert strove not only for humor but also for poeticism. His most successful plays avoid mawkishness by using wit to leaven evocative, poetic imagery. Audiences forgive failed poeticism less than they do failed wit. We extend a groaning tolerance to *H. M. S. Pinafore's* "Your position as a topman is a very exalted one," but the same opera's "Hast ever thought that beneath a gay and frivolous exterior there may lurk a canker-worm which is slowly but surely eating its way into one's very heart?" prompts mutters and unintended laughs. It is through trite images and poetic clichés that the early works most often lose a modern audience's attention.

Trial by Jury is altogether different, bereft of good and bad poetry alike. The show is virtually without poetic language or imagery. The characters sing exactly what they have to say, in clear, unconvoluted language. The contrast with the other early shows is striking: *H. M. S. Pinafore's* Ralph Rackstraw says, "She is the figurehead of my ship of life, the bright beacon that guides me into my port of happiness." *Trial by Jury's* Angelina simply sings "I love him, I love him."

Only one song in *Trial by Jury* is at all imagistic—"Comes the Broken Flower," whose hackneyed flower imagery makes it the least engaging spot in the show. Otherwise, the lyrics are direct and matter-of-fact. The characters tell stories, make their cases, and maneuver for advantage without a single word being wasted.

Brevity produces clarity. In a full-length show, both men probably would have been seduced into trying to do more than they were capable of doing. Flowery language would mar the clean lines of the show, the recitatives would be drawn out, extra characters would muddle the story, thematic considerations would be introduced, "serious" music would dilute the wittiness of the score. The show might have more high points, but it would also be encumbered by more conventional boilerplate. It would, in short, resemble *Thespis* or *The Sorcerer.*

Instead, *Trial by Jury* sticks to the point. The short form itself is less convention bound than full-length opera, leaving Gilbert & Sullivan freer to be themselves, to have fun without feeling guilty about it.

All of which is not to say that *Trial by Jury* lacks artistic merit. Given its cameo form, it is actually one of the best Gilbert & Sullivan shows. It is particularly funny—Gilbert is as witty as he ever was. But it is wittiness achieved through manipulating stereotypes, not through the clever, original, and even believable characters of later shows.

Trial by Jury is so much a one-joke show that it would probably drag if it were any longer. Again and again, Gilbert plays the same card—that, behind the respectable veneer of justice, everyone in the courtroom is a hypocrite out for personal advantage. But *Trial by Jury* is short enough that the repetition never grows tiresome.

The show's most cynical passages focus on love and money, which it portrays as essentially the same. Except for Edwin, its characters unhesitatingly barter their romantic/matrimonial connections for economic advantage.

Angelina is probably the most blatant about it. Despite her professed love for Edwin, she makes it clear that she is not especially distressed over losing him ("I am no unhappy maid," she rebukes the pitying chorus). But she means to get every penny she can out of him: Her apparently passionate "I love him, I love him" ends with a calculated appeal to the jury for "the damages Edwin must pay." Her willingness to marry the Judge is equally venal—"Oh joy unbounded, with wealth surrounded," she celebrates.

The Judge himself says nothing at all about love. Instead, he proclaims "Of beauty I'm a judge, and a good judge too!" But while he prizes beauty, it is hardly his highest priority: He did not hesitate to "fall in love" with the rich attorney's elderly, ugly daughter in order to win her father's patronage. Once he was rich, of course, he dumped her unceremoniously; and if Angelina has the temerity to grow old or plain, he'll surely dispense with her just as quickly.

Angelina's Counsel is of the same mind. His moving oration on his client's tragedy climaxes not with her misery but with her financial loss ("doubly criminal to do so, for the maid had bought her trousseau"). This moves the jury and spectators—who have no objection to a woman being jilted, since both judge and jurymen reveal similar episodes in their past—to a violent denunciation of Edwin. Clearly they, too, value money more than love.

Through this storm of avarice walks Edwin, the opera's true innocent. It testifies to the opera's cynicism that its most naive, sincere songs are those in which he admits dumping Angelina because he tired of her, and offers to marry her if he can also have his new lover. Compared to the conniving, money-hungry people around him, this lothario and would-be bigamist actually looks pure.

Edwin doesn't initially understand what's going on. Even with the jury denouncing him as soon as he sticks his head in the door, he still thinks that if he can only explain, everything will work out. To his credit, however, Edwin does catch on. His early appeals for understanding are wasted, but his "I smoke like a furnace" plays effectively to the jurors' contempt for him.

While far from a fully drawn character, Edwin manages to display a distinct personality even in his small amount of stage time. The same holds true for the Judge, with his self-interest and utter lack of legal knowledge or decorum. Angelina, too, has a cleverness that, paired with her mercenary streak, makes her immediately amusing.

The smaller characters—the shrewd Counsel, angling everything for his client's advantage, or the punctilious Usher with an eye for feminine charms—also enjoy their brief moments. Almost any production proves that there is more for actors to work with in these small parts than in the secondary roles in *Thespis, The Sorcerer,* or *H. M. S. Pinafore,* despite those operas' greater room for development. Even the jurymen have a collective identity that, in protean form, foreshadows the authors' later mastery of chorus characterization.

Trial by Jury offers a smattering of other hints of things to come. Edwin's use of an onstage guitar suggests Dr. Daly's flageolet in *The Sorcerer,* Captain Corcoran's mandolin in *H. M. S. Pinafore,* and Lady Jane's cello in *Patience.* There's Gilbert's first sneer at aging women. And "When I, Good Friends" is a clear progenitor of "how I got here" patter songs such as *H. M. S. Pinafore's* "When I Was a Lad" or *Iolanthe's* "When I Went to the Bar as a Very Young Man."

But of other characteristic Gilbert & Sullivan song genres—the madrigal or part song, the one-person-too-many "mathematics song" of confusion, the love song of separation, the flamboyant male chorus—there is no sign. Similarly, such favorite Gilbertian plot devices as long-hidden secrets, twist endings, or multiple tellings of a single story are nowhere to be found.

In one sense, this lack of continuity with future operas is surprising. After all, within the year its creators were to set to work on *The Sorcerer,* which in form and content is clearly a "rough draft" for the mature operas to come. But ultimately the lack of continuity simply reflects the different priorities at work in *Trial by Jury* and *The Sorcerer.* The latter is the work of prominent artists with a track record in the genre; they are taken seriously, and thus they take their work seriously.

Trial by Jury, though its success made the greater aspirations of *The Sorcerer* possible, is the work of two relatively young men having fun with a genre that neither takes very seriously. Their delight in the form comes through clearly, as does their irreverent attitude toward its many constraining conventions—an attitude that soon led them to begin a wholesale reshaping of the genre.

But that sense of fun may be the most important aspect of *Trial by Jury.* For all of their brilliance, Gilbert & Sullivan couldn't have achieved so much if they hadn't loved comic opera. And it is in *Trial by Jury*—precisely because of its lack of ambition, pretension, or even seriousness—that we see that love most clearly.

Facing page: FIGURE 5.1. A sinister John Wellington Wells (George Grossmith) conjures up evil in the original 1877 production of *The Sorcerer,* as Alexis and Aline (George Bentham and Alice May) shrink from him. *Source:* Illustrated London News, *February 23, 1878. By permission of The British Library.*

5

The Sorcerer

In writing the libretti for *Thespis* and *Trial by Jury*, Gilbert had not imagined Sullivan as the composer; similarly, Sullivan's task had largely been limited to writing tunes for the existing words. Though in later years the composer was to be intimately involved in shaping the story and characters, for their first two joint works Sullivan worked only marginally more closely with Gilbert than he had with Shakespeare on his incidental music to *The Tempest*.

The success of *Trial by Jury* changed all that. Richard D'Oyly Carte envisioned Gilbert & Sullivan as the cornerstones of his new Comic Opera Company, and *The Sorcerer* was a true collaboration from the beginning. It was thus the first show initially conceived as a Gilbert & Sullivan opera—or, as the team was then usually known, Sullivan & Gilbert.

The Sorcerer is in many ways a prototype for the Savoy operas to come. Structurally and thematically it is actually closer to the later operas, es-

FIGURE 5.2. A D'Oyly Carte poster from 1919, drawn by H. M. Brock and modeled after Henry Lytton as John Wellington Wells. Lytton's Wells is far less grotesque—though he has an ominous shadow, he is more picturesque than sinister. *Source: The Pierpont Morgan Library, Gilbert and Sullivan Collection.*

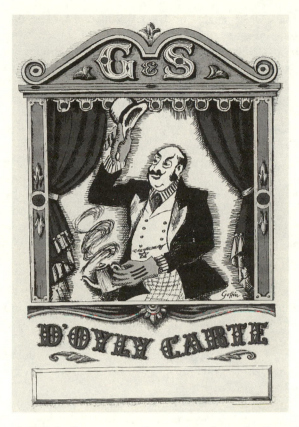

FIGURE 5.3. A D'Oyly Carte poster from 1971, drawn by Peter Goffin and modeled after John Reed as John Wellington Wells. By this time Wells has completed his evolution from a sinister fomenter of evil to a fast-talking carnival barker—a far more sympathetic portrayal but one that blurs the thematic point of the character. *Source: The Pierpont Morgan Library, Gilbert and Sullivan Collection.*

pecially *Patience*, than to its immediate successors, *H. M. S. Pinafore* and *The Pirates of Penzance*.

The Sorcerer introduced the collaborative mode that prevailed for the rest of the partnership: Gilbert drafted a plot (in this case, a thorough revision of his 1869 short story, "An Elixir of Love"), which he and Sullivan hashed out at length before agreeing on its details. Gilbert then set to work on the lyrics, first Act 1 and then Act 2, sending each song on to Sullivan as he completed it. The dialogue was the last element to be written. Meanwhile, Sullivan, as was his wont, put off writing much of the music until deadlines forced him to buckle down.

It was likewise with *The Sorcerer* that Gilbert & Sullivan first had full control of the casting of their work. With *Thespis* and *Trial by Jury* they had been obliged to accommodate certain principal performers of existing companies, which chafed both men. With *The Sorcerer*, they were writing for actor/singers whom they themselves had chosen, whose attitudes and abilities perfectly matched what each man was looking for.

In casting their performers, they ignored box-office appeal—indeed, established stars virtually never appeared in the Savoy operas (though the American singer/actress Lillian Russell was originally engaged to appear as Princess Ida).[1] Gilbert & Sullivan were the true stars, and their artistic judgments were the sole criteria in casting—a unique idea for the time and one that contributed much to the success of the operas.

Future Savoy stalwarts such as Rutland Barrington (Dr. Daly) and Richard Temple (Sir Marmaduke) were first signed for *The Sorcerer*. The title role was conceived for Frederic Sullivan, the composer's brother, who had scored a hit as the Judge in *Trial by Jury*, but his illness and subsequent death opened a space for piano entertainer George Grossmith, who as the original "patter man" was to become the most popular of all the stars at the Savoy.

In short, the arrangement with Carte finally offered Gilbert & Sullivan the opportunity to create real work of lasting importance, and both men took the opportunity seriously. If *Thespis* and *Trial by Jury* suggest talented creators on something of a lark, *The Sorcerer* reflects more serious musical, dramatic, and comedic aspirations. For the first time, both men seem aware that their professional images will be at stake, and accordingly put forth their best work.

For all three men, *The Sorcerer* inaugurated a crusade against the domination of the British comic-opera stage by Offenbach and his French imitators. Carte had long aspired to establish a true school of English comic opera, and he saw in Gilbert & Sullivan the means to realize that ambition. (He was later to see in Sullivan the means to a true school of English grand opera, in the ill-fated Royal English Opera that produced *Ivanhoe*.)

As for Sullivan, his outlook on Carte's crusade can be seen in a letter to a friend shortly after *The Sorcerer* opened: "We are doing tremendous business at the Opera Comique I am glad to say. I was on the stage last night and heard three encores before I left. If it is a great success it is another nail in the coffin of Opera Bouffe from the French."[2]

Neither Gilbert nor Sullivan previously had written any musical-theater work as ambitious as *The Sorcerer*. Sullivan had succeeded only with the vest-pocket operettas *Cox and Box* and *Trial by Jury*. His two full-length ventures, *The Contrabandista* and *Thespis*, had been disappointments, as had a third one-act operetta, *The Zoo*. He was generally familiar with opera of the day, of course, but his own experience lay primarily in popular ballads, hymns, and instrumental music—all of which strongly influenced his score for *The Sorcerer*.

Gilbert had worked in musical theater a bit more, but his German Reed shows had been in most respects little more ambitious than Sullivan's

early works. *Ages Ago, Our Island Home*, and their ilk supplied some interesting plot elements and theatrical effects for future Savoy operas, but
stylistically they were very different. They were small in scale and tight in
focus, performed by small casts and aiming at little more than winning
laughs.

Thus, the creators of *The Sorcerer* were novices to the genre. Gilbert's
most serious aspirations had been for his straight plays, as Sullivan's had
been for his instrumental and choral music. In applying themselves to a
serious-minded comic opera, they brought to the task tools honed in
other genres, tools that they themselves weren't quite sure how to apply
to their new undertaking.

It is hard to escape the technical problems of *The Sorcerer*. Even its authors
found it charming but ungainly: It is the only one of their shows that they
substantially reworked after its original run.[3]

When it was revived in 1884 following the unexpectedly early demise
of *Princess Ida*, Sullivan wrote a new overture (there had been none previously). The Act 2 setting, formerly a marketplace half an hour after Act
1, was changed to the same scene as Act 1, but at midnight. Accordingly,
a new ending for the Act 1 finale was written, showing the characters
falling asleep, and a new Act 2 opening to show them awakening.

The new material, from the big finish for "Oh Marvelous Illusion" to
the spooky trio " 'Tis Twelve, I Think" and the rollicking chorus number
"If You'll Marry Me" (with its accompanying country dance), is the best
sustained sequence in the show. The falling-asleep/waking-up sequence
is theatrically strong, while making Act 2 a nighttime scene (as "previously" done in *H. M. S. Pinafore*, *The Pirates of Penzance*, and *Iolanthe*), instantly imparts a more evocative dramatic atmosphere. As for "If You'll
Marry Me" and the preceding "Why, Where Be I," this is the only scene
in the opera offering anything approaching the rich chorus material of
later Gilbert & Sullivan.

Apparently the mature Gilbert & Sullivan were a bit embarrassed by *The
Sorcerer's* clunkiness and in their revision fixed as much as they felt they
could, given that the show had, after all, been a resounding success in its
original form.

Their perspective was much more sophisticated in 1884: By then they
had thrown precedent to the winds and created their own form of comic
opera—in fact, they had accomplished the revolution that they had aimed
for with *The Sorcerer*.

In 1877, however, they were still clinging to the established genre and
its conventions. These conventions were primarily drawn from ballad
opera. Pioneered by John Gay in *The Beggar's Opera* (1728) and later stan-
dardized by custom, ballad opera consisted almost exclusively of short
choruses and solos, strung together by recitative or brief dialogues. As the
name "ballad opera" suggests, the songs were designed to be easily de-
tachable from their dramatic context, and indeed were often previously

5.1. *Statistical Breakdown,* The Sorcerer *vs.* The Mikado

	Sorcerer (original version)	*Mikado*
Total musical numbers	23	29
Choruses	7	6
Solos	11 (3 w/chorus)	12 (7 w/chorus)
Duets	4	3
Trios	0	4
Quartets	0	2
Quintets	1	2
Recitatives (excluding act 1 finales)	10	2
Dialogues	9	18

existing songs interpolated into the operas. They featured strongly marked rhythms, conventional lyrics and short verse-chorus structures that made it easy for the public to exit whistling the tunes—and for under-rehearsed actors to learn them.

Applied to *The Sorcerer*, these conventions produce a musical structure strikingly bland compared to those of the later Gilbert & Sullivan. Where *The Sorcerer* is almost half solos, for example, *The Mikado* is barely one-third solos, uses the chorus more often, and employs more ensemble numbers and far fewer recitatives (excluding connecting tissue from Act 1 finales), as table 5.1 shows.

Sullivan was to become a master of chorus writing, but there are few signs of it in *The Sorcerer*. Only 10 of the songs use the chorus, including three versions of "With Heart and with Voice" and two of "Now to the Banquet We Press"; only the combined-chorus "With Heart and with Voice" shows Sullivan's real capabilities in chorus writing. (So does the opening of Act 2, of course, but it was written later, as was *The Sorcerer's* only trio.)

The sheer number of solos is reinforced by their content. They are "ballad opera" solos, clichéd genre songs that could be given to many operatic characters. Alexis's "For Love Alone," Constance's "When He Is Here," or Aline's "Happy Young Heart" would all work equally well for the equivalent characters in *Ruddigore*—but "I Shipped, D'Ye See," "I Once Was a Very Abandoned Person," or "Ghost's High Noon" could hardly replace them. The songs in *Ruddigore*, like those in most later Gilbert & Sullivan, are site specific, grounded in the characters and situations of that opera. Many of those in *The Sorcerer* are generic, with little connection to who sings them or what's going on.

The recitatives are as generalized as the solos and far more tiresome. They have little or no humor, and the information they convey would be expressed just as well, and far more quickly, as dialogue. The excruciating Constance/Partlet recitative that opens *The Sorcerer* could be done in four lines of dialogue.

But recitative was a conventional part of comic opera, so Gilbert & Sullivan provided it. As they grew accustomed to the genre, they used recitative less and less, primarily as a connecting element in Act 1 finales. Gilbert learned to make them shorter and funnier, while Sullivan began to score his recitatives more dramatically, using strong instrumental bridges for added musical interest. Compare the tedious, by-the-book Daly/Marmaduke/Alexis recitative "Sir Marmaduke—my dear young friend Alexis" in *The Sorcerer* with the engagingly funny (and character-specific) King/Ruth/Frederic recitative "Young Frederic/Who calls?" in *The Pirates of Penzance.*

The same conventionality that marks the recitatives hampers Gilbert's lyrics. A few of the songs have the distinctive Savoy touch, most notably Daly's "Time Was When Love and I Were Well-Acquainted," which is everything most of the songs are not—concise, polished, funny and character specific.

Many others, however, have no point at all. Most of the other solos consist of stale, hackneyed imagery, while the choruses are unfailingly banal.

Only two years later, the choruses in *The Pirates of Penzance* would have spark and wit, humorously commenting on the situation and interacting so much with the principals as to become virtually collective principals in their own right.

In *The Sorcerer*, however, the choruses' interaction with the principals is limited to echoing them. And the full choruses are a world away from the swagger of the pirates or the hilarious "Tarantara" chorus: "Ring Forth Ye Bells" repeats the same phrases over and over again, without any noticeable humor; "With Heart and with Voice" is similarly repetitious and humorless, with men and women reiterating the same obvious sentiment; and "Now to the Banquet We Press" is nothing more than a menu set to music.

The dramatic structure of *The Sorcerer* is similarly awkward. In keeping with the loosely knit structures of most previous opera, *The Sorcerer's* scenes rely heavily on the "revolving door" technique, wherein one set of characters enters, speaks and sings a song, then exits together as another set enters for the next scene.

The problem with the revolving-door technique is that it breaks narrative momentum: Each scene is followed by a momentary pause, after which new characters take up new issues instead of developing the ideas in the previous scene.

In later operas, Gilbert became skilled at making each scene flow seamlessly into the next—using Captain Corcoran, for example, as the centerpiece for the entire second act of *H. M. S. Pinafore*—but *The Sorcerer* staggers along fitfully, with five blank-stage moments scattered through its two short acts.

The dialogue is equally rough and convention bound—surprising, since by 1877 Gilbert was an experienced playwright, and his straight plays, while still conventional, are far less leaden than his *Sorcerer* dialogue.

There are comparatively few dialogues in *The Sorcerer* (nine, versus 18 in *The Mikado*), and they serve only to set up songs or convey plot information. Gilbert was soon to become a master of situational comedy, shaping dialogues in which clearly defined characters address their particular situation (usually a crisis of some kind). In *The Sorcerer*, however, the dialogue is conventional, heavily dependent on puns and lacking in wit or situational comedy.

Perhaps Gilbert didn't consider the dialogue in a comic opera to be worth much effort. Evidence of his inattention is ample: Two of the first three scenes are written in blank verse, for example, but the rest of the show is in prose, as if Gilbert meant to write it all in verse but simply lost interest. And after making plot changes for the 1884 revision, he neglected to square several dialogue and lyric references, so that the workings of the love potion are unclear and contradictory.

As to Gilbert's dramatic craftsmanship, even he regarded it only indifferently. The next year, writing *H. M. S. Pinafore*, he wrote to Sullivan, "It seems to me that there is plenty of story in it *(The Sorcerer* rather lacks story)."[4]

His retrospective judgment is entirely accurate. No subsequent Gilbert & Sullivan plot can be summed up in a single sentence as simply as *The Sorcerer:* "A young man puts a love potion in the teapot at a wedding feast, causing everyone to fall in love with the wrong people, but ultimately the spell is lifted and everyone goes back to their proper loves."

Moreover, what there is of story is awkward and poorly executed. Though the subsequent operas are far more complex, they generally hang together better in terms of plausibility and character motivation. Not so with *The Sorcerer*, where the plot has all the slapdash quality of opera as Gilbert & Sullivan found it.

Daly and Constance do come together at the end, as do Sir Marmaduke and Lady Sangazure, but there is no explanation of why—their earlier obstacles vanish in a manner only marginally more rational than the Notary's sudden pairing-off with Mrs. Partlet, whom the play gives no indication that he has met previously.

And the 1884 revision left the love potion's mechanism thoroughly confused. Originally it was to take effect in half an hour, without anyone falling asleep; in the revision, as Wells says, it takes effect "[i]n twelve hours. Whoever drinks of it loses consciousness for that period, and on waking falls in love as a matter of course with the first person he meets who has also tasted it, and his affection is at once returned."

But after waking, Sangazure falls in love with Wells, who has not tasted it, and her affection isn't returned; Aline doesn't fall asleep at all but starts to wander offstage before conveniently meeting Dr. Daly as he enters for his solo. And, despite Wells's revised dialogue, he, Alexis, and Aline still watch the chorus drinking the tea and sing "Their hearts will melt in half an hour, then will be felt the potion's power!"

The greatest weakness of *The Sorcerer* is not its plot, however. It may be simplistic, but its romantic mix-ups offer plenty of room for both situational and character comedy. These aspects are explored only on the most superficial level, though, and are worked out only haphazardly.

The reason, of course, is the lack of meaningful characterization. With the exception of Daly, Wells, and possibly Aline, the characters are stick figures defined by stiff dialogue and platitudinous songs. Thus the romantic confusion lacks the humor it might have had.

Constance's love for the Notary, for example, is played only for the humor in a young girl being passionately in love with an elderly man. This is unavoidable, because the Notary is nothing more than elderly—nothing distinguishes him from any other elderly character, and nothing contrasts him with Constance except their ages. On the other hand, if a similar potion were to make *Ruddigore's* Rose Maybud fall in love with Old Adam, the results would be funnier, because we know more about these characters and how ill suited they would be for each other.

The same applies, to a lesser extent, to Lady Sangazure's affection for Mr. Wells or Sir Marmaduke's for Mrs. Partlet. In short, a potentially serviceable plot fails to be more than broadly funny because the play lacks the detailed characterizations that would make it so.

Anyone wanting to throw critical stones at Gilbert & Sullivan can find plenty of targets in *The Sorcerer*. In many ways it's a ragged work that has more in common with *Thespis* (written five years before) than with *Patience* (written five years later).

Still, there is much in *The Sorcerer* that works well and lays the groundwork for operas to come. Its plot structure, for example, is the same that Gilbert used for all of the operas from *Patience* through *The Grand Duke*.

In this simple but dramatically solid framework, Act 1 establishes an apparently stable equilibrium, only to introduce an outside force (in this case, Wells and his potion) that brings out the inherent instabilities in that equilibrium. In the Act 1 finale, diverse plot elements come together in a "false solution" to set up a new, superficially stable equilibrium that, in Act 2, is shown actually to be worse than before.

The second act explores the comic implications of the "false solution"—often introducing several alternative "false solutions," each worse than the one before—until a final twist brings about a final "true solution" that establishes a new, presumably more stable equilibrium.

Along with this new dramatic framework come the prototypes of certain stock characters who were to recur often in later operas (not coincidentally, so were the same actors). *The Sorcerer* introduces the patter man, an outsider thrown into the midst of the action (Thespis had filled the outsider function without the patter, *Trial by Jury's* Judge the patter function without being an outsider); the aging woman in love with a younger man; and the comically idealistic romantic hero.

For these recurring types, Gilbert & Sullivan devised the first examples of songs that were to become Savoy staples. *Trial by Jury* had seen the first patter song of introduction, but "My Name Is John Wellington Wells" liberates it from the awkward verse/chorus structure to create the team's first virtuoso patter song, the male equivalent of the flashy aria conventionally given to the leading soprano. (Both types of showpiece number were to become rarer after *The Pirates of Penzance*, as soprano and baritone alike were more fully integrated into the operas.)

"She Will Tend Him" inaugurates a long series of Gilbert & Sullivan quasi-madrigals, interwoven part songs for trio, quartet, or quintet. It is unlike mature examples of the form—such as *H. M. S. Pinafore's* "A British Tar Is a Soaring Soul," *Iolanthe's* "In Friendship's Name," *The Mikado's* "Brightly Dawns Our Wedding Day," or *The Yeomen of the Guard's* "Strange Adventure"—in that it is (ironically) more related to the actual characters singing it; later ones tend to be generalized plot summaries or paeans to some abstract virtue. But musically it sets the mold for songs to come.

There is a smorgasbord of other "firsts" to *The Sorcerer*. The "Oh, my adored one! / Beloved boy!" reiterations, for example, foreshadow such musical running gags as *H. M. S. Pinafore's* "What, never?"

The mathematics problem (one man or one woman too many—"no one left to marry me") looks ahead to future operas: The "death" of Wells prefigures operas in which the extra person has to go (as in *Patience* and *The Yeomen of the Guard*), while in other operas *(The Gondoliers* and *The Grand Duke)* a new person is introduced to even out the math.

In these and many other ways, *The Sorcerer* is a lens through which we can see the Savoy operas emerging.

But the most important new element to *The Sorcerer* is thematic. However much the opera's technical flaws may recall *Thespis*, its thematic elements link it to the later operas and to *Patience* in particular. From a thematic point of view, *The Sorcerer* can legitimately claim to be both the first of the "real" Savoy operas and an interesting, even compelling work in its own right.

Thespis hadn't been about anything beyond a story level: It is about some actors taking over Mount Olympus, a plot that provides an occasion for humor on everything from classical myths and theatrical egotism to the temperance movement—but only individual lines, scenes, or characters were about these subjects. The play as a whole wasn't about anything.

Trial by Jury moved to a second, slightly more substantial level. Beyond its story level, about a breach-of-promise case, it had a subject: Its satiric barbs at mercenary lawyers, mercenary lovers, and the hypocrisy of the legal system all added up to a somewhat coherent whole. It may have been a story about a breach-of-promise case, but its subject was hypocrisy.

The great genius of the Gilbert & Sullivan works, however, is the mature operas' attainment of a thematic "third level." On a story level, for example, *Princess Ida* is about a princess who runs away from home; on a subject level, it's about women's equality; and on a thematic level, it's about generational conflict and the need for the young to transcend old ways of thinking.

This third level is what the operas have in common with most truly great works of art, from Shakespeare or Dickens through Sondheim or Kubrick—an underlying thematic story line that treats universal human concerns, independent of the more topical elements of its story and subject levels. It is in *The Sorcerer*, however falteringly, that Gilbert & Sullivan for the first time work on this level.

Of all complaints against *The Sorcerer*, the most common is that its ending is unsatisfactory. The audience accepts that either Wells or Alexis must die—after all, they're the ones responsible for the whole mess. But between the clever, amusing Wells and the arrogant, bullying Alexis, most audiences would rather penalize the latter.

This point of view is understandable, given the clumsiness of the writing and the way the two characters are usually performed. The awkwardness of Gilbert's characterization is such that his intentions are hard to grasp, making it easier for directors and performers to go astray.

Such is the case with John Wellington Wells. He is one of the better, more rounded characters in early Gilbert & Sullivan, but over the years directors and performers have diverged from the original sense of the character, softening his villainous side and making him more likable than he was written to be.

A fine example of this evolution is provided by three diverse depictions of the character (see figures 5.1–5.3). On the front cover of the 1979 D'Oyly Carte Opera Company recording of *The Sorcerer*, a jovial, chubby Wells, complete with jaunty mustache and sideburns, doffs his hat from within a puppet stage, his teapot puffing smoke rings. On the back cover, however, a 1920s D'Oyly Carte poster shows a leaner, hungrier-looking Wells, sparks flying from his teapot as, behind him, an ominous gray shadow looms. Finally, on the inside jacket is an 1878 newspaper illustration in which Alexis and Aline recoil as fire, smoke, and lightning erupt from the teapot brandished by a grimacing, black-garbed Wells whose facial makeup strikingly resembles Lon Chaney's in *The Phantom of the Opera* (1926). Taken together, the three provide graphic evidence of the century-long transformation of an evil figure into a sideshow barker.

This is not to say that Wells wasn't intended to be funny. But, like most of the best Gilbert & Sullivan characters, he has both comic and serious sides. Gilbert can make Pooh-Bah hilariously funny, for example, while still having utter contempt for him; Wilfred Shadbolt is a disgusting creature but still draws laughs.

So it is with Wells. The humor of the character derives from his being both a black magician and a matter-of-fact businessman. Wells as charlatan wouldn't be as funny as he is when played as exactly what he appears to be—a supernatural being who consorts with the most evil demons and is ready to deliver their services to anyone with the money to pay.

"My Name Is John Wellington Wells" long ago became the character's signature song, but it is the ensuing "Incantation" that is most revealing:

> Now, shriveled hags
> with poison bags,
>   discharge your loathsome loads.
> Spit flame and fire,
> unholy choir—
>   belch forth your venom, toads.
> Ye demons fell,
> with yelp and yell
>   shed curses far afield.
> Ye fiends of night,
> your filthy blight
>   in noisome plenty yield.

There is nothing in the text or Sullivan's dramatic setting (which echoes the supernatural music of Weber) to suggest that this sequence is meant anything but seriously. Wells actually is raising demons, and in the Victorian age of *Faust* and a thousand imitations (versions of the story by Marlowe, Goethe, and Gounod were only the most prominent among the many popular at the time), the conventions of such a portrayal were readily understood by audiences. An 1870s audience would have readily recognized Wells as a villain—a comic villain, to be sure, but still a villain.

Gilbert himself was fascinated by *Faust*. He called it "the grandest philosophical work of the century,"[5] and his own play *Gretchen*, written the year after *The Sorcerer*, was a somewhat free adaptation of the Faust story.

The Sorcerer is very much in the vein of Faustian drama, except that the leading role is split into two: Alexis provides the requisite hubris, the arrogance that leads man to tamper with forces he cannot control; Wells provides the mystical knowledge, the arcane learning that invariably corrupts its bearer.

As in *Faust*, the devil (Ahrimanes, who in an early draft of the opera was intended to appear onstage)[6] is both honest and deceitful: The spell delivers exactly what Alexis asks for, but the consequences are nonetheless disastrous. And, in the end, the audacious mortal must pay with his soul.

The only question is, since Faust's sin has been divided between Alexis and Wells, which will have to pay? Again, the conventions of the Faustian genre dictate that the only way to emerge alive (or at least with soul intact) is to accept responsibility—which Alexis does and Wells does not.

Faced with punishment for his actions, Alexis responds simply, "True. Well, I am ready." It's what we expect from a character who, however wrongheaded, has always been well intentioned and anything but timid.

Wells, on the other hand, attempts to duck responsibility.

"I would rather it were you," he says. "I should have no hesitation in sacrificing my life to save yours, but we take stock next week, and it would not be fair on the company."

His response amounts to "It wouldn't be good for business," exactly his motive for getting involved in the first place. Wells is a hustler, a self-promoter, and a liar. (In his opening speech he announces his penny curse as his most popular item, but as soon as Alexis inquires about the love potion, it becomes his leading article; and, for all his Act 2 regrets over the "ill I can't undo," he could easily undo it if he were willing to pay the price—just as, when pursued by Sangazure, he reflexively lies and claims to be already engaged.)

He sells Alexis the potion because it's good business. As his opening song makes clear, if Alexis wanted to raise the dead, murder someone through voodoo, or simply curse somebody, Wells would be every bit as accommodating—and at a very attractive price. The whole joke about Wells is that he sells evil the way a shopkeeper sells cheese.

Wells dies because he has selfishly used his knowledge for monetary gain. Like many other Victorian works, Gilbert & Sullivan's operas detest greed above all other motivations and have nothing but contempt for venal characters such as *The Mikado's* Pooh-Bah, *Utopia, Limited's* Mr. Goldbury, *Trial by Jury's* Judge, the title character in *The Grand Duke*, or *The Gondoliers'* Duke of Plaza-Toro. Wells is one in a long line of people willing to do anything for money, and he is literally damned for it.

To sum up, George Grossmith's Wells was unquestionably funny but villainous as well. Gilbert the director saw to it that the invocation scene and the final damnation scene were appropriately fiery, keeping the comic and demonic elements in proper balance. It is only over time that the ending has come to seem unsatisfactory, and the fault lies not in the opera but in its performance.

If Wells is the key to the Faust story that is *The Sorcerer's* dramatic skeleton, Alexis and Aline are the key to its thematic flesh and blood. In this regard Wells is simply a plot device, a convenient means to teach Alexis an important lesson.

The lesson aspect of the story is crucial. *Faust* is quintessentially a morality tale, and so is *The Sorcerer*. It introduces for the first time two central concerns of the Gilbert & Sullivan operas: the importance of free will—the ability to choose our own destinies—and the search for the true nature of love.

The lesson on free will is the most immediately obvious. Alexis is determined to impose his own ideas about love onto the village, and must nearly die in order to learn how wrong he is.

On the other hand, Aline, who with Daly functions as the opera's moral center (she's afraid of Wells, sees nothing wrong with the socially inappropriate Partlet–Sir Marmaduke match, and accepts her love for Alexis on its own terms), has nothing more to learn. Her first reaction to the idea is absolutely right: "Oh, Alexis! I don't think it would be right. I don't indeed. And then—a real magician! Oh, it would be downright wicked."

Alexis thinks he knows better, of course, and sets himself on the road to disaster by overriding the free will of others. Throughout the next 10 operas, Gilbert & Sullivan repeatedly show characters torn between their own hearts and external forces such as legal law, fairy law, etiquette, and social rank. In every case, the constraints on free will are ultimately discarded. This theme is never again as central as in *The Sorcerer*, but it is a running motif in every opera through *The Yeomen of the Guard* and perhaps accounts in part for Gilbert's shaky moral reputation with the Victorians, to whom free will was untrustworthy and external constraint a way of life.

(In his *W. S. Gilbert* Max Keith Sutton offers an interesting, largely persuasive analysis of this element in several of the operas, though he tends to overestimate its importance to a given opera while overlooking more dominant thematic elements.)[7]

Alexis's central error is one of misunderstanding, and what he misunderstands is love itself. *The Sorcerer* is an opera obsessed with love—of its 11 solos, for example, nine are about love. As the central figure, Alexis is the most love-obsessed. But unlike the title character in *Patience*, which is thematically much akin to *The Sorcerer*, Alexis is not striving to learn about love—he thinks he already knows all about it.

The problem is that he doesn't. To him, love is a drug, a rapturous source of "limpid joy." He equates love with the feeling it inspires in him and out of genuine generosity of spirit longs to share that feeling with everyone he meets.

However, he is misguided. His song "For Love Alone" initially impresses with its heartfelt passion; on further thought, however, it is a massive fallacy. Gilbert surely joins him in rejecting love based on money, on pride, on rank, or on beauty. But when Alexis boils it down to a determination to "love for love alone," he goes off the rails, valuing love itself even over his loved one—in principle, he could love anyone "for love alone."

More to the point, Alexis isn't really in love—at least, not as it manifests itself in Gilbert & Sullivan. Aline is: Her introductory "Happy Young Heart" is about Alexis and expresses her radiant joy in his presence. His

"For Love Alone," on the other hand, isn't about her at all; it's essentially an evangelical exhortation, an assertion of his beliefs on the subject, and thus not about anyone but himself.

Alexis wants to share his ecstasy with everyone, and that's exactly what Wells lets him do. If he is "welling over with limpid joy," so too are Constance and the Notary, Marmaduke and Partlet, and especially Aline and Daly.

Yet they are anything but happy: "Dear friends, take pity on my lot," exclaims Constance on falling for the Notary, while Aline, who previously swore that "[t]rue love, faithfully given and faithfully returned, [is] the source of every earthly joy," now can only wail that "[s]ome most extraordinary spell/on us has cast its magic fell." ("Fell," an interesting word meaning "cruel or evil," occurs only once elsewhere in Gilbert & Sullivan, in the incantation's "Ye demons fell/with yelp and yell.")

Their philter-induced unhappiness mirrors that of Alexis himself, even before the potion goes awry. For one supposedly rapturously in love, Alexis is remarkably argumentative, especially with Aline. She gives up everything for him. The dynamic of her potion-drinking scene is, of course, that of a death scene—which, to Aline, it is: the death of free will. But Alexis won't yield an inch for her. He's so caught up in his own feelings, in his own messianic zeal, that he has no thought for the person he supposedly loves.

This is not true love. What he has is nothing more substantial than what Constance has with the Notary—surface passion, with frustration barely beneath the surface. Alexis has wanted to share his "love" with everyone in the village—and that is exactly what he does, leaving them all as passionate and frustrated as he is.

Squarely in the Faustian tradition, Alexis discovers that getting what he wanted—everyone in the village madly in love and Aline willing to drink the potion—isn't enough to make him happy. In fact, quite the opposite: What he really learns is that he should have been happy all along.

What is true love? The answer is the same as in *Patience*, if not as well-expressed in *The Sorcerer*. It is the loved one, nothing more and nothing less. Aline knew it all along—"Happy Young Heart," her opening song, captures it perfectly, just as the naive Patience does when she initially says, "I seem now to know what love is! It has been revealed to me—it is Archibald Grosvenor!"

In the world according to Gilbert & Sullivan, love cannot be shared, forced, changed, or even explained; it is not sexuality or sympathy or similarity, though those are all aspects of it. Love is the loved one.

Unfortunately for those directing or performing the opera, this thematic substance is present only sketchily in *The Sorcerer*. In years to come, Gilbert would become a master at shaping dialogue and lyrics that would speak volumes, every detail clearly laid out. Sullivan would be able to tellingly enhance characterization with a single well-placed chord. The thematic material would be clearly, concisely expressed, every nuance readily accessible for the actor to work with.

In *The Sorcerer*, this is not the case. The dialogue and lyrics falter; the music is conventional rather than revelatory. The ending, in particular, is abrupt and hard to stage effectively. Alexis's coming to his senses—and possibly to true love?—is there, but it's not explored. The actor must build on what he is given, rather than luxuriating in it, as can an actress playing Patience.

Ultimately, therefore, *The Sorcerer* fails on its thematic level. The story of the love potion and the subject of free will are both effectively explored, but the meaning of love remains elusive—the ideas are there, but they are never resolved into clarity as they will later be in *Patience* and *The Yeomen of the Guard.*

But the mere existence of a thematic level provides a clear road to the future of Gilbert & Sullivan opera, as well as a clear break from what has gone before. The aspirations are clear, even this early—all that's missing are the technical skills to realize those aspirations and the boldness to transcend the crippling conventions of the operatic form. By their next opera, *H. M. S. Pinafore*, they were clearly headed for that goal.

The closest Gilbert & Sullivan ever came to "rewriting" an opera was with *Patience*, for which *The Sorcerer* stands almost as a rough draft. Dr. Daly's lines "Time was when maidens of the noblest station/forsaking even military men,/would gaze upon me, rapt in adoration" contain the distilled essence of Reginald Bunthorne (who was, after all, originally supposed to be a young curate).

The Sorcerer is a comedy about the meaning of love, but it is warped almost beyond recognition by the genre inexperience of its creators. Perhaps that is why they returned to the same ground in later years for *Patience* and even told the same story once more as tragedy in *The Yeomen of the Guard.*

Clearly this is a theme that meant a great deal to both men and inspired some of their best work. It may seem unfair to *The Sorcerer* to compare it to the authors' future works, but after all *The Sorcerer* would rarely if ever be performed today if it had not been created by the authors of *The Mikado* and *The Pirates of Penzance*. So it's hard to resist pushing past the cloggings of convention to see the true Savoy heart underneath.

If Gilbert & Sullivan didn't quite hit their mark the first time out, it certainly was a valuable learning experience for both men and pointed the way toward their later triumphs.

Facing page: FIGURE 6.1. Rutland Barrington as Captain Corcoran in the original production of *H. M. S. Pinafore* at the Opera Comique. Initially one of the opera's most engaging comic characters, Corcoran's impact fades as his central joke is appropriated and enhanced by Sir Joseph Porter, until ultimately the Captain is reduced to a stock heavy. *Source: The Pierpont Morgan Library, Gilbert and Sullivan Collection.*

6

H. M. S. Pinafore

H. M. S. Pinafore was both an ending and a beginning for Gilbert & Sullivan. It closed what was, in retrospect, the first quarter of their collaboration, but it also opened the doors to a whole new world of comic opera, a world they themselves were to create over the next 12 years.

From a career standpoint, of course, *H. M. S. Pinafore* "made" Gilbert & Sullivan. *Trial by Jury* and *The Sorcerer* had made their creators the talk of London, but *H. M. S. Pinafore* made them the talk of England and, with its phenomenal American success, true international celebrities.

It wasn't merely *H. M. S. Pinafore's* 571 London performances (though *The Sorcerer* had been deemed a hit with 178). *The Sorcerer* was a popular comic opera, but *H. M. S. Pinafore* was a popular craze—its sheet music sold furiously, its music was performed in concerts throughout the English-speaking world, and its catch-phrases were on everybody's lips. (Almost literally—when Sullivan met the German crown prince years later, the future Kaiser Wilhelm II astonished the composer by quoting *H. M. S. Pinafore's* "When I Was a Lad.")[1]

With *H. M. S. Pinafore*, Gilbert & Sullivan found themselves a joint phenomenon. Before *H. M. S. Pinafore*, their collaborations had been popular, but each had been better known for other works—Gilbert for *Bab*, Sullivan as a leading English conductor and composer of concert music. After *H. M. S. Pinafore*, each was primarily known as half of the world-famous collaboration.

The two really were world-famous. Touring the American West, Sullivan was reportedly challenged to a brawl in a tavern under the mistaken impression that he was the boxer John L. Sullivan. When he hastened to identify himself as Arthur Sullivan, the burly cowhand responded, "What, the chap that wrote up *Pinafore?*" and offered to buy the relieved composer a drink.[2]

Fittingly, it was during the run of *H. M. S. Pinafore* that Gilbert & Sullivan became themselves. Billed until that time as "Sullivan & Gilbert," for reasons still unknown the team metamorphosed into "Gilbert & Sullivan," well on their way to becoming, in Gilbert's later words, "as much an institution as Westminster Abbey."[3]

H. M. S. Pinafore also saw the institutionalization of their partnership, now clearly understood to be open-ended. *Thespis* and *Trial by Jury* had been one-shot efforts, *The Sorcerer* the first step in a commercial speculation. If *The Sorcerer* had flopped, the collaboration probably would have gone down with it.

But *H. M. S. Pinafore* was a success of a different order. It was the wild popularity of *H. M. S. Pinafore* that both led to conflict between Carte and his fractious partners in the Comedy Opera Company and emboldened him to form the tripartite partnership of author, composer, and producer that was to present the next eight Gilbert & Sullivan operas. Because

Gilbert & Sullivan themselves shared in the profits of the opera rather than the usual simple royalties, the arrangement stood to make them both very rich and, of course, motivated both to continue to work together.

After *H. M. S. Pinafore*, it was clear that each had something to offer that the other could find nowhere else.

The partnership was now also institutionalized in creative terms. *Thespis* and *Trial by Jury* had been written primarily for performers who had been forced on the authors. They had been able to choose their own cast for *The Sorcerer*, but most of the performers were new to both men. Not a single *Sorcerer* principal had sung in any previous Sullivan opera, though a few (notably Harriet Everard, the original Mrs. Partlet and Little Buttercup) had worked with Gilbert.

For *H. M. S. Pinafore* the repertory company was largely in place, and the partners could replace or continue performers at their own will. Thus Mrs. Howard Paul, the formidable Lady Sangazure, was delicately eased out (despite Jessie Bond's decades-later recollection to the contrary, it seems clear that Paul was consciously written out);[4] tenor George Bentham and soprano Alice May were replaced by George Power and Emma Howson; and Bond herself was added to the company. George Grossmith (Wells and Porter), Rutland Barrington (Daly and Captain Corcoran) and Richard Temple (Sir Marmaduke and Deadeye) were all retained.

Those returning actors found parts that were literally written for them and thus made better use of their individual talents. Grossmith may have won the role of Wells because he could sing its already written patter song,[5] but Sir Joseph Porter was created specifically for him, and it showed.

Likewise, the authors made better use of the choruses, mostly the same people who had appeared in *The Sorcerer*. They were given more to do than previously, including some comedy bits, especially for the sailors. *H. M. S. Pinafore* also marks the team's first use of fully differentiated male and female choruses (*Trial by Jury* had partly differentiated them—four bridesmaids and a male jury—but most of its chorus was the undifferentiated courtroom audience.)

In short, *The Sorcerer* had given Gilbert & Sullivan the tools, but it took once around to learn how to use them. From *H. M. S. Pinafore* on, they would have the resources and the artistic freedom to do comic opera however they liked.

The question was: What would they do with this opportunity? Neither man had planned a career in comic opera, and initially neither was fully prepared for it. Gilbert had exhaustively studied both burlesque and verse plays before launching himself in these areas, and had specific, strongly held standards and goals by the time he began writing for the stage. From childhood Sullivan had been trained as a conductor and composer of concert music, so by the time he wrote his first major pieces his own ideas had been substantially formed.

Such was not the case with comic opera, with which neither was as familiar. Their early efforts, including Gilbert's with Frederic Clay and Sullivan's with F. C. Burnand, had paired them with equally untrained collaborators—ironically, Gilbert with one of Sullivan's closest friends, Sullivan with one of Gilbert's greatest rivals. Neither had studied the medium in which they were now working nor shown much desire to do so.

Accordingly, their earliest collaborations reflected outsiders' viewpoints. They parodied the excesses of conventional opera, which as audience members they had long scoffed at, while otherwise adhering fairly closely to those conventions.

Like *The Sorcerer*, *H. M. S. Pinafore* generally follows genre conventions, alternately parodying and embodying operatic clichés. But *H. M. S. Pinafore* shows a more polished touch in words and music alike. Both men learned from their experience with *The Sorcerer* (in their correspondence, each compared the old and new shows frequently), and handled the genre conventions more effectively for *H. M. S. Pinafore*.

Still, one can often see the authors straining against the constraints of the form, itching to do things that they weren't supposed to do according to the genre's conventions. After a partial hiatus for the hastily written, somewhat tongue-in-cheek *The Pirates of Penzance*, their dissatisfaction with the genre as they found it would explode into a whole new approach in *Patience*.

So venerated is *H. M. S. Pinafore* today, so beloved even by non-Savoyards, that it seems almost churlish to point out its many flaws.

(It was not always so acclaimed, of course. In 1881, William Archer published an essay in which he reported of another critic, "Mr. Frederic Harrison is of opinion that the age which can tolerate *H. M. S. Pinafore* cannot read Homer.")[6]

The fact is that *H. M. S. Pinafore* triumphs in spite of itself: Its creators' raw talents transcend a structure that undercuts even the opera's best moments. But, despite their growth since *The Sorcerer*, both men are still new at what they're doing, and their inexperience shows.

Of the two, Sullivan generally is more successful at overcoming the conventional restraints of the genre—the show's popularity owes more to its music than to its words. This may be because, as a past master of hymns and drawing-room ballads, he was more used to tailoring his art to exacting genre constraints.

Nonetheless, those constraints are severe, and the score suffers for it. In particular, *H. M. S. Pinafore* (like *The Sorcerer*) adheres to the ballad-opera tradition in featuring many short songs, averaging one or two minutes instead of the later operas' four or more. Most are solos, and even putative duets tend to have characters singing *at* each other rather than *with* each other.

H. M. S. Pinafore also relies heavily on direct address to the audience in both songs and dialogue. This is most noticeable in the frequent asides in dialogue and in songs such as "Refrain, Audacious Tar" and "Things Are Seldom What They Seem"—a stylistic mannerism reminiscent of English music-hall performance styles. There are also several soliloquy songs ("Sorry Her Lot," "The Nightingale," "Fair Moon") and a number of non-soliloquies nevertheless entirely directed to the audience, such as "I Am the Captain of the Pinafore."

Virtually every character has a song of introduction that is dramatically unnecessary, since the people onstage already know who he or she is. The prime example is the Captain's first song, in which he introduces himself to his crew and reiterates the policies that presumably he has been applying for their last six months at sea.

Such songs make nice showcases for the characters and for the singers playing them, but are dramatically awkward. Not only do they break the dramatic momentum and leave the other characters idly onstage, but also they remind the audience that this is only a play, undermining both dramatic intensity and character plausibility.

The combination of short songs and a heavy reliance on solos is more inhibiting to Sullivan than to Gilbert. A relatively short opera, *H. M. S. Pinafore* features 62 different component pieces—37 songs, nine recitatives, and 14 dialogues, plus two instrumentals. By contrast, *Iolanthe* is nearly an hour longer but contains one less component piece.

This choppiness makes it difficult for the composer to link musical elements as he later would. *Iolanthe* and *Princess Ida* are tightly integrated scores, their musical ideas developed continuously throughout the opera. *H. M. S. Pinafore's* musical ideas are not so much developed as repeated—there are 12 different reprises, compared to only three in *Iolanthe* or two in *The Mikado.*

Similarly, short solos don't allow Sullivan the musical power he would soon find in true ensemble numbers. Compare the Ralph-Josephine "Refrain, Audacious Tar" scene with the Frederic-Mabel "Stay, Frederic, Stay" scene, written only a year later. Both follow the basic pattern of traded solos followed by a joint ending, but the *Pirates of Penzance* sequence is far more elaborated. Sullivan ends the scene not with a few bars of simple harmonies but with a glorious duet many times longer and far more musically and theatrically exciting.

Surely the length of the numbers in *The Pirates of Penzance* is a reaction, on the parts of author and composer alike, to the structural constraints they imposed on themselves in making *H. M. S. Pinafore* the genre-conventional show that it is. *The Pirates of Penzance* is a conscious abandonment of the ballad opera, with longer sequences, more vigorous choruses, and a greater emphasis on duets, trios, and ensemble numbers. It offers a vivid contrast to *H. M. S. Pinafore*, which remains mired in operatic orthodoxy, parodic and nonparodic alike, to the evident frustration of both its creators.

Nevertheless, Sullivan's work on *H. M. S. Pinafore* in some ways far exceeds *The Sorcerer*. He himself didn't think so, probably because of *H. M. S. Pinafore's* smaller, less "operatic" focus. He missed the drama of scenes such as Wells's demonic incantation and found less scope for musical humor.

Five weeks before the opening, he wrote to his mother: "I am in the full swing of my new work. It will be bright and probably more popular than *The Sorcerer*, but it is not so clever."[7]

In this judgment, he was at least partially correct. To many accustomed to later Gilbert & Sullivan, *H. M. S. Pinafore* seems excessively restrained, oddly bloodless. Nothing is very loud or very fast—or, for that matter, very soft or very slow.

The robust vigor that was to be hinted at in *The Pirates of Penzance* and come to full flower in *Patience* and *Iolanthe* is not to be seen. Contrast the energy level of "We Sail the Ocean Blue" with *Patience's* "The Soldiers of Our Queen," for example. The later song is bolder and brassier, with a musical exuberance the *H. M. S. Pinafore* chorus lacks.

H. M. S. Pinafore is peak early Sullivan: graceful melodies and textbook-perfect harmonies that are pretty without being especially original. This is not great music but pleasing music, offering cleverness and theatrical sensibility more than real emotion or dramatic power.

Still, Sullivan does some fine work for *H. M. S. Pinafore*. In particular, he uses his music to elaborate on theatrical ideas, to capture character and situation, and to integrate some of the opera's many disjointed pieces.

He seems consciously to use music to fight against the limitations of genre convention. For example, he several times uses the combination of two different tunes, an idea he had used effectively in *The Sorcerer*, but on a smaller scale.

There, he set the male and female verses of "With Heart and With Voice" to variant tunes, not only enlivening the repetition but also setting up a musical coup when the two versions are combined for the chorus's exit. In *H. M. S. Pinafore* the idea is worked out more ingeniously, combining not variant tunes but completely different ones.

The entrance of the female chorus, for example, is spiced by reintroducing the sailors' "We Sail the Ocean Blue" and setting it in counterpoint with the women's "Gaily Tripping, Lightly Skipping." The effect is musically engaging but also serves to integrate two potentially disparate elements, binding the show together more tightly.

He uses the same device twice in the Act 1 finale, setting Dick Deadeye's growling complaints, "You must submit" and "Our Captain, ere the day is gone," against massed chorus numbers. In each case, two pieces are transformed into one—probably to Gilbert's surprise, since the libretto presents the words sequentially.

Similarly, Gilbert's libretto provides two unrelated blocks of words when the Captain confronts Ralph and Josephine with "Pretty Daughter of Mine" and they respond with the duet "Humble, Poor and Lowly Born." But Sullivan combines the two, using the "Pretty Daughter" melody as orchestral underscoring to "Humble, Poor and Lowly Born" (ex. 6.1): The effect not only ties the scene together more tightly but also increases its theatrical power, sustaining the Captain's anger and building tension beneath the surface beauty of the duet. It is a perfect musical equivalent to the actual scene, with the lovers singing their plea while the fuming Captain prepares to flog Ralph.

The *H. M. S. Pinafore* score abounds in deft musical characterizations. Immediately following the "Pretty Daughter" sequence and "He Is an Englishman," Captain Corcoran's frustration builds to a climactic imprecation:

> In uttering a reprobation
> > to any British tar,
> I try to speak with moderation,
> > but you have gone too far.
> I'm very sorry to disparage
> > a humble foremast lad,
> but to seek your Captain's child in marriage—
> > why, damme, it's too bad!

An inattentive composer might have treated this as a recitative or at best a short, unremarkable melody. But Sullivan, as usual attuned to Gilbert's subtlest touches, picks up the slight stuttering rhythm imparted by the extra syllable at the end of every odd line. He responds to its vaguely drumbeat quality by setting the words with a series of clipped pauses, suggesting the Captain's struggle to control himself, breaking up every odd line until the last one, a spurt of music that captures perfectly the Captain finally losing his temper (ex. 6.2):

This attention to detail characterizes virtually the entire score. The flurried canon of "Did you hear him?" and "He said damme" in reaction to the oath is hilarious, for example. And even if the music lacks the scope of such later scores as *Iolanthe, Princess Ida,* or *The Mikado, H. M. S. Pinafore* ranks as one of Sullivan's best scores for the sheer ingenuity with which he compensates for potentially crippling structural problems.

(Sullivan also deserves credit for one other element of the opera's success: He reportedly suggested "Pinafore" as better than the rhyme Gilbert had chosen for "one cheer more."[8] A good thing, too—even in retrospect, it's hard to imagine the world going mad for *H. M. S. Semaphore!*)

6.1. In "Humble, poor and lowly born" from *H. M. S. Pinafore*, Sullivan uses a dancing instrumental part, played by violins, to reprise Captain Corcoran's "Pretty Daughter of Mine," helping tie together a scene that could easily have been musically fragmented.

6.2. In setting Captain Corcoran's "In uttering a reprobation" from *H. M. S. Pinafore*, Sullivan clips off the rhythmic pattern, introducing crisp eighth and sixteenth rests, unasked-for by the lyric, to produce a musical representation of the Captain's struggle to keep his temper.

As for Gilbert's contribution, it is more mixed. While in some ways he has progressed far beyond *The Sorcerer*, in others his work is frustratingly limited.

After all, he is most responsible for *H. M. S. Pinafore's* adherence to the conventional operatic form, as subsequently he would be most responsible for the team's fresher, freer comic-opera form.

The great strengths of this libretto are its satiric acuity, the smoothness of its lyrics, and its expanded use of the chorus. Its great weaknesses are a lack of focus in lyrics and dialogue alike, and its failure to create characters who are either funny or real.

In general, *H. M. Pinafore* is a structural step forward from *The Sorcerer*. There is still a lot of recitative, though much less in the second act (only one, versus eight in the first act). On a scene level, the play is more tightly structured, so that the revolving-door transitions that broke the flow of *The Sorcerer* are all but absent—there is only one, leading into Josephine's "Sorry Her Lot." In particular, keeping Captain Corcoran onstage for virtually the entire second act makes him the centerpiece of a continuously flowing act that is exemplary in its escalating dramatic intensity.

Gilbert's dialogue has also matured markedly. He still occasionally places inappropriate words in his characters' mouths (the Captain's use of "Elysian," for example), but far less often. The convoluted diction and forced blank verse of *The Sorcerer* have yielded to more conversational speech patterns and rhythms, giving the dialogue a naturalness that is almost impossible to achieve in *The Sorcerer*

In particular, there is more interplay. *The Sorcerer's* dialogue scenes had generally involved one character talking at another, with little real interaction. *H. M. S. Pinafore's* funniest lines tend to be reactions (Josephine's unintentionally ironic "His simple eloquence goes to my heart," for example, in response to an absurdly florid outburst from Ralph).

Granted, Gilbert still doesn't shape dialogues well. *H. M. S. Pinafore's* dialogue scenes tend to stop or be interrupted, rather than coming to satisfying endings, as would those in later operas. On the whole, however, its dialogue is much smoother and more natural than that of *The Sorcerer*.

The lyrics are also much improved. There's only one truly leaden lyric, Ralph's cliché-riddled "The Nightingale." The other songs are fresher and more focused on the character who sings them. Gilbert's love for seaman's lingo helps make his sailors more convincing, as a rule, though as a result occasional inappropriate lines (such as "Hymen will defray the fare") seem all the more jarring.

Technically, *H. M. S. Pinafore* is a better show than *The Sorcerer* in nearly every respect. Gilbert seems more aware of writing for specific characters and of creating realistic interaction between them, all of which is a great step forward.

None of these advances mask the libretto's weaknesses, however. Its song structures are awkward, relying heavily on couplets and matching frustratingly short verses with wearyingly long choruses that echo either the soloists' lines or the previous chorus.

"When I Was a Lad," for example, has three lines of chorus for each six lines of verse, all repeating Sir Joseph's lines. "Kind Captain, I've Important Information" offers 16 measures of verse followed by 12 of chorus and instrumental bridge for each of four verses, all but the last identical.

In later operas Gilbert tended to use longer verses—eight or 12 lines, as opposed to the four lines typical in *H. M. S. Pinafore*. He also virtually abandoned repetitive choruses in favor of evolving choruses that commented on the verses, such as the sarcastic choral responses to "The Criminal Cried" in *The Mikado*.

H. M. S. Pinafore may be a comic opera, but its jokes aren't funny. It has only a few character laughs and virtually no dialogue laughs. The "joke" lines are labored puns—the Bos'n's response to Ralph's saying that he "lacks birth" ("you've a berth on board this very ship") or Sir Joseph's "your position as a topman is a very exalted one" are typical. "He loves, alas / he loves a lass" wouldn't be out of place in *Thespis*.

As for the songs, most lack any comic point. This is surprising, because Gilbert later would bring wit even to love ballads and plot summaries. He might mine the humor in a tender situation (*The Mikado's* "Were You Not to Ko-Ko Plighted") or find the tenderness in a humorous situation (*The Pirates of Penzance's* "Stay, Frederic, Stay"). He might create an overblown parody of a love song (*The Mikado's* "Titwillow") or linger on a romantic paradox (*Utopia, Limited's* "Sweet and Low"). Always he had a knack for simultaneously serving the plot and being funny.

In *H. M. S. Pinafore* this is far from the case. Most of the songs merely serve the plot, and few are at all funny. The love songs ("The Nightingale," "A Maiden Fair to See," "Sorry Her Lot," "Refrain, Audacious Tar") aren't excessive enough to be parodies or fresh enough to be convincing; they don't even try to be funny.

Other songs might have been funny but aren't. "I'm Called Little Buttercup" is a virtual clone of "My Name Is John Wellington Wells," simply a list of items for sale, except that Wells's items were funny, while Buttercup's are commonplace and uninteresting. Many performers have found it hard to memorize, simply because there's no order to it beyond the rhyme scheme, nor any real structure.

Most of the other songs have no raison d'être, conveying neither humor nor dramatic content. "We Sail the Ocean Blue," "Gaily Tripping, Lightly Skipping," "Things Are Seldom What They Seem, "Never Mind the Why and Wherefore," "Kind Captain, I've Important Information," "A British Tar Is a Soaring Soul"—all lack humor. They don't fail to be funny, they simply fail to try—there are no jokes in their lyrics. Of *H. M. S. Pinafore's* 30 songs, at most nine are even marginally comic in intent.

Nor do they serve any dramatic point. "We Sail the Ocean Blue" and "Gaily Tripping" don't tell us anything important about the characters or the situation. "Things Are Seldom What They Seem" and "Never Mind the Why and Wherefore" are musically engaging, but their lyrics merely repeat at length what has already happened in the dialogue.

In general the lyrics are platforms to be built on by the composer and by the performers, not worthwhile pieces in their own right. They give Sullivan room to strut his stuff, and many can be made funny by sufficiently capable comedians. But this is a far cry from the real creative fusion of music and words in the later shows.

Character humor, soon to become the lifeblood of Gilbert & Sullivan comedy, takes a few steps forward in *H. M. S. Pinafore*—but they're short ones.

Sir Joseph Porter is easily the best comic role the team has created to this point, and the use of the sailors as a collective character, as in their agreement that they all hate Deadeye, is an engaging foreshadowing of operas to come.

But other than the parodic element embodied in his diction, there's nothing particularly funny about Ralph as a character, nor about Josephine, Hebe, Buttercup, the Bos'n, or the Carpenter. They are essentially unhumorous characters occasionally involved in humorous goings-on.

Captain Corcoran starts out well, with his genial coddling of his crew. It's a funny idea (one Gilbert first used in his 1868 Bab Ballad "Captain Reese"), playing off the Captain Bligh image of the Royal Navy. "I Am the Captain of the Pinafore" sets up the idea well. Think of it—a high-ranking naval officer who treats his crew delicately and detests bad language of any kind! Obviously, this captain will provide many good laughs.

Unfortunately, Sir Joseph embodies exactly the same joke. He too is a high-ranking naval official who treats his crew delicately and detests bad language of any kind. Indeed, "I Am the Monarch of the Sea," with its emphasis on seasickness and decorous language, is lyrically a virtual reprise of "I Am the Captain of the Pinafore."

But Sir Joseph is even higher ranking and has the added irony of never having been to sea—even his name, "Porter," evokes a landlubber. The joke is funnier embodied in him, leaving Captain Corcoran to evolve into a straight man (in the act 1 dialogue with Sir Joseph) and finally into something close to a villain (by the time he's about to lash Ralph).

As originally introduced, the Captain and Sir Joseph are too similar to coexist. The joke works better if one of the two is a rigid disciplinarian, and as a result the Captain is forced into that role. But it's not a good fit—the kindly Captain Corcoran, who says "Good morning" to his crew and inquires about their health, probably *would* say "if you please."

The mature Gilbert & Sullivan would never allow such duplication of a comic idea. Ko-Ko, Pish-Tush, and the Mikado all have their jokes, but none is the same as Pooh-Bah's. As a result, their opera is funnier.

The most successful humor of *H. M. S. Pinafore* comes from its parody elements.

Naturally, these elements are the hardest to appreciate today, since the nautical melodrama is long gone. But on examination they reveal a good deal about the opera and its structure. And they show that, while Gilbert's skill with character humor still leaves much to be desired, he thoroughly understands parody.

Such devices as long-held secrets, concealed identities, and switched babies were, of course, standard in Victorian melodrama. The discovery of long-lost noblemen hidden among the peasantry was also a staple, serving the Victorians' desire to allow change yet keep things as they were: They could cheer a noblewoman's right to marry a peasant, but it was much neater and less disruptive of social norms if, after ringing declarations of equality, it turned out that the peasant was himself a nobleman all along.

It also supported the notion that an actual peasant wouldn't appeal to a noblewoman: Given the right to marry whomever she wanted, she would instinctively choose one of her own class.

There was, after all, such a thing as "breeding" or "sensibility." An aristocrat, even raised as a peasant, would be a cut above the norm, just as a peasant, even raised as an aristocrat, would have an earthy, ignoble side. "Blood will tell," as the saying went.

In short, the Victorian creed believed 100 percent in nature, 0 percent in nurture. In *H. M. S. Pinafore*, Gilbert uses his depiction of Rackstraw and Corcoran (and to a lesser extent Josephine) to spoof this idea, a spoof as delightful to Victorians as it may be incomprehensible to modern audiences raised in a society that accords nature and nurture equal value.

It is a commonplace to note that Ralph speaks like an aristocrat. Some have even used this fact to attack Gilbert's dialogue skill, ignoring the fact that the other sailors have a clearly differentiated, much rougher diction.

Less noted but equally important to Gilbert's comic point is that Captain Corcoran speaks like the sailors. Compare the two men as they rhapsodize over their respective unattainable loves:

Ralph: A maiden fair to see,
　　　the pearl of minstrelsy,
　　　　　a bud of blushing beauty
　　　for whom proud nobles sigh
　　　and with each other vie
　　　　　to do her menial's duty.
Captain: A plump and pleasing person!

With only occasional lapses, each man's diction is consistent throughout the opera. Ralph is lofty and refined, Corcoran bluff and to the point.

Gilbert is foreshadowing the opera's "surprise" ending, in a way that was far more obvious (and funnier) to 1870s audiences, familiar with the conventions he was parodying, than it is today.

Beyond the words, the plot continues the idea that "blood will tell." Corcoran, for example, has all the hearty egalitarianism of the sailors. He can't even swear at Ralph without prefacing it with an apology: "I'm very sorry to disparage a humble foremast lad."

By contrast, Ralph is outspoken, even insulting, in rebuking the Captain: "Proud officer, that haughty lip uncurl! Vain man, suppress that supercilious sneer!" There is no hint of apology—even as a humble sailor, he has the quarterdeck swagger that Corcoran lacks.

Ralph's apparent dilemma between his heart and his head, between love and duty, is actually a crisis of social misplacement—his heart reacts to what he is, his head to what he is supposed to be. His heart draws him to an aristocrat's daughter, while his head tells him it's improper. (This is, of course, exactly the same dilemma Josephine faces between the "God of Reason" and the "God of Love" in her aria, "The Hours Creep On Apace.")

As always in Gilbert & Sullivan, the heart knows best. As soon as Ralph is elevated to his proper rank, everything falls into place, and heart and head are reconciled. (Josephine is still the right match for him, of course, but it's because of who her mother was—presumably an aristocrat's daughter—not her lowborn father.)

Corcoran suffers similar problems of social misplacement. He catalogues his problems in "Fair Moon, to Thee I Sing": "But now, my kindly crew rebel, / my daughter to a tar is partial, / Sir Joseph storms, and sad to tell, / he threatens a court martial." And, of course, he can't love Buttercup, whom he would "were we differently situated." Like Ralph, he yearns for a woman whom his head tells him is inappropriate.

Also like Ralph, he sees his problems vanish when he is restored to his proper rank: The crew is now someone else's problem; his daughter can marry the man she wants with perfect propriety; Sir Joseph is out of the picture; and Corcoran can marry Buttercup. He seems happier at the final curtain as "a member of the crew" than at any time previously.

Again, a modern audience will miss much of this, but to Victorians it wasn't so subtle. Today audiences often find the opera musically delightful and lyrically clever, but wonder how the Victorians found so much humor in it. The fault, of course, lies not in *H. M. S. Pinafore* but in the social changes wrought by more than a century.

Satire tends to outlive parody, however, and *H. M. S. Pinafore* still flourishes as a satire, tweaking Victorian ideas of status and power.

The opera's ending has been widely criticized as illogical and inconsistent: According to the famous *"Pinafore* age paradox," Captain Corcoran is apparently roughly the same age—or at least within bounds of conventional marriagability—as both the woman who nursed him as a baby and the man who marries his daughter. If Josephine is perhaps 20, the Captain should be 40 and Buttercup perhaps 60; Ralph himself should be 40, the same as the Captain. Yet, even as directed by the detail-obsessed Gilbert, the roles were never played at those ages.

This paradox is only a flaw, however, in the light of later Gilbert & Sullivan operas, most of which revel in their coherence. *H. M. S. Pinafore* isn't meant to be logical: Victorian audiences didn't particularly care about narrative consistency or plausibility, and Gilbert is after something different here from what he would seek in future operas.

Critics have often seen *H. M. S. Pinafore* in the light of later Gilbert & Sullivan satire—Gilbert taking an essentially conservative position by allowing his characters to espouse an apparently attractive ideal (*Patience*'s aestheticism, for example, or republican equality in *The Gondoliers*), only to take it to a ridiculous extreme and expose it as idealistic and impractical. This interpretation makes Sir Joseph a Bunthorne equivalent, and *H. M. S. Pinafore* an argument in favor of Victorian class distinctions as they were.

However, this interpretation doesn't hold up under closer analysis. To be sure, Sir Joseph is depicted as an ass, and his pronouncements of egalitarianism are shown to be hypocritical and unrealistic. But the idea of class distinctions doesn't come out any better, especially in the changed-babies ending whose utter absurdity is its entire point.

H. M. S. Pinafore is actually satire in the classic sense, in this case targeting class distinctions. In an approach reminiscent of Swift, Gilbert does not explicitly state his own opinion that the Victorian idea of class distinctions by birth is absurd. Instead, he posits the contrary—such distinctions are natural and proper—and then carries that idea to its logical extreme, proving that the idea itself is ridiculous.

The ending of *H. M. S. Pinafore* represents the logical extreme of the concept of distinction by birth and is *intended* to produce the reaction "Isn't that ridiculous?" The idea, of course, is that showing the absurdity of the extreme version may cause audiences to think anew about the less extreme versions by which they live.

Like any good satirist, Gilbert initially presents his contrary premise—"Captain's daughters don't marry foremast hands"—so reasonably that most of his audience would reflexively agree. But he puts it in the mouth of Deadeye, the obvious villain of the piece. The alert audience member will realize that what Deadeye is saying is the simple truth . . . but also sense that perhaps it shouldn't be.

Gilbert continues by introducing the inane Sir Joseph, a political manipulator who supposedly represents the alternative to distinction-by-birth. Sir Joseph talks a great deal about equality, though always excepting himself from it, but he's such an obvious buffoon that his pronouncements argue against themselves: As Deadeye says, "When people have to obey other people's orders, equality's out of the question."

But Gilbert is not attacking the idea of people obeying other people— clearly, he's in favor of that throughout. The question is: Who obeys whom, or how should status be determined? The opera explicitly raises two possible options, but Gilbert actually endorses a third which, as in Swiftian satire, is not explicitly stated.

Distinction of birth is one way of awarding status, of course, and this is the way the *Pinafore* (like Victorian society as a whole) is run. Captain Corcoran may indeed be a fine sailor, able to "hand, reef and steer / or ship a selvagee," but he owes his rank not to these accomplishments but to being "related to a peer." (In any event, these accomplishments are— understandably, in light of the ending—those of a fine sailor, not a fine captain.) The first verse of "I Am the Captain" is defensive, acknowledging that he owes his position to his birth but insisting that he deserves it anyway.

Many observers misunderstand Captain Corcoran's social and financial standing, misled by Sir Joseph's assertion that the Captain and Josephine "occupy a station in the lower middle class."

While the nouveau-riche Sir Joseph may wish that were the case, we know otherwise: Josephine's song "The Hours Creep On Apace" offers a convincing portrait of "papa's luxurious home, / hung with ancestral armor and old brasses, / carved oak and tapestry from distant Rome, / rare 'blue and white,' Venetian finger-glasses, / rich oriental rugs, luxurious sofa pillows, / and everything that isn't old from Gillow's."

Obviously Captain Corcoran is a younger son of an "old money" family and in fact is socially superior to Sir Joseph (which is, of course, why the wealthy Sir Joseph wants to marry Josephine in the first place). Corcoran is captain of the *Pinafore* for the same reason that the Duke of Plaza-Toro led a regiment—because he was born to leadership. As Sir Joseph correctly observes, "That you are their captain is an accident of birth."

The arbitrariness of the ending is a strong argument against status-by-birth. The revelation of the switching of babies gives Ralph the rank of captain, and presumably that luxurious home, as a matter of course. He will probably be a good captain, but that has nothing to do with it: Because of who his father was, he is a sailor; when he turns out to have had a different father, he becomes a captain.

It's laughably arbitrary—and of course laughter is exactly what Gilbert as satirist is after. The idea that a ship should be entrusted to someone based on birth alone is so silly and yet so logically consistent with the existing practice that real-life status-by-birth is implicitly discredited by the opera's resolution.

The second possible way of determining status is embodied in Sir Joseph Porter, another character who is frequently misunderstood.

Sir Joseph is often viewed as the opposite of the high-born aristocrat, a commoner who worked his way to the top, as he recounts in his famous "When I Was a Lad." But Sir Joseph's commentary isn't necessarily reliable. A closer examination shows him in a much different light.

It is true that Sir Joseph has risen from humble beginnings. (His "Sir" derives from being a KCB, or Knight Commander of the Bath, a title that is conferred, not inherited.) And his low birth indeed underlies his radical views on equality. He sneers at Captain Corcoran's "accident of birth," implying (more accurately than he knows) that without it Corcoran would be no better than the sailors he commands.

In fact, Sir Joseph scorns Corcoran. His opening dialogue is a continuous humiliation of the Captain, and he interrupts even his joyous "Never Mind the Why and Wherefore" for a gratuitous dig at him—"though your nautical relation / in my set could scarcely pass," he tells Josephine. He can't stand the Captain, because Corcoran is the embodiment of status-by-birth, a system in which the low-born Sir Joseph can never attain status.

But the nouveau-riche, self-aggrandizing Porter hardly embodies the rising man of the people. From "I Am the Monarch of the Sea" on, Sir Joseph's lack of qualifications is readily apparent. He knows nothing about the sea but presumes to know everything; he preaches equality but abuses the Captain and his other subordinates; he's vain and gullible and generally funny but far from admirable.

In reality, Sir Joseph's story represents anything but hard work made good. "When I Was a Lad" does not depict a nose-to-the-grindstone toiler but rather a born politician, making his way through flattery and subservience, not talent: He polishes handles. He smiles blandly. He prepares for an exam by dressing up in a new suit, not by studying. He wins political prominence through wealth, not leadership—elected from a "pocket borough," a district controlled by one or more powerful landowners, so he need only please his sponsor, not any electorate. And he advances to the Cabinet by doing as he's told—"I never thought of thinking for myself at all."

Sir Joseph's only real skill is his legal knowledge, and to the failed lawyer Gilbert law was little more than decorous venality. (See *Iolanthe's* "When I Went to the Bar," *Utopia, Limited's* "A Complicated Gentleman," or practically anything in *Trial by Jury.*) In short, Sir Joseph is an embodiment of status-by-politics, a longstanding Gilbertian bugaboo. With his politically obtained title and his zeal to marry Josephine to acquire social standing, Sir Joseph is a perfect match for the "supple MPs" in *Ruddigore's* "Henceforth All the Crimes" who will gladly sell their "country's good name, her repute or her shame" for a baronet's title. Social advancement is clearly his sole motive, given how quickly he drops Josephine after the "change in [her father's] condition."

Captain Corcoran is as guilty in this respect as Sir Joseph. He has only one reason to want Josephine to marry Sir Joseph—power. He already has money and prestige, but Sir Joseph has power that Corcoran can only dream of: "My only daughter is to be the bride of a Cabinet Minister," he sighs. "The prospect is Elysian."

Clearly, status-by-politics is no more desirable than status-by-birth. Run by Sir Joseph, the ship is if anything even more topsy-turvy than under Captain Corcoran. In fact, the cynical Gilbert implies that Victorian society itself is going off the rails because these are the only two routes to power, leaving society in the hands of incompetent aristocrats and ambitious self-promoters.

The option Gilbert prefers and implicitly endorses in *H. M. S. Pinafore* is predictably that which applies to both himself and Sullivan: status-by-talent.

Neither author nor composer had any status by birth. And while Sullivan was more socially skilled than Gilbert, he was by nature a courtier, not a politician. Both had made good use of their talents, earning their way to power and influence.

If this is the preferred option, what character in the opera embodies it? Ralph Rackstraw, of course. He is in the Bos'n's judgment "the smartest lad in all the fleet" (with "smart" referring to general fitness, not merely intelligence). So accomplished is he that when Sir Joseph asks for "that splendid seaman to step forward," Captain Corcoran calls for Ralph without hesitation.

(The traditional comic business of Deadeye coming forward instead was not Gilbert's, incidentally.[9] It is a performer's interpolation that got a laugh, though 30 years later Gilbert permitted its use in a revival at the Savoy.)

What makes *H. M. S. Pinafore* a comedy rather than a dark satire is that the perverse machinations of politics and status-by-birth unpredictably bring the right person to the top. The ship is safe with Rackstraw at the helm, because he's clearly the best qualified for the position, despite his seeming lack of either birth or political skill.

In real life Rackstraw could never become a captain, however talented he was—a fact of which the original audience would have been well aware and which supports Gilbert's real point that both Corcoran and Sir Joseph represent "real world" circumstances that are to the long-term disadvantage of England.

As satires go, *H. M. S. Pinafore* is well balanced and effective, neither bludgeoning the audience with opinion nor submerging it in silliness. Gilbert did not undertake a full-fledged satire again until *Utopia, Limited* (though several intervening operas would include satiric elements), and by 1893 he had forgotten many of the things he'd known when he wrote *H. M. S. Pinafore.*

The most intriguing number in *H. M. S. Pinafore*, and the one most foreshadowing of things to come, is Josephine's song "The Hours Creep On Apace."

In one respect, this is a conventional number, a virtuoso display for the soprano (and Emma Howson indeed won raves singing it). It offers a simple emotional structure—Reason versus Love—and plenty of room for grand musical flourishes, which Sullivan duly provides.

But unlike similar numbers in earlier operas, most notably Aline's "Happy Young Heart" in *The Sorcerer* (and for that matter such earlier *H. M. S. Pinafore* songs as "The Nightingale" and "Sorry Her Lot"), it is not a "shop ballad"—generalized, padded with clichéd imagery, and ready for drawing-room pianos throughout England. Reviewers justly criticized such ballads in this and earlier shows,[10] but "The Hours Creep On Apace" is different.

For one thing, it is longer. For another, it is sharp, specific, and closely tied to the character and her situation. Instead of being a generalized expression of romantic happiness ("Happy Young Heart") or lovelorn sadness ("Sorry Her Lot"), it is a detailed evocation of Josephine's particular situation, complete with details of "papa's luxurious home" and her vision of the squalid dwelling of a sailor's wife.

It is, in short, the only moment in the opera when Josephine Corcoran ceases to be a generic "lass that loved a sailor" and becomes a believable young woman, torn by believably conflicting emotions.

In the later Gilbert & Sullivan operas the funniest characters are usually men, but the most intriguing are women. Aline had been a hesitant step in that direction, but with "The Hours Creep On Apace" Josephine surpasses her and points the way to such memorable characters as Patience, Iolanthe, Princess Ida, Rose Maybud, Mad Margaret and Phoebe Meryll.

(It is no coincidence that, when director Wilford Leach needed an extra soprano solo for Linda Ronstadt in his 1980 Broadway production of *The Pirates of Penzance*, he picked "Sorry Her Lot." This song could be sung by the heroines of at least 10 Gilbert & Sullivan operas and any number of other shows; "The Hours Creep On Apace" and most of its successors could be sung only by the women who sing them.)

None of the other numbers in *H. M. S. Pinafore* live up to the standard of "The Hours Creep On Apace," and the opera itself lacks the unity of later works. Gilbert was only just beginning to appreciate the effectiveness of thematic and imagistic integration.

The use of moon imagery in Rackstraw's "The Nightingale" and Corcoran's "Fair Moon" helps to tie together these linked characters, but it is clichéd and, in any event, is carried no further. Imagery of height and distance, appropriate to the story, figures in several of the scenes, but not enough to become an imagistic leitmotif in the way that death imagery would in *Iolanthe*, for example.

Too often, the images are stock clichés—"buds of blushing beauty," "pearls," "fairest, purest gems," and the like. This is in keeping with typical ballad usage but not extravagant enough to be truly parodic. By the next year, in *The Pirates of Penzance*, Gilbert was writing lines for Frederic that were so broad that the parody was unmistakable. But Ralph Rackstraw is exactly the young hero he seems to be—"a sailor that a lass loved." The play is structurally a parody, but the characters themselves are not.

Indeed, *H. M. S. Pinafore* uses stock characters to a degree that no future Gilbert & Sullivan opera would. It's no coincidence, for example, that Deadeye is the only pure villain in Gilbert & Sullivan (except for *The Yeomen of the Guard*'s offstage Sir Clarence Poltwhistle). In subsequent operas, villainous deeds are carried out by people such as Richard Daunt-less or Katisha, three-dimensional characters with motivations deeper than generic villainy. In those operas, someone as simple and blatant as Dead-eye just wouldn't work; in *H. M. S. Pinafore*, however, he fits right in.

Stock characters are defined by their roles in the plot, which dictate how much stage time they get. *H. M. S. Pinafore* is therefore hurt by its use of stock figures: Sir Joseph, the most engaging character in the opera, has the misfortune to be peripheral to the plot. His is the traditional role of the wealthy-but-objectionable spurned suitor—a bit part. Thus, for all the depth, interest, and welcome humor he brings to the opera, he has little to do.

The same goes for Deadeye, the second most interesting character, whose role as villain similarly marginalizes him. Between them the two have barely 15 minutes of stage time.

Later Gilbert & Sullivan operas would be theme- and character-driven. *Iolanthe*, for example, allows ample time to the Lord Chancellor, an in-triguing character who is only marginally relevant to the plot per se, be-cause he is so central to the opera's thematic exploration. Pooh-Bah is all but irrelevant to the plot of *The Mikado*, but he's a great character in a character-driven opera, so he gets plenty of stage time to develop.

Had the Gilbert & Sullivan of those years written *H. M. S. Pinafore*, Sir Joseph surely would have been given more to do, even if it meant com-plicating the story. But a plot-driven opera doesn't encourage such flexi-bility.

Gilbert's characters have long been criticized as mere puppets, even by those who loved the operas—"To complain that they are not human is to be guilty of irrelevance," the critic Deems Taylor wrote. "They do not pretend to be. There is no question of plausibility in any of their acts. . . . They are the Little People, and have no souls."[11]

This criticism is generally unfair, but it does apply to *H. M. S. Pinafore* and the earlier operas. Gilbert wants to tell a funny story, not introduce us to funny people, so he never lets them off their strings long enough for us to get to know them.

Only in "The Hours Creep On Apace" are we allowed a glimpse of what Gilbert could do if he chose, and was later to do so brilliantly—creating funny, real characters to tell a story that was itself both funny and real.

Even at the time, people didn't know what to make of *H. M. S. Pinafore*. In reviewing the D'Oyly Carte production when it reached America, months behind numerous pirate productions, a New York critic wrote: "We've seen it as a comedy, we've seen it as a tragedy, but the play these Englishmen have brought over is quite a new play to us, and very good it is."[12]

Such interpretive disagreements have continued to the present day, only heightened by the fading of the genre the play parodies. It is a conflicted work, sometimes serious, sometimes funny, and sometimes not quite either. No wonder people were confused then, and still are.

In later years Gilbert & Sullivan were to create operas that were funny and serious, comic and tragic all at once. In fact, it was to be the secret of their success. In *H. M. S. Pinafore*, we see the seeds of those triumphs.

But those seeds are not yet grown. Compared to their work in the later operas, in *H. M. S. Pinafore* Gilbert & Sullivan lack the technical skills to be really sharp, the originality to be really funny or the depth to be really moving. It remains a brilliant piece of superficial work, both the height of achievement in the genre of operatic parody and an embodiment of that genre's limitations.

Thus it is no surprise that its creators weren't quite satisfied with *H. M. S. Pinafore*. After two ventures in conventional comic opera, it was clear that their ideas weren't compatible with the genre's constraints: In *The Sorcerer* they had tested many of the structural and thematic ideas that were to reappear in future operas, only to find that they didn't quite fit the form they were working in. In *H. M. S. Pinafore* they take the other approach, committing themselves more fully to the genre. This lets them utilize the form more effectively but forces them to abandon many of the ideas they'd explored earlier.

The solution, clearly, was to be a re-visioning of the form, a wholesale jettisoning of conventions not compatible with their own creative vision. They would need to commit themselves fully to comic opera as a form of artistic expression and bring their own ideas back to center stage, at whatever cost to the accepted rules of the genre.

It was the success of *H. M. S. Pinafore* that made it possible for Gilbert & Sullivan to throw out so much of what had made it successful. Its amazing popularity bred dozens of imitations in England and abroad, but ironically its creators themselves more or less turned their backs on it. Others churned out comic operas laden with running gags, reprises, and melodrama parody, but Gilbert & Sullivan were already thinking along different lines.

After rushing through *The Pirates of Penzance* for the American market, the two men approached their next collaboration more carefully. Surprisingly enough, given *H. M. S. Pinafore's* acclaim, *Patience* and its successors proved to have relatively little in common with it (save for a tune that reappears in *Utopia, Limited),* and a great deal more with its less successful predecessor, *The Sorcerer.*

Perhaps it's appropriate that the *Pinafore* is a ship, because Gilbert & Sullivan used it as a means of transportation. It made it possible for them to get where they wanted to go, and they always appreciated that (as late as the 1890s, Sullivan's telegraph address was still "Pinafore 1"). But they moved quickly away from it, in directions that even they themselves can have envisioned only vaguely at the time.

Facing page: FIGURE 7.1. An advertising poster for the original New York production of *The Pirates of Penzance* on December 31, 1879. Note the use of proper names for the Pirate King and the Sergeant of Police, which were dropped in the London premiere on April 3, 1880. Samuel, Edith, Kate, and Isabel retained their character names, though none is ever referred to by name in the opera. *Source: The Pierpont Morgan Library, Gilbert and Sullivan Collection.*

7

The Pirates of Penzance

The most revealing line in *The Pirates of Penzance* may be the passage in which Major-General Stanley exclaims, "Then I can hum a fugue of which I've heard the music's din afore, / and whistle all the airs from that infernal nonsense *Pinafore!*"

In *Utopia, Limited,* the only other Savoy opera to refer to a predecessor, references to *H. M. S. Pinafore* and *The Mikado* reinforce a sort of pageant on Gilbert & Sullivan themes, establishing that King Paramount lives in the same world as Captain Corcoran and the Mikado. Not so in *The Pirates of Penzance.* In the Major-General's world *H. M. S. Pinafore* is not a ship but a comic opera, one that any very modern man of culture would know intimately.

The Pirates of Penzance was begun in a London buzzing about *H. M. S. Pinafore* and completed and premiered in a New York utterly mad for it. Gilbert and Sullivan arrived in New York to a reception unparalleled since Dickens's day. They found themselves world-class celebrities. Interviewers flocked to them before they had even come ashore, and everything they said or did was snapped up by the press. No British visitors until the Beatles were so lionized.

"Of course it is an exciting state of existence—too exciting for me," Sullivan wrote to his mother.[1] "I live in a semi-public state all the time, everything I do watched—every word I say noted and probably commented on, so that I get bewildered and dazed, and long for a little rest and quietness."

The greatest subject of interest was their operatic work in progress. The newspapers bulged with rumors, largely unfounded. But the biggest question, one that led off virtually every review of *The Pirates of Penzance,* was: "Is it as good as *Pinafore?*"

This furor was new for both men. *Trial by Jury* and *The Sorcerer* had been popular, and neither man was a stranger to independent success, but the *Pinafore* rage was something else entirely. Henceforth everything they did, together or apart, would be compared to *H. M. S. Pinafore.* In particular, *The Pirates of Penzance* faced almost impossibly high expectations.

Only in New York, it seems, did they fully realize how much *H. M. S. Pinafore* had changed their careers. Suddenly they were "Gilbert & Sullivan," a permanent conjunction. From *H. M. S. Pinafore* on, every composer writing an opera with Gilbert would be compared, however unfairly, to Sullivan; every librettist for a Sullivan opera would be measured against Gilbert.

In response, both men largely curtailed their independent careers. In the 10 years between *Thespis* and *The Pirates of Penzance,* Gilbert had written 26 plays, only three of them with Sullivan; in the 10 years between *The Pirates of Penzance* and *The Gondoliers,* he would write only 11, eight of them with Sullivan.

Sullivan continued conducting, especially for the triennial Leeds Festival, but as a composer he worked almost exclusively with Gilbert. Over the next 10 years, his stream of orchestral and choral music was to dwindle to *The Martyr of Antioch* (1880), a cantata (featuring a libretto arranged by Gilbert) contracted for prior to the *Pinafore* rage, and his final oratorio, *The Golden Legend* (1886).

For better or worse, the 1880s were to be the age of Gilbert & Sullivan. Both would at various times chafe at this fact, but neither could do much about it.

The most important aspects of *H. M. S. Pinafore's* impact on *The Pirates of Penzance* were the tremendous haste with which the new opera was written and the greater scrutiny (and higher standards) set by *H. M. S. Pinafore's* success.

Hasty composition was nothing new to either man. Both *Thespis* and *Trial by Jury* had been written rapidly—Sullivan in particular was a confirmed last-minute worker. But *The Pirates of Penzance* took deadline pressure to another level. Their "authentic" *H. M. S. Pinafore* (as opposed to the many previous pirated versions) opened in New York on December 1, two weeks after their arrival, with *The Pirates of Penzance* set to debut on December 31. Amid the New York social whirl, they had to mount *H. M. S. Pinafore* while simultaneously finishing and rehearsing *The Pirates of Penzance.*

Sullivan's diary records weeks of frenzied activity, with writing, rehearsals, performances, and social obligations depriving the composer of any real rest.[2] This marathon culminated in an all-night session after the rehearsal on December 30, with Sullivan frantically composing the *Pirates* overture while Gilbert, loyal friend Frederic Clay, and conductor François Cellier sat beside him, copying orchestral parts as fast as their ink could dry. Sullivan and Cellier finished at 5 A.M. (Gilbert and Clay had knocked off two hours earlier). Sullivan got no sleep whatever and, as he recorded in his diary, on opening night "went into the orchestra, more dead than alive."

Under the circumstances, it's no wonder that *The Pirates of Penzance* shows more signs of haste than any other Savoy opera. The reuse of "Climbing over Rocky Mountain" from *Thespis* is only the most obvious example.

Also reflecting the rush, Gilbert & Sullivan revised *The Pirates of Penzance* after its opening night more than they did any other Savoy opera, including radical revisions of the finales for both acts. During the four months between the New York and London openings the creators redid much of their initial work—so much that even today exactly what was and wasn't in the New York premiere is not known.

I will discuss some of these changes later; my point here is that their very existence attests to the partners' conviction that the new opera had been too rushed for its own good.

The pressure to finish *The Pirates of Penzance* was matched by the pressure to make it as good as *H. M. S. Pinafore*—which, in practice, meant even better. *H. M. S. Pinafore* was literally more popular than it was good. An equally good show, without its fluke popularity, would be a disappointment; to match *H. M. S. Pinafore*, they would actually have to exceed it.

To do so would require their very best efforts, a creative commitment to their collaboration that neither man had previously made. Given the race to finish *The Pirates of Penzance*, the full impact of this new commitment would not be seen until *Patience*, but even so *The Pirates of Penzance* is clearly a more ambitious work than *H. M. S. Pinafore*.

Reviewing the show for his mother, Sullivan wrote: "The music is infinitely superior in every way to the *Pinafore*—tunier, and more developed—of a higher class altogether."[3]

And so it is. Sullivan rarely looked back, but had he done so he might have seen *The Pirates of Penzance* as a promising path not taken. Many of the things he was later to demand from Gilbert, and not fully get until *The Gondoliers* a decade later, actually materialize in *The Pirates of Penzance*. The "plausible, human story" that obsessed the composer did not begin to emerge until *Patience*, but in terms of its relative amounts of music and dialogue *The Pirates of Penzance* resembles *The Gondoliers* more than any other Savoy opera.

Compared with its six immediate successors, *The Pirates of Penzance* has an astounding amount of music. There are only seven pure dialogue sequences in the entire show, with only two in the second act. This is all the more remarkable in that the preceding *H. M. S. Pinafore* contains 13 dialogue scenes, and the following *Patience* 17.

The Pirates of Penzance is built operatically, around a series of musical scenes. The opening of *The Gondoliers*, much touted for its 20-minute musical sequence, is actually only the second-longest nonfinale sequence in Gilbert & Sullivan. The longest is the brilliantly paced sequence beginning with Frederic's "Stop, ladies, pray!" and running unbroken through "I Am the Very Model of a Modern Major-General."

Granted, this musical flow is achieved through the extensive use of recitative. But Sullivan's *Pirates* recitative far excels the pro forma recitative (in operatic terms, recitative secco) in *H. M. S. Pinafore*.

For example, the Captain-Buttercup sequence in Act 1 of *H. M. S. Pinafore* (beginning "Sir, you are sad—/ the silent eloquence of yonder tear") conveys key plot information, but it's long and musically uninteresting—a series of chanted lines over held chords, with little drama or excitement (ex. 7.1a).

A similar scene in Act 2 of *The Pirates of Penzance*, beginning "Young Frederic!" is as exciting as anything in the opera. In place of lengthy chanting, Sullivan sets Gilbert's blank verse in small snatches of melody, each flowing effortlessly into the next. Frederic's "Know ye not, O rash ones, that I have doomed you to extermination?" may be clichéd as a lyric, but Sullivan's soaring tune makes it seem fresh. The recitative is so musically strong, and so funny, that we hardly notice when it segues into the actual song, "A Most Ingenious Paradox" (ex. 7.1b).

As for the songs, they offer muscular orchestrations and an emotional power almost entirely lacking in *H. M. S. Pinafore*. The hallmark of *H. M. S. Pinafore* is tasteful restraint—even confrontational songs such as Ralph and Josephine's angry "Refrain, Audacious Tar" are unfailingly decorous, with the characters politely trading verses without ever interrupting one another.

By contrast, *The Pirates of Penzance* rings with emotion. The decorum of "Refrain, Audacious Tar" pales before the venom of Frederic and Ruth's "Oh, False One, You Have Deceived Me." The two trade accusations, interrupt each other, and finally end screaming at complete cross-purposes. The scene may not be as musically pretty, but it has an emotional intensity beyond anything in *H. M. S. Pinafore*.

The romantic numbers show the same growth. *H. M. S. Pinafore's* "Sorry Her Lot" and "The Nightingale" express sadness, but they are pretty, elegantly structured songs that convey no real sadness to the audience. By contrast, the Frederic-Mabel musical scene built around "Ah, Leave Me Not to Pine" conveys an aching misery that transcends the silliness of Frederic's dilemma to achieve emotional resonance.

Or, again, compare *H. M. S. Pinafore's* "Kind Captain, I've Important Information" with *The Pirates of Penzance's* "Away, Away!" The situations are similar—a secret betrayal is revealed and the baritone vows vengeance. But the Captain-Deadeye duet is laboriously formal, with the characters trading four neat verses before ending with a fugal chorus; it is musically clever but dramatically thin.

The Frederic–Ruth–Pirate King trio, on the other hand, is structurally complex and anything but neat. The verse structure completely breaks down by the end, as the infuriated pirates and the horrified Frederic repeatedly interrupt one another's lines. Meanwhile, a storming orchestration and vigorous harmonies reflect the characters' emotional turmoil.

The music isn't as pretty as "Kind Captain," to be sure, but it seethes with dramatic energy. Listening, we forget that the King is a namby-pamby who invariably gets thrashed, that Ruth can't tell the difference between "pilot" and "pirate," and that Frederic is a duty-obsessed monomaniac.

The Pirates of Penzance sets the pattern that, after hints in *The Sorcerer* and *H. M. S. Pinafore*, would guide the rest of the operas: Two conflicting ideas not only exist simultaneously but strengthen one another. Characters can be hilariously comic one moment and absolutely dramatically credible the next, or even both at once.

The cliché is that Sullivan humanized Gilbert's amusing puppets, but this was only rarely the case. "Away, Away!" is exciting, "Ah, Leave Me Not to Pine" heartbreaking, and "Oh, False One, You Have Deceived Me" harrowing not despite their lyrics but because of them.

Ruth's pathetic "My love without reflecting, / ah, do not be rejecting," for example, is the perfect sad, despairing acceptance to follow her tumultuous confrontation with Frederic. Sullivan provides a powerful setting, but it is Gilbert's lyrics that provide the dramatic framework that makes the music work.

7.1a. "Sir, you are sad" is representative of *H. M. S. Pinafore's* pedestrian recitatives in the secco style, little more than chanting over sustained chords. By *The Pirates of Penzance's* "Young Frederic," however, Sullivan is scoring his recitatives freely, with nearly the same musical inventiveness that he would apply to conventional melody.

My daugh-ter, Jo - se - phine, the fair - est flower that ev - er blos - somed on an - ces - tral tim - ber, Is sought in mar-riage by Sir Jo - seph Por - ter, Our Ad - mi - ral - ty's First Lord, but for some rea - son She does not seem to tac - kle kind - ly to it.

Gilbert never hesitates to veer sharply from sentiment to comedy and back again. The misery of "Ah, Leave Me Not to Pine" gives way to the tongue-in-cheek recitative "In 1940 I of age shall be . . . / It seems so long" and the comic "she will be faithful to her sooth / 'til we are wed and even after," which in turn yield to the couple's heartdrawn farewells. Each turn of mood is made wholeheartedly, and Sullivan is there every step of the way, intensifying the comic as much as the pathetic and making every word emotionally credible.

This pure, resonant human emotion is what had been missing to this point, except for *H. M. S. Pinafore's* "The Hours Creep On Apace" and scattered moments in *The Sorcerer.*

With *The Pirates of Penzance*, the shows begin to live up to their billing as operas. Sullivan pulls out all the stops, giving everything he has to offer as a composer and producing his best music to this point, symphony and oratorios included. He shows himself to be at heart a theatrical composer,

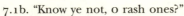

7.1b. "Know ye not, o rash ones?"

King
na - tion? Have mer - cy on us!

Hear us, ere you slaugh - ter! I do not think I ought to lis - ten

Fred.

to you. Yet, mer - cy should al - loy our stern re - sent - ment, And

so I will be mer - ci - ful — say on!

at his best when inspired by a believably characterized, strongly emotional human situation.

Shortly before the New York opening of *The Pirates of Penzance*, the orchestra at the Fifth Avenue Theater went on strike.[4] They had been engaged at operetta rates, they argued, but *The Pirates of Penzance* was grand-opera music, and they insisted on being paid accordingly.

Ever diplomatic, Sullivan thanked them for the compliment, but he took a hard line: If the musicians didn't yield, he said, he would send for the orchestra of London's Covent Garden Opera House.

Facing this polite ultimatum, the musicians backed down and ended their strike. But a simple comparison of the scores for *H. M. S. Pinafore* and *The Pirates of Penzance* shows that their argument was far from unjustified. This is indeed music "of a higher class altogether."

As for Gilbert, his share of *The Pirates of Penzance* also shows substantial improvement, at least in some areas.

The opera is far more structurally integrated than *H. M. S. Pinafore*, giving it better dramatic momentum. The previous opera had been built around short solos, sung directly to the audience. In *The Pirates of Penzance*, most of the songs are sung to other characters, not the audience: The Major-General is plausibly introducing himself to a group of strangers, as is not the case with Captain Corcoran's introduction of himself to his own crew, while the Pirate King presents his "comparatively honest" philosophy as a rebuttal to Frederic's moralizing.

Not breaking the dramatic frame helps make these characters more plausible: The King's not acknowledging the audience makes it easier to believe that he is what he claims to be—and to fear his anger. Mabel's big scenes are not soliloquies sung to the balcony but emotional interactions with other characters, making it easier to accept her as real—and to share her sorrow.

Moreover, the opera's songs are fewer and longer, and the primary dramatic unit is not the song but the scene. Act 2 of *H. M. S. Pinafore* is a series of seven vignettes, all but the last based on single songs. By contrast, Act 2 of *The Pirates of Penzance* is built on four long musical scenes: The opening daughters-police scene, with three lengthy numbers; the Frederic–Ruth–Pirate King scene, with three numbers; the Frederic-Mabel scene, with three; and then the final scene, beginning with the police alone and adding other characters with each song until finally the entire company is assembled.

If Gilbert the dramatic craftsman breaks new ground in *The Pirates of Penzance*, Gilbert the humorist also excels himself.

A few forced puns aside, *H. M. S. Pinafore's* humor is very gentle. The genial Captain Corcoran may evoke a smile, the snobby Sir Joseph even a chuckle, but they aren't hilarious, if only because they rarely say things that are funny as such.

By contrast, *The Pirates of Penzance* is hilarious. The opening dialogue, in which Frederic explains to the pirates why they can't make piracy pay, is funnier than anything in any preceding opera. However strained the "orphan/often" sequence may seem, in performance it invariably brings the house down. And the police scenes are among the biggest laugh-getters in all Gilbert & Sullivan.

The police are only the most obvious example of the opera's brilliant use of the chorus by author and composer alike. Earlier choruses had offered occasional comic moments—the sailors' unison declaration of their hatred for Dick Deadeye, the flirtatiousness of the *Trial by Jury* jurors—but in *The Pirates of Penzance* the choruses emerge as full comic characters in their own right.

Beyond the police, whose appeal is all but universal, the pirates are funny and, at the same time, lovable in a way no previous chorus had been. Their genial ineptness, from their weeping at the word "orphan" to their determination to carry off the girls and . . . marry them, is unfailingly winning.

If earlier male choruses were generally bland, earlier female choruses were virtual ciphers. The sisters, cousins, and aunts are essentially one joke repeated endlessly, while the female choruses in *Thespis, Trial by Jury,* and *The Sorcerer* are hardly even distinguishable from their male counterparts. It is certainly possible to stage any of these choruses to get laughs, but the performers will get virtually no help from script or score.

All this changes in *The Pirates of Penzance.* The female chorus has at least three sure-fire comic scenes: their flirtatious carryings-on with Frederic in "Oh, Is There Not One Maiden Breast" (along with their vexation at his reference to "homely face and bad complexion"); their not-very-subtle eavesdropping in "How Beautifully Blue the Sky"; and their overzealous "Go, Ye Heroes, Go to Glory" to the police. It's no wonder that Sullivan produces such stellar female-chorus material for *The Pirates of Penzance* (atoning for his unremarkable work on the earlier operas)—Gilbert gives him ample comic material to work with, and the composer comes through with flying colors.

In all, *The Pirates of Penzance* represents a long-awaited return of the Gilbert who was considered one of England's funniest men. *The Sorcerer* and *H. M. S. Pinafore* had drawn most of their humor from plot parody; in *The Pirates of Penzance,* for the first time since *Trial by Jury,* the richly inventive comedian of the *Bab Ballads* steps back onto the stage.

The lyrics for *The Pirates of Penzance,* however, are less advanced than its dramatic structure. While their content is substantially improved over *H. M. S. Pinafore,* in form they yet betray the hand of an author who is still not mature.

Written overwhelmingly in either straight or interlocked couplets, the lyrics are generally metrically sound but often labor under forced rhymes. "Vile lot/pilot" and "din afore/*Pinafore*" are the sort of excessively clever forced rhymes that worked in the *Bab Ballads* but that marred early operas such as *The Sorcerer* (with its excruciating rhymes such as "is to be next her / Pointdextre").

There are some fine lyrics in *The Pirates of Penzance*, but on the whole Gilbert's skill at crafting effective musical scenes still runs ahead of his lyrical skills. The "How Beautifully Blue the Sky" scene, for example, is theatrically brilliant, but the actual lyrics sung by Mabel and Frederic are banal. Gilbert has his moments (the police-daughters scene in Act 2 is as lyrically fresh as it is theatrically clever), but the sure-handed lyricist of *Iolanthe* and *Princess Ida* is yet to be seen.

The story of *The Pirates of Penzance* is in some ways even less polished. Here and there can be seen hints of the thematic approach that will emerge full-blown in *Patience*, but on the whole *The Pirates of Penzance* is a flatter show that is less than the sum of its parts.

A canny London *Times* critic wrote of the opera:

> Music is fully able to deal with broadly comic phases of human life, but Mr. Gilbert's characters are not comic in themselves, but only in reference to other characters chiefly of the operatic type, whose exaggerated attitude and parlance they mimic. He writes in fact not comedies but parodies, and the music has accordingly to follow him to the sphere of all others most uncongenial to it—the mock-heroic.[5]

This is not entirely fair. "I Am the Very Model of a Modern Major-General" is more than parody, and the police are valid comic creations in themselves. But much of the appeal of *The Pirates of Penzance* does rest in the mock-heroic—brave generals, pirates, and policemen who turn out to be anything but.

Nor has *The Pirates of Penzance* any real satiric point. After *H. M. S. Pinafore* Gilbert was rarely a satirist—in the sense of a humorous social critic— as much as he was a parodist and a thematic playwright.

The Pirates of Penzance tilts at no social windmills—it doesn't imply that British generals are unqualified imbeciles, nor that the British police are all bumbling cowards, only that these specific ones are. The spoofery is too good-humored to have any real sting.

Major-General Sir Garnet Wolseley, the primary victim of the opera's spoofing, actually memorized "I Am the Very Model of a Modern Major-General" and loved to rattle it off to guests. Clearly, he didn't find it biting.

Originally, *The Pirates of Penzance* had more social commentary than it does today and followed more closely in the satiric footsteps of *H. M. S. Pinafore*. That satire—targeting the absurdity of aristocratic privilege—remains in the revised opera as we know it, but only in embryonic form.

This subject is prefigured in the Pirate King's assertion that, in the world of respectability where "pirates all are well-to-do,"

> many a king on a first-class throne,
> if he wants to call his crown his own,
>   must manage somehow to get through
>   more dirty work than ever I do.

The point is developed further, when the apparently respectable Major-General enters to the same piratical tune, and climaxes when, after their arrest, the pirates are all revealed to be noblemen who have gone wrong—and immediately pardoned.

As the opera stands today, however, the King's comment—deprived of a more substantial context—is more a generalized philosophic comment than a satiric attack, while the all-noblemen ending feels like a thin, tacked-on rehash of *H. M. S. Pinafore's* switched-babies resolution. There is no coherent message to tie together these threads.

Once upon a time, though, there was. Cut from the original New York production before opening night (though it was sung in the British copyright performance in Paignton the night before) was a "Hymn to the Nobility" that followed the King's remark and was anything but subtle:[6]

General: Let foreigners look down with scorn
> on legislators heaven-born;
>   we know what limpid wisdom runs
>   from Peers and all their eldest Sons.
> Enrapt the true-born Briton hears
> the wisdom of his House of Peers.

Sergeant: And if a noble Lord should die
> and leave no nearer progeny,
>   his twentieth cousin takes his place
>   and legislates with equal grace.

Ruth: But should a Son or Heir survive,
> or other nearer relative,
>   then twentieth cousins get you hence—
>   you're persons of no consequence.
> When issue male their chances bar,
> how paltry twentieth cousins are!

Mabel: How double blest that glorious land
> where rank and brains go hand-in-hand,
>   where wisdom pure and virtue hale
>   obey the law of strict entail.
> No harm can touch a country when
> it's ruled by British Noblemen.

It's understandable that this number was cut. Its pungency is out of place in an opera that generally has nothing to do with such issues. It is an overtly political song, steeped in sarcasm, in an opera that otherwise has little of either.

Gilbert would return to the subject of aristocratic privilege in several other operas, most notably in *Iolanthe, The Gondoliers,* and *Utopia, Limited.* But these operas were far more political, and the later treatments were generally less blatant than the earlier "Hymn."

Much has been written about the treatment of the idea of duty in *The Pirates of Penzance.* The word runs throughout the opera, leading some critics to view the opera as a strong thematic satire of the Victorian sense of duty.

Certainly, there was satiric material here. Duty (like its cousin, honor) was a virtual religion to Victorian culture. One of the era's central artistic works was Tennyson's phenomenally popular poem "The Charge of the Light Brigade" (1854). Tennyson's attack on the officerial incompetence that led to the Crimean War slaughter of an entire light brigade inspired a reworking of the British military command.

But the poem also glorifies the soldiers themselves, who did their duty and charged, "though the soldier knew / someone had blundered."[7] A soldier refusing to obey an obviously inept, clearly suicidal order would have been court-martialed; those who obeyed at the cost of their lives were exalted as paragons of honor.

In one sense, Frederic fits this picture well. "Duty over brains" would be an appropriate motto for either poem or opera. But *The Pirates of Penzance* isn't really a thematic satire, because neither Gilbert nor Sullivan is really attacking the idea of duty. Gilbert, a militia officer for many years, demanded blind obedience to orders, whether in his regiment or on the stage of the Opera Comique. As for Sullivan, he was anything but a radical. Born outside the system, like many self-made men he took on its coloring once he had succeeded in gaining entrance, becoming its staunch defender.

The Pirates of Penzance can't be a satire on duty because it refuses to take sides for or against it, the way *H. M. S. Pinafore* pillories status-by-birth in favor of status-by-talent.

The opera doesn't endorse lying and deceit—Ruth and the Major-General are both caught in their falsehoods, and neither is seen as admirable. But the King's superficially appealing motto, "Always act in accordance with the dictates of your conscience, my boy, and chance the consequences," is hardly more credible, since the King himself is a gullible, hypersentimental buffoon.

Moreover, Frederic's adherence to duty doesn't reflect loyalty to a higher ideal or any real morality. He's an absurd literalist with no sense of proportion. It may be consistent with his own view of duty, but an audience can only see his rejoining the pirates, revealing the Major-General's secret, and assisting the pirates in their plan to murder him as deplorable. As the police correctly observe, "He has acted shamefully."

Frederic isn't a comic equivalent of the Light Brigade heroes, setting right above his own self-interest. He's a laughable fool, placing a legalistic quibble over what's right *or* good for him—it's his very obtuseness that makes him funny.

The police are actually more in the Light Brigade mode in singing, "When constabulary duty's to be done, / a policeman's lot is not a happy one." Their song is a comic spin on the idea of placing their duty above their humane sympathy for even the criminal. But there is no irony in the song, no suggestion that they really ought to let the criminals go. The song is comic, with no satiric edge whatever.

The opera's most characteristic outlook on duty is provided by Mabel. She finds Frederic's earnestness charming and even admirable, but by the second act she clearly also finds it irritating. Her "Oh, Frederic, cannot you . . . reconcile it with your conscience to say something that will relieve my father's sorrow?" suggests that Frederic has been criticizing the Major-General's "terrible story" (as he might be expected to), and that she wishes he wouldn't.

When that sense of duty actually leads him to desert her, Mabel tosses duty to the winds: To Frederic's call of duty, she responds "They have no legal claim, / no shadow of a shame / will fall upon thy name"—true enough, but irrelevant from Frederic's point of view.

Mabel is clearly offended. In a line that was cut after the New York run, she observes: "But if it is his duty to constitute himself my foe, it is likewise my duty to regard him in that light!"

But her opposition is purely personal, not philosophical. She cares only about getting what she wants—a refreshing change from the Major-General's hypocrisy, the pirates' innate generosity, and Frederic's punctiliousness, perhaps, but hardly a foundation for effective satire.

If *The Pirates of Penzance* is (as Max Keith Sutton asserts)[8] to some extent a debate between pragmatism and idealism (he calls it "duty"), with the sportsmanlike pirates embodying idealism and the wily Major-General embodying pragmatism, it is ultimately an empty one, because (unlike *H. M. S. Pinafore's* debate over matters of status) this debate is never resolved.

Frederic is never forced to face the consequences of his philosophy, as for example is the Lord Chancellor in *Iolanthe* or Robin Oakapple in *Ruddigore*. The Major-General never pays for his lie, and the revelation that the pirates are all aristocrats fudges the question by suggesting that idealism and pragmatism are really two sides of the same coin—which we know is not the case.

In short, *The Pirates of Penzance* contains the elements of a coherent opera, but the pieces don't fit together. Gilbert's normally exhaustive process of revision was swept away by the tide of events, while Sullivan never had time for his usual thinking-through of the story and characters.

The result is a highly unusual opera. Besides its unique history and uncharacteristic, quasi-operatic format, it offers diverse offbeat elements unlike anything else in Gilbert & Sullivan before or since—the character of Ruth, for example, the Major-General's funny-plaintive "Sighing Softly to the River," or the out-of-left-field "Hail, Poetry!" It has a flamboyant, anything-goes self-indulgence beyond even *Trial by Jury*.

Thus, while *The Pirates of Penzance* in some ways begins the partnership's mature period, it isn't itself a mature work. The next decade was to yield progressively more serious operas, highly polished works of art reaching for ever-higher levels of artistic integration and thematic drama. In this context, *The Pirates of Penzance* is strikingly unpretentious, the work of two men approaching artistic maturity but not above having a good time doing it.

Anything but integrated—the police sequences, for example, have virtually nothing to do with the rest of the opera—*The Pirates of Penzance* shows both men kicking back and being funny, exciting, dramatic, or moving as the fancy seizes them, reveling in the sheer scope of their talents.

It is this spirit of fun that makes the opera so beloved today. *The Pirates of Penzance* succeeds in outdoing *H. M. S. Pinafore* on nearly every front, but it's neither as funny nor as musically effective as its successors. Its humor is broad and occasionally crude—most notably in its mockery of Ruth—and its drama is clichéd and often overwrought. The partners have come a long way from *The Sorcerer* (let alone from *Thespis*) but still have a long way to go to *Iolanthe*.

But there's a loosely knit sense of fun to *The Pirates of Penzance* that tops even the famously good-natured *The Gondoliers*. It is, perhaps, Gilbert & Sullivan's last "young" opera, a final kick of the heels before maturity sets in. And that youthful exuberance still makes it a delight to see, or to perform, more than a century later.

In retrospect, we know the path that the collaboration took after *H. M. S. Pinafore*. But it was by no means obvious at the time. Despite *Pinafore's* 571-performance run, Gilbert & Sullivan could easily have been one-hit wonders: A few years later Alfred Cellier and B. C. Stephenson wrote *Dorothy* (1887), which ran a staggering 931 performances. But neither man was to have any significant success again, including Cellier's 1892 collaboration with Gilbert on *The Mountebanks;* Cellier's follow-up to *Dorothy*, the highly imitative *Doris*, was a failure.

In light of this, if the "infernal nonsense" passage is perhaps the most revealing in *The Pirates of Penzance*, the most revealing passage *not* in it is one included in the initial New York production but cut by the London premiere:[9]

Ruth: They are all noblemen who have gone wrong!

General, Police & Girls: What! All noblemen?

King & Pirates: Yes, all noblemen!

General, Police & Girls: What! All?

King: Well, nearly all.

All: They are nearly all noblemen who have gone wrong.
    Then give three cheers, both loud and strong,
    for the twenty noblemen who have gone wrong!
    Then give three cheers, both loud and strong,
    for the noblemen who have gone wrong!

The inclusion of so obvious an *H. M. S. Pinafore* swipe attests to the temptation to cash in on that opera's sensational success. Gilbert & Sullivan knew what the public wanted, which was *H. M. S. Pinafore*, and chances are that this reprise was greeted with the same glee that welcomed a similar echo in *Utopia, Limited*, 24 years later.

But the decision to cut it was crucial. It would have been easy for both men to live off *H. M. S. Pinafore's* success, writing a series of cheap knock-offs for as long as the market would bear. There was no obvious need to cut the passage or make any other substantial revisions—after all, *The Pirates of Penzance* was a hit in its original form and would surely have been so in London where, as Sullivan noted to his mother "all the local allusions, etc. will have twice the force they have here."[10]

The decision to rework *The Pirates of Penzance*, making it simultaneously stronger and less like *H. M. S. Pinafore*, was a key one. It signified that there was to be more to Gilbert & Sullivan than "the men who wrote *Pinafore*." In exorcising *H. M. S. Pinafore* from *The Pirates of Penzance*, they exorcised it from themselves as well. Whatever else they were to do in days to come, they would not succumb to facile self-imitation.

H. M. S. Pinafore was to be a beginning, not an end.

8

Patience

If *H. M. S. Pinafore* and *The Pirates of Penzance* ended the early stage of the Gilbert & Sullivan collaboration, *Patience* marks the threshold of their mature period. Not quite a masterpiece itself, it establishes the context for the masterpieces to come.

The Sorcerer had demonstrated the potential of the Gilbert & Sullivan team, while the phenomenal success of *H. M. S. Pinafore* had put pressure on the two men to put their best efforts into the collaboration. The hastily written *Pirates of Penzance* had been too rushed for substantial innovation, so *Patience* is their first real stab at a new form, and predictably shows some growing pains.

Not everything in it is new, and some of the new ideas don't work. In particular, Sullivan's score is wildly inconsistent, ranging from brilliant integration to musical boilerplate only a short step above *The Sorcerer*. But despite occasional fumbling, *Patience* clearly stands as the prototype of mature Gilbert & Sullivan opera. Thematically, structurally, and dramatically, it resembles *The Yeomen of the Guard*, written seven years later, more than it does *The Pirates of Penzance*, written the previous year.

Most particularly, *Patience* provides the first full look at the form that was to define all the subsequent operas (except, to some extent, *The Mikado*).

The hallmark of mature Gilbert & Sullivan opera is integration. *H. M. S. Pinafore*, a half-hour shorter than *Patience*, had featured 62 different songs, dialogues, and recitatives; *Patience* has only 54. Fewer, longer segments give the opera greater structural integrity and offer richer opportunities for composer and librettist alike.

Integration is more than a counting game, however. The primary theatrical unit of mature Gilbert & Sullivan is no longer the individual song or dialogue but rather the integrated scene. Music, lyrics, and dialogue (as well as staging and production design) function as component parts to the overall scene, enhanced by their relation to one another. *Patience* is inconsistent in this regard, but the first two scenes of act 1 provide an excellent example of the integration that was to become the team's standard.

After the overture, the act begins with an elegiac instrumental dominated by the four-note horn theme (F–G–F–F) subsequently sung as "Ah, misery" (ex. 8.1).

This leads directly into the chorus "Twenty love-sick maidens we," whose first statement ends with the words "twenty love-sick maidens still," with the final four syllables recapitulating the F–G–F–F "misery" theme (ex. 8.2).

Angela's solo ("Love feeds on hope") is punctuated by the chorus singing "Ah, misery," a third lower; the solo ends with Angela singing a variant "Ah, misery" (F–A–G–F; ex. 8.3).

Another chorus ending in "Ah, misery" is followed by Ella's solo ("Go, breaking heart"), with the chorus again intoning "Ah, misery." The closing

8.1. The instrumental introduction to the opening number of *Patience* begins and ends with the musical pattern that will subsequently be set to the lyric "Ah, misery!"

chorus recapitulation ends with the same theme on "-sick maidens still" and a final "ah, misery" (ex. 8.4).

Already this is more structurally sophisticated, both musically and lyrically, than the short introductory choruses that opened *The Sorcerer, H. M. S. Pinafore,* and *The Pirates of Penzance.*

But once finished, those songs were essentially over (one *Pinafore* reprise excepted). In *Patience,* the opening song's elements continue to appear in various guises. A brief dialogue follows, after which Patience enters for a recitative and her song, "I Cannot Tell What This Love May Be" (its central theme already introduced instrumentally during the recitative). Sullivan contrasts her bubbling bliss to a lugubrious chorus response, complete with, at the very end of each verse, a reprise of the "Ah, misery" theme (ex. 8.5).

After a dialogue combining the subjects of the first two songs, the ladies exit, singing "Twenty Lovesick Maidens We" as they go. The scene ends on "Ah, misery"—the same notes that began the opening instrumental. Thus the "Ah, misery" theme serves to bind together six separate pieces (chorus-dialogue-recitative-solo-dialogue-chorus)   into   an   integrated

8.2. Subsequently Sullivan sets the words "twenty love-sick maidens still" to a rhythmic variation on the same "Ah, misery!" tune.

whole. The scene is more unified and coherent than any previous Gilbert & Sullivan effort; in fact, among its operatic contemporaries, only Wagner had practiced this degree of integration.

It is important to note that this integration is a collaborative effort. Just as Sullivan had greater influence on the operas' stories and characterizations than is generally acknowledged, so Gilbert had greater influence on their music. His lyrical structures shaped the resulting musical structures and provided crucial inspiration for Sullivan.

8.3. At the end of Angela's solo, Sullivan sets the words "Ah, misery" to an appoggiatura variation (F–A–G–F instead of F–G–F–F) of the passage that opened the number.

8.4. Sullivan closes "Twenty Love-sick Maidens We" by having the chorus repeat the opening instrumental motif of the song, to the words "Ah, misery!"

For example, Gilbert presumably never envisioned "-sick maidens still" relating in any way to "Ah, misery"—as lyrics, they have nothing in common. But when he has Patience allude to the women's phrase "misery" (in quotation marks in the libretto: "Think of the gulf 'twixt them and me,/'Fal la la la!'—and 'Misery!' "), he surely suggests to Sullivan another musical use of the motif. By ending the scene on the same words, he inspires the composer to begin the scene with that motif. The resulting integration is a triumph for both composer and author.

The next scene proves the value of integration, both exploiting it and enhancing it to brilliant effect. The entrance of the Dragoon Guards, with their rousing "Soldiers of Our Queen," has been justly hailed as the first

8.5. Sullivan wittily ends Patience's "I Cannot Tell What This Love May Be" by setting her closing words, "and misery," to the same motif he used as the linking "ah, misery" theme for "Twenty Love-sick Maidens Still," with the chorus providing a gloomy harmony. It requires some ingenious scoring, as the two songs are in different keys.

"big entrance" of the Savoy operas, the ancestor of *Iolanthe's* "Loudly Let the Trumpets Bray" and others to follow. But it is not itself a particularly impressive song—it gains its impact from the previous, highly integrated scene.

This contrast works on every level. Musically, Sullivan uses the swaggering brasses to great effect, after having withheld them almost entirely from the preceding scene, creating a brilliantly theatrical contrast. Similarly, Gilbert (as his own costume designer) dressed the aesthetic ladies in cobwebby costumes that were entirely without primary red or yellow, setting up a striking contrast with the red-and-yellow dragoons. Meanwhile, Gilbert as director gave the aesthetes a droopy sway that served as a perfect foil for the stiff-necked precision marching of the soldiers.

That contrast is, in fact, the raison d'être of the entire second scene. Once the Dragoons have been given a song and a dialogue to establish themselves, the ladies reenter. Their "In a Doleful Train" is not a reprise of "Twenty Love-sick Maidens We," but Sullivan craftily relates the tunes: The opening instrumental theme, later sung as "Woe is me," is a variant on "Ah, misery," reflecting the characters' consistent mood (ex. 8.6). This contrasts vividly with the martial "Now Is Not This Ridiculous," to delightful effect.

Next follow solos for Angela and Bunthorne, then Saphir and Bunthorne. All four are written to the same scansion, and Gilbert probably intended them to share the same tune. But Sullivan cannily gives Bunthorne a hopping, distinctly unaesthetic line that perfectly reflects his

8.6. The female chorus's reentry evokes a variation on the "ah, misery" theme, a third higher, later sung to the words "woe is me."

unaesthetic revelations. As for Angela and Saphir, their solos use the tune from "Twenty Love-sick Maidens We," tying this scene to the first one.

Finally, of course, the composer pairs the aesthetic "In a Doleful Train" with the military "Now Is Not This Ridiculous" in a musical combination so deft that it invariably draws applause—so much so that one hardly notices the women's reprise of "Twenty Love-sick Maidens We" trumpeted over the din.

The next dialogue draws its humor from the same stylistic contrast between the dragoons and the ladies, a contrast reflected perfectly in their dialogue style—the aesthetes lush, wordy, and flowing, the dragoons crisp and to the point. Finally the women strike up "Twenty Lovesick Maidens We" once more, exiting on "Ah, misery," and the military blare of "When I First Put This Uniform On" reprises the contrast between the earlier "Ah, misery" and "The Soldiers of Our Queen"; like the first scene, the second scene ends by recalling its beginning.

Together, the two scenes are a fully integrated 20-minute sequence that shows the creators in complete control of every aspect of their play— music, lyrics, dialogue, costumes, and staging alike. The engine driving the sequence is the tension between consistency and contrast, with the ladies and the dragoons stylistically consistent throughout but forcefully contrasting with each other. The upshot is a sequence that feels not like a collection of 14 separate pieces but like one ingeniously linked whole.

In short, it is a quantum leap beyond *The Pirates of Penzance* and very much in the integrated style of *Iolanthe.*

Unfortunately, the show does not sustain this high level of integration. In particular, the music falls apart, so that scenes that Gilbert wrote in integrated form (for example, the opening sequence of Act 2, from the offstage "Turn, Oh Turn" to "The Magnet and the Churn") become musically fragmented and inconsistent. Similarly, Gilbert uses a single concept as the impetus behind four different scenes: Men assume new clothes in order to impress women in four different songs: "When I First Put This Uniform On," "If You're Anxious for to Shine," "It's Clear That Medieval Art" and "When I Go Out of Door." In a later show, Sullivan would surely have musically linked these songs in some way, reinforcing the irony of the twist ending in which Grosvenor proves that after all it isn't clothes that make the man. But here the opportunity passes unmarked.

But the keynote has been sounded, and by the upcoming *Iolanthe*, both men will be up to sustaining integration through the entire opera.

By the time *Patience* was written, "the House That *Pinafore* Built" was already well underway.

Carte's new Savoy Theatre was built specifically for the presentation of Gilbert & Sullivan's operas. (Only ten days before it opened, Sullivan inspected it and insisted that the orchestra pit be raised by eight inches; it was.)[1] *Patience* was transferred to the new theater six months into its run, complete with an enlarged chorus to fit the bigger stage and new costumes and scenery designed to show to best effect under the electric light that was the Savoy's pride and joy. (It was the first time a London theater had been lit wholly electrically.)

It might be expected that, with new reputations and a new theater, Gilbert & Sullivan would produce a new kind of opera, and indeed they did.

The innovations of *Patience* were not limited to matters of structure. Its substance was also quite different from that of its predecessors. *Patience* was the first Gilbert & Sullivan opera that was not significantly a burlesque of operatic conventions, and perhaps as a result seems more comfortable than any of its predecessors in ignoring those conventions when necessary.

The previous operas had featured occasional topical jokes, even topical characters (Sir Joseph Porter and Major-General Stanley). But *Patience* was their first opera with an overtly topical story, as well as their first to include characters of what Sullivan called "human plausibility" and, by far, their most thematically integrated and theatrically powerful to date.

Patience's topicality was apparent from the start, of course. With Oscar Wilde himself in the opening-night audience (he was a client of Carte's booking agency and rather enjoyed being spoofed), there was no chance of anyone missing the contemporary allusions.

Of course, W. H. Smith had been widely recognized behind the mask of Sir Joseph Porter and Sir Garnet Wolseley behind Major-General Stanley. In fact, with Grossmith playing Bunthorne as a composite of Wilde, James Whistler, and Algernon Swinburne, and Barrington's Grosvenor combining elements of William Morris and Walter Pater, the barbs of *Patience* were actually less specific than those in *H. M. S. Pinafore* or *The Pirates of Penzance.*

But Sir Joseph and the Major-General were small parts of larger pictures—*H. M. S. Pinafore* was no satire on political office-holders, nor *The Pirates of Penzance* on incompetent military officers. *Patience,* on the other hand, is a broad parody of the entire aesthetic movement and has an edge to it: Bunthorne and Grosvenor are shown to be essentially a fraud and a fool, respectively, and their followers to be self-indulgent twits. It might easily have been taken as a mean-spirited attack on their entire movement.

Yet it wasn't, then or since. Later in 1881, the critic William Archer examined the question:

> There is a general inclination to attribute to these operas, or at any rate to the last three, a serious satiric purpose. Nothing could be more mistaken. Not even *Patience* is to be taken as a satire. It is an extravaganza, pure and simple, and so are its predecessors. Genuinely satiric touches are no doubt interspersed, but we are no more meant to conclude from *Patience* that Mr. Gilbert believes "aestheticism" as a whole to be a sham and a craze, than we are to conclude from *The Pirates* that he believes our police as a body to be arrant cowards. That they are not satires in the true sense of the term is proved by the fact that they leave everyone's "withers unwrung." Satire which meets with universal acquiescence is unworthy of the name.[2]

In short, Archer thought that if it didn't offend anyone, it couldn't be real satire. And indeed, the program for *Patience* bore a careful note explaining that the authors were not attacking poetry or true aestheticism but rather pretenders to that art. As Gilbert was later to have Giuseppe say in *The Gondoliers,* "When I say that I detest kings, I mean I detest *bad* kings."

Except in *Utopia, Limited,* this would always be the case in Gilbert & Sullivan. Sir Joseph's sin wasn't being first lord of the admiralty but rather not being qualified to be, any more than General Stanley was qualified to be an army officer. *Patience* is even less explicitly satiric in that there aren't any real aesthetes in the play, any more than there are poets or intellectuals—everyone is pretending. If Gilbert has anything to say about aestheticism, it's simply "Good aesthetes are good; bad aesthetes are bad"—hardly a revelation.

(Gilbert wouldn't have spoofed intellectuals or artists anyway, as he considered himself to be both an intellectual and an artist. Upon being knighted, he complained of the official recognition of him as "William S. Gilbert, playwright," which he felt sounded too much like mere manual labor.[3] Noting that nobody spoke of "poemwrights" or "picturewrights," he preferred to be called a "dramatist.")

If *Patience* is more parody than satire, however, its longevity is all the more remarkable.

Parody is by its nature ephemeral. It relies on recognition, and the specific objects of parody seldom have lasting recognition. In 1881, when George Grossmith played Bunthorne wearing an eyeglass like Swinburne's, a lily like Wilde's, and a silver streak in his hair like Whistler's, he entered to a prolonged ovation; in the 1970s, a similarly made-up John Reed got only mild chuckles at his eccentric appearance. Parody doesn't last, and *Patience* is no exception.

Yet since it first appeared people have suspected that there was something more to *Patience* than a parody of aestheticism or artistic pretension in general. But no one has put the pieces together—commentators appear to have been blinded by received wisdom, by excessive interest in exactly who is being parodied, by undue efforts to force the opera into a satiric mold or simply by refusal to take the opera on its own terms.

The critic who came closest to the truth is probably W. A. Darlington, in his 1950 study *The World of Gilbert and Sullivan*.[4] He perceptively notices that "If You're Anxious for to Shine" "is the only number in the first act that gets away from the theme of love." Instead of pursuing this intriguing observation, however, he returns to a further discussion of art and aestheticism.

The fact of the matter is that *Patience* isn't about art, aestheticism, pretension, or anything of the kind, any more than *H. M. S. Pinafore* is about naval practices or *Iolanthe* about the House of Peers. Aestheticism provides a story line and a production concept, a comic framework through which Gilbert & Sullivan can pursue a more serious subject matter.

Through the previous three operas, they had struggled for a way to achieve true thematic depth; with the new form of *Patience*, they finally have the creative freedom to do exactly that. Henceforth, except perhaps in *The Mikado*, thematic considerations will lie at the heart of every Savoy opera.

In November 1880, as he was working on the libretto of *Patience*, Gilbert wrote an intriguing letter to the critic Clement Scott:

"I have to rewrite *The Sorcerer* for early performance & I have to finish the new libretto as soon as possible—& I have just had to begin it all over again after I had finished two-thirds of it."[5]

Reginald Allen, in *The First Night Gilbert and Sullivan*, concludes from this that Gilbert initially saw *Patience* as a rewriting of *The Sorcerer*.[6] This seems unlikely. The letter sounds as if Gilbert viewed the *Sorcerer* rewrite and "the new libretto" as two separate projects. Besides, the re-beginning clearly refers to his decision of that month to change his two rival curates into two rival poets; by this time, that almost finished libretto (which survives) could hardly be considered a revision of *The Sorcerer*, even if it had originated as such.

In any event, the rival-curates libretto had been based closely on the Bab Ballad "The Rival Curates." In later years the author explicitly credited that poem as the inspiration for *Patience*, and never again alluded to *The Sorcerer* in this context.

Still, Gilbert clearly had *The Sorcerer* fresh in his mind while writing *Patience*, and it shows. The theme of *Patience* is exactly the same as that of *The Sorcerer:* What is love?

The earlier opera had been thematically muddled, partly because both creators were relatively new to the genre and partly because Gilbert's libretto was too unfocused and awkwardly shaped to allow room for thematic maneuvering. *Patience* is far more focused, primarily because it follows a classical model for using a narrative framework to explore a question: Center the story on a character who sets out on a quest for an answer to that very question.

It is no accident that the opera is called *Patience*. In fact, it is the first of three consecutive operas titled after women who are not the operas' most prominent figures but nevertheless are the real focuses of the action. From a standpoint of fair billing, *Patience, Iolanthe*, and *Princess Ida* should have been called *Bunthorne, Strephon*, and *Hilarion*—but, though the male characters enjoy more stage time, such retitling would have grossly distorted the operas.

Patience is a classic questing youth in the folk tradition of Aladdin, Dick Whittington, Oliver Twist, and Dorothy of *The Wizard of Oz*. The opera's youngest character, she begins as a true innocent. Her defining characteristic is that she knows nothing whatsoever of love: Her introductory song is the lilting "I Cannot Tell What This Love May Be," a paean to ignorance as bliss. She is so pure that "I won't go to bed until I am head over ears in love with somebody," which from anyone else would be a ringing double-entendre, from her is completely innocuous.

Subsequently, she is exposed to a diversity of opinions on love. She embraces the most grievously wrong one, propounded by Lady Angela. Angela presents love as a quasi-religious duty, a transfiguring pain and sorrow taken on for its own reward.

Angela is merely posturing, of course. She knows nothing about love, nor even knows that she doesn't know. Her wandering affections take her from the Major to Bunthorne to the Major to Grosvenor to the Major to

Grosvenor and back again to the Major over the course of the opera. Her real point of view is perfectly expressed in the song "If Saphir I Choose to Marry," in which all five singers celebrate the irrelevance of who marries whom. Now that the dragoons are aesthetes, Angela is perfectly happy with any of them, because she has no real love in her.

Patience does, however, and thus trying to follow Angela's example all but ruins her. The ladies can skip blithely from Bunthorne to Grosvenor because to them there is no difference between the two poets. But Patience longs for Grosvenor with all her heart.

To Patience, Angela's frivolous idea is catastrophic. It leads her to her fourth song about love, "True Love Must Single-Hearted Be." In this song, she takes Angela's hypothesis to its logical conclusion: If love is suffering, whatever causes the most pain must be the greatest love. Therefore the loathsome Bunthorne, who frightens her to death, is the perfect mate, while the perfect Grosvenor, whom she adores, is the worst possible match.

Bunthorne is quite right when he says to Patience, "I don't believe you know what love is." Still under Angela's misguided sway, Patience responds with the finest lyric in the opera—perhaps in all the operas:

> Love is a plaintive song
>   sung by a suffering maid,
> telling a tale of wrong,
>   telling of hope betrayed.
> Tuned to his every note,
>   sorry when he is sad,
> blind to his every mote,
>   merry when he is glad.
> Love that no wrong can cure,
>   love that is always new,
> that is the love that's pure,
>   that is the love that's true.
>
> Rendering good for ill,
>   smiling at every frown,
> yielding your own self-will,
>   laughing the tear-drops down.
> Never a selfish whim,
>   trouble, or pain to stir;
> everything for him,
>   nothing at all for her.
> Love that will aye endure,
>   though the rewards be few,
> that is the love that's pure,
>   that is the love that's true.

The brilliance of this ballad lies in two aspects, both tied to the words. (The tune, unfortunately, is one of Sullivan's least distinguished, a routine waltz that shows virtually no sense of the words, character, or situation.)

First, the images are comparatively fresh and to the point. Gilbert has come a long way from the strung-together clichés of *The Sorcerer* or *H. M. S. Pinafore.* "Blind to his every mote" is a compelling image—she's so attentive to him that when he gets dust in his eye, she can't see—and entirely fresh. "Laughing the tear-drops down" is another perfect image, simple and free of artifice or rhetorical excess.

Furthermore, the lyrics relate strongly to the preceding love songs "I Cannot Tell What This Love May Be" and "True Love Must Single-Hearted Be." "I Cannot Tell" is a question, for which "Plaintive Song" is an answer. The former is all innocence while the latter is all experience, both using images of falling tears and red eyes to similar effect—by Act 2, Patience has become what initially she mocked.

"True Love Must Single-Hearted Be" is also an answer to the question asked by "I Cannot Tell," but it is an innocent's answer, a description of an idealized martyr's role. By contrast, "Love Is a Plaintive Song" is specific and detailed, a flesh-and-blood woman's moan of misery. Together the three songs make up a triptych of the passage from innocence to experience.

With "Love Is a Plaintive Song," Patience is brought to rock bottom, as all questing youths must be. And, as is traditional in such story lines, the youth must reject outside help in order to find the answer. In so doing, she finds that she has known the answer all along, if only she had known she knew it.

It is not enough, however, to tell a story about a youth's quest for an answer—the story must supply that answer, the lesson from the tale. And while Gilbert had nothing to say about aestheticism, he had something powerful to say about love.

It's easy to overlook Patience's second song about love. Among other things, "Long Years Ago" has a mundane tune and routine orchestration, while its subject matter (babies in love) seems silly to modern viewers. (Indeed, to most Victorian ones—the song didn't go over well in the original production, and its second verse was cut shortly after opening.)

But to Gilbert the song is quite serious. Its lyrics and music are entirely in earnest, with no hint of humor or sarcasm. Angela's risqué quibbling at the end proves only that she misses the point. Associating love with sex, she emphasizes the fact that Patience's childhood friend "was a little *boy.*" Patience, shocked, insists "he was a *little* boy," denying any sexual implication. (Emphases in original.)

And indeed, there is no sexual insinuation here. The song's key line is not "he was a little boy" but "how pure our baby joy." To Gilbert, in *The Sorcerer* earlier and in other works later, love is entirely distinct from sex.

The bond between Patience and Grosvenor is indeed true love, all the purer for being asexual, just as the infant bonds between Ida and Hilarion and between Luiz and Casilda will be true love.

Theirs is love purified. Even more than the average Victorian, Gilbert venerated childhood in general and infancy in particular as the age of moral purity. (Needless to say, his was a pre-Freudian age!) He used his own baby nickname "Bab" to sign his poems, and to the end of his life enjoyed the company of children more than adults, hosting parties for as many as 100 children at Grim's Dyke, where he read them his own poems, Dickens stories, and other works.

He approved special all-child productions of *H. M. S. Pinafore* and *The Pirates of Penzance* at the Savoy, and in his final years produced children's-book adaptations of two of the operas. Even his wife, Lucy, was 17 when they met (Gilbert was 29), and throughout his operas 17 remains a magical age, the cusp between innocence and adulthood.

To Gilbert, then, the child's answer was usually the right one. Amid the clouds of rank, money, art, politics, self-interest, war, and all the other adult things blowing through *Patience*, the love of Patience and Grosvenor shines through as something literally pure and simple. Patience has the answer all along, buried in her heart: "I seem now to know what love is! It has been revealed to me—it is Archibald Grosvenor!"

But despite this revelation, and despite all her instincts telling her to love Grosvenor and spurn Bunthorne, Patience suppresses her feelings and does as she has been told she should. This is of course a great mistake, but Patience is a child and has to learn through experience.

It may seem simplistic to say "love is . . . Archibald Grosvenor," but Gilbert means it sincerely. In his romantic vision, consistent through all his works, love is not sexual, mechanical, political, dynastic, familial, social, or any of the other adult-world viewpoints on which Victorian society based its affairs. Love is the loved one, as simple as that.

The child-woman Patience (who naively accepts everything she's told and is addressed by the ladies as "happy girl" and "pretty child" throughout) and the child-man Grosvenor (author of faux-aesthetic nursery rhymes) know more than all the practical adults on the stage—or, by implication, in the audience.

In keeping with the questing-youth tradition, it is up to Patience to save herself, and eventually she does. In this she is unlike her predecessors: Aline, Josephine, and Mabel are saved by, respectively, Wells's sacrifice, Buttercup's revelation, and the Police Sergeant's appeal to the pirates. In these operas the good characters, male and female alike, owe their rescue to external agents. Patience, on the other hand, is the first in a line of characters who make their own salvation: After her, the Chancellor, Princess Ida, Ko-Ko, and Robin Oakapple will all triumph through their own wits (except for Ida, who triumphs through her courage).

At first glance, it may seem as if Patience's salvation is nothing more than a byproduct of Bunthorne's ironic downfall. Actually, however, it is she who turns the situation to her own advantage, even more so than the Chancellor, Ko-Ko, or Robin.

Within the context of their operas, their convoluted logic makes sense as a plot resolution, but the same is not true for Patience. Her leaving Grosvenor for Bunthorne had nothing to do with aestheticism, after all— by her own admission, "I don't like poetry." It was motivated by Grosvenor's perfection and Bunthorne's loathsomeness: "To monopolize those features on which all women love to linger—it would be unpardonable!" versus "It follows then a maiden who/devotes herself to loving you/is promoted by no selfish view."

The consummate egotist, Bunthorne assumes that Grosvenor's appeal lies solely in his meeker brand of aestheticism—he can't imagine that Grosvenor might merely be more attractive. He is as much an ass as the three dragoons who become aesthetes: Having lost their loves to Grosvenor, all four decide to start acting like Grosvenor to win them back. But only Bunthorne has the added inspiration of simultaneously bullying Grosvenor into ceasing to be aesthetic.

This backfires, of course, because Grosvenor's appeal to women is not his aestheticism but his perfection: "Archibald the All-Right cannot be all wrong," Angela says blithely. "And if the All-Right chooses to discard aestheticism, it proves that aestheticism ought to be discarded."

This irony frustrates Bunthorne, and by rights it ought to frustrate Patience as well. After all, Grosvenor still has "those features on which all women love to linger"—in fact, as she begins her final dialogue, all the women are lingering on those very features. (Her "I am shocked—surprised—horrified" presumably refers not to his change of clothes but to his dancing onstage with all the young ladies, whom he now admires as much as any commonplace young man would.)

Patience also realizes that changing his mode of aestheticism doesn't make Bunthorne perfect. Her first reaction to his new style is "What in the world is the matter with you?" If she stuck to her previous logic, she would continue to spurn the universally attractive Grosvenor in favor of Bunthorne.

Instead, Patience adopts the pretense that what attracted her to Grosvenor was his aestheticism. This is obviously untrue—she loved him years before he became a poet—but it gives her a pretext to dismiss Bunthorne and go to Grosvenor, the man she really loves.

In principle, Patience could have done this at any time. But, like any questing youth, she must strike bottom before she learns what she already knows. It is only by having all social pretenses stripped away and reaching the depths of "Love Is a Plaintive Song" that she can realize the truth. The next time we see her, it is a different Patience, stronger and more in control of herself and her situation.

Bunthorne's final situation is the crowning irony. From our first glimpse of the opera's subtitle, we have been waiting to see "who shall be our Bunthorne's bride." Yet he winds up the only man without a bride, forced to turn for consolation to his lily, the very affectation he has previously admitted adopting only out of "a morbid love of admiration."

Despite the title, Patience is not to be Bunthorne's bride. At the beginning, they seemed potential mates, both renowned deniers of love (he "remains icy insensible . . . the love of maidens is to him as interesting as the taxes"). But Patience has learned, and Bunthorne has not. She, a child, has become an adult (the quest to learn "What is love?" obviously suggests the quest for adulthood and sexuality); Bunthorne hasn't grown at all. He ends up exactly where he started, and deserves nothing better.

In the two operas prior to *Patience*, Gilbert & Sullivan had shown substantial growth in the technical aspects of their work, while failing to master the thematic aspects. *Patience* is the reverse: The thematic level is stronger and more developed, while both creators show signs of technical uncertainty.

This is in part the perhaps inevitable consequence of abandoning the trappings of conventional comic opera to devise their own conventions. This radical re-visioning did not escape the notice of contemporary critics. Looking back on their career in 1893, an anonymous critic in *The Speaker* wrote:

> Comic opera, as a rule, being an unsavory compound of ribald buffoonery and sentimental twaddle, we all hailed with delighted surprise the decent and yet humorous exception invented by Mr. W. S. Gilbert and Sir Arthur Sullivan and reproduced under superficially varying but fundamentally identical forms in their series of extravaganzas at the Savoy Theatre.[7]

Given that they were rethinking the entire genre, it's natural that here and there in *Patience* each man falters. In addition, for different reasons each was working under time pressure—Sullivan, as he admitted at the time, out of "my natural indolence," Gilbert owing to the revamping of the rival-curates libretto at a relatively late date.

In Sullivan's case, his music retreats from the greater theatricality that had marked *The Pirates of Penzance*. The first 20 minutes of *Patience* are musically brilliant, but thereafter the tunes are often catchy but seldom particularly suited to the characters or the situation; the overall effect resembles *H. M. S. Pinafore* or even *The Sorcerer*.

For example, "I Hear the Soft Note of the Echoing Voice" is a gorgeous chorale, but it stops the action dead. Nothing in it is in musical character for the six people singing it, nor for the chorus. Gilbert seems to have been at a loss to stage it—Francois Cellier, the Savoy's music director, notes (approvingly) that Gilbert simply had the entire company stop, turn to the audience, and sing without movement of any kind.[8]

If "I Hear the Soft Note" sounds more like a church than a theater, "The Magnet and the Churn" sounds more like a music hall than either. It is one of the show's catchiest tunes, but is stylistically out of character for the Grosvenor of "Prithee, Pretty Maiden."

Moreover, Sullivan skews the emphasis of a clever lyric that plies three separate levels of meaning: The tune catches the first level, as a collection of intricate puns, but the composer misses the second level, as an allegory for the futile love of the ladies (as the magnet) for Grosvenor (as the churn), which is Grosvenor's supposed reason for singing it, and also the third, as an allegory for the love of Grosvenor (the "most aesthetic, very magnetic" lure to all the ladies) for Patience (the milkmaid represented as a churn). It's a deft lyric, funny and perfectly expressing the character's state of mind as established in the preceding dialogue. How Sullivan might have reflected this in the music is impossible to say—integrating something of "Prithee, Pretty Maiden," perhaps?—but the tune shows no signs of his having tried.

Again and again, Sullivan's score fails to live up to its first two sequences. The Act 1 finale is barely integrated at all, a collection of fragments without cohesion until the very end, when Grosvenor's entrance inspires Sullivan to a sparkling finish that even incorporates the dragoons' "Now Is Not This Ridiculous?" once again.

Similarly, the tune to "Silvered Is the Raven Hair" is a sentimental parlor ballad that doesn't suit the pun-filled lyric or the hard-edged character; it did work well when subsequently adapted as a parlor ballad, "In the Twilight of Our Love." The tune for "Love Is a Plaintive Song" fails to reflect the misery of the lyric. "If Saphir I Choose to Marry" is a bouncy tune that simply ignores the fact that all the characters are now supposed to be aesthetic in speech and movement. "So Go to Him and Say to Him" is catchy but violently out of character for Jane and Bunthorne as their musical styles have previously been established.

There are plenty of other examples, but the point is clear: While Gilbert has moved to another level, with scenes and lyrics that are tightly linked to character and resonate with several levels of meaning, Sullivan stands still or even goes backward.

Ian Bradley has remarked, with some justice, that "[a]ltogether, the music for *Patience* shows a greater maturity and originality than that of the earlier Gilbert & Sullivan operas. There are fewer recitatives and solo arias imitative of the grand-opera tradition, and more duets, trios and other concerted pieces."[9] However, credit for these structural improvements belongs less to Sullivan than to Gilbert, who laid out the structure of the show and thus is most responsible for the new, more integrated form.

Sullivan would later embrace this concept, but he does not for most of *Patience.* In fact, his work often runs contrary to Gilbert's efforts at integration. It is only in the following *Iolanthe* that Sullivan catches up to Gilbert, and in some respects even passes him, on the road to a new operatic form.

As for Gilbert, in most respects *Patience* is one of his finest librettos. His greatest failings are attributable to his hasty revision, in which certain inconsistencies are hastily dealt with in implausible ways.

The first act of the rival-curates opera, for example, was to have as its setting "Exterior of [a] country vicarage," the home of the Bunthorne prototype, the Reverend Lawn Tennison. (The loss of excruciating puns in the names was one benefit of the revision!) In adapting, however, Gilbert hastily made the new scene the exterior of Bunthorne's home—"Exterior of Castle Bunthorne."

This setting was duly presented on the Savoy stage and since, yet it makes no sense. The opera makes clear that Bunthorne is new in town: The dragoons, after only a year's absence, do not recognize him. ("Who is the gentleman with the long hair?") Moreover, Jane explains the ladies' aestheticism by saying, "Bunthorne! . . . He has come among us, and he has idealized us." Obviously, Bunthorne is a wandering poet, as much a stranger as Wilde was in London when he arrived from Ireland via Oxford.

There are a variety of other awkward relics of the rival-curates version. As several critics have pointed out, rural clergymen were known for holding charity raffles, so the Reverend Tennison putting himself up as a raffle prize would have been hilarious. For an aesthetic poet, it's funny, but only in a non-sequitur sense—there is no inherent link between raffles and poets. Similarly, lines such as "your style is much too sanctified, your cut is too canonical" are right for clergymen but don't apply to either poet. The threat of a curse would probably have seemed funnier directed at an ultramild clergyman than at an aesthetic poet—again, the resulting laugh is from non-sequitur, not substantive, humor.

Even Sullivan is caught once by the switch. His opening line for "Twenty Lovesick Maidens We" is an exact quote of a tune in William Vincent Wallace's 1845 opera *Maritana*, the words for which are "Hark, those chimes so sweetly sounding."[10] In the context of maidens sighing outside a vicarage, the quotation is witty; in its existing context, it actually drew charges of plagiarism.

Not every lyric is as perfectly executed as "Love Is a Plaintive Song" or "The Magnet and the Churn." Colonel Calverley's song "A Heavy Dragoon," for example, recalls "I Am the Very Model of a Modern Major-General" in rattling off a formidable array of historical, scientific, and fictional characters. But there is a comic point to the Major-General's song—that none of his examples have anything to do with modern warfare, making him vastly qualified for everything but his current position.

By contrast, some of the Colonel's examples are relevant and others absurd, but the song as a whole is without a comic point. It's nothing more than a list set to music, and as such is a step backward. (And, like "When I Go Out of Door," its plethora of local references made it incomprehensible almost before the original production closed.)

Gilbert also loses track of certain aspects of his story. The Duke's personality is wildly inconsistent, for example: He begins as a comic figure, a bumbling nobleman who enlists in the army in quest of bullying; he becomes smoothly romantic in "Your Maiden Hearts, Ah, Do Not Steel"; and he finishes as a querulous aesthetic convert who seems to resent being bullied by the Colonel and the Major. In later operas, Gilbert would excel at developing characters' comic and dramatic potential. Here, apparently, he simply forgets.

Other than these revision-related problems, however, Gilbert's work is easily his best so far. His passion for integration gives the opera a structural solidity that was to characterize the subsequent operas (except *Utopia, Limited,* gutted by last-minute cuts).

For example, twice in Act 2 he reenacts a key scene from Act 1, Bunthorne's poetry-reading scene. The contrasts are deliberate—the stage direction for Grosvenor's entrance reads "Enter Grosvenor, followed by maidens, two and two, each playing on an archaic instrument, as in Act I. He is reading abstractedly, as Bunthorne did in Act 1, and pays no attention to them." Similarly, Bunthorne's later entrance is accompanied by Jane, reprising the Act 1 chorus as "In a doleful train, one and one I walk all day."

The point is not to echo earlier jokes, as with the running gags in *H. M. S. Pinafore,* but rather to develop them. Grosvenor's Act 2 scene is close enough to Bunthorne's Act 1 scene to gain extra humor from the contrast, but its jokes are fresh. His poems are as funny as Bunthorne's but in a different way, while the ladies get as big a laugh from their vacant looks on "Let us think of nothing at all" as they did from their droopy aestheticism on "To understand it, cling passionately to one another and think of faint lilies."

The continuity adds humor, but these lines would be funny in their own right. When Sir Joseph asks Captain Corcoran "What, never?" it is funny not in itself but only in its reminder of the earlier scene, whereas "Let us think of nothing at all" would be almost as funny even if the previous poetry-reading scene had never occurred.

This extra humor is a result of Gilbert's crucial leap: He is now thinking of his operas as unified works rather than collections of individual pieces. It is the logical outcome of a progression he began as a lyricist in the 1860s, translating a foreign opera lyric as a concert song; continued in the early 1870s, writing original lyrics to established opera tunes for his burlesques; evolved in the mid-1870s, writing lyrics to be set to original music for his early operas with Clay and others; and most recently manifested in *H. M. S. Pinafore* and *The Pirates of Penzance* with his use of reprises.

Those reprises had served as mere tub-thumping, reminding people of the most popular songs in the show. In *Patience*, however, reprises are used as connective tissue to tie the opera together. "Twenty Lovesick Maidens We," "In a Doleful Train," and "Now, Is Not This Ridiculous" are not the "hit tunes" of *Patience*. Had the opera been written a few years earlier, Gilbert & Sullivan would probably have served up multiple reprises of "Prithee, Pretty Maiden," "If You're Anxious for to Shine" and "So Go to Him and Say to Him." Now they reprise the less catchy but more integrative tunes for a greater theatrical purpose. It is in every way a major step forward.

So too is the characterization. Previous Gilbert & Sullivan operas had offered some delightfully funny characters—most notably the Judge, Dr. Daly, John Wellington Wells, Sir Joseph Porter, and Major-General Stanley. But, however funny, they were hardly plausible or psychologically convincing characters. To this day, these roles require engaging performers more than convincing actors.

In *Patience*, this changes. Patience, Bunthorne, and Jane are every bit as funny as their predecessors, but each is also a comparatively rounded character who tests an actor's full range of resources.

Patience is the first really interesting female character in the operas, leading a series of well-rendered women who grace the mature operas. Her innocence is her dominant characteristic, reminiscent of the similarly duty-bound Frederic in *The Pirates of Penzance*, and the character's humor stems largely from her naiveté. She is so pure that Bunthorne's attempt to seduce her fails because she literally doesn't understand what he is saying: "If you please, I don't understand you—you frighten me."

But there is more to Patience than the wide-eyed innocent of the early scenes. Her fear and discomfort in the seduction scene and her alarmed bafflement in her scene with Angela add dimension to the character. By "Love Is a Plaintive Song" she's as naive as she ever was but not at all funny. If the role is well played, the audience will be entirely sympathetic to her song, reacting to a humanity that is only glimpsed in the operatic anguish of Aline, Josephine, or Mabel.

This is why Patience, unlike her predecessors, has an active role in the resolution of the opera. The earlier heroines were neither convincingly human nor substantially comic. They were peripheral to the action, which was sorted out by the men (and, in *H. M. S. Pinafore*, by Buttercup). Patience, on the other hand, is at the core of her opera. Its resolution depends on her and derives both its comic appeal and its satisfying quality from her humor and believability.

Bunthorne is the most unpleasant Gilbert & Sullivan character so far, except for the stock-villainous Dick Deadeye. While Wells is more evil and Sir Joseph arguably is as egotistical and manipulative, both characters have a certain whimsy that Bunthorne lacks. The sight of him in Act 2 consumed by jealous frustration, hectoring Patience while simultaneously bullying Jane, is far more off-putting than Wells's conjuring of demons or Sir Joseph's harassment of Captain Corcoran.

The reason, of course, is that the *Patience* characters are far more real. Because we see the impact of Bunthorne's hurtfulness on characters whose feelings are convincing, his conduct makes him far more unpleasant—unpleasant enough that his final downfall is unambiguously satisfying.

Still, while we may not like Bunthorne, we understand him far more than we do Wells, Porter, or Stanley. It's a question of motivation: Wells's is presumably commercialism (though we never even see him present a bill), and Porter's is egotistical social climbing, while the Major-General is without any motivation beyond self-preservation. All three are essentially stick figures, their motivations rarely explored.

Bunthorne is amply motivated. Narcissistic to the point of masochism, he is never happy, because he obsessively wants what he can't have: When all the ladies but Patience love him, he wants only her; but as soon as he has her, he is consumed with outrage at having lost the others. So great is his "morbid love of admiration" that he'll tolerate even Jane, whom he detests, if she will admire him.

Actually, Bunthorne detests everyone. He despises Grosvenor, he despises the dragoons, he despises Patience (once he has her), he even despises his own aesthetic persona. In a word, Bunthorne is hollow. Behind his aloof, transcendental facade is a mean, spiteful, self-obsessed cad as detestable as King Gama.

In an opera that never gets far from the difference between outward appearance and inner truth, it is Bunthorne who loses the most by the contrast. He would be pitiable if he weren't so despicable. As it is, the audience is happy to see him get what he deserves at the end. He's believable enough to be detestable.

Jane too is far more real than her Gilbert & Sullivan predecessors. Her strong-willed pursuit of Bunthorne gives her a clarity they lack. Jane is so human, in fact, that audiences usually take her side against her creator, Gilbert himself. "Silvered Is the Raven Hair" expresses a fear of aging and loss of beauty that still resonates for women everywhere, and audiences don't like seeing it made fun of.

Obviously, this type of humor is less popular today than in the 1880s. Modern audiences are unlikely to share the critical consensus that, as *The Era* said, "Nothing could be better than the song of Lady Jane at the opening of the second Act."[11]

Nevertheless, the lyric's craftsmanship is truly ingenious, offering a series of puns as deft as "The Magnet and the Churn." At the same time, its "too-little, too-much" structure is a witty parallel to "I Cannot Tell What This Love May Be," the first examples of a particularly Gilbertian paradoxical structure that was to peak with "Is Life a Boon?" in *The Yeomen of the Guard*. But today it plays more often as a tasteless author picking on a woman who has trouble enough already.

Jane is not only convincing but also funny. Her overheated aestheticism (with a sarcastic undertone that reveals that she doesn't buy this stuff for a minute) gives the opera some of its best lines: "Still, there is a cobwebby gray velvet, with a tender bloom like cold gravy, which, made Florentine 14th-century, trimmed with Venetian leather and Spanish altar lace and surmounted with something Japanese—it matters not what—would at least be Early English!"

Jane is a vital element in the "What is love?" theme, serving as a constant counterbalance to Patience, age to her youth, experience to her innocence. To Jane, there is no such thing as love. Her approach is practical and hard-nosed, even tactical: She wants a mate, she knows that the time is running short for her, and she targets Bunthorne as the most likely candidate. No more drawn to Grosvenor's beauty than to Bunthorne's sham poeticism, she never wavers: "The fickle crew have deserted Reginald and sworn allegiance to his rival, and all, forsooth, because he has glanced with passing favor on a puling milkmaid. Fools! Of that fancy he will soon weary—and then I, who alone am faithful to him, shall reap my reward."

Jane seems to have targeted Bunthorne on the assumption that he is too unpleasant to ultimately appeal to any woman but so dependent on admiration that he will accept even her fading charms if they are the only ones available. She stomachs his abuse, is effulgent in praising him, and even helps him in what she knows is a doomed pursuit of the other ladies. But she doesn't love him in the least: When a better match comes along, she abandons Bunthorne without a second thought.

Jane and Patience are true opposites. They are the only women who see through Bunthorne's posturing, but they do so from different directions—Patience from an "emperor has no clothes" innocence, Jane from a hard-nosed realism that penetrates his pretension effortlessly.

Throughout the opera, the two women are rivals, constantly juxtaposed: First in Jane's opening-scene speech, "Oh, Reginald, if you but knew what a wealth of golden love is waiting for you, stored up in this rugged old bosom of mine, the milkmaid's triumph would be short indeed!" and then as Patience prevents Jane from drawing the raffle ticket for Bunthorne's hand. The contrast is picked up again in Jane's "puling milkmaid" speech in Act 2; then in the "Crushed again" dialogue, as Jane repeatedly takes Bunthorne's side against Patience, forcibly contrasting her own supportiveness with Patience's longing for Grosvenor; then at the finale, as Bunthorne settles for Jane when Patience jilts him; and finally when Jane too jilts Bunthorne for a more desirable suitor.

The two are contrasted because Jane represents a worst-case scenario for Patience's future. Jane probably fully endorses both "I Cannot Tell What This Love May Be" and "Love Is a Plaintive Song." She doesn't believe in romantic love and submits uncomplainingly to Bunthorne's bullying because she considers it the natural order of things. If Patience never met the adult Grosvenor, she might grow older and wiser, more attuned to her own interests, but would never know what love really was; as her beauty faded, she might become a lonely, desperate old maid. In a word, she might become Jane.

In other words, the two characters offer two "alternate" scenarios for the same basic story, with Jane's example providing extra resonance for the main story line. This multiple-story technique is soon to become a hallmark of Gilbert's Savoy style: The next opera, *Iolanthe*, offers three alternate fairy-loves-mortal scenarios, establishing a triple-scenario structure that will hold for every subsequent opera except *The Mikado* (and *Utopia, Limited*, in which it will become a quadruple structure).

The advantage of the multiple-story technique is that instead of having their characters simply discuss their options, Gilbert & Sullivan can explore those choices dramatically. Instead of having Robin Oakapple discuss different ways of dealing with his curse, for example, *Ruddigore* presents three different bad baronets (and three innocent women in love with them) to make the options concrete and real. The same is true of *Iolanthe's* three fairies in love with three mortals, *Princess Ida's* three children rebelling against autocratic parents, and so forth.

It's so effective a structure that Gilbert & Sullivan return to it again and again. As with so much else in the mature operas, it begins in *Patience*.

Coupled with this new narrative structure, tightly keyed to thematic issues, *Patience* presents a new, more effective dramatic structure, based on ideas first employed in *The Sorcerer* and in *H. M. S. Pinafore*.

By this scheme, the opera opens with a peaceful but flawed equilibrium: The ladies are all in love with Bunthorne, who in turn is in love with Patience. Over the course of the first act, as the various characters are introduced, this equilibrium becomes unstable. We meet the "right" lovers for the ladies in the dragoons and for Patience in Grosvenor. But obstacles arise in all these matches, and it becomes clear that the success or failure of the effort to resolve the instability will depend on the resolution of the central story line, in this case Patience's quest for love.

Until the Act 1 finale, the audience has realized more than the characters how unstable their equilibrium is. We know, for example, that there is an irresistibly perfect man wandering around town, but none of the other characters (except Patience) knows until the finale.

In this prototype structure, the Act 1 finale presents two apparent resolutions: First, the "false happy ending" in which every element but one is resolved,[12] and second the "new flawed equilibrium."

The "false happy ending" for *Patience* pairs off Bunthorne with Patience and the ladies with the dragoons in "I Hear the Soft Note of the Echoing Voice." (Subsequent "false happy endings" will include *Iolanthe's* "When Darkly Looms the Day," *The Mikado's* "The Threatened Cloud Has Passed Away," and *Ruddigore's* "When the Buds Are Blossoming.")

The "false happy ending" collapses, however, with the arrival of that one unresolved element. At this point, the characters catch up with the audience and see the full complexity of the situation. (The unresolved element in *Patience* is Grosvenor; in *Iolanthe* the half-fairy Strephon and the Fairy Queen; in *The Mikado* Katisha; and in *Ruddigore* Sir Despard. In every case, the audience has been warned, but most of the characters have not.)

Finally the act ends with what is supposedly a new equilibrium but is obviously fatally flawed (and usually captured in a final ensemble that sets the aggrieved people against the happy ones). The ladies migrate to Grosvenor, leaving both the dragoons and Patience frustrated, as well as Grosvenor himself. It is apparent that this resolution cannot last. (The dragoons' shouted complaints mirror the Peers' threats in *Iolanthe* or Katisha's vow to seek out the Mikado; an antecedent is Deadeye's vow to seek out the Captain in *H. M. S. Pinafore.*)

Time passes during the intermission, days or weeks that allow the strains of the new equilibrium to become pronounced. The early part of Act 2 is devoted to showing us just how bad things have gotten—how miserable Patience is, how miserable Grosvenor is, how frustrated Bunthorne is. Obviously, something must be done.

The remainder of Act 2 then consists of a series of increasingly preposterous attempts by various characters to find a better equilibrium—the dragoons going aesthetic, Bunthorne attempting to be insipid, Grosvenor attempting to be imperfect. Here Gilbert & Sullivan cash in the chips they have accumulated over the first one and a third acts, producing rich humor and one memorable scene after another.

Finally, two resolutions—one of the narrative, the other of the theme—are achieved at once, to bring about the happy ending. The thematic resolution is always achieved first, whether it be Patience's renunciation of Bunthorne, Iolanthe's sacrifice for her child, Princess Ida's acceptance of Hilarion, Robin's rejection of evil, or whatever.

All that then remains is the gimmick, a narrative twist to resolve the superficial problem without anyone losing face (or, often, their lives). In *Patience* it's the Duke's last-minute choice of a bride; in *Iolanthe* the Chancellor's legal quibbling; in *The Mikado* Ko-Ko's ingenious semantic twist; and in *Ruddigore* a similarly intricate argument from Robin.

In every case, the ending is neatly tied up with a final laugh, bringing the story line into sync with the thematic narrative. Finally, an upbeat and almost content-free finale ends the opera on a joyful note. It celebrates a new equilibrium, similar to the opening one but clearly more stable. The

Act 2 curtain falls on a world that has been put through a wringer but is finally at peace with itself.

Elements of this bare-bones formula had appeared in *The Sorcerer* and *H. M. S. Pinafore* (indeed, some go back to Shakespeare and earlier). But it is in *Patience* that the pieces come together, producing the dramatic structure that will be the skeleton of *Iolanthe, Princess Ida, The Mikado, Ruddigore, The Gondoliers, Utopia, Limited,* and *The Grand Duke. (The Yeomen of the Guard* has the same structure until a somewhat different ending.)

It is also in *Patience* that Gilbert develops a new style of dialogue—again, one that will last through the remainder of the operas.

Shorn of all its songs, *Patience* would still be a fairly amusing play. Its libretto *reads* much better than that of any of the early operas, because it features more dialogue and that dialogue is far stronger. Prior to *Patience,* Gilbert's dialogue had been sketchy and utilitarian, little more than music-less recitative. Now the dialogue gains a far greater prominence (the *Patience* libretto contains 20 pages of dialogue, that of *The Pirates of Penzance* less than 10), assuming almost as significant a role as the songs.

That the dialogue can sustain this greater length derives from two primary elements: expanded use of multicharacter dialogues and the development of character humor.

Gilbert had been moving toward multicharacter dialogue for some time. *The Sorcerer's* dialogue was stiff, mostly two-person scenes with one character talking *at* another, not *with* him or her. In *H. M. S. Pinafore* and *The Pirates of Penzance,* Gilbert learned to balance his dialogues. Buttercup and the Captain, the Captain and Josephine, Deadeye and the Captain converse as equals.

But these are still essentially two-person scenes. Even when other characters are present, the core of the scene is two people: Despite the presence of the full crew and all Sir Joseph's relatives, the "remarkably fine crew" dialogue remains essentially a parley between Sir Joseph and Captain Corcoran, while in *Pirates* all the pirates and daughters can't make the "orphan/often" scene more than a one-on-one exchange between the Pirate King and the Major-General.

That is not the case in *Patience.* Of 14 dialogues, only six are between two people. In the major dialogue scenes, talk time and laughs are distributed freely, giving every character a chance to shine. Bunthorne's poetry-reading scene lets eight different characters speak (plus the full dragoon chorus), with six (plus the dragoons) getting laugh lines.

This wider distribution of dialogue results in scenes that are less predictable, keeping the audience alert and involved. There's a great deal more interplay, and hence more opportunities for jokes.

Just as important, the type of joke is different. The primary joke form of the early shows was the pun, a la Sir Joseph's "Your position as a topman is a very exalted one" or the "orphan/often" scene. Granted, the Victorians valued puns more than do modern audiences. Still, a pun is by nature less integrated, since as a play on words it can come from almost any character. The "topman" line needn't have been said by Sir Joseph—the Bos'n, Ralph, or Hebe could have said it equally well.

With *Patience*, Gilbert shifts from word humor to character humor. He creates characters who are funnier in themselves and gives them room to express themselves humorously.

The poetry-reading scene's humor is based entirely on the characters as they've already been established. The dragoons' unison "No!" to Bunthorne's proposed reading is funny not in itself but in its perfectly capturing the dragoons' vehement opposition to poetry (it also sets up a bigger laugh when the dragoons reappear in Act 2 as aesthetes). Similarly, Bunthorne's flamboyant poetry is funniest not in itself but in the reactions it provokes from the ladies and the dragoons.

Once Gilbert found the idea of character-based humor, he never abandoned it. *Patience* and its successors are far funnier than their predecessors because their characters are funnier. Pooh-Bah is different in kind from Captain Corcoran, as the Lord Chancellor is from J. W. Wells or the Fairy Queen from Little Buttercup. They are humorous in their own right.

Where previously Gilbert had taken bland characters and put them in self-consciously funny situations, he now has characters funny enough that the humor doesn't have to be forced. The comic effect of bringing Grosvenor and Bunthorne together is enough to sustain a five-minute dialogue with ease, while it's hard to even imagine a five-minute dialogue between, say, Frederic and the Major-General—their characters are simply too sketchy to bear explication.

The character-comedy concept was to reach its zenith in *The Mikado*, for which Gilbert actually wrote the characters before creating the plot. But it got its start in *Patience*.

The crux of the comic-opera revolution represented by *Patience* is that every individual advance both reinforced the others and made them necessary. Because the humor is now based on character instead of words, for example, Sullivan is able to reflect that characterization in the music. The music for Pooh-Bah will sound like Pooh-Bah a lot more than Captain Corcoran's music sounded like him.

Again, the evolution of Gilbert's dialogue increases the variety of scene structures possible. In *The Sorcerer* or *H. M. S. Pinafore*, scenes were built around songs, with dialogue and recitatives setting them up; the "revolving door" structure of "enter-recite-sing-exit, enter-recite-sing-exit" reflected the song-based scene structure.

In *Patience*, however, the scenes are based on the characters, opening up a wider array of structures: A song can bookend a dialogue scene, as in the "Prithee, Pretty Maiden" scene; a scene can begin with a song and build to a dialogue, or even dispense with the song entirely, as in the Bunthorne-Patience seduction scene.

The songs now serve as capstones, expressing and intensifying the characters' emotions as established in the dialogue. It's a method foreshadowing the musical-theater revolution wrought in a later generation by Rodgers & Hammerstein.

But having so many different kinds of possible scene structures demands greater structural integration, to keep the opera from disintegrating. Hence the use of musical motifs, lyric echoes, scenes that evoke previous scenes, and the other devices that so tightly unify the early sequences of *Patience*—which, in turn, demand greater lyrical and musical sophistication than previous shows had required.

By building humor into all the characters, Gilbert also finds himself obliged to do the same with the choruses.

As early as *Trial by Jury* he had worked to make the chorus of jurymen into something of a collective character. In *The Pirates of Penzance*, the policemen arguably had collectively constituted the funniest character in the opera. But just as the individual characters in *Patience* are funnier and more effective, so the aesthetic ladies and the dragoons are the funniest Gilbert & Sullivan choruses yet.

And, as always, the higher the standards achieved in one area, the higher the expectations in others. That the Duke's character is inconsistent is a flaw in *Patience* but would not have been in *The Pirates of Penzance*, in which there was so little real characterization that an important character such as Ruth could completely disappear without comment. That Sullivan's music doesn't always match the situation is noticeable only in *Patience*, because previously no one expected the music to be so tightly integrated.

In short, *Patience* is the first of Gilbert's truly great works, and at times comes close to being the first of Sullivan's. Whatever its weaknesses, it established the context by which their work would subsequently be judged: A highly comic story, laced with satire and contemporary social commentary, is countered and supported by a broader, more universal thematic narrative that is absolutely serious.

The comic surface draws the greatest audience attention, but the deeper thematic narrative is the engine driving the play. The creative tension between the comic and the serious makes *Patience* a dynamic, involving show in a way that its predecessors, however enjoyable, never were.

In the four years since their collaboration had officially begun with *The Sorcerer*, the two men had moved from an essentially derivative operatic style to one all their own, which Gilbert was later to describe to Sullivan as "humorous work, tempered with occasional glimpses of earnest drama."[13]

From subject matter that was primarily parodic, burlesquing the conventions of comic and grand opera, they had moved to a thematic style characterized by structural integration, serious subjects treated with comic flair, characters with one silly element who are otherwise consistent and believable in their behavior, and above all by the highest standards for music, lyrics, dialogue, story, and production values that English musical theater had ever known.

With the Savoy Theatre almost finished, with the D'Oyly Carte company and chorus by now fully trained to meet the exacting requirements of both author and composer, and with their own mastery of their genre essentially achieved, Gilbert & Sullivan were in position to dominate the world of English musical theater, as they would for the next decade.

At the end of that decade, Gilbert wrote to Sullivan, "We have the best theatre, the best company, the best composer and (though I say it) the best librettist in England working together—we are world-known, and as much an institution as Westminster Abbey."[14]

Even after the phenomenal success of *H. M. S. Pinafore*, some might have quarreled with that evaluation. But after *Patience*, it clearly was true.

Facing page: FIGURE 9.1. Henry Lytton as the Lord Chancellor in *Iolanthe.* The role is one of the most demanding in the Gilbert & Sullivan repertoire, a comic part that evolves into a dramatic one as the opera progresses. *Source: The Pierpont Morgan Library, Gilbert and Sullivan Collection.*

9

Iolanthe

With *Iolanthe*, Gilbert & Sullivan hit their stride. *Iolanthe* is the team's first masterpiece, both a pulling-together of what had come before and a signpost to their next six operas, each in its own way a triumph. Unequivocally serious but at the same time funnier than any of its predecessors, *Iolanthe* displays a breathtaking ability to combine apparently contradictory elements without strain. As Strephon is half fairy and half mortal, so *Iolanthe* itself is half opera and half comedy, and the combination works wonderfully.

It is no surprise that *Iolanthe* is more serious in tone. Its story line ups the ante beyond that of *Patience*, making the stakes nothing less than life and death. Except for the unexpected, ambiguous demise of Wells in *The Sorcerer*, every preceding Gilbert & Sullivan opera had concerned itself with matters of marriage and social rank—not trivial to the characters, naturally, but more likely to amuse an audience than to involve them emotionally.

In *Iolanthe*, however, questions of mortality are omnipresent, whether in Strephon's descriptions of his mortal/immortal body, Mountararat and Tolloller threatening one another's lives or, most notably, in the story of Iolanthe herself. The Queen's threat to execute her is real—while it can misguidedly be played for parody, there is nothing in Gilbert's words or Sullivan's music for the final confrontation that suggests humor. The Queen's spear is real, as real as the swords of the warriors in *Princess Ida*, the Mikado's torture racks, the agonies of Robin Oakapple, or the executioner's block in *The Yeomen of the Guard*. *Iolanthe* is the first in a series of operas in which darkness coexists equally with light.

With the stakes so high, the humor gains an edge that is missing in the earlier operas. As in the best moments in *Patience*, and unlike the typical humor of *H. M. S. Pinafore* or *The Pirates of Penzance*, the laughter in *Iolanthe* comes not from puns or local references but from character and situation. The humor of the Lord Chancellor is subtler but funnier than that of Sir Joseph Porter because where Porter is essentially a one-joke caricature, the Chancellor is a rounded, believable figure.

Sir Joseph never has a moment such as "He Loves," evoking the passion of the character's youth, and thus can never have a moment as powerful as the Chancellor's simple "Iolanthe, thou livest." Everything the Chancellor does leads up to this devastating, powerful moment—and yet, he is no melodramatic hero: Five minutes before the audience is engrossed in the drama of "He Loves," it is laughing at the "Nightmare Song." The genius of the mature Gilbert & Sullivan is their ability to combine such elements without compromising either one.

The laughter in *Iolanthe* is also integral to the story and its situations. "This lady's my mother!" invariably gets as big a laugh from the audience as from the characters onstage, precisely because the audience has bought the whole story—the fairies, Iolanthe, Strephon the half-mortal, and all—and can anticipate how the other characters will, quite plausibly, react to

Strephon's apparent lie. It is a bigger, stronger laugh because of the coherence of the story, and is a far cry from "often/orphan." It is also distinctive to *Iolanthe* and could occur in no other opera.

So well woven is *Iolanthe's* story that one tends to remember characters rather than individual lines. Lord Mountararat, the Fairy Queen, and Strephon are funnier than the sum of their parts because the humor derives not from what they say or do but from who they are. Like such subsequent characters as Pooh-Bah, Rose Maybud, or the Duke of Plaza-Toro, these are people who are both "realistic"—in that, given who they are, they act consistently and believably throughout the opera—and innately comic.

But because the humor of *Iolanthe* is so enhanced by its dramatic power and because the sources of that power are so often overlooked, it is worth exploring these elements in greater detail.

It is in thematic areas that we find the greatest continuity between the operas—not in subject matter, which varies as much as do the settings and characters, but in the thematic approach that gives the operas their power. This thematic approach, first experimented with in *The Sorcerer* and developed in *Patience*, flowers in *Iolanthe*, and it is this approach that makes it and the following operas the world-class theater they are.

The watchword for *Iolanthe* is duality, manifested in everything from the characters themselves (the Chancellor's battling capacities, the Queen's battle between her conflicting impulses, Phyllis's engagement to two peers, Strephon's dual nature) to the tone of the opera (simultaneously serious and comic). It finds its strongest manifestation in the two primary themes of the opera, Gilbert's great anti-Victorian theme of head versus heart and the mythic story of life, sexuality, and death. These themes are interwoven throughout the opera, coming to a climax in the final scenes.

Iolanthe is in the most literal sense a fairy tale, and must be understood in the context of Victorian fairy tales for its power to be understood.

The Victorian era was the great age of fairy tales. The poles of the age were set by the great collectors of classic tales, Hans Christian Andersen (1805–75) in Denmark and the Brothers Grimm (Jacob, 1785–1862, and Wilhelm, 1786–1859) in Germany. Older fairy-tale–influenced works were much in vogue: Two of the Victorians' favorite Shakespearean plays were *A Midsummer Night's Dream*, for which Mendelssohn wrote the incidental music that so heavily influenced Sullivan's score for *Iolanthe*, and *The Tempest*, for which Sullivan wrote the incidental music that earned him his initial fame. This was the age that produced James Barrie, Lewis Carroll, and L. Frank Baum, and audiences for *Iolanthe* would have immediately placed much of the show into a fairy-tale context.

Our understanding of the workings of fairy tales—the source of the resonance that makes certain supernatural-influenced stories become classics when others vanish—has been much influenced by the works of post-

Victorian commentators, most notably C. G. Jung and Bruno Bettelheim.[1] These and other critics have pointed out the subtext that provides the social function of these fairy tales, what they do on a conscious or subconscious level that makes them worth retelling as an ongoing part of the culture.

The classic fairy tale is a metaphor of gain and loss. Its "purpose" is to present to children (and, in the Victorian era, to adults), in suitably abstracted form, a central truth of their own existence: that they cannot remain children forever, but must grow up to take their own place in the world—a place that can be cleared only by the death of their parents.

In the traditional fairy tale, such as Little Red Riding Hood, Puss in Boots, or Cinderella (and in such Victorian analogs as *Peter Pan, The Wizard of Oz*, or *Alice in Wonderland*), a child is separated from his or her parents and forced to fend for him- or herself in a world that is strange but somehow also familiar. This world is full of looming threats but also has many wonders to offer. Along the way, the child proves to be up to the challenges of this world, and returns home at the end as a stronger, wiser person, better equipped to face the "real world."

The stories themselves can have different endings and different tones. Most traditional fairy tales have alternate endings in different tellings. The "real ending," as in many Grimm tales, involves the actual death of the parents and the accession of the child to adulthood: The grandmother is eaten by the wolf, and Red Riding Hood and the Woodman live happily ever after in her cottage.

In the "fantasy ending," as in many Andersen tales, the child proves him or herself but is restored to the protection of the parents (however less it may be needed): The Woodman slices open the wolf and the grandmother emerges alive and unhurt.

The Victorians preferred Andersen to the Grimms. A culture that idealized childish innocence did not want to rush children into adulthood. The fantasy ending of eternal childhood may be less satisfying on one level (after all, we all know that aging and death are practical inevitabilities) and certainly less plausible (wait a minute—you mean the wolf swallowed her whole, without even chewing?), but it does make it easier for the children to sleep at night.

Even today, in our supposedly tougher-minded world, we still straddle the fence. Consider the reluctance of the many stage and screen adapters of *Peter Pan* to acknowledge Barrie's original ending ("the tragedy," he calls it[2]) in which Wendy grows old and can no longer fly, or the insistence of Hollywood filmmakers that *The Wizard of Oz* prove ultimately to be only a dream—unlike the original book, which left the question ambiguous.

Iolanthe is very much in this tradition. The inherent shape of the story is clear from early in the show. Just as a parent's protection often also serves, ironically, to smother a child and keep him or her from reaching true maturity, Iolanthe and the Chancellor—Strephon's parents—stand in the way of his happiness with Phyllis. Iolanthe's paradoxical youth drives Phyllis away from him, while the Chancellor is his rival for Phyllis.

In the "real" ending of the opera, Iolanthe reveals her existence to the Chancellor. As Phyllis says, "Upon his realizing that Strephon is his son, all objection to our marriage will be at once removed." This revelation, of course, mandates Iolanthe's death—as she says, "for him, for her, for thee I yield my life." Clearing herself and the Chancellor from the scene, Iolanthe makes room for Strephon and Phyllis to be happy.

It is important not to get caught up in our knowledge of the opera's actual ending or in our after-the-fact assumption that Gilbert & Sullivan couldn't have chosen otherwise. A darker ending is entirely plausible, just as are the murder of Hilarion by Princess Ida, Nanki-Poo's being beheaded, Robin Oakapple perishing in horrible agonies, or Colonel Fairfax being executed. As they would demonstrate in *The Yeomen of the Guard*, Gilbert & Sullivan didn't feel themselves to be constrained by the genre dictates of comic opera (and indeed they never described their plays as such—*Iolanthe*, for example, was billed as "an original fairy opera" and *Ruddigore* as "an original supernatural opera," with no assurance of comedy).

Not only is a dark ending perfectly possible, and one that Gilbert & Sullivan might plausibly have pursued (both men wrote other works that ended tragically), but also it is the ending to which the entire course of the opera naturally leads.

Even the overture, in which Iolanthe and the Chancellor's "He Loves" is superseded by Strephon and Phyllis's "If We're Weak Enough to Tarry," which is in turn crushed by the Fairy Queen's authoritarian "O, Foolish Fay," establishes this scenario. It is reinforced in the initial dialogue that establishes the death penalty Iolanthe has incurred and, later, in her frightened insistence on avoiding the Chancellor. Iolanthe's final "Aye, I live, now let me die" could well mark a coherent, consistent end of the opera—sad, but not without its bittersweet joys ("for him, for her, for thee"). More important, it is psychologically "right."

The same cannot be said for the "fantasy ending" which actually closes the opera. This provides a "happy" ending, to be sure, and Andersen would have approved. But it's hardly plausible.

It is not the Chancellor's "insertion of a single word" that provides the "fantasy ending." We will examine that plot element later. Here, however, it is sufficient to note that it doesn't actually solve anything—it merely defers the problem inherent in love between mortals and immortals.

The shadow hanging over *Iolanthe* is that of Ovid ("Ovidius Naso," as the Fairy Queen calls him). In his *Metamorphoses*, Ovid tells several stories of immortals in love with mortals, and they never end happily. The tragedy of mortals who marry immortals is to die, Ovid wrote; the tragedy of the immortals is to watch their loved ones die.

This dilemma is treated several times in *Iolanthe*, in different forms: Strephon's grotesque-but-hilarious "What's to become of my upper half when I've buried my lower half," for example, obliquely acknowledges that Strephon is what the ancients called a monster—the child of a mortal and an immortal—and in his own way as "wrong" as the Minotaur. The repeated reminders of Iolanthe's age—"a couple of centuries or so"— serves to remind us that, though she looks like a 17-year-old human being, she is actually something quite different.

But the point is most tellingly made in the final recognition scene between Iolanthe and the Chancellor. Its power comes not only from his realization that she is still alive but also from their mutual realization that, while he has aged, she is exactly the same as she ever was. When last they met, he was a young man of roughly Strephon's 24, she 17; now he is an old man, but she is still 17; in not so long, he will be dead . . . and she will still be 17.

Picking up the multiple-story line technique he first used in *Patience*, Gilbert provides a de-facto look at the Chancellor and Iolanthe as they were 25 years before, in the form of the immediately preceding scene between Strephon and Phyllis. In it, we see that their passionate young love already has been tempered by the passage of time—their Act 1 "None Shall Part Us from Each Other," with its ardent defiance of reality, has become the Act 2 "If We're Weak Enough to Tarry," acknowledging that they'd better marry while there's still time—before their own mutability or external pressures sweep them apart. And time will indeed part them from each other: 50 years from now, Phyllis will be 69 and Strephon still only 24.

In this context, the Lord Chancellor's insertion of a single word resolves little. It merely means that, instead of the peers watching as the fairies are slaughtered, the fairies later will have to watch as the peers grow old and die. The tragedy is merely postponed.

The "fantasy ending" that resolves this tragic dilemma is that, as Phyllis sings, "Everyone is now a fairy." This is hardly plausible—if marrying a fairy makes a mortal into one, why didn't the Chancellor become a fairy years ago? And if it's the Queen who makes them all fairies ("Then away we go to Fairyland"), why didn't she do this for Strephon to start out with?

Obviously, this is the "fantasy ending," and it doesn't have to make sense, any more than a wolf who doesn't chew or a little girl who can outrun three bears. The entire context of the opera makes clear that mortals and immortals are fundamentally different and that they intermingle at their peril—as far as the opera reveals, after all, the only way a fairy can die is as the result of marrying a mortal.

But the Savoy audience was doubtless much happier with an ending that let them sleep at night, and so Gilbert & Sullivan take a leaf from "Andersen's library."

Fairies themselves had a particular significance to the Victorians, however, and through that significance we can get to Gilbert's aforementioned theme of head against heart. As the most consistent theme in all of the operas, it is the building block on which the entire Gilbert & Sullivan canon is based, and deserves close attention.

To the Victorians, fairies embodied innocence—specifically, the purity of children. Today we think of 17-year-olds as sexual, hormone-driven creatures, but to the Victorians the age was more like what we think of as 12 or 13—the sexy-but-not-sexual purity of children just before sexual awakening. It was seen as the golden age of life, and the great tragedy was that even as one reached it, it was gone—tainted by the arrival of sexuality.

It is no great insight to notice that *Iolanthe* is, among other things, a tale of sexual awakening—in the opera itself, that of the Queen and the fairies, but more significantly that of Iolanthe herself, which occurs before the opera.

From a metaphorical point of view, it is obvious why "by our laws, it is death to marry a mortal." Thanos and eros are intertwined, if only by the basic fact that sex leads to children, and children's places in the world are cleared by their parents' deaths.

While it is on the face of it ironic that the fairies who, as they proclaim, "live on lover" can die only by tasting love themselves, it makes perfect sense if their status as children is understood: Children come into being through the act of love, but can remain children—with all the purity the pre-Freudian Victorians associated with that stage of life—only as long as they are themselves asexual.

The Queen, who is both of and above the fairies, knows full well what Iolanthe has done to deserve death. Love is a contagion, a disease that will inevitably spread throughout the entire band if it is allowed to exist. (Gilbert had already explored this notion in his 1873 fairy comedy *The Wicked World.*) The Queen allows Iolanthe to live in exile out of compassion, but in doing so all but dooms the fairies.

The all-knowing Queen's surprise and dismay that Iolanthe has a child—and this talkative character's silence for some time after the revelation—speaks to her anticipation of the inevitable consequences. Sure enough, within days of Iolanthe's return the fairies are sighing after mortal men and the Queen herself is infected; soon they are all married, and all is lost.

As he had demonstrated in *Patience,* Gilbert strongly believed in love as a pure emotion distinct from sexuality. But this belief in the purity of true love in no way made him a stereotypically repressive Victorian. Sexuality is an important element in Gilbert & Sullivan, and except in cases of deviant sexuality (as in the rape imagery of *Princess Ida* or the sadistic elements of *The Yeomen of the Guard*) it is never portrayed negatively.

Gilbert's emphasis on ethereal love does not mean that sexuality is bad but merely that it is less important than the spiritual aspects of love—and that real sexuality moves in tandem with idealized love. Where some Victorians saw the central element as the groin and others saw it as the head,

Gilbert looked to the heart. (Richard Dauntless in *Ruddigore* is not wrong in stressing the importance of the heart—merely in mistaking his groin for his heart.)

In every one of Gilbert & Sullivan's mature operas, the central characters are confronted by a conflict between what they instinctively want to do and what's expected of them. In some cases, this conflict is externally imposed, as in Rose Maybud's etiquette book, the Mikado's law against flirting or Hildebrand's expectations of his son; in other cases, it is internal, as in Frederic's sense of duty. In either case, however, Gilbert & Sullivan come down strongly on the side of the heart.

Iolanthe's dualities constantly manifest themselves in this form. The Queen's "I should be marble, but I am clay"; Strephon's "I suppose one ought to enjoy oneself in Parliament . . . but I'm miserable"; the Chancellor's "I am here in two capacities, and they clash"; the Queen's "If I yielded to a natural impulse, I should fall down and worship that man, but I mortify this inclination"—all are conflicts between "would" and "should."

More significant, in nearly every case the characters' failure to trust their own instincts leads to disaster. Strephon and Phyllis hold aloof from each other, despite their longing; the Chancellor brings nightmares on himself; and the Queen comes to the brink of slaughtering her whole company.

The case of the Chancellor is particularly intriguing, and his resolution of his conflict is the most revealing as to Gilbert & Sullivan's intentions. His conflict is simple, he believes: He's in love with a woman whom the law says he can't marry, and he is killing himself over it—he can't sleep, he can't eat ("three months ago I was a stout man").

Gilbert finds a great deal of fun in the Chancellor's torment, but the psychological portrayal of the character is absolutely convincing. Here we have a young man, a lawyer, who falls madly, passionately in love with an "unsuitable" young woman of whom he knows nothing. Throwing caution to the winds, he marries her, only to have her disappear—to the best of his knowledge, dead.

From his "When I Went to the Bar," we have his reaction to his loss: Numbing his heart, he throws himself into his work. Where others take shortcuts, he dots every *i* and crosses every *t*. When Strephon reproaches him for heartlessness (applying "the prosaic rules of evidence to a case which bubbles over with poetical emotion"), the Chancellor proudly agrees.

The law is his refuge from a broken heart. As he says when he first appears, "The law is the true embodiment / of everything that's excellent. / It has no kind of fault or flaw, / and I, my lords, embody the law."

His progression from this first moment to his final dialogue—in which he acknowledges that the law has flaws and turns it on its head—is a massive shift, and indeed it is the Chancellor who, in many ways, is the opera's hero. While Strephon is the "romantic lead," it is the Chancellor who undergoes the greatest change over the opera and whose revival is central to its resolution.

The Chancellor himself doesn't know what is happening to him. He believes that he is being destroyed by his love for Phyllis, but the audience, seeing the situation from outside, knows that actually he is still in love with Iolanthe and that it is his "wrong" attraction to Phyllis that is destroying him. Her eventual "The Lord Chancellor is . . . my husband" is a revelation only to the characters, not to the audience: Even today, viewers know what to make of her early "The Lord Chancellor—oh, if he did but know," and the Victorians were much more used to this convention.

The story of the Chancellor is the story of the reawakening of a human heart. Two much different aspects of the Chancellor are displayed in the punctilious, officious detail of "When I Went to the Bar" and in the volcanic outpouring of turmoil in the "Nightmare Song." He is a troubled man, flailing about helplessly for something he can't identify.

But when he does identify it—"Iolanthe, thou livest"—his world changes. He unhesitatingly tampers with the law, and doesn't see it as flawless or himself as its embodiment. In fact, he is (as the final song says) happy—a word never used to describe him previously.

This is why the "insertion of a single word" ending is so satisfying on a performance level, even though it neither accords with the tone of the preceding scenes nor really resolves the fairies/mortals dilemma. It resolves the Chancellor-Iolanthe story line, completing the rebirth of a long-lost man. On this basis, it is in its own way as resonant as could be.

By the end of the opera, all of the conflicted characters have resolved their conflicts in favor of the heart over the head. Strephon and Phyllis have moved past the jealousy that inflamed their earlier relationship—his of the peers, hers of Iolanthe. The Queen and the fairies have set childhood behind and found happiness in the adult world of marriage. Iolanthe has found a way to be both a wife and alive, and the newly revitalized Chancellor has resolved to leave the law. This may be the "fantasy ending," but it feels right, for them and for us.

Of course, it may be asked, how much of this is a critic's imposition and how much is what Gilbert & Sullivan had in mind? This question can't definitively be answered, of course, but I would suggest that these two masters, by now in full control of their art, knew what they were doing.

Consider the two songs that most explicitly define the head-versus-heart conflict: The Queen's "O, Foolish Fay," a hymn to quashing the feelings and obeying the law at all costs, and Mountararat and Tolloller's "If You Go In," a go-for-it testimonial to "love that makes the world go round."

These two songs stand in direct antithesis to one another—a point made all the stronger, as conductor Raymond Osnato has pointed out, by

9.1a. The Fairy Queen's "Oh, Foolish Fay," which argues in favor of suppressing natural impulse, begins with a four-note musical motif that later reappears in transposition as the beginning of the trio "If You Go In," an effective rebuttal to the Fairy Queen's song.

the fact that Sullivan uses the same introductory four-note passage (in the former, the words are "Oh, foolish fay" and in the latter "If you go in") to begin both songs (exs. 9.1a, b).

In earlier operas this might be written off as a coincidence or at best a subconscious echo. *Iolanthe*, however, is the opera in which Sullivan most regularly uses Wagnerian leitmotif as a compositional tool—the Lord Chancellor's fugal theme that precedes each of his entrances, for example, or the four-note "Iolanthe" theme that is the title character's leitmotif. His repeated use of such devices shows him to be alive to the extent to which musical echoes can evoke and enhance nonmusical ideas and emotions.

This use of musical themes to embody ideas and attitudes begins as early as the overture—the first one he had actually composed himself, after years of leaving this last-minute task to assistants, and thus obviously one more important to him than most. (Of all the subsequent operas, only *The Yeomen of the Guard* and *The Grand Duke* would open with Sullivan

9.1b. "If You Go In" (opening)

overtures, though *Ruddigore's* assistant-written overture was later replaced with a Sullivan original.)

Sullivan sets the tone for Act 1 by introducing two love songs (the Iolanthe/Chancellor "He Loves" and the Strephon/Phyllis "If We're Weak Enough to Tarry") only to have them obliterated by the renunciatory "O, Foolish Fay." But when it comes to the finale, he repeats and expands the upbeat "If You Go In." The movement from repression to freedom, from the head to the heart, is mirrored perfectly in the music.

Obviously, this message is counter to the moral thrust of the Victorian age and accounts in some degree for the fact that Gilbert in particular was viewed as radical and untrustworthy—despite the fact that, unlike Sullivan, he lived a personal life that embodied classic Victorian rectitude. The operas in which this message was the most obvious—most notably *Princess Ida* and *Ruddigore*—would be some of the team's least commercially successful ventures. But this would remain the most consistent theme in their work.

In many ways, *Iolanthe* was a turning point for Gilbert & Sullivan. It marks the beginning of their mature stage, which would produce five more operas of outstanding quality.

Many of the weaknesses of their previous works are no longer to be seen. Sullivan's music, for example, reaches a new level of consistency and ambition. The early operas had been skillfully scored but had been composed in short sequences, repetitive and emotionally restrained. In *Iolanthe*, the music is more forthrightly romantic than in any preceding show—it is a music of extremes, of faster accelerandos, slower allargandos, louder crescendos, and softer decrescendos.

The composer doesn't let Gilbert's verse structure intimidate him—sometimes, as in the "Nightmare Song," he through-composes so meticulously that the verse structure is almost indiscernible. Here, as throughout the opera, he varies his orchestrations on different verses to keep the music evolving and to ingeniously illustrate Gilbert's lyric—as, for example, in the flute-clarinet motif that marks the words "crossing the Channel and tossing about in a steamer."

Under the influence of Wagner, Sullivan also gives himself more room to maneuver. Writing his own overture produces a far higher caliber of music, establishing a stronger musical tone from the outset. There are fewer breaks in the opera's music and fewer obvious pauses for applause, and overall there is much more music. *Iolanthe* runs 20 minutes longer than any previous Gilbert & Sullivan show, and it's all music. The Act 1 finale is the longest single number in any of the operas, and the composer takes the time to develop such sequences as the March of the Peers, the opening of Act 1 and the raising of Iolanthe from the stream into major musical scenes.

The difference between *Patience's* swaggering but perfunctory "The Soldiers of Our Queen" and *Iolanthe's* virtuoso "March of the Peers" is as between night and day; so too the contrast between the pro-forma "We Sail the Ocean Blue" and the magical "Tripping Hither, Tripping Thither." Throughout, in fact, Sullivan's musical characterization of the choruses is remarkable—henceforth his chorus work would be perhaps the strongest element of his scores.

Sullivan also pays more attention to setting and characters, as will be the case in every subsequent opera. The score for *H. M. S. Pinafore* had employed a certain nautical roll now and then, but nothing like the subtle shadings of *Iolanthe's* Act 1 Arcadia or the grand pomp of its Act 2 London. Henceforth the war-torn land of King Hildebrand, the serene veneer of Castle Adamant, the Eastern ambiance of Titipu, the horror of Castle Ruddigore, the majesty of the Tower of London, and the surging waters of Venice would all be strongly evoked, with their own distinct musical textures.

Taking another page from Wagner, Sullivan utilizes leitmotifs for all of his principal characters, from the sublime Iolanthe theme that opens the opera and runs through the climactic "Iolanthe, thou livest." (That this line is sometimes spoken instead of sung is a travesty, since it eliminates the final, most powerful use of Sullivan's "Iolanthe" leitmotif.) (ex.9.2a–d).

The piping call of Strephon and Phyllis is another leitmotif, while the knotty fugue that introduces the Chancellor gets more complex and tangled with each successive entrance, until it suddenly vanishes without a trace upon the Chancellor's resolving his inner conflict.

In short, Sullivan now seems to be seeing his work with a new, broader scope, as if the greater depth of *Iolanthe* had made him realize that there could be more to comic opera than jaunty amusements for the Victorian public. More than mere financial pressures may have kept him from pursuing his much-vaunted dream of writing grand opera—from *Iolanthe* on, he was putting the same depth of purpose into his work with Gilbert.

As for Gilbert, the sea change that Sullivan experienced with *Iolanthe* had started for him with *Patience. Iolanthe* takes it further. Gilbert seems more

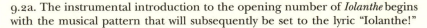

9.2a. The instrumental introduction to the opening number of *Iolanthe* begins with the musical pattern that will subsequently be set to the lyric "Iolanthe!"

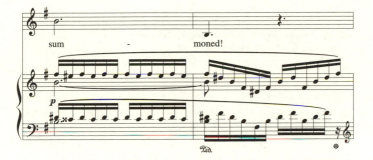

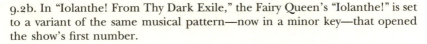

9.2b. In "Iolanthe! From Thy Dark Exile," the Fairy Queen's "Iolanthe!" is set to a variant of the same musical pattern—now in a minor key—that opened the show's first number.

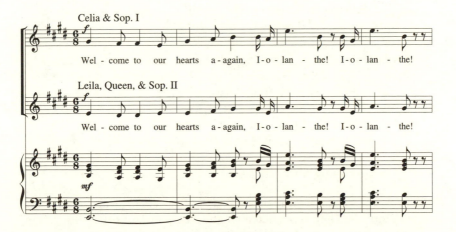

9.2c. When the chorus sings "Welcome to our hearts again," the word "Iolanthe" is once again set to the same musical leitmotif that opened the opera, now returned to a major key.

9.2d. When the Lord Chancellor recognizes his long-dead wife, he responds by singing her name in the same variant leitmotif used earlier by the Fairy Queen in "Iolanthe! From Thy Dark Exile."

confident with his voice, more willing to write serious songs without the veneer of clichés and technique that had limited his work prior to *Iolanthe*.

To appreciate the new cleanness of his work, it is only necessary to compare two songs of powerful emotional content, one from Alexis in *The Sorcerer*, the other from Iolanthe. Both are Act 2 songs, with the characters in emotional extremis, venting powerful feelings without restraint. But Gilbert puts very different words into their mouths:

> *Alexis:* Thine is the power and thine alone
> to place me on so proud a throne
> that kings might envy me!
> A priceless throne of love untold,
> more rare than orient pearl and gold,
> but no! Thou wouldst be free!

> *Iolanthe:* He dies! If fondly laid aside
> in some old cabinet,
> memorials of thy long-dead bride
> lie dearly treasured yet,
> then let her hallowed bridal dress—
> her little dainty gloves—
> her withered flowers—her faded tress—
> plead for my boy—he loves!

The Alexis lyrics are florid, rhetorical, and in keeping with the operatic style of the day. They were good enough to help make a hit of *The Sorcerer*. But they are generalized and artificial, distancing the audience from any real feeling for the character. The Iolanthe lyrics, on the other hand, are simple and cut to the bone. In their specificity and their lack of rhetorical flourish, they are vastly more effective, more affecting.

These two excerpts capture their shows' styles admirably. *The Sorcerer*, and *H. M. S. Pinafore* and *The Pirates of Penzance* after it, were generally tailored to the operetta form of the day, showing the talents of their creators but largely playing by the rules. *Iolanthe*, like *Patience* and the shows that followed them, shatters the rules, throws out conventional operetta form, and creates something altogether new and different, a work of genius.

Moving toward a simpler, less artificial lyrical style (one mirrored in his dialogue, which grows cleaner, shorter, and all but punless) didn't make Gilbert's task easier, however. Indeed it became harder, because he now had to pay strict attention to consistency in characterization, not only in what his characters said and sang but in how they said it.

It had been a clever bit of foreshadowing in *H. M. S. Pinafore* when Gilbert had Ralph speak like a stage aristocrat and the Captain like a commoner, anticipating their change in positions; unfortunately, in some other scenes Ralph spoke like a commoner and the Captain like a lord. And other characters had no real distinctive manners of speaking.

Not so in *Iolanthe*. In foreshadowing the fact that Strephon is the Chancellor's son, Gilbert not only makes their speech patterns similar (he has each open with a long two-capacities speech, for example), he establishes a physical resemblance ("but he's inclined to be stout" / "three months ago, I was a stout man"). He links Strephon's and Phyllis' emotional condition with parallel speeches in Act 2 ("I can't think why I'm not in better spirits; I'm engaged to two noblemen at once, that ought to be enough to make any girl happy" / "I suppose one ought to enjoy oneself in Parliament, when one leads both parties, as I do, but I'm miserable"). He even makes the effort to consistently distinguish the points of view of Leila (soft, semipractical, and romantic), Celia (light, hard-edged, and mischievous) and Fleta (young, curious, and unsure) far more than he ever did with, for example, the Bos'n and the Carpenter.

Following up on his innovations in *Patience*, Gilbert again uses the problem/conflict/false-resolution/attempted-solutions/serious-ending/final-happy-twist structure that he had roughed out in *The Sorcerer*.

But in *Iolanthe* Gilbert is more economical in his plot-related matters, trusting his audience to piece together past events and character motivations without resorting to long plot explications, periodic recapitulations of what's going on, lengthy asides to the audience revealing true feelings, and so forth. His use of recitative is much less frequent—he's now willing to dive straight from dialogue into a song, or out again—and more focused when he does use it.

Prior to *Iolanthe* (with the partial exception of *Patience*), Gilbert & Sullivan had written performer-oriented shows. *The Sorcerer*, *H. M. S. Pinafore*, and *The Pirates of Penzance* had all too frequently stopped dead for the "obligatory" tenor or soprano solo, the "mandatory" introductory patter song, and so forth. These shows lived or died by the performances—there was basically only one joke to the Police in *The Pirates of Penzance*, for example, but then as now strong performances can make their scenes hilarious; with poor performances, they can be deathly.

Iolanthe takes a different tack in being, like most later Gilbert & Sullivan, story-based. Its character- and situation-based humor is so invincibly funny that, even with bad performances, there are laughs. Even when simply read in a book, the show is funny.

In *Iolanthe*, nothing is "obligatory." The putative leads, Phyllis and Strephon, never really get full-fledged solos, while the minor character Private Willis gets a "big" song just because it's needed to set the scene (and to provide a touch of satiric bite). Casting clichés are thrown aside—the romantic lead is a baritone and the tenor is a comic character—and Sullivan feels no need for virtuoso cadenzas and flourishes to show off the singers' voices. Everything is subverted to the needs of the story.

In short, with *Iolanthe* we see the mature Gilbert & Sullivan, two creative artists at their peaks, in harmony with each other and committed enough to their work to reconceptualize their entire genre. Their talent is as great as it ever was, but both have grown markedly in confidence and range. Now they are applying that talent to something distinctively their own.

The Sullivan and Gilbert who had created *Trial by Jury, The Sorcerer,* and *H. M. S. Pinafore* had been perhaps the best practitioners ever of an art form that they had found waiting for them. The Gilbert & Sullivan who emerged with *Patience* and found full fruition in *Iolanthe* were the only practitioners of an art form all their own.

The stage was set for seven years that would change musical theater forever.

Facing page: FIGURE 10.1. Tennyson's Princess Ida, as depicted by Howard Chandler Christy. Tennyson's Ida lives in a world in which the greatest evil is miscommunication. *Source: Illustration for* The Princess *(Bobbs-Merrill, 1911). Author's collection.*

10

Princess Ida

No Gilbert and Sullivan opera is more misunderstood than *Princess Ida.* The general consensus is with Isaac Asimov, who calls it "of all the plays, the one . . . most uncomfortable for contemporary enlightened taste. It satirizes 'feminism' or what we today call 'the women's movement,' and some of the laughter it elicits is rather hollow."[1]

Despite its prevalence, this consensus reflects a complete misunderstanding of the opera. This is ironic in that, of all the operas, *Princess Ida* should be the easiest to understand. While relatively unfamiliar, it offers the unique advantage of being the only Gilbert & Sullivan opera based entirely on a work by another author—Alfred Tennyson's poem "The Princess," which inspired Gilbert's 1870 play *The Princess,* which he in turn adapted as *Princess Ida.*

In analyzing any literary work, we can understand the author's purpose by examining the choices he or she makes. In Arthur Miller's *Death of a Salesman,* for example, that Willy Loman is a salesman and not, say, a railroad conductor is obviously significant. Miller invented Loman and could have given him any profession; that he chose to make him a salesman provides insight into Miller's thematic intentions.

FIGURE 10.2. A newspaper illustration of Princess Ida (right in elaborate costume) as seen in Gilbert's 1870 play *The Princess.* The conventions of English burlesque shaped Gilbert's treatment of Tennyson's poem: Notice, at center, three women playing three men disguised as three women. *Source:* Illustrated London News, *January 29, 1870. Courtesy of The MacPhail Gilbert & Sullivan Collection.*

FIGURE 10.3. King Hildebrand and his soldiers attack in *Princess Ida*, as depicted in a London newspaper illustration. The world of Gilbert & Sullivan's opera is far grimmer than that of Tennyson's poem and far less funny than that of Gilbert's play. *Source:* Illustrated Sporting & Dramatic News, *January 19, 1884. By permission of The British Library.*

The difficulty with this approach lies in what Robert Neil, one of my college professors, called "the tyranny of the actual": After the fact, it's hard to imagine events happening any other way. Hypothetically, for example, the male chorus in *Iolanthe* might have been lawyers rather than peers—and indeed Gilbert originally planned it that way. But now that we know the opera, it's hard to imagine. Nor can we realistically consider every possible option not chosen—a chorus of farmers? Roman soldiers? no male chorus at all? As a result it is easy to overlook roads not taken, even when the choice had a tremendous impact on the opera.

Obviously, however, choices that are known to have been considered and rejected are more significant than those that apparently never occurred to the author. It would be highly significant if, for example, Gilbert had originally planned to have Buttercup be Dick Deadeye's mother; absent any evidence of such authorial consideration, however, such a thought is meaningless.

In the case of *Princess Ida*, "The Princess" is a virtual guidebook of alternative choices. When Gilbert chose to change anything from Tennyson's original, it's fair to conclude that he at least considered leaving it the way it was, and that he must have had some point in making that change.

After all, Tennyson was England's poet laureate, and "The Princess" one of his best-known works. As in any adaptation, the adapters' tendency had to be to leave it as written: If one adapts a well-known work faithfully and the adaptation fails, the audience will be understanding; but an author who makes radical changes in an adaptation that fails is risking charges of blasphemy. Just ask the filmmakers of *Bonfire of the Vanities* or Barbra Streisand's *A Star Is Born.*

Nevertheless, most analysts of *Princess Ida* seem not to have read "The Princess." Even Ian Bradley, normally a keen observer, writes: "In both his play and his opera libretto, Gilbert closely followed the details of the poet laureate's story."[2]

Actually, his reworkings are enormous: To name only one, Gilbert changes the outcome of the climactic battle—in Tennyson, Arac defeats the prince! This is a radical change indeed, and would have been glaringly apparent to any Victorian audience.

The relationship between "The Princess" and *Princess Ida* (the intervening play generally resembles the opera, though there are a few significant differences) is generally misunderstood. Most critics would say that "The Princess" is an argument for the equality for women and that the opera is a parody that defends male superiority. The truth is almost exactly the opposite.

First of all, the reason *Princess Ida* seems less funny than most Gilbert & Sullivan is that it isn't a comedy; productions based on the assumption that it is fail out of hand. Certain aspects are meant to be humorous— King Gama's sequences, for example, or the early Act 2 parodies of women's education. But 20 of the opera's 34 songs are in no way intended humorously.[3] Where most of the operas are comedies with serious touches, *Princess Ida* is, like *The Yeomen of the Guard,* a drama with comic touches.

Nor is it a parody of "The Princess." Gilbert attacks neither Tennyson's content nor his style (and the poet certainly provides an inviting target, at least to modern eyes). Further, his outlook on women's issues is close to Tennyson's—generally sympathetic in the abstract, though with a conservative wariness of the practical implications of women's equality.

It is, after all, a hallmark of Gilbert & Sullivan that their smartest characters are women, from *The Sorcerer's* Aline and *Patience's* Lady Jane through *The Gondoliers'* Duchess of Plaza-Toro and *Utopia, Limited's* Princess Zara. In *Princess Ida* alone, the practical and intellectual knowledge of Ida, Psyche, Blanche, and even Melissa outshines that of any of the men, at least at the outset.

The fact is, *Princess Ida* is not about women's education nor even women's rights. The satire of feminism is no more central than the political satire of *Iolanthe* or *The Gondoliers.* The actual theme lies deeper: *Princess Ida* is the first and best working-out of a theme that was to inform the subsequent *Mikado* and *Ruddigore*—the necessity of young people breaking with the past (and especially with the sins of their parents or ancestors) to achieve the hope of progress.

Some of Gilbert's revisions of Tennyson are clearly motivated by practical dramatic considerations: Tennyson's framing story and first-person narrative, for example, would be difficult to stage effectively, while actors and audiences alike would probably have been disconcerted if the operatic Ida, like her poetic counterpart, had been accompanied by a pair of pet leopards.[4]

But many other changes are not dramatically motivated: Besides having Hildebrand's forces defeat Ida's, Gilbert also removes Hilarion's warm, loving mother from the story. Ida's mother, likewise a loving one, is also removed, and Gilbert makes her father a monster instead of the beaming sentimentalist portrayed by Tennyson. Her brother Arac becomes a thundering dolt rather than the articulate paragon presented by Tennyson. Gilbert turns Ida's realm from a Christian domain to one that worships Minerva and has it forbid marriage permanently rather than merely for three years. While Tennyson's Ida frees Hilarion from captivity in gratitude for his saving her life, Gilbert's comes close to killing him before holding him as hostage for her brothers' lives; and there are many other changes as well.

(Obviously, the usually insightful Bradley has not read Tennyson as carefully as he has read Gilbert.)

The question is: Why would Gilbert take such tremendous liberties with a popular work by the age's most respected poet (who was also a social acquaintance and former collaborator of Sullivan's)? It wasn't done on a whim—the line of least resistance lay in fidelity to the poem.

Nor was it done to be funny, as is sometimes suggested. To say that Gilbert made Gama a "twisted monster, all awry" to get laughs gives the playwright too little credit. Most obviously, if he wanted to create such a character, he could have given all the same characteristics to Hilarion's father, the brutal "hard old king" Tennyson describes, instead of creating a second brutal king. More generally, Gilbert was a master humorist and could easily have made the whole opera vastly funnier if he had wanted to.

Besides, most of Gilbert's changes make the opera less funny, not more. Ida's near-killing of Hilarion, for example, or the change in the ending, can't have been intended to get laughs. To understand Gilbert's decisions, we need to examine their effects.

Tennyson's Ida is as much a crusader as Gilbert's, but nevertheless a warmer, more humorous woman. She has the memory of a loving mother recently deceased, along with the support of a loving father (when she wanted use of his castle, Tennyson's good king Gama recalls, "I said no, but being an easy man, gave it") and a sympathetic, intelligent, and loving brother. ("I thought her half-right talking of her wrongs," the poem's Arac says, and adds "I take her for the flower of womankind.")

The circumstances of her proxy marriage are similarly different. In Tennyson, it is a marriage of state, symbolizing a union between the fathers' kingdoms. These kings are friendly—Hildebrand apologizes for taking Gama hostage, and Gama takes no umbrage—and both do everything they can to avoid a confrontation.

Gilbert's Ida is a battle prize, extorted from Gama on the threat of war—Hildebrand makes clear that, if she is not handed over, war is inevitable. Her forced marriage with Hilarion represents a land grab on Hildebrand's part, seizing Gama's kingdom for his son. (By all indications, Ida is Gama's heir—Arac is never referred to as Prince Arac—and, once the marriage is consummated, the only thing standing between Hildebrand's son and the throne of Hungary will be Gama's life. No wonder Gama is so upset!)

Gilbert's Ida has also endured a much grimmer upbringing than Tennyson's. The only mention of her mother is Gama's "If your mamma had looked on matters from your point of view (I wish she had)," regretting that Ida was ever born. Gama never praises the brilliant Ida, except as a means of insulting Hildebrand, but virtually fawns on her brainless brothers.

In the grim, martial world of *Princess Ida*, military strength is all that counts. Gilbert's Ida has grown up with a nasty father continually demeaning her (as Gilbert's father also did his son, incidentally), scorning her intelligence in favor of the brute muscle of Arac, Guron, and Scynthius.

It is natural, then, that the two princesses react differently to being rescued. When the ladies plead for mercy for Hilarion, Gilbert's Ida rejects their appeal, while Tennyson's freely releases her prince. Each Ida reflects her upbringing—Tennyson's the warmth and fairness she has always known, Gilbert's the bleak, violent, confrontational world of Gama and the warriors three. Gilbert's Ida condemns the prince for the same reason that Tennyson's Ida frees him: It's the kind of woman her world has made her.

Gilbert's changes result in a harder, more driven princess. Throughout Act 2 she is more absolute than Tennyson's Ida: She requires her women to forswear marriage forever, where Tennyson's asks only three years; her sermons are more fanatic, her laws more draconian. It's the way of her world.

It's also the way of Hilarion's world. Where Tennyson's prince grew up with a "mother mild as any saint, / half-canonized by all that looked on her,/ so gracious was her tact and tenderness," Gilbert's is apparently motherless. The bullying King Hildebrand is even harsher than Tennyson's king, who for all his male chauvinism is blunt but affectionate with his son.

Hilarion's is an all-male world (women are allowed not a single word in Act 1, appearing only in the chorus), built on violence and power, and it creates a different prince. Where Tennyson's prince is a gentle, epileptic philosopher and poet, Hilarion is a somewhat effeminate dandy more suited to the arid wordplay of "Ida Was a Twelve-Month Old" than to poetry. In all of Act 1, he shows no sign of true nobility of character.

The World of Man portrayed by Tennyson is a land of gently misguided people who are struggling to adjust to a changing world. Gilbert's version is a harsh, ultraviolent world in which absolutism comes naturally.

King Hildebrand is this world's dominant force, its alpha male, commanding the most power and hence free to rule absolutely. His is a black-and-white world in which the only options are submission or death—"for as King Gama brings the princess here or brings her not / so shall King Gama have much more than everything / [or] much less than nothing," he declaims. To Hildebrand, to even conceive of a middle ground is unmanly.

After the violent hell of Act 1, Castle Adamant initially seems a paradise. In place of the harsh, claustrophobic, percussive chord clashes of Act 1, Sullivan uses lush scales and harmonics to create a sense of edenic openness that is thoroughly Tennysonian. "Toward the Empyrean Heights," with its promise of learning and progress free of any competitiveness or envy, seems the antithesis of Hildebrand's world.

Soon, however, snakes begin to appear in this Eden. Psyche recommends a series of great authors—but she wants them bowdlerized, or censored of sexually explicit passages. Then the simple question "What is man?" spurs her to a blistering diatribe (one that Sullivan captures perfectly in his disparate settings for the two verses of her solo—the first, about learning, is sweet and pretty, while the second, about man, is strident and dogmatic). Blanche's punishments reinforce this fanatic fear of sexuality and, through it, men.

Princess Ida's sermon reveals the extent of this corruption. Her goals are as extreme as her rules are harsh. Tennyson's Ida seeks freedom for women but is not explicitly hostile toward men. In fact, there is even a place for marriage in her world: She aims to educate her women "that so, / some future time, if so indeed you will,/ you may with those self-styled our lords ally / your fortunes, justlier balanced, scale with scale." Needless to say, Gilbert's Ida feels otherwise. All she has to say on marriage is: "Will you undertake / that you will never marry any man?"

But her goal is not simply cloistered seclusion. Her kingdom is armed and ready for war. As she says in her sermon, "a hundred maidens here have sworn to place their feet upon [Man's] neck." Her goal is conquest, and she can match Hildebrand's absolutism blow for blow: "But if we fail, why, then let hope fail too! . . . In other words, let Chaos come again!"

The irony is that, for all that he ignores her, Gama's spiritual heir is not Arac but Ida. She proves herself a master of the same canny manipulation that he uses to sow dissension in Hildebrand's court, setting his enemies against each other. Ida handles Blanche with similar dexterity, coaxing her out just enough to be quashed.

Even more impressive is the way Ida controls her kingdom. Like Gama, she lacks military power; but she makes herself not only princess and principal but also priestess. She doesn't implore Minerva to bless the women with insight but rather pleads, "let fervent words and fervent thoughts be mine, / that I may lead them to thy sacred shrine." Ida herself is the intermediary, without whom the women will never reach enlightenment. It is a brilliantly *political* moment, one worthy of Gama at his best.

(The same is true of the cultlike veneration with which the ladies greet Ida in "Mighty Maiden With a Mission":

We are blind and we would see,
we are bound and would be free,
    we are dumb and we would talk,
    we are lame and we would walk.

Most of a Victorian audience would know who it was "who maketh the blind to see, who setteth the captive free, who maketh the dumb to talk and the lame to walk." What in Tennyson's Ida is only a messianic tinge in Gilbert's Ida verges on blasphemy.)

Throughout, *Princess Ida* stresses the similarity between the worlds of Man and of Ida. Lady Blanche proves herself as Machiavellian as Gama ever was, and her "Come, Mighty Must" is as absolutist as Hildebrand at his worst. In choosing not to reveal the presence of the interloping men in the hope that they will bring about Ida's downfall, she reveals herself as an utter pragmatist, discarding all of the antimale rules she has herself earlier enforced so stringently.

But the clearest equating of the two sides comes in the Act 2 finale, as Hildebrand and Ida come head to head, neither flinching. When Hildebrand takes up arms, so does Ida; when he takes hostages, so does she. When he threatens her with death if she doesn't "let Hilarion claim his bride," she responds, "I will die before I call myself his wife." The act ends with the male and female warriors howling at each other "Defiance! Defiance! Defiance!"

In short, other than the change in the ending, all of Gilbert's major changes serve, in one way or another, to tighten the screws on Hilarion and, especially, on Ida.

Again, to what end? It cannot be to sharpen the attack on feminism: Hildebrand's world is no paradise, while Gilbert's Ida is so fanatical as to be a straw target, no more representative of feminism than Torquemada is of Christianity.

Tennyson's Ida, an intelligent, kind and warm young woman led astray by good intentions, is a better argument against feminism than Gilbert's Ida, warped by family and societal pressures into a dictator. An antifeminist would also surely prefer Tennyson's intelligent, kind, and warm men to Gilbert's harsh, implacable, brainless warriors.

In a sense, Gilbert has transmuted "The Princess" from social commentary into family drama. Tennyson's poem is essentially a comedy of misunderstanding; Gilbert's play is a drama of confrontation. Instead of clashing ideas, *Princess Ida* is about the conflicts between and within three dynastic, highly dysfunctional families: Gama, his daughter, and his three sons; the tyrannical Hildebrand and his heir, Hilarion; and Blanche, oppressor of all the women and especially of her daughter Melissa, the play's youngest and purest character (in Gilbert & Sullivan, youth and purity always go together).

All three parents see their children as chess pieces, Hildebrand and Gama in their maneuvering against each other, Blanche in her campaign against Ida. This ruthlessness is passed on to the children themselves: Caught in a lie by Blanche, Melissa uses Blanche-like manipulation to turn her mother's lust for power to her own advantage, while Hildebrand would surely second Hilarion's arrogant condescension in "Expressive Glances" and "They Intend to Send a Wire to the Moon."

Ida's Gama-like skill at power politics has already been noted. In fact, Ida's emotional manipulation, her rock-hard "Castle Adamant" determination to meet force with even greater force and her willingness to bend philosophical, scientific, and religious ideas to her own purposes make her a sort of fusion of Gama, Hildebrand, and Blanche—the worst of three worlds.

Against this grimness, the opera sets only one counterbalancing force: the love between Ida and Hilarion.

Love has no place in the world of their parents. It is as foreign in the court of Hildebrand, where infants are married off for political purposes, as in Castle Adamant, where a girl can be expelled for possessing chessmen.

The opera's dominant imagery is sexual, but it is a violent, unhealthy sexuality. Again and again, *Princess Ida* couples sex and violence in imagery of rape. The Act 1 finale is particularly ingenious, with its three main sections each offering a different blending of sex and violence. "Perhaps If You Address the Lady" uses a two-verse parallelism to contrast the love that Gama recommends (with a violent undercurrent, since "address" means both "to speak to another" and "to face off at swordpoint") with the force that Hildebrand threatens. It is followed by "Expressive Glances Will Be Our Lances," which begins with an extended metaphor comparing love tokens with military armaments and segues into a virtual pledge of rape, and "For a Month to Dwell," whose quasi-erotic approach to violence ends with Hildebrand's "when Hilarion's bride has at length complied."

Sullivan's setting for "Expressive Glances" is particularly impressive, with its initially honeyed melody gradually darkening as the song progresses. The orchestration evolves from the lyric beauty of Hilarion's first verse, with its sweetly sinister images of seduction, through the grimmer undertones of Florian's verse, ending with the explicitly threatening "little heeding / their pretty pleading, / our love exceeding we'll justify."

Act 2 continues the implicitly violent tone, with Psyche's bestial images of men (donkey, goose, and finally ape). Ida's sermon culminates in a nihilistic rant that combines irrational fury with bizarrely sexual imagery: "Let hairpins lose their virtue; let the hook / disdain the fascination of the eye—/ the bashful button modestly evade / the soft embraces of the button-hole!"

Florian's boast that, however much the college teaches its girls, "I'll teach them twice as much in half an hour outside it" is clearly sexual, as are the jests about the girls coming to the college "weary of the world and all its wooing, and penitent for deeds there's no undoing, looked at askance by well-conducted maids" and "waiting with open arms to receive us." Even Cyril's joking about him and Hilarion riding the same horse ("astride," as Ida says) seems to imply sexual innuendo.

The rape imagery returns full throttle with the Act 2 finale, as the men smash through the gate with a battering ram while the women shriek "Shed the shameful tear, man has entered here."

In Gilbert's World of Man (of which Castle Adamant is merely an inversion), love does not exist, and the only sex is rape, violent and impersonal. This stain taints even the noblest characters. Where Tennyson's prince is first seen rhapsodizing on a picture of Ida and a tress of her hair, Gilbert's can only make a quibbling joke out of their ages; until they meet, his attitude toward her is sarcastic and condescending.

Similarly, Ida is at best distantly curious about him. She is thinking about him—understandably, since Act 1 takes place on her 21st birthday, the day she was to be turned over to her husband—but her attitude toward men is entirely hostile.

Hilarion's attitude toward Ida changes when he meets her. She isn't at all what he expected (she doesn't intend to send wires to the moon), and "The World Is But a Broken Toy" strikes a chord in him. Its cynicism befits the daughter of Gama but also suits the son of Hildebrand.

While the other two men mock her, he listens to her—he joins in her song before they do, and there is nothing in words or music to suggest that he is insincere. And while Cyril and Florian continue to deride the women's college, after "Broken Toy" Hilarion never has another negative word about it.

The couple's conversation at lunch is one of Gilbert's most effective dialogues, with Hilarion probing Ida to discern her true feelings while she tries to pump him for information without revealing her interest. Already, it is clear, he is drawn to her, and she (without knowing it) to him.

Hilarion reaches an epiphany of sorts when his disguise is revealed. As in Tennyson, he gives himself away by hitting Cyril when Cyril sings a crude song. But while Tennyson's prince hits Cyril to stop his song, Gilbert's Cyril has already finished it by the time Hilarion hits him. Cyril has not revealed their disguise, either—Ida is expelling him not as an interloping man but as an "infamous creature," an immoral woman. It is Hilarion who heedlessly gives away the masquerade.

Yet Hilarion hits him nonetheless. The motivation is obviously different: Unlike Tennyson's Cyril (whose song is mentioned but not transcribed), this Cyril sings a song that he reports as having been sung, not long ago, by Hilarion himself. But now the changed Hilarion is repulsed by it (and by his former self?).

When Ida falls into the river, Hilarion comes to a crossroads. One day earlier, he would surely have escaped in the confusion; now, however, he rescues Ida, knowing that it means certain death. And when Ida prepares to execute him, he surprises her and perhaps himself by responding not with threats or defiance but with a declaration of his love and his willingness to die for it. Again, while "Whom Thou Hast Chained" can be played as a cynical manipulation by a desperate man, both lyricist and composer present it without irony.

It is a *coup de théâtre* that the alarm sounds at this point, before we see how Ida will respond. For two measures she stands silent, taken off-guard—surely, no one has ever told her that he loved her. Ida the woman and Ida the princess are brought face to face . . . and then Hildebrand's forces attack, dispelling whatever doubt she may have had. The next time she deals with Hilarion, it is as a hostage.

Which brings us to the opera's ending. Up to this point, Gilbert's major changes have related to characterization. From the Arac/Hilarion fight scene through the finale, however, he all but deserts Tennyson's story line. Why?

In "The Princess," Arac's victory is so complete that the wounded prince remains in a coma for weeks. Moved by the fallen hero, Ida has him brought into the castle. There she nurses him back to health and gradually falls in love with him.

This Ida proves herself a paragon of Victorian womanly virtues. The prince brings out her nurturing side, a sort of royal Florence Nightingale.

It is a gentle ending, befitting a world in which misunderstandings can be talked out. Tennyson's prince and princess don't even really have to *do* anything—he lies comatose, she thaws.

Gilbert's characters don't get off so easily. In *Princess Ida*, much more is wrong with the world. In fact, wrongness is the way of the world. Relations between men and women, parents and children, neighbor and neighbor—all are awry.

In this world, a tragic ending is quite plausible—in fact, the opera seems to be heading that way. Ida's troops, however willing, are not fit to fight. Ida reacts with frenzied defiance—she'll do the fighting, heal the wounded, play several instruments, and everything else. From this manic height, she plummets into depression in "I Built upon a Rock."

At this point, the opera could end tragically indeed, with Hildebrand's soldiers slaughtering the women as Ida flings herself from the ramparts. Avoiding the "tyranny of the actual," we must admit that it fits: Hildebrand warned Ida to submit or die, and she proclaimed that she would rather die than submit. Given the stubbornness on both sides, a tragic ending is entirely plausible.

Instead, Ida steps away from the brink. Instead of screaming "Defiance" to the end, she compromises. She accepts Hildebrand's offer, borne by Gama, to have Arac, Guron, and Scynthius fight on her behalf. This is important, because it demolishes the common view that Gilbert's ending depicts the failure of the Castle Adamant ideal, a satiric attack on feminism.

In fact, that failure comes well before the ending. Blanche is absolutely right when she responds to Ida's concession by screaming "Infamous!" By Ida's own principles, this is blasphemy: She is not only welcoming men into the castle but also making herself, in her own words, "a stake for fighting-men." For Ida, this is truly a surrender.

But Gilbert does not depict this compromise satirically, as a betrayal of an ideal. Made out of concern for her father, her hostage brothers, and surely her students, with whose inability she has just been brought face to face, Ida's concession is actually a triumph of humanity over ideology.

Agreeing to open the gates (with, of course, the continuing sexual imagery) represents her first step away from her prior extremism. It is only a first step, and a forced one, but it is crucial in the development of her character.

As to the battle itself, one can only imagine the reaction of the many readers of "The Princess" upon seeing the "wrong side" win. It would be as if a modern production of *Princess Ida* were to be staged so that Arac won. It has the effect of derailing the story line and spilling the audience into unknown territory.

It is also apparently implausible: Arac and his brothers have been raised for war, Hilarion and his friends for courtly life. While the warriors three long for "the rattle / of a complicated battle, / for the rum-tum-tum / of the military drum / and the guns that go boom-boom," Hilarion and his friends are content that "expressive glances / shall be our lances, / and pops of Sillery / our light artillery." How could they possibly defeat these "three rude warriors?"

The answer lies in a miscalculation by King Gama. His dialogue prior to the battle is designed to infuriate Hilarion, making him too angry to think. He taunts the three men, and even Hildebrand, about their being dressed as women, impugning their masculinity and challenging Hilarion's bravery. He succeeds admirably in goading Hilarion into a frenzy.

But then he errs. "You've this advantage over warriors/ who kill their country's enemies for pay—/ you know what you are fighting for—look there!" he says in conclusion, waving toward the watching women. To Gama, of course, risking one's life for a woman, especially Ida, is utterly ridiculous. Power, for which he fights, is the only meaningful prize. Gama hopes to demoralize Hilarion by convincing him that his prize isn't worth fighting for.

But Gama miscalculates. Hilarion cares nothing for power, having already told Ida that "a loveless life apart from thee / is hopeless slavery." But Ida herself is worth winning. Hilarion is inspired, and it is that inspiration that lets him win a fight that everyone (including the audience members, who have read Tennyson) expects him to lose.

And that victory sets up one of the richest and most telling dialogues in all of Gilbert & Sullivan:

Ida: Hold! Stay your hands—we yield ourselves to you. . . .
            Is this the end? How say you, Lady Blanche—
            can I with dignity my post resign?
            And if I do, will you then take my place?

Blanche: . . . Can you resign? The prince May claim you; if
            he Might, you Could—and if you Should, I Would!

Ida: I thought as much. Then to my fate I yield—
            so ends my cherished scheme! Oh, I had hoped
            to band all women with my maiden throng,
            and make them all abjure tyrannic Man!

Hildebrand: A noble aim!

Ida: You ridicule it now,
            but if I carried out this glorious scheme,
            at my exalted name Posterity
            would bow in gratitude!

Hildebrand: But pray reflect—
            If you enlist all women in your cause,
            and make them all abjure tyrannic Man,
            the obvious question then arises—how
            is that Posterity to be provided?

Ida:	I never thought of that. My Lady Blanche, how do you solve the riddle?
Blanche:	Don't ask me— Abstract Philosophy won't answer it. Take him—he is your Shall! Give in to Fate!
Ida:	And you desert me. I alone am staunch!
Hilarion:	Madam, you placed your trust in Woman—well, Woman has failed you utterly—try Man. Give him one chance, it's only fair—besides, women are far too precious, too divine to try unproven theories upon. Experiments, the proverb says, are made on humble subjects—try our grosser clay, and mold it as you will.
Cyril:	Remember, too, dear madam, if at any time you feel aweary of the Prince, you can return to Castle Adamant and rule your girls as heretofore, you know.
Ida:	And shall I find the Lady Psyche here?
Psyche:	If Cyril, ma'am, does not behave himself, I think you will.
Ida:	And you, Melissa, shall I find you here?
Melissa:	Madam, however Florian turns out, unhesitatingly I answer, no!
Gama:	Consider this, my love, if your mamma had looked on matters from your point of view (I wish she had), why, where would you have been?
Blanche:	There's an unbounded field of speculation on which I could discourse for hours!
Ida:	No doubt! We will not trouble you. Hilarion, I have been wrong—I see my error now. Take me, Hilarion—"We will walk the world yoked in all exercise of noble end, and so through those dark gates across the wild that no man knows! Indeed, I love thee—come!"

With Hilarion's victory, the Act 2 finale stands reversed. Then Hilarion was at Ida's mercy, now she is at his. He has won her fairly, and honor requires her to submit to him.

"Is this the end?" Ida asks. And, of course, it should be. The story has come to its end. Hildebrand and Blanche have won, Ida and Gama have lost; as far as the three parents are concerned, there's nothing more to be said.

If this were indeed the end, it would be a tragic one, representing the triumph of the violent world of Hildebrand. Hilarion would have embraced his heritage and triumphed through force. And this is exactly what Hildebrand and Blanche think has happened, as each rubs Ida's nose in her defeat. "Give in to Fate," Blanche tells her scornfully.

But for the victorious Hilarion, the story is not over. He finds himself in a position of strength that Tennyson's defeated prince never enjoys, but he rejects the right to command Ida as her conqueror. Instead, he appeals to her (in a speech that has a vastly different tone in the play, in which it is Hildebrand who delivers it) as her best and sole remaining student. As indifferent to power now as he was when helpless in "Whom Thou Hast Chained," he gives up the hand he has won in quest of the heart he craves.

"Experiments, the proverb says, are made on humble subjects," he says to Ida. "Try our grosser clay, and mold it as you will."

That Hilarion is ceding his right of conquest, that Ida is now being offered a choice, is made clear by the next lines, from so unlikely a source as Cyril: "Remember, too, / dear lady," he adds, "if at any time you feel / aweary of the prince, you can return / to Castle Adamant, and rule your girls / as heretofore, you know."

This is truly a revolutionary sentiment. Ida is not only being offered a choice between the World of Man and Castle Adamant, but Cyril even concedes that she may tire of Hilarion—and allows that, if she later desires, she can return to her previous life. We could hardly be further from Hildebrand's "But if you choose / to sulk in the blues / . . . I'll storm your walls / and level your halls / in the twinkling of an eye."

Offered this choice, Ida is stripped of her armor. She can no longer stand as the fiery crusader against man or as the defiant martyr she had cast herself as in her "So ends my dream" speech. Now the choice is hers: She must embrace or reject Hilarion, not as a princess, but as a woman.

For the first time in the opera, she asks for help: "And shall I find / the Lady Psyche here [if I return]?" To which Psyche responds, "If Cyril, ma'am, / does not behave himself, I think you will."

This is hardly the traditional "Gilbert & Sullivan" rapture of couples at the end of the opera, but it befits the man-fearing Psyche and her loutish suitor. Cyril is on probation, as it were—Psyche explicitly reserves for herself the same choice that is being offered Ida, and accepts Cyril only on those terms.

Finally, confirming her uncertainty, Ida turns for advice to a most unlikely source—Melissa, the opera's youngest character, its most innocent and the embodiment of its intergenerational theme: "And you, Melissa, shall I find you here?"

And Melissa replies, "Madam, however Florian turns out, / unhesitatingly I answer no."

Hers is the boldest choice, recognizing that there are options beyond the World of Man (as represented by Florian) and the World of Woman (and the college now ruled by her mother, which she categorically and "unhesitatingly" rejects). If the former fails her, Melissa will not retreat to the latter—she will find a new way.

It is Melissa's rejection of "either/or" that inspires Ida's final decision. "I have been wrong—I see my error now," she says.

Many critics have judged her "error" to be having dared to presume female equality or (as Hildebrand's "posterity" speech suggests) having overlooked man's indispensability. But neither judgment is valid.

Even after losing the battle, Ida still calls her dream "a glorious scheme." Having her women's physical weakness demonstrated has not caused her to reconsider her extremist ideals. Nor does her "error" have anything to do with the question of posterity. Even after Hildebrand's sarcastic comments, Ida still says, "I alone am staunch." If anything, in her martyrdom she remains more firm in her beliefs than ever.

Instead, responding to the examples of Psyche and especially Melissa, she realizes that her "error" lies in having unintentionally emulated her father, remaking his world in her own image. Instead of creating a new world free of oppression, while rejecting victimhood she has claimed the oppressor's role for herself. Melissa's stepping away from both worlds is an inspiration to Ida, leading her forward to a new ideal.

Ida's last speech quotes the final speech in "The Princess," but it is recast to give it a much different meaning. In Tennyson's poem it is the prince who has the last word, saying to Ida:

> My wife, my life! O, we will walk this world
> yoked in all exercise of noble end,
> and so through those dark gates across the wild
> that no man knows. Indeed, I love thee; come,
> yield thyself up; my hopes and thine are one.
> Accomplish thou my manhood and thyself;
> lay thy sweet hands in mine and trust to me.

Gilbert not only switches the speech to the princess but also cuts it substantially, in the process completely changing its meaning. Ida finishes:

> Take me, Hilarion—"we will walk this world
> yoked in all exercise of noble end,
> and so through those dark gates across the wild
> that no man knows. Indeed, I love thee—come!"

Obviously, there is a huge difference between the prince coaxing her to submit herself to him—"yield thyself up . . . lay thy sweet hands in mine and trust to me"—and Ida's freely giving herself.

But more significant are where Gilbert ends the speech and his change in punctuation. Both Tennyson's prince and Gilbert's princess speak of walking the world "yoked in all exercise of noble end"—a powerful image of plowing and planting seeds for the future, betokening not mere surrender but joint submission for the sake of accomplishment. But Tennyson's "come," is a cajoling inducement to surrender; Gilbert's "come!" is a call to action.

In short, both Gilbert and Tennyson play on the paradox of the victor ultimately ceding one prize to win a greater one—Tennyson's Ida wins her freedom only to yield to love, while Gilbert's Hilarion wins his princess only to surrender her in the name of freedom. He realizes he has won only her hand, and is willing to yield that in hope of winning her heart.

But because Gilbert has Hilarion win the battle, his happy ending actually requires two surrenders. First Hilarion surrenders his prize, then Ida surrenders her independence. Both man and woman must make sacrifices for true love. This is not true of Tennyson's prince, who, having lost the battle, has nothing left to surrender.

The upshot of Tennyson's poem is reconciliation. His princess finally realizes that her point of view is not so different from that of the prince and their fathers—as he tells her, "my hopes and thine are one." A world temporarily thrown out of kilter is made whole through love and understanding.

The upshot of Gilbert & Sullivan's play is emancipation. Prince and princess alike must leave the world of their fathers, rejecting the birthright of power and violence that has driven the dynastic feud. They learn this through being humbled. Gilbert humiliates both characters far more than Tennyson does, bringing them far lower, because in the grimmer world of *Princess Ida* they must be stripped of everything before they can grow anew.

The power of this ending is reflected in a finale that is far more substantial than most in Gilbert & Sullivan. While (like all their previous finales) it is a musical reprise, it significantly reworks the thematic material. The song originally heard as "little heeding / their pretty pleading, / our love exceeding we'll justify" now emerges as "with joy abiding, / together gliding / through life's variety / in sweet society." The song has been stripped of its violent images, which are replaced by images of peace, togetherness, and idyllic happiness. A sharper contrast could hardly be imagined.

Sullivan matches this contrast in setting the music. This is the team's only finale that is neither a chorus number nor a string of solos. Instead, it is a tenor-soprano duet, the first in the show. Mirroring the distance between the characters, *Princess Ida* has been the only Savoy opera in which the hero and heroine never sing together. But the ending brings them together, and the finale follows suit.

The composer's setting is a triumph. Not only is the finale's orchestration lusher than that of the Act 1 version of the song, but he brings the two voices closer and closer, first as matching solos and finally entwined in a duet soaring over the chorus on the words "with scented showers of fairest flowers, the happy hours will gaily fly."

The effect is magical, and gives *Princess Ida* something few Gilbert & Sullivan shows can boast—an ending that is truly satisfying in narrative, musical, and thematic terms.

Why has the substance of the opera proven so elusive to audiences, readers, and directors alike—especially with so much evidence to draw on, both in the opera itself and in comparison with Tennyson?

Part of the problem is well expressed by Geoffrey Smith, who writes that "Perhaps *Princess Ida's* fundamental flaw is simply that it is two productions stitched . . . together. One is the silly old play of the dialogue, the other the quite brilliant comic opera of the songs."[5]

Hopefully, we have seen that Gilbert's *The Princess* is more than a "silly old play." But it cannot be denied that Gilbert's reliance on his earlier play for much of the dialogue leaves *Princess Ida* with a book far below the mark of *Iolanthe* or *The Mikado*.

Since writing *The Princess*, Gilbert had improved greatly as a dialoguist, and it is too bad that, whether out of laziness or out of affection for his 1870 play, he didn't rework it more thoroughly. As it stands, some of the punning is quite lame, and he is in general less effective in conveying ideas than he otherwise was in the 1880s.

There's also the blank verse, which made the opera a bit old-fashioned at the time and can pose serious problems for modern-day performers. (The answer, often, is simply to treat it as prose. Blank verse done badly is dire indeed.) It can also be difficult for audiences. In his memoirs, Savoy music director François Cellier tells a possibly apocryphal anecdote of a Yorkshireman whose verdict on leaving *Princess Ida* was, "Well, I do like the music well enow; 't be bang up to date and full o' tunes I can whistle, but t' words sounds too much like Shakespeare for t' likes o' me to understand."[6]

In point of fact, *Princess Ida* is Shakespearian in both subject and style, and doesn't necessarily conform to people's expectations of the normal Gilbertian model. The play is laced with Shakespearian quotations, and its plot and characters are heavily influenced by Shakespeare as well.

Even its dramatic structure shows Shakespeare's influence. Awkward as three acts (with the second act more than twice as long as either of the others), it breaks naturally and evenly into Shakespeare's five-act form. In this structure, act breaks (marked by the traditional Elizabethan clearing of the stage rather than by a curtain) would occur after the exit of the women prior to "Gently, Gently" and before the entrance of the women for "Merrily Ring the Luncheon Bell."

It is my belief, based on this structural evidence, that Gilbert intended it to be a five-act play on the Shakespearian model but then telescoped it into three to make it more familiar to the Savoy audience. Certainly the audience's familiarity was a consideration at the time—*Princess Ida* was originally presented at the Savoy as a two-act opera, with the first act disingenuously termed a "prologue."

Whether or not it came about as a result of Gilbert's altering a planned five-act form, however, it cannot be denied that the final result is an awkward three-act structure that renders satisfactory placement of an intermission impossible.

Obviously, *Princess Ida*, with its "strange realm" of Castle Adamant, cross-gender disguises, philosophical musings on the responsibilities of nobility, and so on, has many of the characteristics of Shakespearian comedy. The most relevant is *Love's Labours Lost*. The skeleton of Tennyson's plot is drawn from this story of three aristocrats who retreat to a secluded forest for a year of study, forswearing all female companionship, only to have their seclusion infiltrated by women in disguise.

The Hildebrand-Hilarion relationship also draws on *1 Henry IV*. Like *Princess Ida*, Shakespeare's play tells the story of a young prince coming of age and learning the meaning of responsibility. Gilbert's choice of names for king and prince (neither named in Tennyson) echoes Henry and Hal, as do his portrayals of the strong, demanding king and his dissolute son, hanging around in taverns and singing love songs to the tavern wenches—Mistress Lalage, in the case of Hilarion's "Would You Know the Kind of Maid" (sung by Cyril but apparently the prince's song).

Fittingly, the opera's only direct Shakespearian quote is from *1 Henry IV*, with Psyche's reference to "villainous saltpetre" recalling Hotspur's line, "this villainous saltpetre should be digged / out of the bowels of the harmless earth."[7]

There are other Shakespearian touches as well. Melissa's first meeting with the men is reminiscent of Miranda's first encounter with Ferdinand in *The Tempest*, for example. There are two references to *Hamlet:* Hilarion and Hildebrand, in their "'I think I see her now'—'Ha, let me look!' / 'in my mind's eye, I mean,'" echo the dialogue between Hamlet and Horatio, " 'methinks I see my father' /—'where, my lord?'—'In my mind's eye, Horatio,' " while Gilbert picks up from Tennyson the final lines "and so through those dark gates across the wild / that no man knows," which evoke death, which in *Hamlet* is called "the undiscovered country from whose bourn / no traveler returns." The *Macbeth* parody, with " 'are men' stuck in her throat" echoing Macbeth's " 'amen' stuck in my throat,' " is obvious.

These quotations and allusions serve to create a consciously Shakespearian context for the play. To understand it, therefore, one has to view it with a Shakespearian eye. The characters in *Princess Ida* are more complex

than those in previous operas, and Gilbert employs a Shakespearian economy of words in presenting them, using inference more than description—perhaps to a fault, as the character inferences, especially couched
in blank verse, often escape an audience unfamiliar with the play.

Psyche, for example, is a fully drawn and convincing character but has
no "I will tell you what I am" song to explain herself—only a few lines
and references in passing. But they are rich enough to offer the convincing story of a brilliant young girl, petted and praised for her intellectual
achievement, until one day she is no longer a child, and finds that brilliance is considered charming in a little girl but off-putting in a woman.

There is evidence of a possible love affair gone wrong in Psyche's vehement resentment of men, especially of their coarse, animalistic physi-
cality; but in any event she runs away from home, fleeing what, from her
brother's status and her history as a playmate of the young prince, would
seem to be a position of power and privilege at Hildebrand's court. Coming as a refugee to Hungary, she becomes companion to the princess,
influences Ida's plans for her new school, and ultimately becomes a tutor
there.

This is a strong, intriguing, and very human role, one that calls for a
talented actress. But its subtleties can pass unnoticed by those accustomed
to the more blatant characterizations of *H. M. S. Pinafore* or *Patience*, leaving Psyche to seem merely a not-so-big role with one clever song about
an ape.

Lady Blanche, too, is an intriguing figure. She is the play's only English
character (save her daughter, who may be only half English), apparently
either exiled because of political reversals or perhaps sent to Hungary for
the marriage that produced Melissa. Her line "For years I've writhed beneath her sneers / although a born Plantagenet" is not, as Asimov says,
merely a clever rhyme for "imagine it." Blanche's connection to the House
of Plantagenet, which ruled England throughout Shakespeare's history
plays (including, of course, *1 Henry IV*) is also evidenced in her monologue
prior to "Come, Mighty Must": "I should command here—I was born to
rule," she begins, and later observes, "I once was Some One—and the
Was Will Be."

In short, Blanche is one of the royal pretenders common in Shakespeare's comedies and histories, a Richard III or Don John to Ida's Edward or Don Pedro.[8] She is acutely political, nursing a personal grudge
against Ida and a sense of entitlement so great as to make her utterly
ruthless, as is chillingly shown in the implacable "Come, Mighty Must."

The role is an important one—she is the counterpoint to Hildebrand,
as Ida initially is to Gama, nailing down Gilbert's portrayal of ruthless
absolutism not as a specifically male trait but as a state of mind common
to both sexes.

Cyril likewise plays an important schematic role, representing the "old
Hilarion." Initially, Hilarion, Cyril, and Florian are three of a kind—their

verses of "Oh, Dainty Triolet" or "I Am a Maiden" have only minor differences in tone. Cyril, whose reformation (such as it is) comes late, serves as a ground point to show Hilarion's progress.

"Would You Know the Kind of Maid" caps this function. In it, Cyril explicitly recalls Hilarion to himself, or rather to the man he was: It is, after all, Hilarion's song, not Cyril's. In lashing out at Cyril, the prince is rejecting his own past, vaguely akin to Prince Hal's rejection of Falstaff at the end of *Henry IV.* (Hilarion does not speak to Cyril again in the opera.)

There is a suggestion of Cyril's reformation in his protecting Gama from Hilarion's anger and, of course, in his final speech to Ida, but the challenge of depicting this change is primarily the actor's, as Gilbert & Sullivan give him insufficient material to make such a change explicit.

Ultimately, however, *Princess Ida* is not about a prince's coming of age. It is about a generation—any generation—coming of age and rejecting the ways of the past.

It is ironic that Hildebrand, Blanche, and even Gama end the opera thinking themselves victorious, since in a greater sense all three have lost.

Hilarion may have won the fight, but he will never be the conqueror that Hildebrand is and wants his son to be. In submitting himself to Ida for guidance ("try our grosser clay, / and mold it as you will"), Hilarion rejects his father's example, just as Ida turns her back on Gama and the dynastic feud that has driven her family for 20 years. And while Blanche may have won the college, she has lost her daughter, who "unhesitatingly" is leaving the school for good.

In this sense, the ending is a happy one. The influence of Hildebrand, Gama and Blanche has been unqualifiedly negative, and we can unreservedly applaud their children's emancipation.

But overall the ending is at best bittersweet. In addition to the three principal couples, Tennyson has many others fall in love: "Not only these; Love in the sacred halls / held carnival at will, and flying struck / with showers of random sweet on maid and man."

Gilbert's ending is not so happy, nor so universal. There is no traditional "Gilbert & Sullivan" ending to pair off the soldiers and maidens in unqualified rapture. (The "traditional" ending is a fallacy, anyway. In 14 operas, there are only four in which the entire ensemble marries—*The Pirates of Penzance, Patience, Iolanthe,* and *The Gondoliers,* plus perhaps *The Sorcerer.*)

Moreover, even for the three principal couples the ending is tinged with uncertainty, even pessimism. The possibility that Cyril will not behave himself and that Florian will not turn out well is explicitly raised—Ida may even grow aweary of the prince. This happy ending is only provisional.

Even for Hilarion and Ida, whose love we most believe in, the tone is one of hope, not faith. They do not take flight to Fairyland or rejoice

"Take heart, no danger lowers." Instead, Ida sounds the keynote, evoking the journey ahead "across the wild that no man knows." The young lovers, having turned their backs on the past, face an unknown future, with only one another for support.

Unlike any of the other operas, *Princess Ida's* finale celebrates not the end but the beginning: "Indeed I love thee—come!"

In crafting this subtle, multilayered story, both Gilbert and Sullivan excel themselves. Sullivan's score is arguably his best, with a grander, more operatic feeling to match the story's high stakes and confrontational style. Where strings filled *Patience* and woodwinds *Iolanthe*, *Princess Ida* is a brass-driven score, with the blare of trumpets and the crash of cymbals evoking the rattle of armor and the clash of swords.

Sullivan also shines in his use of sweet melodies to underlie unsettling words. His music is seductive as often as it is battering. For every "Now Harken to My Strict Command," "For a Month to Dwell," or "When Anger Spreads His Wing" there is an "O, Dainty Triolet," "I Am a Maiden," or "Mighty Maiden with a Mission"—dangerous sentiments clothed in sweet refinement. Small wonder that the Victorians found the show less appealing than its predecessors.

As for Gilbert, his not having reworked the preexisting dialogue diminishes the opera's impact substantially, but his lyrics are considerably more sophisticated, from a structural standpoint, than even those for *Iolanthe*. With each successive show Gilbert had given Sullivan a broader palette to work with, and in *Princess Ida* he continues to expand his range.

In particular, he begins alternating his couplets with triplets. He previously had used triplet structures occasionally, but in *Princess Ida* they are common. "The Lady and the Ape," for example, begins with a normal couplet structure but diversifies at the end of the verse into a triplet, giving Sullivan something fresh to work with: AABB–CC–DEEDD. The unexpected five-line finish, instead of the more conventional DDEE, rewards the ear with an unexpected twist.

The same is true of the tripping interlocked triplets that close "They Intend to Send a Wire to the Moon"—ABABCDCDEFEFGGGF. Conventional couplet structure might have produced:

> and weasels at their slumbers
> > they'll trepan,
> to get sunbeams from cucumbers
> > they've a plan.
> they've a firmly rooted notion,
> > so have they,
> that they'll cross the polar ocean,
> > so they say.

Gilbert not only sets up the triplet "firmly rooted notion / polar ocean / perpetual motion" but also concludes it with a third "-an" rhyme:

> and weasels at their slumbers
> > they'll trepan,
> to get sunbeams from cucumbers
> > they've a plan.
> they've a firmly rooted notion,
> they can cross the polar ocean,
> and they'll find perpetual motion
> > if they can.

In doing so he gives Sullivan a much richer form to draw on musically. He also heightens the impact of the final "if they can," capturing the sardonic quality of the young men's diatribe.

Gilbert even ventures altogether away from strict rhyming. "I Built upon a Rock" is his first major song that features unrhyming lines:

> I built upon a rock,
> > but ere destruction's hand
> > > dealt equal lot
> > > to court and cot,
> > my rock had turned to sand.

"Rock" and its successors "oak," "steel," and "fire" are not rhymed, except when repeated in the chorus ("fire" is not rhymed even then, because the chorus is "false fire indeed / to fail me in my need").

Obviously, this structural looseness gives Sullivan a great deal of freedom in setting the lyric. But it also has a dramatic point: The first line, establishing Ida's hope, is left isolated and without reinforcement, a classic instance of form reflecting content.

Overall, Gilbert's ability to use his lyrics to convey dramatic ideas reaches full maturity with *Princess Ida*. The contrast between the dialogue's fuzziness and the razor-sharp acuity of the lyrics demonstrates Gilbert's remarkable growth (due, in large part, to Sullivan's influence) over the course of their collaboration. (*The Princess* dated from barely a year before *Thespis*.)

It also promised well for their next collaboration, when Gilbert was to provide entirely original dialogue and lyrics alike for *The Mikado*.

All in all, *Princess Ida* is a remarkable show. It is not the polished gem that *Iolanthe* had been or *The Mikado* would be. In addition to its dialogue problems, its pacing occasionally drags because of problems involving the constraints of the Savoy company. (For example, "Don't the Days Seem

Lank and Long" is discordant in tone, unrelated to the situation at hand and disruptive to the momentum of an otherwise propulsive final act, but it had to be included in order to give the popular George Grossmith a second solo.)

Despite these weaknesses it remains a powerful work. It is the team's most ambitious opera, exceeding even *The Yeomen of the Guard* in scope and in the seriousness of its subject matter. Its flaws reflect its ambition as much as anything else: For earlier shows, fairly straightforward expansion of ideas from Gilbert's previous works had sufficed, but not for a project as bold as *Princess Ida.* If Gilbert had applied himself to rebuilding his play from the ground up, it might well have become their greatest work.

As it is, it remains a stunningly accomplished, emotionally stirring work when approached in the right way. It is testimony to the remarkable level of artistic achievement to which Gilbert & Sullivan had risen in only six years of serious collaboration, and it sets a high standard for what was to come.

Facing page: FIGURE 11.1. Sybil Grey as Peep-Bo (left), Leonora Braham as Yum-Yum (center), and Jessie Bond as Pitti-Sing (right) in the original production of *The Mikado.* In a reversal of his usual procedure, Gilbert actually created the characters for *The Mikado* before addressing plot or theme. *Source: The Pierpont Morgan Library, Gilbert and Sullivan Collection.*

11

The Mikado

The biggest problem with *The Mikado* is that it's the most famous and most widely performed of the Savoy operas. As a result, it's the opera most people think of when they think of Gilbert & Sullivan—which is a pity, because while it is arguably their best opera, it is far from typical.

Extrapolating from the opera they know best, many people jump to insupportable assumptions about the Gilbert & Sullivan operas as a whole—and, in particular, assume that the least serious of all the mature operas is representative of what they take to be a string of frivolous works.

The success of *The Mikado* is readily understandable. While other Savoy operas may be better in some ways—*Iolanthe, Princess Ida*, and *The Yeomen of the Guard* all have greater depth, a wider scope, and more impressive music—its charms cannot be denied. Among other things, it represents one of the most perfect fusions of composer and librettist ever achieved in music theater.

Yet the opera is a puzzling one. Alone among the Savoy operas, it has achieved lasting popularity in non-English-speaking countries, and many observers sense that it is somehow different from the others, without being able to put their fingers on exactly how.

I would submit that this is primarily because they are looking in the wrong place. Instead of examining *The Mikado* in an attempt to uncover its differences from the Gilbert & Sullivan norm—or, rather, what it leads them to think of as the norm—they ought to look at the others in a different light. After studying the thematic dimension that adds weight to the other mature operas, they may find that *The Mikado's* difference is, paradoxically, that it actually is what they mistakenly think the others to be.

The substantial difference in *The Mikado* is most likely attributable to the circumstances of its creation. Of all its siblings, *The Mikado* is most like *The Pirates of Penzance*. It is far better from a technical point of view, to be sure, but like *The Pirates of Penzance* it was created comparatively hurriedly and, perhaps as a result, stands outside the main stream of the evolution of Gilbert & Sullivan as thematic playwrights.

Where *The Pirates of Penzance* had been thrown together quickly to cash in on the popularity of *H. M. S. Pinafore, The Mikado* was born out of the opposite cause—the relative unpopularity of *Princess Ida*. It was also delayed in gestation, owing to the first major dispute between Gilbert and Sullivan.

Princess Ida was by no means a failure. *The Sorcerer*, which had taken London by storm, ran for a total of 178 performances; *Princess Ida* notched 246. But Gilbert & Sullivan had since defined a new standard for themselves. Compared to *Iolanthe's* 398 performances, *Princess Ida* was a disappointment.

But neither Gilbert nor Sullivan was a free agent, able to write when he pleased or, if he felt like it, not write at all. Under their contract with Richard D'Oyly Carte, the producer could inform the two at any time that a new opera would be required within six months, as indeed he did on March 22, 1884. As Gilbert reminded Sullivan on 30 March, "we are bound to supply Carte with a new opera on receiving from him six months' notice, and, if from any reason, we fail to do so, we are liable with him for any losses that may result from our default."[1]

However, the two found themselves initially unable to agree on a successor to *Princess Ida*. Gilbert worked out a new story in considerable detail, but when he submitted it to Sullivan, the composer rejected it. Reminiscent of Gilbert's play *The Palace of Truth*, it concerned a magic lozenge that compelled people to speak the truth and, indeed, to become what they claimed to be. (Ultimately, it was to become Gilbert's 1892 opera *The Mountebanks*, with music by Sullivan's former assistant Alfred Cellier.)

Sullivan didn't like it. He wanted to write more serious operas, free of supernatural devices and implausible characters. *Princess Ida* had been a step forward from the "implausible" *Iolanthe*, but the "lozenge plot" was a step backward—"it is going back to the elements of topsyturvydom and unreality which I had hoped we had now done with," he wrote to Carte.[2]

Moreover, he added, it reminded him excessively of a previous opera in the series: "It bears a strong resemblance to *The Sorcerer*, inasmuch as in both pieces by means of a charm, people all fall in love with each other . . . and if, as is probable, we revive *The Sorcerer* after *[Princess Ida]*, people will not fail to observe the resemblance." (As it turned out, *The Sorcerer* was indeed revived, so the composer's caution was well advised.)

Sullivan wanted something fresh. Gilbert reworked the proposal extensively, but to no avail. Carte's deadline was approaching, and they appeared to be at an impasse.

Whether or not there is any truth to the story of Gilbert being inspired by a Japanese sword falling from his wall (I think not), it is certain that when in May he finally proposed a completely new idea, Sullivan was thrilled. He wrote back saying that, as long as it didn't resort to "supernatural and improbable elements," he would agree "to set it without further discussing the matter, or asking what the subject is to be."[3]

The resulting opera is indeed free of supernatural influence, though it would be a stretch to consider it free of "improbable elements."

The new opera had to be written more swiftly than its predecessors: *Iolanthe's* opening had followed *Patience's* by 19 months, for example, whereas *The Mikado* premiered only 14 months after *Princess Ida* (with most of its first two months consumed in arguing about the lozenge plot).

Moreover, the authors were starting from scratch. Every previous opera except *Thespis* had been based, at least in germ, on some previous work by Gilbert. From *The Mikado* onward, all were to be original creations.

In some ways, the play shows its comparatively hasty composition. It is more loosely constructed than the previous operas, whose hallmark had been tight plotting and "site-specific" songs firmly connected to the characters who sing them and the situations in which they are sung. It is almost impossible to imagine rearranging the songs in *Patience* or *Princess Ida*, for example, though each did undergo some minor adjustments during the creative process. But *The Mikado* was constantly being reworked, right up to opening night and indeed afterward.

The first-night audience heard Yum-Yum's "The Sun Whose Rays Are All Ablaze" directly after "So Please You Sir, We Much Regret" ("The Sun Whose Rays," which had originally been meant for Pitti-Sing, ended up somewhat awkwardly placed in the second act). And without a last-minute appeal from members of the chorus no one would ever have heard the Mikado's "My Object All Sublime," which had been cut after the final dress rehearsal.

"I've Got a Little List" actually had three locations, being tried immediately after "I Am So Proud" and then immediately before it (in either context, it made more sense than in its eventual position) before finally being turned into a quasi-introduction song after "Behold the Lord High Executioner." The fact that so many of its songs could function effectively in several different places testifies to the relatively loose construction of the play.

Moreover, the songs rarely relate to the opera's thematic substance, such as it is. In place of the thoroughly integrated songs of *Iolanthe* and most of *Princess Ida*, many of *The Mikado's* songs are entirely unnecessary from a story standpoint, serving merely to recapitulate what has gone before, such as "Young Man, Despair"; "The Flowers That Bloom in the Spring"; "So Please You, Sir"; and others.

The songs are also remarkably similar in mood: Except for Katisha's two solos and perhaps "Titwillow," every song has the sole purpose of being funny. The emotional range of *The Mikado* is much narrower than that of *Iolanthe* or *Princess Ida*. Even songs whose subject matter would suggest grim treatment, such as "I Am So Proud" or "The Criminal Cried," are pitched to bring out their humorous elements.

In short, in *The Mikado* Gilbert & Sullivan step back from their previous evolution toward seriousness in tone and subject matter. Indeed, they commit themselves to an almost antithetical course: From beginning to end, the audience is distanced from any real sympathy for the characters and their situations, and invited to laugh at even their grimmest plights.

Part of the brilliance of Gilbert & Sullivan had been their ability to swing from the comic to the dramatic on a moment's notice. Never, however, had they tried to achieve both simultaneously—characters might be both funny and serious, as Strephon or Patience are, but in a given scene they would be one or the other, not both.

When Iolanthe or Princess Ida face death, for example, the authors craft "He Loves" or "I Built upon a Rock," entirely serious songs that crystallize the characters' emotions, involving the audience deeply in their crises.

Not so in *The Mikado*, in which even the grimmest situations—Nanki-Poo's planned suicide or the imminent agonizing deaths of Ko-Ko, Pitti-Sing, and Pooh-Bah—are played for laughs. The effect is to produce an extremely funny show, but one that is virtually never moving.

Laughter is a distancing response, disrupting intimacy of character and audience: In a serious song the audience's response is intended to be empathic, mirroring the character's emotions—Mabel weeps, and the audience weeps with her. A comic song, however, invites the audience to have a different response from the character's—Ko-Ko weeps, and the audience laughs. Emotionally distanced from the character, they can witness his fear, doubt, sorrow, anguish, or despair without themselves sharing those emotions.

This distancing is especially notable in *The Mikado's* comic device of the breaking of the "fourth wall" that conventionally separates the audience from the characters. This is rare in the operas. Though many critics have suggested otherwise (Isaac Asimov, for example, writes that "The truth is that Gilbert didn't care a maravedi for consistency of time or place in these operettas, and neither should we"),[4] Gilbert strove for authenticity in his sets, costumes, dialogue, and characters. He rigorously suppressed actors' out-of-context ad libs and usually refrained from topical references unless he was writing a show, such as *The Pirates of Penzance* or *Patience*, that was set in the England of his day.

When he did go against this, it was with a specific purpose in mind. In *Princess Ida* he consciously plays with time and place to create a timelessness appropriate to the subject matter; in *The Grand Duke*, self-reference and fourth-wall tricks are a key part of the opera's central metaphor.

It is a commonplace to say that *The Mikado* isn't about Japan but about England, and this is surely true. The same is true, of course, about the Greece of *Thespis*, the Venice of *The Gondoliers*, and so forth. These shows show little concern for authentic Greek or Venetian institutions, social forms, and the like, any more than Sullivan abandons English song forms for an authentic Greek or Italian musical idiom (as opposed to stylistic flavorings, which the composer often employed for "local color"). It could hardly be otherwise, because neither Gilbert nor Sullivan knew anything substantial about Japan, Greece, or classical Venice.

But in these cases, and indeed in all of the other operas, they lay out a set of consistent ground rules for "their" Venice, Greece, or wherever, rules they do not break. The basis of the rules, of course, are the traditional theatrical ground rules—the actors will pretend not to see the audience, for example, and if they talk to the audience it will be "as" the characters, not as the actors. In addition, it is understood that in *The*

Gondoliers the Italians will nonetheless speak English (most of the time), have afternoon tea, and so forth.

Audience members have to accept these rules as givens—to employ what Coleridge called a willing suspension of disbelief. And they do so without even thinking about it, because the conventions of theater are so generally understood that it never occurs to an audience member to say, "Why do all the people face the same way when they speak?"

But this acceptance of convention carries with it a reciprocal obligation. The authors are expected to work within the context that the audience has accepted and not to change the rules in midstream.

In particular, the rules work only if they are tacitly accepted—to express them ruins them. Marco never says, "I'd take this case to the doge, if only I were really Venetian," and Gianetta never says, "As I often sing in my musical Italian way . . ." If they did, of course, the effect would be comic. By underlining the artificiality of the story and its telling, it would distance the audience from characters whom Gilbert & Sullivan want us to take seriously. We couldn't laugh with them, or cry with them, if that artificiality were constantly thrown in our faces—continually reminded of their nonreality, we could only laugh at them.

In *The Mikado*, that artifice is constantly apparent. Again and again, Gilbert & Sullivan shatter the apparent "realism" of their Japan with playful abandon. For example, "The Japanese equivalent for 'Hear hear hear!' " breaks the tacit agreement that audience members will assume that the characters are speaking Japanese, even though they hear it in English.

The opera has literally dozens of such moments. Virtually unheard of elsewhere in Gilbert & Sullivan, they are everywhere in *The Mikado:* "[B]ut Japanese don't use pocket handkerchiefs!" jars the audience's agreement to forget that the actor is only an actor, not a Japanese executioner. "I often sit and wonder, in my artless Japanese way," is about the same as saying, "I'm not Japanese, but if I were I'd sit and wonder." And so on.

Some of the fourth-wall breaks are explicit, others implicit, but they fill the opera right from its start—"our attitude's queer and quaint" is hardly how a real Japanese gentleman would describe himself. (Try to imagine Marco singing "We all wear funny-looking caps, because that's what Venetians do.")

These lines get laughs, but they arise largely from the audience's surprise at seeing the convention broken, not from the lines themselves. There is nothing intrinsically funny about the Japanese not using pocket handkerchiefs. The laugh is the same sort that Laurence Olivier would have gotten by walking downstage and saying "To be or not to be—sheesh, why'd those Danes have to wear such itchy tights? Anyway, that is the question . . ."

But Olivier never would have done such a thing, because he didn't want to hinder the audience's ability to take Hamlet seriously. Such an ap-

Like a fine old Eng-lish gent - le-man   one__ of the ol - den   time!

11.1a. The opening of the 1836 English song "He's a Fine Old English Gentleman," by Henry Russell (1812–1900), serves as source material for *The Mikado's* wittily metatheatrical "Behold the Lord High Executioner," which was of course sung by an actual Englishman, despite the character being a Japanese executioner.

Be-hold the Lord   High   Ex - e - cu - tion-er!   A
per - son-age of no - ble rank and ti - tle

11.1b. "Behold the Lord High Executioner" (opening)

proach can succeed only in works such as Marx Brothers movies, which are not at all intended to be taken seriously. Nobody really believes in Rufus T. Firefly, including Groucho Marx himself, so he feels free to regularly break the fourth wall to talk to the audience as Groucho.

This distancing is reinforced in other ways. Except for the "Miya Sama" march (whose melody is based on an actual Japanese tune), Sullivan's music doesn't provide Japanese "local color" the way his Italian and Spanish rhythms tinge *The Gondoliers* or his Mendelssohnian echoes create a Fairyland ambiance in *Iolanthe.*

Indeed, *The Mikado* may be his most English score, with glees, madrigals, and other characteristic English song forms turning up repeatedly. "Behold the Lord High Executioner" is even set to a tune highly reminiscent of an old song called "A Fine Old English Gentleman," readily familiar to a Victorian audience (and to several 1885 critics, who missed the joke and accused Sullivan of plagiarism or lack of imagination) (ex. 11.1a, b).

Finally, Gilbert resolutely dilutes the seriousness of scenes that might otherwise mar the bright tone of the opera. He makes extensive use of alliteration, which in other operas he uses only occasionally—probably precisely because his dramatic intentions are usually serious, and alliteration interferes with seriousness.

Consider, for example, a possible lyric without alliteration:

To wait in quiet stillness in an unlit cell,
in a roach-infested prison where for life you'll dwell
     awaiting the sensation of that one last shock
     from a rusty, painful cleaver on the headsman's block!

This is a striking lyric, but it's unsettling. The subject matter isn't innately amusing, and its content would disturb an audience, then or now. Indeed, Gilbert had deftly mingled comedy and grimness in a very similar number, *Princess Ida's* "For a Month to Dwell in a Dungeon Cell," only the year before.

However, Gilbert's infusion of alliteration produces a much different effect:

To sit in solemn silence in a dull, dark dock
in a pestilential prison with a lifelong lock,
     awaiting the sensation of a short, sharp shock,
     from a cheap and chippy chopper on a big black block!

The ideas are exactly the same, but Gilbert's use of alliteration makes it a much different song. The audience is amused, smiling reflexively . . . and in the process losing any empathy for the characters and the horrible situation they face.

In this and other instances ("The Criminal Cried" and "There Is Beauty in the Bellow of the Blast," for example), alliteration turns the song into a stunt. We are more aware of the lyricist, and also of the performers as they try to get out all the words; consequently, we are less aware of the characters.

Finally, *The Mikado* features the team's most flamboyant fourth-wall–breaking moment, as the Mikado observes, "Virtue is triumphant only in theatrical performances"—the next best thing to a narrator reassuring us, "Don't worry, it'll come out all right, it's only a play."

The observation gets a laugh, but it undercuts what would otherwise be the grimly ironic plight of Ko-Ko, Pitti-Sing, and Pooh-Bah, condemned to a horrible death for a crime that never even took place.

None of this distancing makes *The Mikado* a poor opera, of course. It isn't a lesser work than its predecessors, only a less ambitious one—the infectious sense of play engendered by the fourth-wall game-playing is, in fact, one of the strongest elements in its uniquely broad-based appeal.

Given the creators' conscious efforts to undercut the opera's seriousness, the greatest "wrong note" in *The Mikado* lies in the character of Katisha.

Her two solos, "The Hour of Gladness Is Dead and Gone" and "Alone, and Yet Alive," were probably written to reflect Sullivan's growing distaste for Gilbert's stock "repulsive old lady" characters, as epitomized by the Ladies Jane and Blanche. They may also reflect a desire to give the popular Savoy actress Rosina Brandram a bit more to do. And in their own right they're fine songs

In context, however, they feel as if they'd been dropped in from another show. Those two songs apart, Katisha is a magnificent comic creation, a dragon lady who manages to be a memorable villain while, at the same time, getting some big laughs with her right elbow and her left shoulder blade. She is bloodthirstiness personified, and her characterization of Nanki-Poo as "my prey . . . I mean, my pupil" is one of her funniest lines.

What, then, is one to make of "Alone, and Yet Alive?" ("The Hour of Gladness" is basically the same song.) There is nothing in its lyrics or music to suggest that it is meant at all farcically—quite the contrary. But if the audience takes it seriously, the following scene will play as Ko-Ko tormenting a grieving lover (or at least a desperately lonely woman) rather than trying to coax a smile out of a dragon.

The fact is that, given "The Hour of Gladness" and "Alone, and Yet Alive," Katisha seems to love Nanki-Poo more truly than Yum-Yum does. The latter is quite prepared to marry Ko-Ko if she can't have Nanki-Poo ("what good would [refusing him] do? He's my guardian, and he wouldn't let me marry you"), while Katisha wails to the heavens that all has perished, "save love, which never dies."

This attitude is incompatible with her dialogue or, for that matter, her other songs. In her dialogue, after "Alone, and Yet Alive," she shows every indication of wanting to watch Ko-Ko and his associates die (presumably for having interfered with her rise to the exalted rank of "daughter-in-law elected") but no sign whatever of wanting to die herself.

Many directors deal with this problem by simply cutting the two solos. This certainly makes the character more consistent but does violence to the authors' intentions while losing two excellent songs. Retained, they serve to create a softer side to Katisha, making her response to "Titwillow" more comprehensible.

But even the most ardent Katisha fan will have to admit that they are simply jarring from the standpoints of tone and character alike. In an opera otherwise dedicated to artificiality, real sentiment doesn't fit.

The opera's artificiality is mirrored in the structure of its plot. Artifice is everywhere in *The Mikado*, in which an irrational world gets by only through legal fictions and mutually agreed-on pretenses. In Titipu, after all, the pretty face gets painted and the already-coral lip dyed, and even "these divisions of time are strictly arbitrary."

Ko-Ko, obviously, is a tailor whose real skill is cutting and trimming the truth. He has accepted the position of lord high executioner only on the understanding that he won't actually do the job, just as his colleague Pooh-Bah has a hundred titles but no real job.

(Incidentally, though Pooh-Bah generally has been played by older men since Rutland Barrington's later years, he is actually described in "The

Criminal Cried" as "this haughty youth." He is the first embodiment of Gilbert's satire of latter-day aristocrats who sell their nobility to the highest bidder. His "I go and dine with middle-class people on reasonable terms" speech is the direct ancestor of *The Gondolier's* "Small Titles and Orders.")

As Max Keith Sutton has amply demonstrated, the relationship between people and the law is prominent in several Gilbert & Sullivan operas.[5] The most obvious case is in *Iolanthe*, in which characters such as the Lord Chancellor and the Fairy Queen are sincerely torn between a law they respect and their personal sense of what is right.

The Mikado, however, is closer in spirit to *Trial by Jury*, in which the law is merely a mask for venality. The question in *The Mikado* is not whether to obey the law but how to get away with not obeying it. The Mikado's laws are so arbitrary and so excessive ("flirting is the only crime punishable by decapitation," so presumably more substantial crimes are punished far more severely) that there is no real respect for them. The only reason to obey them is fear of the awful punishments, and normal living requires finding ways to disobey them.

Hence the townspeople of Titipu collectively agree to violate the spirit, if not the letter, of the law against flirting. Ko-Ko is first in line to die, and if he kills himself, there'll be no one to enforce further sentences of death. And, to judge by the usual behavior of the three little maids, there seems to be a considerable amount of flirting going on!

Even the heir to the throne runs afoul of the law and is forced to flee his father's arbitrary judgment. The law's absurdity is amply proven by the fact that, should Nanki-Poo fail to marry Katisha, the Mikado would have him instantly beheaded, which would in turn render himself guilty of compassing the death of the heir apparent, with its humorous but lingering punishment to follow.

The most common way of violating the law in Titipu, however, is simply to claim to have obeyed it. Yum-Yum and Nanki-Poo set the tone, "obeying" the flirting law through declaring that they're obeying it, complete with detailed demonstrations of what they're not doing.

Ko-Ko follows suit. "Why should I kill you," he asks, "when making an affidavit that you've been executed will do just as well?" And indeed it does: Nanki-Poo's legal death (which foreshadows those of Ernest and Rudolph in *The Grand Duke*) is, from the Mikado's point of view, fully sufficient. Despite the three witnesses' highly unlikely testimony, neither he nor Katisha asks to see the body or any corroborating evidence whatsoever.

The crowning touch, of course, is Ko-Ko's explanation to the Mikado: Essentially, he says, your majesty's word is law; your majesty says, let a thing be done, and it's as good as done—practically, it is done. And if it is done, why do it?

In other words, the Mikado is so omnipotent that his merely decreeing a law makes it so, hence there's no real reason to bother obeying or enforcing it.

Sullivan's worries about "improbable elements" notwithstanding, it is a very unusual world that Gilbert & Sullivan create in *The Mikado*. However, it is also a highly consistent one, even in its inconsistencies—after all, a single instance of fourth-wall–breaking would be much more jarring than the repeated instances that fill *The Mikado*.

While its content lies outside the mainstream of the collaboration, *The Mikado* shows a continuing evolution in Gilbert's lyrical style. Sullivan's appeals for more diverse lyrics continue to be met with understanding and cooperation from Gilbert.

The verses to the songs in *The Mikado* are much longer than in earlier shows: In *Patience*, for example, the longest non-patter-song verse form was 12 lines (used in three different songs); "Our Great Mikado" logs in at 14, "Young Man Despair" at 20.

Besides offering the composer more room for musical expression, longer verses produce greater structural diversity. "Our Great Mikado" adds an extra rhyme to an apparently normal couplet scheme to produce the highly unusual AABBCDDDC–EEE, where AABBCDDC–EE would be expected. The addition of the extra line (in the first verse, it's "unless connubially linked") creates a stuttering rhythm that is very distinctive.

The oddly shaped "Young Man, Despair" uses one of the most original rhyme schemes ever: ABABBBC–DEDEEEC–FGFGCC (in the first verse, adding to the complexity, the D and G rhymes are the same "-ay"):

A	Young man despair,
B	likewise go to,
A	Yum-Yum the fair
B	you must not woo.
B	It will not do,
B	I'm sorry for you,
C	you very imperfect ablutioner.
D	This very day
E	from school Yum-Yum
D	will wend her way
E	and homeward come
E	with beat of drum
E	and a rum-tum-tum
C	to wed the lord high executioner!
F	And the brass will crash
G	and the trumpets bray,
F	and they'll cut a dash
G	on their wedding day—
C	She'll toddle away as all aver
C	with the lord high executioner!

And of course "I Am So Proud" carries its mock-obsessive subject matter into a verse of AABBCCDDCCCC, followed by a chorus of-EEFFFFFF (although / go / pine / shine / line / fine / condign / decline) and the final coda of GGGG (dock / lock / shock / block).

Gilbert also carries on his practice, begun in *Princess Ida,* of using occasional lines that don't rhyme at all—as in "There Is Beauty in the Bellow of the Blast," whose rhyme scheme leaves the first and ninth lines unrhymed (in verse one, they are "blast" and "grim").

Another unrhymed line pops up in "The Criminal Cried," where Gilbert is particularly clever in using rhyme scheme to convey character: Ko-Ko lays out the "bare bones" of the story in an ABABCDEED–FFDGGD verse (the unrhymed C line is "I seized him by his little pig-tail"). Pitti-Sing follows suit. But when Pooh-Bah takes over the story, Gilbert not only throws in a triple internal rhyme in the first line ("Now though you'd have *said* that *head* was *dead*") but also makes the B and D rhymes the same "he / pedigree" rhyme, to create a bizarre (AAA)BABCBDDB–EEBFFB, perfectly capturing the ornate pomposity of Pooh-Bah's character.

(Gilbert even seems to be tweaking Sullivan's often-voiced dislike for couplets when he sets Ko-Ko's "Taken from a County Jail" to a scheme of ABABABABABAB!)

It's natural that Gilbert would use a rhyme scheme to express characterization in *The Mikado,* because the opera's strength is its comedy, and the comedy's strength is its characters. This is hardly surprising, since in this case—unusually for him—Gilbert literally created the characters first, then developed the plot around them.[6]

After seeing the earlier operas, one tends to remember scenes over characters, the "I like you very much—but not, perhaps, as much as you like me" scene, for example, over Lord Tolloller specifically, or the "You Hold Yourself Like This" scene over Major Murgatroyd.

In *The Mikado,* the situation is reversed. Pooh-Bah is more memorable than any given scene in which he appears. His "big song," in fact, is "Young Man, Despair," a simple plot explication that is one of the opera's few songs that didn't become classics.

From this strong characterization stems the opera's distinctive "riff" feeling, a jazz-like sense of almost improvisatory looseness to its dialogue and songs. Many of its scenes are not built on what happens as much as how it happens—"character riffs" on a simple premise.

The first scene between Ko-Ko and Pooh-Bah, for example, is a prototypical one-joke scene in which nothing really happens. The question of how much Ko-Ko's wedding will cost is irrelevant to the opera—it's merely a device to bounce the two characters off one another for laughs.

The same is true of the dialogue leading into "I Am So Proud." Nothing really happens after the first three lines—but, once the basic situation is tossed out, the three characters are freed to riff on it, producing a less goal-oriented humor that is just as hilarious as the more focused scenes in other operas. (The apparent spontaneity of this and other dialogues in

The Mikado is not deceiving—many of the lines arose as actors' ad libs, to which Gilbert was more receptive than usual.)

In this regard, the show is much different from its predecessors and its successors alike, probably because its hurried composition gave Gilbert & Sullivan less time to shape deeper themes and tighter structures.

It is looser, offering its performers more room to maneuver. Its humor is character based, probably accounting for a good part of its international success: The Bunthorne-Patience "Hollow, Hollow" scene, with its puns, parodic elements, and thematic linkages, is hilarious, but translating it would be virtually impossible. But with the opening Ko-Ko/Pooh-Bah scene, a reasonably literal translation will serve admirably.

The Mikado is a show whose strengths and weaknesses are inseparable. Watching *The Sorcerer,* one can see ways that it could be substantially improved through relatively minor adjustments, and one wishes that the partners' revision of 1884 had been more thoroughgoing. Watching *The Mikado,* on the other hand, one delights in the hilarity of the characters and the all-but-unfailing brightness of words and music; whatever flaws there are occur only on reflection.

One may wish that there were more substance to it, more of the depth that made *Iolanthe, Princess Ida,* or *The Yeomen of the Guard* such impressive accomplishments, but the delight of *The Mikado* stems precisely from that lack of depth, and no amount of minor adjustments could do anything but, probably, spoil the fun. *The Mikado* is what it is, and is perfect as what it is.

The opera has something of the charm of a clever clockwork. We don't get involved in it or feel emotionally committed to it to the extent that we may even with *The Sorcerer* or *H. M. S. Pinafore.* Nor should we—the clockmakers don't expect us to and didn't build it with that in mind. But the ingenuity of the machinery is so remarkable, so flawlessly meshed, that it remains a source of joy on many repeated viewings.

If all of Gilbert & Sullivan's other operas really were better or worse attempts to match *The Mikado,* as many people seem to think, they'd be a pretty shallow lot. But as a lighthearted diversion from the generally ambitious Savoy operas, it stands as a remarkable achievement.

12

Ruddigore

"We are credited—or discredited—with one conspicuous failure, *Ruddigore; or, The Witch's Curse,*" Gilbert said in a famous 1907 speech.[1] "Well, it ran eight months, and, with the sale of the libretto, put 7,000 pounds into my pocket. In the blackness of my heart, the worst I wish to my rival dramatists is that they may each have a dozen such failures, and retire upon the profits."

And to be sure, *Ruddigore's* reputation as a failure is undeserved. Its 288 performances falls about halfway between *The Sorcerer's* 175 and *The Pirates of Penzance's* 363, and both were considered solid successes. But *Ruddigore* followed *The Mikado,* whose 672 performances had changed the calculus of success. Following such a blockbuster, almost any opera would have seemed inadequate.

As the *Times of London* critic noted in a generally favorable review of *Ruddigore,* "It is the misfortune of Messrs. Gilbert and Sullivan that they are their own rivals, and every new work makes their task harder."[2] Still, after more than a century, one might expect comparisons to *The Mikado* to have waned. After all, modern audiences rarely know what order the operas were written in.

But *Ruddigore* remains problematic. Most Savoyards love it, cherishing it as a neglected gem, but the general public has never taken to it as warmly. What are we to make of it today?

The greatest obstacle to a fair evaluation of *Ruddigore* is its text, which (excepting *Thespis*) is the most irregular of the operas. After the opening night Gilbert & Sullivan made substantial changes, and severe cuts were made in D'Oyly Carte Opera Company revivals after the creators' deaths.

Many of the post-opening changes were minor, no more affecting the overall text than did the change of title from *Ruddygore* to the less-offensive *Ruddigore.* And some—such as the decision not to revive all the ghosts for the Act 2 finale—reflected practical problems of stagecraft. (That is, the picture frames didn't work much better at the Savoy than they have in hundreds of productions since!)

But some changes played hob with the creators' original intentions, leaving *Ruddigore* as we know it something of a mess. Until one understands the various textual variants and their claims to authenticity, anything like an informed judgment is impossible.

(For reference purposes, these changes may be found in appendix B. I encourage readers to examine them before continuing, as they are integral to my discussion of the opera and its themes.)

In addition to these changes, the first revival by the D'Oyly Carte Opera Company, in 1920, made four even more significant changes that drastically marred the opera's structure, in the process giving the lie to the Carte company's vaunted claims of historical authenticity.

1. The Richard-Rose love duet in Act 1, "The Battle's Roar Is Over, O My Love!" was deleted, not to be restored to the Carte productions until 1977. This was a serious change, rightly or wrongly eliminating any romantic or sentimental aspect to Richard's character.

2. The second verse of the Richard-Rose duet in Act 2, "Happily Coupled Are We," was cut and never permanently restored. This is also a serious change—Rose's response to Richard's flirting expresses her lingering doubts about him, an attitude otherwise not clear.

3. "Henceforth All the Crimes" was also cut, never to be restored in a Carte production. This was a particularly bad change, taking the slow-fast-slow sequence of "Painted Emblems"–"Henceforth All the Crimes"–"I Once Was a Very Abandoned Person" and making it a slow-slow sequence that is significantly less effective.

4. Finally, the solo verses to the Act 2 finale were cut, reducing it to a vestigial reprise of "Oh, Happy the Lily." This change, not reversed until 1971, cut a 34-line song to six lines, by far the shortest Savoy finale, and made a mockery of Sullivan's structural intentions for the finale's music.

Fortunately, the material cut in 1920 was never eliminated from the published scores and libretti, and other companies generally retained some or all of it in performance.

Together, the alterations have made *Ruddigore* problematic on page and stage alike. Audiences, critics, and scholars have based their opinions on versions of the show that are, to one degree or another, unrepresentative of the opera that Gilbert & Sullivan spent much of 1886 writing.

For analytic purposes, I will consider the pre-1920 text the "authentic" one. It was finalized after fewer than 10 performances and remained consistent thereafter. It therefore reflects the more-or-less-final word of the creators themselves.

(Gilbert was not entirely satisfied. After Sullivan's death, he wrote to Helen Carte to discuss a series of revised revivals, saying "The alterations would probably be very material, especially in *Ruddigore, Utopia, Limited* and *The Grand Duke.*"[3] However, the series fell through, and those alterations were never made—probably for the best, given Sullivan's absence.)

The material eliminated after the opening night is not wholly "authentic," since it was cut by the creators themselves. But it is evidence of their original intent, and thus I also consider it here, with appropriate caution.

Fans of *Ruddigore* point to a number of gems from the opera. "I Once Was a Very Abandoned Person" has always been one of the team's most popular songs, while "My Boy, You May Take It from Me" and the "Matter Matter Matter" trio are considered peaks of Gilbert's patter repertoire. Sullivan wins kudos for the lovely madrigal "When the Buds Are Blossoming" and for the operatic sweep of "Ghosts' High Noon," among others.

Detractors of the opera rarely question its high points but find it woefully inconsistent. Sullivan wrote in his diary after the opening: "Production of *Ruddygore* at Savoy. Very enthusiastic up to the last 20 minutes, then the audience showed dissatisfaction. Rivivication of ghosts, etc., very weak."[4]

The critics agreed. *The Times* wrote, "With the rapturous applause of a more than sympathetic first-night audience . . . a small but very determined minority mingled its hisses. . . . We have no hesitation in attributing them to the feebleness of the second act."[5]

The ghost scene, today generally considered a high point of the opera, was controversial. Some raved. The *Daily News* critic wrote:

> The whole of the music of the picture scene is far removed above the ordinary level of comic opera, and is among the best things of this sort that Sir Arthur Sullivan has ever written. It is almost serious in aim, but although somewhat after the style of grand opera, there is many a whimsical touch of burlesque in the orchestra.[6]

Those whimsical touches escaped some, however. The *Times* critic wrote:

> The musical treatment of these scenes appears to us pitched in the wrong key. Sir Arthur Sullivan, in a parallel situation of *The Sorcerer*, has shown that the mock-ghastly as well as the mock-heroic is quite within his reach . . . but the present ghost-scene has evidently not found him in a happy mood. He treats Mr. Gilbert's grotesque spectres as if they were a dread reality coming straight from the charnel house. . . . The innate seriousness of the music, the sincerest of all arts, has evidently been too much for the composer, and the result is one evidently quite different from that which he and the dramatist intended.[7]

Gilbert himself shared this opinion. In a letter to a friend he wrote:

> My own impression is that the first act led everyone to believe that the piece was going to be bright and cheery throughout, and that the audience were not prepared for the solemnity of the ghost music. That music seems to my uninstructed ear to be very fine indeed, but—out of place in a comic opera. It is as though one inserted fifty lines of *Paradise Lost* into a farcical comedy. I had hoped that the scene would have been treated more humorously by Sullivan, but I

fancy he thought his professional position demanded something grander and more impressive than the words suggested.[8]

Given its patter-song meter and the *Hamlet* parody "Alas, poor ghost" leading into it, "Ghost's High Noon" clearly could have been a comic song, if Sullivan had treated it as such. But the opera's inconsistency goes beyond the ghost music. Though it is one of the most thematically integrated of the operas, *Ruddigore* has a variety of flaws—some technical, some in characterization and plotting—that undermine its many virtues.

Writing for a standing repertory company let Gilbert & Sullivan tailor each role to the actor's particular capabilities. It also meant, however, that an actor could grow bored with a series of similar parts.

Fortunately, the creators were willing to vary their approach on occasion. In *Iolanthe,* for example, the cavernous bass/baritone Richard Temple, who had shone in comic authority roles such as the Pirate King in *The Pirates of Penzance* and the Colonel in *Patience,* was cast as Strephon, the romantic lead; tenor Durward Lely took on the comic role of Lord Tolloller.

The *Iolanthe* switch worked well, because both Gilbert and Sullivan followed the idea through completely. Lely's songs were comic, Temple's romantic. Instead of letting Lely indulge his fans with a melting love ballad, for example, they gave him two sentimental ballads about his own prestige, "Blue Blood" and "Of All the Young Ladies I Know." Despite his lower voice, Temple was given all the romantic music.

Ruddigore offers a similar switch. The hero Robin was played not by Lely, the popular former Nanki-Poo, but by George Grossmith, the erstwhile Ko-Ko. Lely took the role of the comic, all-but-villainous sailor Dick Dauntless.

But this time Gilbert & Sullivan failed to follow through on the switch. Dauntless's "The Battle's Roar Is Over" is treated by lyricist and composer alike as a typical tenor-soprano duet—perfectly effective but rampantly out of character. The rough, unsentimental wooer turns into a smooth tenor at the first notes of the song, then reverts to form immediately afterward.

The post-1920 D'Oyly Carte tenors reportedly enjoyed not having to sing "The Battle's Roar," and understandably so—without it, the character is far more consistent.

Similarly, Grossmith scored a hit with the comic "My Boy, You May Take It from Me," but it no more suits the diffident Robin than "The Battle's Roar" suits Richard. In both cases, a momentarily effective song undercuts the long-term strength of the character.

It's no coincidence that the opera's two most successful characters are also its most consistent. Sir Despard and Mad Margaret virtually never lose their focus, whether for easy sentiment or a quick laugh (the only exception being the ending of the "Matter Matter Matter" trio). Even in Act 2, their superficial alteration is perfectly compatible with what we've seen of them previously, making it funny in a richer way than "My Boy, You May Take It from Me" could ever be.

Unfortunately, the other characters are less consistent. Sir Roderick goes from Grand Guignol in "Ghosts' High Noon" to simple passivity in "There Grew a Little Flower." Dame Hannah begins as "a nice old person" in Act 1, but in Act 2 metamorphoses into "a tigercat." Rose starts out as a deftly comic mixture of primal neurosis and calculating self-interest but in Act 2 becomes a stock melodrama figure.

The plot, too, is strikingly inconsistent. Why do Richard and Rose need Robin's consent for their marriage, for example, when Robin and Rose didn't need Despard's? How does Margaret know that Despard plans to kidnap Rose? Why do Sir Despard's "evil crew" begin as sharp urban womanizers before suddenly joining gaily in the country wedding of people they don't even know? Whatever happened to Adam being madly in love with Dame Hannah? Why don't the ghosts know that Robin is still alive? And why is Despard so eager for Robin to reform and die, since the curse would then presumably revert to Despard himself?

For all their conceptual implausibility, the plots to *Iolanthe* or *Princess Ida* are virtually airtight on their own terms. Even the tongue-in-cheek *Mikado* has a solid plot structure to hold its eccentricities together. But *Ruddigore* is full of holes. This fragmentation would be increasingly prevalent in the team's final operas—the next, *The Yeomen of the Guard*, makes *Ruddigore* look tight and cohesive.

In this regard, *Ruddigore* shows the first signs of decline for Gilbert & Sullivan. They would rebound commercially with their next two operas—combined, *The Yeomen of the Guard* and *The Gondoliers* would run nearly a thousand nights—but they were never again to produce such coherent, integrated operas as they had previously.

This level of inconsistency is not fatal. Indeed, *Ruddigore* is a consummately theatrical play that can work well onstage. But it takes a firm and insightful director, as well as strong performers in the principal roles, to pull it together.

Iolanthe and *The Mikado* are so rich and so structurally tight that even a bad production can't entirely fail. A bad *Ruddigore*, however, can be very lame indeed.

Despite its flaws, however, *Ruddigore* is one of the most interesting Gilbert & Sullivan operas. Its story is an engaging one, particular on a thematic level, and both author and composer do some of their best work for it.

Whatever the problems of its story level, on the subject level *Ruddigore* is a delightful parody of what used to be called "transpontine melodrama" (literally, "across-the-bridge melodrama," because it flourished in cheap theaters on the far side of the Thames).

Gilbert & Sullivan have great fun with such melodramatic staples as curses, ghosts, evil noblemen abducting maidens, and, especially, the Gothic confrontation between the evil villain and the frightened maiden, which is burlesqued twice in Act 2, once with an inept villain, again with a tigercat maiden.

Most likely, no modern viewer of *Ruddigore* has ever seen a transpontine melodrama; the genre lives on only in parodies, *Ruddigore* included. Those parodies have made virtual archetypes of its conventions—the girl tied to the railroad tracks, the sneering, mustached villain, and the eloquent, dashing hero. Gilbert chose his subject well—melodrama was rich with opportunities for parody, then and even now, more than a century after it breathed its last.

Still, even at the time, the subject was outdated. Transpontine melodrama had peaked in the 1840s and by 1887 was essentially dead. One critic growled, "The author . . . has further chosen to dig up the bones of long-buried melodrama to make a cockshy of. He has elected to burlesque a form of entertainment, the recollection of which only survives in the memories of the oldest play-goers."[9]

Though it hasn't obsolesced, *Ruddigore*'s melodrama parody is inconsistent. As always when parodying theatrical excesses, Gilbert & Sullivan can't quite escape them.

Some of the parody is deft: Sullivan's swooping setting for "Oh, Why Am I Moody and Sad" is just excessive enough to be humorous without being silly, while Gilbert makes a delightful bit role out of Old Adam, a stereotype who glories in his own stereotypicality.

Often, though, the parody lapses: The Union Jack sequence is overblown enough to be corny but not enough to be funny. In her introductory stage direction, Mad Margaret is called "an obvious caricature of theatrical madness" but in practice is neither obvious nor a caricature.

Actually, Margaret is better than a caricature, just as many of the nonparodic songs ("My Boy, You May Take It from Me," "I Know a Youth," "When the Buds Are Blossoming") are better than parody could make them. When parody would get in the way of character humor or effective drama, Gilbert & Sullivan jettison it without a second thought.

In the Savoy operas parody is never more than a means to an end, which is why their parodies have outlasted their expected shelf life. Like *Patience*, *Ruddigore* uses parody for humor but never lets it dominate the play. Its parody aspects are attention-grabbing, but the opera itself is no more about melodrama than *Patience* was about aestheticism.

It is on the thematic level that *Ruddigore* is most successful, indeed perhaps the strongest and most integrated of the entire Savoy series. Had its technical and structural execution matched its thematic development, *Ruddigore* might have been the team's greatest opera. It works on many levels and displays the creators' thematic technique in its fullest development.

Ruddigore is the third consecutive Savoy opera to focus on an aristocratic hero/heroine who has run away from home to escape a "family curse"—Ida and Nanki-Poo the loveless marriages ordered by their fathers, and Robin the curse of the Murgatroyds.

None of the earlier or later operas employ such a device. That this idea was so fixed in Gilbert's mind at this particular time suggests thematic connections between the operas. And indeed *Ruddigore* is a culmination of the ideas of accountability and free will that drive *Princess Ida* and even the light and airy *Mikado.*

Like *Princess Ida, Ruddigore* focuses on the conflict between family responsibility and personal choice. Both operas are essentially morality stories, though more sophisticated than the typical Victorian drama and preaching an almost antithetical morality.

Like Ida (and Hilarion), Robin inherits a family legacy of violence and immorality. Her birthright is one of war and his one of crime, but Ida and Robin both react by fleeing—Ida to a world of her own, Robin (like Nanki-Poo) to the life of an anonymous commoner.

These flights take place before the opera, however, and the story itself proves that evasion is no answer. Ida, Hilarion, and Robin must ultimately face their birthrights and take responsibility for who they are. (Purely comic, *The Mikado* offers so weighty a message only in embryo.)

Each must first accept that legacy (Hilarion and Ida in the opera's final battle, Robin in assuming his title from Despard) before facing a final choice: Hilarion, whether to risk the prize he has won in quest of true love; Ida, whether to risk letting go of her grim, confrontational view of the world and give love a chance; and Robin, whether to choose sin or death.

The moral lessons, of course, come in the choices they make, at the end of the opera and previously.

Where *Princess Ida* addresses a variety of other issues, *Ruddigore* sticks closely to morality.

Patience, superficially about aestheticism, was packed with songs about love. *Ruddigore* is equally packed with songs about morality. Virtually all of its songs are about duty verses inclination: "Sir Rupert Murgatroyd," "If Somebody There Chanced to Be," "I Know a Youth," "In Sailing o'er Life's Ocean Wide," "Oh, Why Am I Moody and Sad?" "You Understand?" "As Pure and Blameless Peasant," "Within This Breast There Beats a Heart," "I Once Was as Meek as a Newborn Lamb," "In Bygone Days," the entire ghost scene, "Henceforth All the Crimes," "I Once Was a Very Abandoned Person," the "Matter Matter Matter" trio, and the Act 2 finale.

The entire opera might have been subtitled "Duty, duty must be done, the rule applies to everyone." Its wide-ranging story comes together in a rigorous morality play—or did, until the various changes undercut its textual integrity, blurring it for future audiences.

Ruddigore offers three conflicting views of duty, each embodied in one character and countered in another. Its drama and comedy alike arise from clashes between these views:

- Personal self-interest: Its prime exponent is Richard Dauntless, who always does what will benefit him, regardless of any moral obligation. Its prime opponent is Sir Despard, a fervent moralist who in Act 2 becomes a virtual evangelist against self-interest. (As usual in Gilbert & Sullivan, Dauntless couches his self-interest in moral terms, while the moralist Despard is the opera's greatest hypocrite.)
- Morality: Everyone invokes morality, but few practice it. Robin supposedly possesses "the morals of a Methodist," but only at the very end do they come to the fore. Morality's prime opponent is Sir Roderick, who assumes that self-interest is everything (it never occurs to him that a baronet might actually choose to die rather than sin) and to whom Robin's morality is an incomprehensible quirk to be worked out through torture.

    The catalyst to the opera is, of course, "The Witch's Curse." The curse forces each Murgatroyd into a daily confrontation between morality and self-interest: The only way to survive is to sin. Despard and Robin both know that the moral choice is to defy the curse and perish, but neither initially has the courage.
- Social expectations: The third source of duty, largely played for comic relief, is Rose Maybud's etiquette book.

    Gilbert detested etiquette (though he was always quick to resent a breach of manners in others). In several of the operas—most notably in *Iolanthe's* Act 2 argument between Mountararat and Tolloller over Phyllis—he depicts etiquette as a mask by which self-interest is passed off as morality.

    It comes off no better here. Its prime exponent, Rose, is neurotic to the brink of madness—her Act 1 charity is as misguided as Margaret's Act 2 charity, while her convoluted response to Robin's courtship nearly ruins her life. By contrast, the mannerless Margaret is the opera's most charming character.

Structurally, *Ruddigore's* thematic treatment goes a step beyond its predecessors. *Patience* and *Iolanthe* employ double story lines, and *Princess Ida* adds a sketchy third parallel story—the parent-child dynamic of Blanche-Melissa echoes that of Gama-Ida and Hildebrand-Hilarion, but it is purely a subplot, never equaling the other two.

In *Ruddigore*, however, the triple story line is complete. "The case of a maiden about to be wedded to one who unexpectedly turns out to be a baronet with a curse on him" may not be considered in Rose's book of etiquette, but it is the dominant theme of the opera. Rose-Robin,

Margaret-Despard, and Hannah-Roderick are all fully developed story lines, each providing an implicit moral commentary on the others.

As the opera opens, Sir Despard holds the title. His essentially moralistic response to the curse lies in compensation: "I get my crime over the first thing in the morning, and then for the rest of the day I do good."

Despard's glee at apparently outwitting the curse is infectious, and his sense of scale is also amusing—building an orphanage atones for stealing a child, for example, but so pristine is Rose Maybud that her lost virtue demands nothing less than a cathedral.

But Despard knows that his approach isn't really moral, that a crime is still a crime. He is consumed by guilt—"It's the workings of conscience, of course." His Act 2 reformation allows him to speak his mind, and he unhesitatingly condemns his own prior acts: "Think of all the atrocities you have committed," he tells Robin, "by attorney, as it were."

In reality, Despard is simply a hypocrite. His only motive for his crimes is fear: "But what is a poor baronet to do, when a whole picture gallery of ancestors step down from their frames and threaten him with an excruciating death if he hesitate to commit his daily crime?"

His hypocrisy is underlined when, in Act 2, he urges Robin to reform, even at the cost of a horrible death. In the original dialogue, Robin himself points out Despard's hypocrisy: "You didn't seem to be of this opinion when *you* were a bad baronet."

Not that Robin is at this point any less hypocritical. He hasn't personally committed any crimes, but by his own admission he shares responsibility for Despard's. And facing the ghosts' torments, he submits as readily as his brother did. In fact, he sets out on exactly the same crime—carrying off a maiden.

Robin's original response to the curse, of course, was evasion. Gilbert is especially harsh in condemning Robin's flight, which, because it left the curse to fall on Despard, is far worse than Ida's or Nanki-Poo's.

In the original dialogue, Despard's "No, because *I* had no good brother at my elbow to check *me* when about to go wrong" draws from Robin a flat admission of guilt: "A home-thrust indeed!"

Despard renews this reproach in the "Matter Matter Matter" trio—"If I had been so lucky as to have a steady brother . . . my existence would have made a very interesting idyll, / and I might have lived and died a very decent indiwiddle"—but it's hardly necessary.

After all, Robin feels guilty right from his first scene. In contemplating his chances of winning Rose, he says to himself, "I sometimes think that if she wasn't quite so particular I might venture—but no, no—even then I should be unworthy of her!"

In other words, what holds him back is only in part Rose's rigorous standards, which he feels he can't meet. More important is his sense that he is morally unfit for her—which is why Adam's innocent mention of Robin's real name prompts a frenzied torrent of confession that non-pluses even Adam, culminating in the admission: "My younger brother, Despard, believing me to be dead, succeeded to the title and its attendant curse."

The only morally appropriate response to the curse is that advocated by Despard, eventually practiced by Roderick (and indeed all the other ancestors) and ultimately embraced by Robin.

As he says, "Oh, my forefathers, wallowers in blood, there came at last a day when, sick of crime, you, each and every, vowed to sin no more, and so, in agony, called welcome Death to free you from your cloying guiltiness."

Or, as Despard says in the original dialogue, "Oh, better that than pursue a course of life-long villainy. Oh, seek refuge in death, I implore you!"

Robin is initially too weak to face this truth. The ghosts are quite right in calling him "coward, poltroon, shaker, squeamer." Even after being forced to accept his curse, he embarks on what Adam in the original dialogue calls "a series of evasions which, as a blameless character, I must denounce as contemptible." Finally subjected to the agonies, he caves in and agrees: "henceforth all the crimes that I find in the *Times* I promise to perpetrate daily."

The opera doesn't end there, but it easily could: The traditional melodrama format had two possible endings, one of which would call for Robin to meet a horrible end at the hands of the heroic Richard Daunt-less.

But this doesn't happen. Instead, Robin is won over by Despard's moral appeal. "I *will* defy my ancestors," he proclaims. "I *will* refuse to obey their behests, and thus, by courting death, atone in some degree for the infamy of my career!"

In 10 years Despard never reached this point. Both brothers are weak, but at this moment Robin proves himself the stronger of the two.

Thus far, however, the story is still within the confines of classic melodrama. In the second traditional ending, the villain realizes the enormity of his evil (often upon learning that the maiden he abducted is his own daughter or something of that nature) and, overcome with remorse, commits suicide.

Ruddigore takes this one step further. In the original version the ending was not as unexpected and abrupt as it seems now, since Robin several times had spoken of suicide. In either version, though, the resolution is particularly appropriate, in that it reveals the witch's spell to be not a random curse (or an arbitrary plot device) but an explicit test of morality.

Robin's triumph may seem to be legalistic quibbling, a la the Lord Chancellor's in *Iolanthe*, but it is anything but. The key is that Robin isn't really emulating his ancestors: There has not come a day when, "sick of crime," he vows to sin no more. He is driven not by guilt over what he has done but by a moral determination never to sin at all.

It is only appropriate that this choice breaks the curse forever. Imposed to punish the first baronet's lack of principle, the curse is lifted by the first baronet who truly has principle. In a properly Gilbertian paradox, the curse compels evildoers to wallow in evil until their guilt destroys them, but cannot harm a truly good man. To resist the curse is to perpetuate it, but to submit on principle is to break it.

In this respect *Ruddigore* offers a comic variation on *Princess Ida.* Just as the cycle of violence setting Hilarion and Ida against each other can be broken only by each in turn ceasing to resist, so the curse of the Murgatroyds demands a similar victory through submission. The curse cannot be beaten on its own terms, any more than Hilarion or Ida can by force of arms win what they seek.

The message is consistent: True success lies only in doing what is right, at the utmost risk to self-interest and in the face of whatever outside pressure is exerted, societal or otherwise.

It is especially significant that Robin's resolve is stirred by Despard's appeal to him as a brother.

In most Gilbert & Sullivan operas, the characters are tied to one another through a web of social and familial bonds. At most one character—Wells, Bunthorne, or Nanki-Poo—is (at least apparently) outside this web, and it is this character who is the catalyst for the plot.

In *Ruddigore*, quite the opposite is true. Robin is a disguised runaway, "dead and buried" for 20 years; Roderick is literally dead and buried for 10. Richard is a just-returned sailor, "home again after 10 long years at sea." Rose is a foundling, "hung in a plated dishcover to the knocker of the workhouse door, with naught that I could call my own," so hungry for connection that she bonds to an etiquette book as a surrogate mother, "a voice from a parent's tomb." Margaret is a lunatic, "wildly dressed in picturesque tatters." Despard is "the greatest villain unhung," loathed by everyone in the village. Even the male choruses—both the bucks and blades and the ghosts, are outsiders.

In particular, the opera lacks family relationships. The parental relationships that so fascinate Gilbert are missing here. There are no family ties beyond the long-estranged Murgatroyd clan—even the foster-brothers Robin and Richard have not seen each other in a decade. (Hannah is presumably the foundling Rose's foster-aunt.) *Ruddigore* also opens without the usual existing engagement—in fact, it opens with a chorus bemoaning the lack of engagements.

In all the Savoy operas, *Ruddigore's* world is the most fragmented. It is no wonder that the characters are so eager to establish connections, especially family connections. Not only does Despard "claim young Robin as my elder brother," but Margaret implores Rose "You pity me? Then be my mother!" Robin welcomes his foster-brother home and meets his long-dead uncle and other ancestors. Despard and Margaret marry between acts and embrace domesticity. And Rose ricochets from engagement to engagement.

But these attempted connections go sour, and the root cause is irresponsibility, even immorality. The foster-brothers Robin and Richard are quickly rivals for Rose, while Despard welcomes Robin not as a brother but as a means to "transfer to his shoulders the hideous thralldom under which I have labored for so many years." Reunited with Robin in Act 2, Despard has nothing for him but reproaches. Robin's uncle tortures him, and despite their marriage Margaret is as mad as ever and Despard as hypocritical.

By the opera's end, however, Robin's moral responsibility has changed everything. All the Murgatroyds are free (even the dead Roderick) and can marry the women they love. Richard, finding contentment with another pretty woman, can reconcile with Robin. (In the original ending, even the ghostly ancestors are "brought in from the cold" and restored to social integration.)

The only question mark concerns Rose. Either she gives up her etiquette book, or Gilbert has nodded: Her verse in the finale has her leaving Richard to join Robin in obedience to her book's instructions on "when a man has been a naughty baronet"—yet earlier she claims that the book doesn't cover such cases.

Perhaps she is now using the book as an excuse to do what she wants rather than as a reason not to; but the scene can be read either way.

Perhaps the most impressive aspect of *Ruddigore* is its linking of poetic imagery with thematic content—especially through the use of flower imagery.

Gilbert was most likely first pointed in this direction by "To a Garden Full of Posies." He had actually written this poem six years before, for *The Illustrated Sporting and Dramatic News*, yet it doesn't seem at all like an interpolation, since its tone and imagery are so tightly linked to the rest of the opera.[10] Chances are that Gilbert found in it the inspiration for the imagistic motifs that permeate the opera.

The flower imagery is most intriguing not because it is so all-pervasive but because it is so consistent and so keyed to the dramatic situations of the various scenes. In no other Savoy opera is there such unified imagery, not even in the more obvious (and less evocative) prison imagery in *The Yeomen of the Guard*.

Throughout *Ruddigore* flowers are associated with women, and specifically with love and the man-woman relationship. "To a Garden Full of

Posies" embodies Margaret herself as a flower, the violet that grows, wild and isolated, "in a nest of weeds and nettles." The gardener who overlooks the violet's beauty is Despard, who we soon learn has deserted Margaret.

But the song is specific to the scene itself, not merely the general situation. When we meet him moments later, Despard is coming to carry off Rose—a woman named after a flower, of course. To Margaret's "poor mad brain," crazed with jealousy, the woman and the flower become one—and the vision is of roses as prostitutes, "who uprising from their beds / hold on high their shameless heads / with their pretty lips a-pouting."

(This lyric may have suggested to Gilbert his heroine's name; it almost certainly inspired him to have Margaret determined to kill Rose, an idea otherwise irrelevant to the story.)

The imagery of "To a Garden Full of Posies" was again associated with the Despard-Margaret relationship in Gilbert's staging for Despard's first song, "Oh, Why Am I Moody and Sad." Gilbert's original promptbook direction reads: "Sir Despard offers flower to ladies right. They shrink from him as he does so—he stamps—they scream and exit. He does the same business with ladies left and again to ladies up stage right centre. He then stamps upon the flower and strikes attitude of disgust."[11] (see fig. 12.2).

This bit of staging is especially resonant and argues strongly that Gilbert's use of flower imagery throughout the opera is anything but accidental. The flower is here used as a symbol of love, giving a sexual tone to both Despard's offer and the women's aversion. His final destruction of the flower not only expresses his frustration but also recalls "To a Garden Full of Posies" and, perhaps, foreshadows his intention to carry off Rose.

Flower imagery also encapsulates the Hannah-Roderick relationship in "There Grew a Little Flower." Here the woman is once again the flower—but this time, the man is a sheltering oak that all too soon proves untrustworthy. (Gilbert had used the image before, in *Princess Ida:* "I leant upon an oak, / but in the hour of need, / alackaday, / my trusted stay / was but a bruised reed.")

The tone of "There Grew a Little Flower" is far less hostile than "To a Garden Full of Posies"—Hannah's memory is bittersweet, even forgiving, whereas Margaret's is furious and despairing. But the songs are sisters, twin tales of a woman as a flower, betrayed by man.

The third of the opera's parallel story lines, the Robin-Rose relationship, is linked with flower imagery in the Act 1 finale, where it gains particular resonance through association with seasonal imagery.

Appropriately—since Rose is a happier character than Margaret or Hannah—the flower imagery of the wedding song "When the Buds Are Blossoming" is brighter, showing a world in harmony. These are buds, young flowers evocative of springtime and happiness. Robin and Rose are explicitly linked with springtime and hope by their names, with the women's

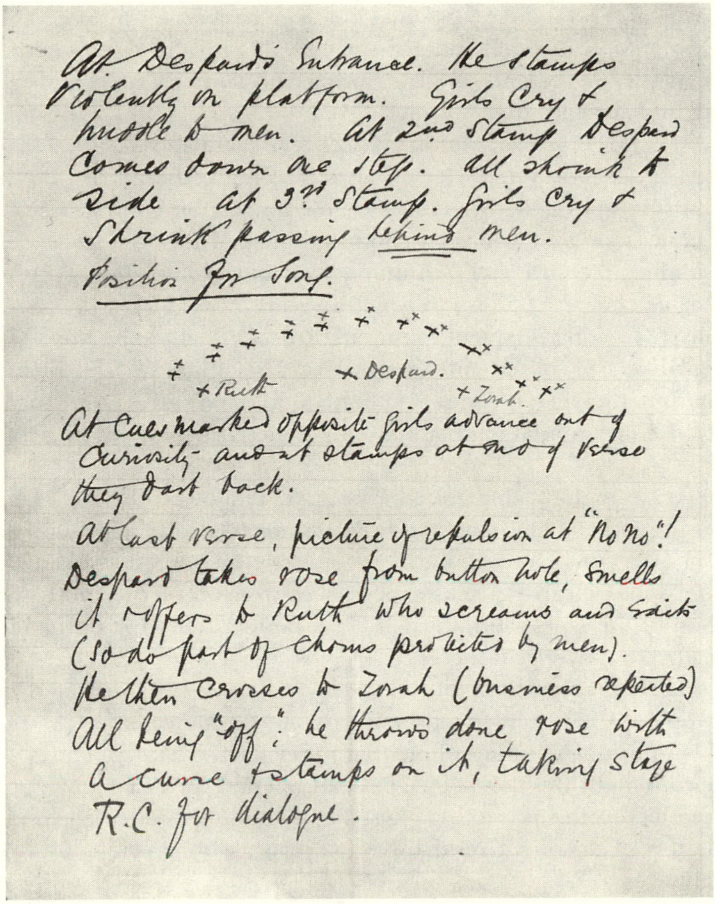

At Despard's Entrance. He stamps
violently on platform. Girls cry &
huddle to men. At 2nd stamp Despard
comes down one step. All shrink to
side. At 3rd stamp. Girls cry &
shrink passing behind men.
Position for Song.

           x x x x x x x x x
      x x x   x x
      x x Ruth   x Despard.   x x
                         x Zorah. x x

At Cues marked opposite girls advance out of
curiosity and at stamps at end of verse
they dart back.
At last verse, picture of repulsion at "No no"!
Despard takes rose from button hole, smells
it offers to Ruth who screams and [exits]
(so do part of chorus protected by men).
He then crosses to Zorah (business repeated)
All being "off": he throws down rose with
a curse & stamps on it, taking stage
R.C. for dialogue.

FIGURE 12.2. A page from Gilbert's prompt book, describing his staging for Despard's initial song. The use of a flower in the staging picks up on imagery previously established in dialogue, lyrics, and even characters' names. *Source: The Pierpont Morgan Library, Gilbert and Sullivan Collection.*

chorus adding effective underscoring as they sing "Spring is green, summer's rose!"

But the audience already knows that this is merely a "false happy ending." Not only do they know Robin's dark secret, but they have seen Richard and Despard plotting to disrupt the wedding. Both Gilbert and Sullivan convey the illusory quality of this brief moment of happiness in remarkably effective ways.

Gilbert's rhyme for "summer's rose" is the unexpectedly shadowy "It is sad when summer goes," followed by the men chiming in with "Autumn's gold—winter's grey." Though the chorus answers reassuringly that

"[W]inter still is far away," the tone has been irrevocably altered. The first verse ends on a distinctly bittersweet tone: "Leaves in autumn fade and fall, / Winter is the end of all. / Spring and summer teem with glee: / Spring and summer then for me!"

The second verse is extraordinary, as Dame Hannah rejects the frivolous naiveté of the first verse. Herself an old woman, she carries the image from springtime seed through autumn's harvest and winter's rest. The song concludes with a massed choral rebuttal of the first verse: "Spring and summer pleasure you, / Autumn, aye, and winter too— / Every season has its cheer, / Life is lovely all the year!"

Sullivan's setting is equally masterful. Rose's initial piping ode to spring is a birdlike trill, blithe and thoughtless. The initial quartet is similarly happy, but the men's choral "Autumn's gold, winter's grey" triggers a troubled contrapuntal chorus that only reluctantly resolves to a final "fa la la."

The verse melody changes to a warmer, mellower line for Hannah's reassuring linkage of spring and winter, life and death. This time the "fa la la" chorus moves from its warm, organ-like close directly into an elegant gavotte whose clean purity is a perfect expression of the unity of ideas resolved in the lyric—and, theatrically, a perfect setup for Despard's dramatically percussive entrance.

The entire sequence is one of the most seamlessly integrated in any Savoy opera. Character, situation, poetry, music, dance, and theatrical effect blend into a stunning whole that never fails to win applause.

Appropriately, the flower imagery that opened the Act 1 finale returns to close it. But this is another "false happy ending," reflected by Gilbert in the use of dissonant resonances that clash with previous uses of the same images.

("Oh, Happy the Lily" is in fact a good example of a basic problem with *Ruddigore:* Imagistically resonant with other numbers, it is sloppily written and features some truly absurd rhymes—"blossom/opossum/come across 'em" is the worst—thrown together to enable the lyricist to follow his imagistic scheme.)

Obviously, Rose and Richard's "Oh, happy the lily / when kissed by the bee, / and sipping tranquilly / quite happy is he" offers another image of woman as flower—this time with the man as a bee, "sipping tranquilly" in apparent peace.

But Rose and Richard are a "wrong" couple, and their lyric recalls a disturbing pair of linked images from Mad Margaret: "Over the ripening peach / buzzes the bee." The word "buzz" recurs shortly thereafter in her dialogue with Rose: "I killed a fly this morning! It buzzed, and I wouldn't have it. So it died—pop! So shall she!" ("She" being Rose herself, of course.)

This evocative imagery is not enough to make "Oh, Happy the Lily" itself sinister but throws it just slightly out of kilter.

The same is true of Despard and Margaret's "Oh, happy the flowers / that blossom in June, / and happy the bowers / that gain by the boon." In any other context, the "June/boon" rhyme would be commonplace, even banal. But with the preceding "When the Buds Are Blossoming" hinting at the impermanence of the flowers that bloom in the spring, it too has its dark side. "When the Buds," after all, was interrupted by the entrance of the bad baronet—just as is "Oh, Happy the Lily" after the next verse.

The second act replaces flower imagery with saturating images of death and darkness. This picks up on imagery introduced in Act 1, of course: Dame Hannah offers a grisly picture of the deaths first of the witch and then of each succeeding Murgatroyd in "Sir Rupert Murgatroyd." Robin and Rose each sing of dying from unrequited love, and Robin describes his exile as being "dead and buried." Margaret's dialogue is filled with allusions to death, from the murder of Rose to the singular death of an affidavit!

As the opera comes to its conclusion, the flower imagery returns. "There Grew a Little Flower" reintroduces it strongly, and then the finale returns to "Oh, Happy the Lily." This time, however, the imagery is less sinister. The couples are the "right" ones, and four solo verses resolve all the outstanding conflicts. Furthermore, this version of "Happy the Lily" is not a duet for mismatched lovers but a unified ensemble, and Sullivan replaces the fragmented canon of Act 1 with a strong unison finale and a concluding dance.

In terms of imagistic expressiveness, *Ruddigore* is Gilbert at his best. The lyrics themselves are frequently flawed, however. Increasingly Gilbert tends to follow his original idea as closely as possible, even if it requires forcing rhymes.

In the earlier operas, he had continually reworked his lyrics so that they captured his meaning while being smoothly natural in rhythm and rhyme. In those operas, he probably wouldn't have resorted to feeble rhymes such as "idyll/indiwiddle" or "blossom/opossum/across 'em"; such rhymes may be mildly "clever" (though only mildly, as they rely on mispronunciation), but they twist the passage beyond any substantive meaning.

On the whole, while Gilbert produces some excellent lyrics in *Ruddigore*—"When the Buds Are Blossoming," "I Shipped, D'Ye See," and "I Once Was a Very Abandoned Person" are among his best—it is not one of his better operas as a lyricist.

In particular, he fails to make his usual strong use of the chorus. The Bridesmaids start out amusingly but by the time they sing "From the Briny Sea" have lost their distinctiveness. "Welcome, Gentry" works only because of Sullivan's musical efforts—its lyrics are downright silly. The act 1 finale begins well but quickly fragments: There's no real point to the "Tara-diddles" sequence, and Rose's "Farewell! Thou Hadst My Heart" lacks the humor previously associated with the character. Only Richard's mock-heroic "Within This Breast" really scores.

On the other hand, the dialogue is Gilbert at a peak, in large part accounting for the number of vivid characters in the opera. Even comparatively minor figures such as the heroically selfish Richard Dauntless and the absurdly honest Old Adam emerge in their dialogue as original, highly comic characters in their own rights.

But the opera's two best dialogues are the Act 1 scene between Margaret and Rose and the Act 2 sequence involving Despard, Margaret, and Robin. For different reasons, they are arguably the best in the entire Savoy canon.

The Despard-Margaret-Robin scene shows Gilbert's continued mastery of character-oriented dialogue. There is a key narrative goal to the scene (motivating Robin's change of heart), but Gilbert is in no hurry to get there. Instead he takes the time to enjoy his characters and their interaction.

The structure of the Despard-Margaret sequence is a familiar one, dating back as far as *H. M. S. Pinafore's* Ralph/Captain costume change. In particular, it's the same joke as with *Patience's* Dragoons-as-aesthetes: Characters from Act 1 reappear for the first time in Act 2, dressed radically differently—as the *Ruddigore* stage direction says, "They . . . present a strong contrast to their appearance in Act I." The initial laugh comes from sheer incongruity—and in both cases, Sullivan cannily provides a long instrumental introduction to wait out the laughter. Subsequently the humor arises from the characters' difficulties in coping with their new roles.

But for two reasons, the *Ruddigore* scene is more effective than its *Patience* counterpart. First, it is longer and more thoroughly developed. All we learn about the dragoon-aesthetes is that they can't do the walk very well. The reformed Despard and Margaret interact at length, discussing a variety of subjects and displaying more of the comic implications of their change of roles. We learn more about what it means for Margaret to be a district visitor than about what it means for the Duke to be an aesthete.

The scene also has a different comic structure. In *Patience* the Duke, the Major, and the Colonel say and do roughly the same things, whereas in *Ruddigore* Despard serves as a stuffy straight man to Margaret's excesses. Despard's more successful change—albeit a lesser one, from a pompously evil hypocrite to a pompously saintly hypocrite—shows what Margaret ought to be, making her failings all the funnier by contrast.

But the "Abandoned Person" scene wouldn't work if we didn't already know Margaret so well. That knowledge comes entirely from the Rose-Margaret dialogue (and its preceding song). This dialogue is every bit as good as the "Abandoned Person" scene, but instead of maximizing ideas from earlier operas it breaks entirely new ground.

Mad Margaret is so striking that it's easy to overlook how minor a character she is. Prior to Act 2, she appears only for a single song and dialogue, plus a cameo in the Act I finale. Even Dame Hannah and Zorah have been given more to do.

But of course quality isn't quantity, and Margaret's lone Act 1 scene leaves an indelible impression. She is one of Gilbert's most vivid characters, and it's her dialogue with Rose that makes her so. Touching though it is, "To a Garden Full of Posies" isn't enough to make the character memorable—it establishes her pathos, to be sure, but the role could easily cloy or become indeed "an obvious caricature."

Gilbert's dialogues are almost always "goal oriented," built around the need to establish some plot development and, of course, to introduce a song. Even in *The Mikado,* so highly character-oriented, plot is crucial—if any dialogue scene were to be omitted, something important would be missing from the story.

The Rose-Margaret dialogue, on the other hand, is not at all goal-oriented. It introduces no song—extraordinary for a Gilbert & Sullivan dialogue—and conveys no plot point, nor is it ever directly referred to again. If it had been cut, no one would notice its absence. Yet it remains in the show, a striking divergence from Gilbert's usual practice.

Obviously, its point is to develop Margaret—Rose has virtually nothing to do in the scene. But even Margaret herself is incidental to the plot—other than to provide a wife for Despard at the end, she has no substantive role. Yet were she eliminated, the play would be much poorer for it.

Given a nonessential scene to develop this nonessential character, Rose is the perfect foil. She is in nearly every way Margaret's antithesis—Rose the maiden so beautiful that "[e]very young man in the village is in love with her," Margaret the outcast lunatic who shuns society so thoroughly that Rose has never even met her.

Their priorities are equally different. As "If Somebody There Chanced to Be" reveals, Rose is puritanically secretive about her love for Robin; Margaret volunteers her love for Despard to a total stranger. Rose is a paragon of manners and morals; Margaret is utterly unmannered and so amoral that she can say, "Did you ever kill anybody? No? Why not?"

Finally, Rose is virtually blind, wearing her etiquette book like a pair of blinkers so thick that she doesn't even realize from "I Know a Youth" that Robin loves her. But Margaret, in her madness, sees and hears everything. Rose's extravagantly ornate language is obvious to the audience, but within the play only Margaret challenges Rose's "Mercy, whom?" Everyone in the opera sings choruses in public, but only Margaret finds it eccentric.

Margaret is so mad she's almost sane, while Rose is so sane she's almost mad. Both women engage in charitable works—Rose taking her absurdly mismatched donations to the villagers and offering her rotten apple in Act 1, Margaret visiting the sick in Act 2—and both are pathetically bad at it. Even the morally upright Hannah finds Rose's etiquette obsession excessive. In short, the two characters are both wildly disparate and surprisingly similar.

It's no surprise that Margaret's first question to Rose is "Tell me, are you mad?" (Rose's denial is so vehement that she feels obliged to decorously add, "That is, I think not.")

Neither character sees the irony of the next two lines, but the audience does: Margaret says "Then you don't love Sir Despard Murgatroyd? All mad girls love him. *I* love him," to which Rose responds, "Thou lovest the bad Baronet of Ruddigore? Oh, horrible—too horrible!" But of course it is Rose who loves the actual bad baronet.

The connections between the two continue in Margaret's apparently pointless wanderings. As Polonius says in *Hamlet,* "Though this be madness, yet there is method in't." *(Ruddigore* contains several *Hamlet* allusions, including Margaret herself, whose madness and obsession with flowers suggest Ophelia.)

Margaret's "You pity me? Then be my mother" and the story of the runaway squirrel with the alcoholic mother may well apply most strongly to Margaret, but both women are alike (so far as we know, anyway) in not having mothers.

The significance of "The cat and the dog and the little puppee / sat down in a . . ." remains obscure, since its source (if any) has never been identified. Perhaps Gilbert is simply having Margaret spout nonsense, but the rest of her dialogue has an offbeat coherence. I suspect that if a source song could be found, and in particular if the broken line could be completed, it would be extremely relevant.

After the entertaining, highly characteristic divergence into a grammar lesson, the scene comes to a head as Margaret announces her intention to kill Rose. There is nothing to suggest either that Margaret's threats are not serious or that she is incapable of carrying them out. Rose takes the threat seriously, and the frenzy of Margaret's ensuing speech seems anything but tongue-in-cheek:

> Aye! I love him—he loved me once. But that's all gone, fisht! He gave me an Italian glance—thus—and made me his. He will give *her* an Italian glance, and make *her* his. But it shall not be, for I'll stamp on her—stamp on her—stamp on her! Did you ever kill anybody? No? Why not? Listen—I killed a fly this morning! It buzzed, and I wouldn't have it. So it died—pop! So shall she!

It's a remarkable speech, disjointedly but tersely recounting her seduction and abandonment by Despard (an "Italian glance" is presumably a leer), and her jealousy and rage come through clearly. Rose's alarm is entirely justified. (The speech also establishes the idea of stamping on flowers, setting up Gilbert's stage business for Despard after "Oh, Why Am I Moody and Sad?")

The same rage is apparent in Margaret's next speech. Like "The cat and the dog," "I would treat you as the auctioneer and the land-agent treated the ladybird—I would rend you asunder!" is obscure. It's apparently an elaborate pun: A land-agent "rents," and "asunder" is close to "a sundry," sundries being the miscellany auctioned after the major lots have been put up; but how this connects to a ladybird, which Americans would call a ladybug, is unclear.

One acquaintance of mine [12] related it to the old rhyme "Ladybird, ladybird, fly away home, / your house is on fire, your children all burned,"[2] but I don't find this persuasive—tempting though it is to find more negligent-mother imagery in the scene. In any event, the speech's real point is Margaret's convincing threat to dismember Rose if she trifles with Despard.

Finally the scene ends on the delightfully fourth-wall–breaking "They are all mad—quite mad! . . . They sing choruses in public. That's mad enough, I think."

It's a remarkable dialogue, and the only instance of a Gilbert & Sullivan dialogue that often garners applause at its end. If in some respects *Ruddigore* shows Gilbert beginning to lose his touch, in others it shows him in top form.

Before leaving the subject of Gilbert's work on *Ruddigore*, it's worth noting that, with the possible exception of *Iolanthe*, *Ruddigore* is the most flamboyantly theatrical of the operas. It offers a splendid case study of the confluence of Gilbert's authorial and directorial visions.

Gilbert's directorial methods were fine-tuned over the course of approximately 40 plays, operas, and burlesques, and were much admired. But because he never saw his mature work directed by anyone else, he never saw his writing as a text separate from its performance; and because he never directed another author's play, he never developed a sense of directing as an interpretive, text-based art form.

Thus, while Gilbert's realism, high standards, and attention to detail were justly praised, he wasn't a director as we use the term today, but more of a three-dimensional writer. Critics praised his remarkable fusion of word and action, but to Gilbert these were two different aspects of the same thing.

His style had its advantages. As director, he had a perfect sense of his author's intentions. And because he directed his own plays, he always wrote them for the stage, not the page. In an age when the densely poetic plays of such "serious" authors as Tennyson were almost unstageable, even Gilbert's most serious works displayed a constant awareness of theatrical effect and pacing.

As a working artist, he also had a strong visual sense of the stage and an abiding interest in scenery, costumes, and choreography. It was this visual sense that inspired his innovative use of electric lights in the *Iolanthe* fairy costumes, for example, or the repainting of the scenery when *Patience* was shifted from the gaslit Opera Comique to the electrified Savoy. This unified theatrical sense was virtually unique among his peers and won Gilbert much critical acclaim.

Conversely, his staging skills could lead him astray. Particularly in the later operas, he sometimes used his directorial skills to let spectacle compensate for weak writing, as for example in the Drawing-Room scene in *Utopia, Limited*.

Ruddigore shows the good side of the linkage between Gilbert the writer and Gilbert the director, especially in the living-portrait sequence that is the opera's theatrical high point.

It is widely known that the idea was lifted from Gilbert's 1869 opera *Ages Ago,* written with Frederick Clay. But, as Frank Moore points out, the scene must have been far more effective at the electric-lit Savoy than it had been at the gaslit Royal Gallery of Illustration.[13] Gas lighting couldn't be extinguished, because each lamp would have had to be manually relit. Thus Victorian audiences were traditionally fully lit, which boosted the sale of Gilbert's libretti but reduced the theatrical illusion.

The *Ruddigore* ghost scene reflects Gilbert's canny sense of the theatrical possibilities of electric lighting—indeed, it may have been inspired by the knowledge that he finally had the technology to do it right. Even given the initial malfunction of some of the portrait equipment, the innovative use of absolute darkness (and Sullivan's illuminated baton) were praised by several critics.

Margaret's initial soliloquy scene is another shrewd innovation by Gilbert. It is neither the first nor the longest solo sequence in the operas, and in fact bears a strong structural resemblance to Bunthorne's "Am I Alone and Unobserved?" But the earlier solo scenes were either comic turns or traditional ballad-opera solos, with little innate theatricality. In fact, they were almost antitheatrical, opportunities for the performer to shine without distractions of plot or character.

Margaret's scene is entirely different and dauntingly complex. Its extended instrumental passages demand dance elements; its long recitative is all the more difficult for having the shortest lines Gilbert ever wrote, the one-metric-foot "no crime / tis only / that I'm / love-lonely"; and, finally, the song, while compellingly beautiful, is so static as to almost defy effective performance.

These hurdles add up to a classic acting challenge for the performer. This is no virtuoso showpiece: Gilbert keeps Margaret rigorously in character and trusts his actress to put over a scene that, for all its choreographic and musical demands, is most of all an acting ordeal, with moods and ideas changing with quicksilver rapidity.

Badly done, it collapses; well done, it is incandescent. Jessie Bond, who had begun her career as Hebe in *H. M. S. Pinafore,* had made a name for herself as Pitti-Sing; Mad Margaret made her a star.

Whatever else may be said about *Ruddigore,* it remains an exciting show to perform or to see. With generous amounts of dance, challenging special effects, and plenty of room for flamboyant performances, it is the most exuberantly theatrical of the operas.

As for Sullivan's score, "inconsistent" again is the byword. His music is never less than charming, but it lacks the cohesiveness displayed by *Iolanthe* or *Princess Ida,* particularly in Act 1. It isn't until Act 2 that Sullivan finds his top form.

For the ghost music—and such related numbers as "Sir Rupert Murgatroyd," "Oh, Why Am I Moody and Sad?" and "I Once Was As Meek as a Newborn Lamb"—Sullivan clearly exerts himself. These stylistically similar numbers use powerful brass lines as the foundation for skittering strings and woodwind special effects; the vocal lines have a rising and falling quality that suggests laborious stairways into and out of deep dungeons (most notably in the opening of "Moody and Sad" and the end of "Newborn Lamb"). They have an epic sweep—many critics remarked on the operatic feel of these parts of the show.

In the rest of the music, however, Sullivan seems less interested. Most of Act 1 is reminiscent of *H. M. S. Pinafore* or especially *Patience,* aiming more for general ambiance than for specific situations or characters.

The composer makes good use of traditional song forms, from the country waltz of "If Somebody There Chanced to Be" through the ballad style of "I Know a Youth" and "There Grew a Little Flower" and the hornpipe of "I Shipped, D'Ye See" to the madrigal "When the Buds Are Blossoming" and its gavotte.

But few of these numbers are either musically distinguished or particularly original. "If Somebody" suggests the waltz tunes from *Patience,* while "I Know a Youth" is enough like *Patience's* "Prithee, Pretty Maiden" to have been remarked on even at the time. The musical flourish of the combined chorus "Welcome Gentry"/"When Thoroughly Tired of Being Admired" is diminished by its being a virtual clone of *Patience's* "In a Doleful Train" / "Now Is Not This Ridiculous?"

In fact, most of Act 1 can be classified as pretty but banal. "Hail the Bridegroom" is not a linking motif, like "Ah, misery" in *Patience* or the "Iolanthe" theme, but simply a running gag. "My Boy, You May Take It from Me" and "Henceforth All the Crimes" are routine patter songs. "In Sailing o'er Life's Ocean Wide" is the type of verse trio for which Sullivan might previously have varied each verse's tune for greater character specificity. Here, he simply repeats it, as he also does with "Happily Coupled Are We." "The Battle's Roar Is Over" and "In Bygone Days" are routine bits of operatic convention that Sullivan handles dutifully rather than imaginatively.

In all these numbers, one senses a composer distracted—as indeed Sullivan was. During the months preceding *Ruddigore's* premiere (on January 22, 1887), Sullivan was hard at work on his most ambitious oratorio, *The Golden Legend,* which had its premiere on October 16, 1886. This massive work, generally considered his best choral composition, had occupied him for months, and listening to Act 1 of *Ruddigore* it is easy to imagine Sullivan's thoughts being elsewhere.

But one can almost feel his eyes light up (like his baton) as the curtain rises on Castle Ruddigore. Suddenly his orchestrations get more intricate, his melodic lines more commanding, and his theatrical sense surer. Throughout Act 2, excepting only the banal "Happily Coupled" sequence and the hastily written "Henceforth All the Crimes," Sullivan's music takes

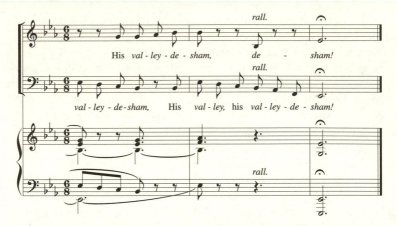

12.1a. At the end of the gloating "I Once Was as Meek as a Newborn Lamb," Sullivan gives Old Adam—now Gideon Crawle—a descending E♭ scale he will later use to end the introduction to Sir Despard's "I Once Was a Very Abandoned Person," wittily implying that Despard's reformation isn't as complete as it seems.

on a whole new life. The gloomy castle seems to inspire him as much as the fishing village left him indifferent.

It isn't only the ghost music. The rest of the act is just as imaginatively composed, even when the emotions are not as operatic and the situation not as innately dramatic. The priggish strut of the introduction to "I Once Was a Very Abandoned Person," for example, restrained but pompous, captures perfectly the Victorian hypocrisy of Despard's new lifestyle.

Sullivan even uses a touch of leitmotif: The introduction for the allegedly reformed baronet ends with a slyly syncopated version of the same seven-note E flat–F bass scale that Old Adam sings as "his valet, his valet de chambre" at the end of "I Once Was as Meek as a Newborn Lamb"—a scale that previously was heard in inverted form (with the same syncopation) in Despard's "Oh, Why Am I Moody and Sad?" as "Observe the unpleasant result" (ex. 12.1a, b). Perhaps this is the composer's way of implying that, under his new clothes, Despard remains the same man.

Or again, contrast the "Matter Matter Matter" trio with "My Boy, You May Take It from Me." Both lyrics are reasonably conventional patter—the Act 2 lyric is, except for its ending, more appropriate to the characters and the situation, but neither is especially musically evocative. A banal setting, with just enough music to avoid getting in the way of the words, would have worked reasonably well in both cases, and indeed this is Sullivan's approach in "My Boy."

For "Matter Matter Matter," however, he proves that, properly motivated, he can still mine musical riches from the patter genre. Gilbert ends

12.1b. "I Once Was a Very Abandoned Person" (intro)

each verse with a single "No, it really doesn't matter" from each singer and then a unison conclusion. Sullivan elaborates this simple concept into a classic of the patter genre, doubling the chorus responses, continuing the "matters" straight on into the next verse, and then building the entire song to a deliriously manic coda.

If "My Boy, You May Take It from Me" is Sullivan as the glorified barrel organ he sometimes felt that Gilbert and Carte considered him, "Matter Matter Matter" is Sullivan as a peerlessly inventive composer at the height of his powers.

The biggest overall problem with *Ruddigore* is not that composer and author are inconsistent, but that they are inconsistently inconsistent. Gilbert does his best work in the first act, with its painstakingly developed flower imagery, clever dialogues, and strongly humorous scenes; in Act 2, even he seems a bit unsure how funny and how serious he means to be. Sullivan, on the other hand, marks time for much of Act 1, before pulling out all the stops for Act 2.

The result is an opera whose dialogue and humor are strongest in Act 1, while its music peaks in Act 2. Instead of one strong act and one weaker one, *Ruddigore* offers many scenes in which one man is doing excellent work, the other somewhat less. There are fewer sequences in which both men are at their best and in full communication.

This lack of communication extends to the basic nature of what they were doing. For Gilbert, the ghost scene was a comic episode, theatrically effective but hardly central—the heart of the opera was "When the Buds Are Blossoming." For Sullivan, on the other hand, the madrigal was a nice musical opportunity but the ghost scene was the defining moment of the opera.

It was inevitable that Gilbert would reproach Sullivan for making too much out of too little, and that Sullivan would feel that Gilbert had made too little out of too much. In retrospect, they should have expected this lack of communication after their disagreements over what was to follow *Princess Ida.* Similar problems had arisen after *The Mikado,* with Gilbert continuing to advocate his "lozenge plot," which Sullivan flatly rejected.

The tremendous success of *The Mikado* had obscured these problems of conceptualization, but the relative failure of *Ruddigore* brought both men back to earth. As popular as *The Mikado* had been, in 1887 the unavoidable fact was that they were increasingly divided over subject matter and that two of their past three shows had been commercial disappointments.

Both might have been expected to resolve that on their next opera they must be in full agreement, and such was indeed the case. After the miscommunications of *Ruddigore, The Yeomen of the Guard* was to be their closest collaboration, and one of their most successful.

Facing page: FIGURE 13.1. George Grossmith as Jack Point in *The Yeomen of the Guard.* The controversy over the character's final collapse has distracted attention from the overall picture of one of Gilbert's most believable—and least likable—characters. *Source: The Pierpont Morgan Library, Gilbert and Sullivan Collection.*

13

The Yeomen of the Guard

From the beginning, *The Yeomen of the Guard* has struck people as unique in the Gilbert & Sullivan canon.

"Their only serious work," one says. "The closest they ever came to grand opera," says another. The London *Daily Telegraph* review said, in part: "The music follows the book to a higher plane, and we have a genuine English opera, forerunner of many others, let us hope, and possibly significant of an advance towards a national lyric stage."[1]

Sullivan himself felt it was something different. When the indefatigable Gilbert appeared on his doorstep on Christmas morning of 1887, the composer showed no signs of feeling imposed on. Indeed, he wrote in his diary: "Gilbert read plot of new piece (Tower of London); immensely pleased with it. Pretty story, no topsy-turvydom, very human and funny also."[2]

It's easy to list the innovations of *The Yeomen of the Guard*, from its opening solo to its much-discussed "tragic" ending. Still, in retrospect, people ought to have seen it coming. Except for the atypical *The Mikado*, the Savoy operas had been growing progressively more serious for years. *Patience* had introduced thematic comedy, while *Iolanthe* brought a more romantic tone. *Princess Ida* was tougher and harder edged, with an ending nearly as ambivalent as that of *The Yeomen of the Guard*.

Most recently, the relative failure of *Ruddigore* had been laid specifically to its seriousness. After being attacked for a work that was half-comic, half-opera, Gilbert & Sullivan responded by letting *The Yeomen of the Guard*'s operatic side clearly dominate.

There had been serious moments in all of the operas since *Trial by Jury*. In fact, part of the collaborators' genius was their willingness to combine broad comedy with serious drama, not by inserting comic relief into a serious story but by making the same characters function both comically and dramatically. *The Yeomen of the Guard* was different only in degree, not in kind. Nothing in it is any more sincere or moving than *Iolanthe*'s "He Loves"; *The Yeomen of the Guard* merely sustains that dramatic intensity through more of the opera. In fact, what's most striking is not how different *The Yeomen of the Guard* is from its predecessors but how little it resembles its successors. Less an innovation than a culmination, *The Yeomen of the Guard* represents the high-water mark for the collaboration's long-rising tide of seriousness. Their final three operas would be far lighter, in both tone and substance.

The Yeomen of the Guard is not a new beginning but an end.

Much has been made of the opera's virtually plagiarized plot, which is notably similar to Vincent Wallace's *Maritana* (1845), in which a condemned knight marries a veiled gypsy dancer. Subsequently he escapes and, returning disguised as a friar, falls in love with a woman whom he does not realize to be his own unknown wife.

However, English theatrical tradition has not particularly prized original plots. Shakespeare's plays drew liberally on other sources, including contemporary hits by other authors, and the tradition continued nearly to the present day. (For example, when Noel Gay's 1930s musical *Me and My Girl* featured a gallery of paintings coming to life to haunt their descendent, critics noted its genesis in *Ruddigore* but made the show a hit anyway.)

Other than a savage attack in *Punch* (which had long pilloried Gilbert, a former writer for the rival *Fun*), critics didn't particularly assail Gilbert's borrowings from *Maritana* (itself an adaptation of a French play). "So obvious, indeed, is the resemblance that one would be inclined to suspect some subtle attempt at parody," said a generally favorable *Times*, "did not the serious tone of Mr. Gilbert's work preclude any such thought."[3]

Whatever *Maritana*'s influence, *The Yeomen of the Guard* is very much a Gilbert & Sullivan opera. In fact, thematically it is a tragic reworking of *Patience*, itself thematically an adaptation of *The Sorcerer*. *Patience* could easily have been a *Yeomen*-style tragedy. If Bunthorne were a more sympathetic figure, genuinely in love with Patience, his final plight would be identical to Point's. Conversely, if Point were more arrogant and dislikable, he wouldn't seem tragic at all—merely a Bunthorne-like poseur getting his just deserts.

Point even resembles *The Sorcerer*'s John Wellington Wells, like the jester a good man with a sales pitch and also the only other Gilbert & Sullivan character to apparently die. Both characters were originated by George Grossmith, as was Bunthorne, and both apparent deaths generally disappoint audiences who would rather see the arrogant tenor die instead.

Gilbert is on record as having had *The Sorcerer* in mind when he began writing *Patience*, and the same is true of *The Yeomen of the Guard*. After seeing an advertising poster of a Beefeater guard, he later explained:

> I thought the Beefeater would make a good picturesque central figure for another Savoy opera, and my intention was to give it a modern setting, with the characteristics and development of burlesque—to make it another *Sorcerer*. But then I decided to make it a romantic and dramatic piece, and to put it back into Elizabethan times.[4]

(Ultimately, he chose to set it in the reign of Henry VIII.)

The Yeomen of the Guard's schematic structure is in fact identical to that of *Patience*—two interlocked triangles: In *The Yeomen of the Guard*, Point loves Elsie who loves Fairfax, while Shadbolt loves Phoebe who loves Fairfax; in *Patience*, Bunthorne loves Patience who loves Grosvenor, while the Dragoons love the Ladies who love Grosvenor (figure 13.2).

(There are no similar interlocked-triangle schema in the operas. A single triangle is standard, but while Ralph and Sir Joseph woo Josephine in

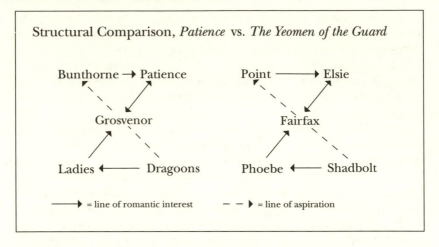

FIGURE 13.2

H. M. S. Pinafore or Robin and Richard woo Rose in *Ruddigore*, those women have no rivals, so the triangles remain single.)

Obviously, the plot resolution is the same in both operas: Elsie-Fairfax and Patience-Grosvenor pair off; so do Shadbolt with the disappointed Phoebe and the Dragoons with the disappointed Ladies. Bunthorne and Point are left alone.

The brilliance of Gilbert's handling of this structure lies in the way he links the outside legs to close the triangles. Shadbolt and the Dragoons aspire to be Point and Bunthorne: Shadbolt asks Point to teach him to be a jester, while the Dragoons try to become aesthetic poets by dressing like Bunthorne. In *The Yeomen of the Guard*, the two legs are also joined when Point and Shadbolt conspire to fake the death of their mutual rival, Fairfax.

The parallels between the two triangles are heightened by Gilbert's meticulous linking of Elsie and Phoebe. Both start out single, with less-than-welcome suitors; soon Phoebe is trading kisses with Fairfax and Elsie is married to him; finally, they become engaged to marry in consecutive scenes and join Dame Carruthers (who has her own parallels with Phoebe) for an ironic trio about the mixture of joy and bitterness.

And, of course, each explains her love in exactly the same way:

Phoebe: Well, [Leonard's] a brave fellow indeed, and I love all brave men.

Fairfax: Dost thou love me, or has thou been insensible these two days?
Elsie: I love all brave men.

In short, *The Yeomen of the Guard* is not only the culmination of Gilbert & Sullivan's arc toward seriousness but also Gilbert's most sustained and effective use of his long-established multiple-story-lines technique.

Ruddigore had added a third story to the usual double format; in *The Yeomen of the Guard* Gilbert not only retains the triple structure (Carruthers and Sergeant Meryll supplying the third strand) but also binds the two primary story lines so strongly that thematically they are all but identical. In *Patience,* the parallels along the various triangles had remained sketchy. In *The Yeomen of the Guard,* each story line further develops the same theme, its impact growing each time.

Most impressive, however, is the opera's imaginative use of songs that present "could-be" parallel plots to comment on the actual course of events, either prophetically or ironically. Often, because they apply equally to either triangle, these songs are prophetic and ironic simultaneously.

The most obvious of these is "The Merryman and His Maid," the Point-Elsie song that also serves as the opera's subtitle and its finale.

On a simple level, the song is initially prophetic, foretelling the love triangle to come (Point as the Merryman, Elsie as the Merrymaid, and Fairfax as the Noble Lord), and ultimately ironic, because its fourth-verse happy ending never comes to pass.

Yet the song actually applies more closely to the Shadbolt-Phoebe-Fairfax triangle. The song's merrymaid laughs the merryman's suit to scorn, pursues her lord, is rejected by him, and ends up marrying the merryman. Elsie never literally laughs off Point's suit, nor does Fairfax ever spurn her—but the story applies perfectly to Phoebe, her noble lord Fairfax, and her would-be-merryman suitor Shadbolt. That the song works so well in both prophetic and ironic terms is particularly ingenious.

But "The Merryman and His Maid" is only one of many such songs in *Yeomen.* For example, Point's "A Private Buffoon Is a Lighthearted Loon" offers, in its final verse, "though your wife ran away / with a soldier that day" and "it's a comfort to feel, / though your partner may flit." Point isn't consciously ironic—at this point, he doesn't know of Elsie's burgeoning romance with "Leonard"—but in retrospect the irony is unmistakable.

Similarly, Phoebe means "When Maiden Loves" purely as an expression of mood. But its "an idle breath / yet life and death / may hang upon a maid's 'heigho!'" foretells both her rescue of Fairfax out of love for him and Point's death over Elsie's rejection. Nor is her "Were I Thy Bride" anything more than a stratagem to distract Wilfred, but in retrospect it is overwhelmingly ironic.

"A Man Who Would Woo a Fair Maid" is doubly ironic. Not only do Point and Phoebe cooperate in their own undoing, but the entire concept of the song is misguided: Wooing gets Point and Shadbolt nowhere, while Fairfax has already won the love of both women without really trying.

Even "Didst Thou Not, O Leonard Meryll" has a powerful irony: Fairfax is forced to accept praise not due him, yet without realizing it the chorus describes not only Leonard's heroism but also Fairfax's less-than-noble escape—an irony that does not escape the witty Fairfax, who ruefully exclaims, "Truly I was to be pitied, / having but an hour to live, / I reluctantly submitted, / I had no alternative!"

Gilbert's ironic intent is clearer in verses cut from the show just before opening:[5]

Third Yeoman: You, when brought to execution
            like a demigod of yore,
         with heroic resolution
            snatched a sword and killed a score! . . .

Fourth Yeoman: Then escaping from the foemen,
            boltered with the blood you shed,
         you, defiant, fearing no men,
            saved your honor and your head! . . .

Fairfax: True, my course with judgment shaping,
            favored, too, by lucky star,
         I succeeded in escaping
            prison bolt and prison bar!

The crowning irony lies in "Strange Adventure," the lovely but unsettling quartet that ends "though the altar be a tomb—Tower, Tower, Tower tomb." The singers think they're merely describing the plot to this point (Elsie is the "modest maid," Fairfax the "gallant groom," and his the tomb), but they actually foreshadow the opera's end, where the tomb will be Point's.

Not everyone accepts that *The Yeomen of the Guard* is a thoroughgoing tragedy. To some it is merely a bittersweet comedy, a slightly darker-than-usual example of Savoy tomfoolery.

Such readers no doubt have objected to my references to Point's death. Surely no word Gilbert ever wrote has been analyzed so exhaustively as the seventh word in the closing stage direction, "FAIRFAX embraces ELSIE as POINT falls insensible at their feet." Unfortunately, "insensible" can mean either "unconscious" or "dead," and Gilbert doesn't specify which he means.

Two secondary citations are contradictory: Henry Lytton, one of several touring Points, claimed that Grossmith made clear that Point wasn't dead, while Lytton himself originated the "really dead" approach.[6] (Actually, another touring Point had already done so, and it isn't even clear that Grossmith "didn't die"—the reviews are contradictory.)

In any event, in his memoirs Lytton reports asking Gilbert if the "really dead" approach was all right, to which the author replied: "Keep on like that. It is just what I want. Jack Point should die and the end of the opera should be a tragedy."

Perhaps unfairly, Reginald Allen has essentially accused Lytton of making up this quotation.[7] But Gilbert's other recorded comment on the scene, to stage manager J. M. Gordon, seems very much in character: "The fate of Jack Point is in the hands of the audience, who may please themselves whether he lives or dies."[8] (Gordon's memoirs also say that Gilbert wanted Point to be "a *coward,* playing on his own grievances.")

At the very least, Gilbert allowed the scene to be played as a death scene and probably countenanced it either way. He easily could have stamped out the "really dead" approach, as he did most interpretive touches by performers, but didn't.

Equally easily, he could have changed the ambiguous phrase to "falls dead" or "falls in a swoon," particularly once he realized that audiences were finding it ambiguous. Again he didn't, even in the 1897 revival, which suggests that he didn't find the question nearly as compelling as later generations have.

That *The Yeomen of the Guard* is a tragedy is etched all over it, and only those blinded by preconceptions of what constitutes "Gilbert & Sullivan" could seriously disagree. Point's final fate is irrelevant—he has already lost everything, and, as he sings, "jester wishes he was dead."

Sullivan's view is much clearer: He uses the same transition device between the finale's "This is their joy-day unalloyed" to "Oh, thoughtless crew" (the orchestra dropping out from under a bright, cheerful song to strike up a somber one) that he uses to introduce Act 1's "The Prisoner Comes"—a funeral march.

From the beginning of *The Yeomen of the Guard,* its tone is all but unrelentingly grim, its tragic nature clear.

To modern American audiences the Tower of London is simply a picturesque tourist attraction. But to Victorians, especially theatergoers, its connotations were sinister. The Tower's theatrical heritage includes the murder of the young princes in Shakespeare's *Richard III* as well as numerous dramatizations of the executions of three English queens—two of Henry VIII's wives and the nine-day queen Lady Jane Gray—explicitly evoked in "When Our Gallant Norman Foes."

A battlefield might evoke blood and gore, or Newgate Prison executions in general, but the Tower suggested the deaths of innocents, trapped in events beyond their control.

Indeed, helplessness is the opera's dominant mood. The Yeomen themselves are aged, withered soldiers who can no longer fight; the Lieutenant, despite his rank, is helpless to save his friend Fairfax, who himself can do little more than sing "Is Life a Boon?"—a witty justification for surrender.

Elsie and Point appear initially at the mercy of a threatening mob, and both end the opera on notes of surrender—Elsie submitting to her supposedly unloved husband (as Phoebe and Meryll have already been forced to do), and finally Point collapsing in despair.

The Tower is embodied in the main theme from Dame Carruthers' majestic "When Our Gallant Norman Foes," the opera's first major number. This remarkable song emphasizes every horrible aspect of the Tower's history—but particularly its standing mute witness to undeserved deaths, as "the flower of the brave have perished with a constancy unshaken" and "the wicked flame may hiss round the heroes who have fought for conscience and for home." Incidentally, for a song that supposedly rebuts Phoebe's image of the Tower as "like a cruel giant in a fairy-tale, [that] must be fed with blood, and that blood must be the best and bravest in England," Sullivan wittily provides an orchestration built on crashing beats like a giant's footsteps.

The Tower isn't merely a place of death but of agonizing and undeserved death. Carruthers's song sets the stage for the introduction of Colonel Fairfax, generally agreed to have been unjustly condemned but nevertheless scheduled to be beheaded.

Nor is the Tower a grim anomaly in a more cheerful world. It is a world unto itself, with its own ruling class (the Lieutenant and his family), middle class (the Merylls) and surging rabble. It has its elderly, its middle-aged, and its young (the Lieutenant's daughters and, once, Leonard and Phoebe). Moreover, it is an all-but-sealed world: People are born, live, and die there; people from outside come there only to die—the aged Yeomen, prisoners such as Fairfax, and, though he doesn't know it, Jack Point.

Actions outside the Tower have little reality. We have no sense of Bridget Maynard, Sir Clarence Poltwhistle, or King Henry himself, and their actions have little impact on what happens in the hermetic world of the Tower. (If Henry's reprieve never arrived, the ending of the opera would be substantially the same.)

The shadow of the Tower underpins the images of death, torture, and imprisonment that permeate the opera, imagery constantly associated with the idea of love.

If *Patience* is a comedy of love, its romantic imagery based on comic excess, *The Yeomen of the Guard* is a tragedy of love. Its romantic imagery begins in tears ("When maiden loves she sits and sighs"), continues in chains ("bound to an unknown bride for good or ill . . . gyves that no smith can weld, no rust devour"), and culminates in death ("though the altar be a tomb").

Love in *The Yeomen of the Guard* is fundamentally the same as it is in *Patience*—an elemental, irrational force that can be neither understood nor controlled. Fairfax's assertion that wooing is "an art in itself" and "purely a matter of skill" is as laughable as the Dragoons' belief that they can rival the adored Grosvenor by dressing like him. The difference is that Fairfax's drivel is purely a stratagem while the Dragoons believe theirs.

Throughout the operas Gilbert creates characters who, given one absurd element, behave logically, consistently, humanly. As the operas progress the characters become more real, with even their absurd aspects having an element of truth to them: Rose Maybud's etiquette book, for example, is both the comic basis of her character and an exaggerated but comprehensible manifestation of an orphan's desperation for a place in society.

The Yeomen of the Guard takes the logical next step, eliminating even that one absurd trait, leaving characters who are wholly plausible—or, as Sullivan said, "very human."

Thus Fairfax is arrogant but not humorously arrogant, like Grosvenor. Shadbolt is grotesque but not theatrically so, like the Mikado. Elsie is prim but not as absurdly prudish as Rose Maybud. Even the grim Dame Carruthers isn't the caricature that Katisha is for most of *The Mikado.*

These are recognizably Gilbert & Sullivan characters, but they are also recognizably real. That reality is what makes their story a tragedy—we believe in them, and thus we care about what happens to them. Bunthorne winds up lovelorn, and we laugh; Point winds up lovelorn, and we cry.

Gilbert & Sullivan had always mixed the good and the bad in their characters. Sometimes it was as simple as Sullivan's sweet music for an otherwise off-putting Lady Jane, but more often it required joint design.

Frederic isn't merely a cardboard embodiment of heroic virtue, for example, but also a bit of a punctilious prig. The Lord Chancellor, apparently a comedian, emerges as an unexpected romantic lead. Patience the cartoon milkmaid suddenly sheds a real tear. Even the sinister Sir Roderick Murgatroyd can warm up to a tender love duet.

In *The Yeomen of the Guard,* this blendedness is crucial. Because the play is less funny, it can't afford to have its characters be two-dimensional. If they were, they'd be nothing but walking clichés—a weeping clown, a heroic soldier, a purer-than-pure heroine, and so on. The opera would, in short, be nothing more than the melodramatic folderol that Gilbert & Sullivan themselves had chased from the stage.

Instead it is something altogether better, a tragedy whose resonance stems not from its derivative plot but from the believability—hence fallibility— of its characters.

Of all the operas' tenor roles, Colonel Fairfax is surely the best, save perhaps the purely comic Lord Tolloller. He stands out precisely because he is a rounded, even contradictory character. Self-centered, even cruel, Fairfax is a far cry from a cardboard hero yet nonetheless possesses some heroic qualities.

We meet Fairfax at his best. His sheer bravery is undeniable, and audiences are as charmed as Phoebe is by the wit and gallantry with which he faces death. "Is Life A Boon?" and the dialogues that flank it reveal a man smart enough to know what he's losing by dying but courageous enough to accept what must be. Lieutenant Cholmondeley, Sergeant Meryll, and his son are as impressed with Fairfax as Phoebe is, and deservedly so.

But, as he himself says, Fairfax is better at dying than living: "It is easier to die well than to live well—for, in sooth, I have tried both." Once freed, he shows a different face.

In particular, as he says, "Coming Death hath made of me a true and chivalrous knight, who holds all womankind in such esteem that the oldest, and the meanest, and the worst-favored of them is good enough for him." Once death recedes, his attitude changes. He is neither true nor chivalrous with Phoebe and Elsie, and his speculations about his unknown wife begin and end with her youth and beauty.

He doesn't become an utter villain, of course. His flirting with Phoebe may exceed respectable limits (Meryll's Act 2 dismay on hearing that Fairfax may be married indicates that the sergeant thinks it does), but he shows commendable discomfort at being forced to accept praises actually due Leonard, as well as a fine wit in accepting them without actually lying. Clearly, honor is important to Fairfax.

But if in Act 1 he is still somewhat modest, by act 2 he has cast off all restraint. He now takes full credit for his escape—more rightly considered a rescue—and is troubled only by his too-hasty marriage.

"Two days gone, and no news of poor Fairfax," he gloats. "The dolts! They seek him everywhere save within a dozen yards of his dungeon. So I am free! . . . [But] [t]he Tower bonds were but a thread of silk compared with these conjugal bonds which I, fool that I was, placed upon mine own hands. From the one I broke readily enough—how to break the other!"

However arrogant this speech, or however cynical the following "Free from His Fetters Grim," they pale before Fairfax's memorable line to Elsie: "Dost thou love me, or hast thou been insensible these two days?" This surely is cockiness personified—only unconsciousness could keep Elsie from loving him after two days in his presence, he believes. (The tragedy is that he's right.)

This early arrogance sets the tone for three consecutive scenes of increasing, gratuitous cruelty.

First, Fairfax uses his knowledge of Elsie's secret to "test her principles"—that is, to take advantage of her affection by coaxing her into sin and apparent bigamy. The more alarmed Elsie gets, the more amusing Fairfax seems to find it.

He follows this wanton cruelty with the "Man Who Would Woo a Fair Maid" scene. Besides his offhand cruelty to Point—knowingly misleading a slower, more gullible man for his own ends—Fairfax's conduct toward Phoebe is all but inexcusable. Regardless of whether their dalliance has extended beyond kisses, Fairfax knows how much Phoebe loves him and also that he owes his very life to her. But with a prettier woman in his sights, he simply dismisses her from his thoughts.

The final scene is crueler yet. On the brink of marrying her beloved "Leonard," Elsie is crushed by the sudden reappearance of the "dead" Fairfax. Her agony and despair fill the ensemble "Day of Terror! Day of Tears!"

Fairfax needs but a word to relieve her anguish. Yet when he speaks, it is only to turn the screw tighter—"Mine is a heart of massive rock, / unmoved by sentimental shock!" Elsie's despairing "Leonard, My Loved One, Come to Me" is entirely unnecessary. She suffers solely because Fairfax wants her to—if not out of sadism than because he simply enjoys the irony of the situation.

All three episodes are basically the same: Fairfax using his role as "Leonard" to humorous effect, ignoring the grief it brings other characters. (Clearly, however, Gilbert & Sullivan don't ignore it—the aching Point and Phoebe verses in "When a Wooer Goes a-Wooing" make their judgment quite apparent.)

Add his trifling with Phoebe and his lying to Meryll, and Fairfax emerges as a reckless, irresponsible lady's man who cares more for his own amusement than for the feelings of others—his is indeed "a heart of massive rock."

To be sure, he is brave and, by his own lights, honorable. Yet one can't help feeling that Elsie's bliss in winning him may last little longer than Phoebe's—especially when Phoebe herself joins Elsie and Carruthers for a triply ironic finale trio:

Tis said that joy in full perfection
   comes only once to womankind—
that, other times, on close inspection,
   some lurking bitter we shall find.

We've already seen the bitter lurking for Phoebe and will soon see what Elsie's happiness does for Point. But, particularly in light of Fairfax's cruelty in the following "Day of Terror" scene, it's no stretch to think that Elsie's faith in the full perfection of her own happiness may be misplaced.

Otherwise, there is little to say of Elsie. A generally passive person (her three major songs—"Tis Done," "O Mercy," and "Leonard, My Loved One" are all complaints), Elsie is driven by emotion, making her a bad match for the witty, heartless Fairfax. Before she even knows him, her heart goes out to him for his bravery (the same attribute that attracts Phoebe) in "Tis Done, I Am a Bride."

Even though it profits her, she weeps for Fairfax's apparent death. In fact, her most spirited speech in the opera is a vigorous defense of those tears: "Still, he was my husband, and had he not been, he was nevertheless a living man, and now he is dead; and so, by your leave, my tears may flow unchidden, Master Point."

Other than this passage, Elsie shows little real character. For a merry-maid she is singularly unhumorous, with none of Phoebe's cheerfulness or ironic realization of her own folly. The contrast is all but diametric—when, for example, each is seemingly abandoned by Fairfax, Phoebe responds with a jealous tirade that is a comic tour de force, Elsie with the plaintive "Leonard, My Own."

Elsie shows no sign of believing in Point's love, much less returning it. Though she knows the jester better than anyone else in the opera, her attitude toward him throughout is indifferent, even dismissive.

Even her final lines, "It's the song of a merrymaid, nestling near, / who loved her lord—but who dropped a tear / at the moan of the merryman, moping mum" are only somewhat authentic, having been written for the 1897 revival. Until that time, including the entire run of the original production, Elsie's final lines were "It's the song of a merrymaid, peerly proud, / who loved a lord and who laughed aloud / at the moan of the merryman, moping mum."

Of course, Elsie's one-dimensionality is vital to the functioning of the play, particularly its final scene. The ending works only if the audience's sympathy rests entirely with Point. If Elsie were as vital and engaging as Phoebe, her happiness would bear greater weight, Point's unpleasant qualities would be easier to remember, and the finale's bittersweet tone would swing excessively toward the sweet. Elsie's shallowness lends Point depth, adding to the pathos of the final scene.

Point as a character is frequently overrated, based in large part on two misconceptions: First, that he is Gilbert's surrogate, and second, that he is unfairly victimized.

Gilbert would hardly have represented himself by a plagiarist ("I will teach thee all my original songs, my self-constructed riddles, my own ingenious paradoxes; nay, more, I will reveal to thee the source whence I get them"). *Maritana* notwithstanding, Gilbert prided himself on his originality—virtually all of his works were labeled "original," and he particularly despised plays cribbed from French sources.

Point's penchant for self-pity is even less Gilbertian. Like Point, Gilbert often saw himself as a victim, but he usually responded with explosive anger (and often litigation), not mere whining.

Furthermore, the perception of "poor Jack Point" as a victim is at best an oversentimentalization, ignoring the fact that Point's actions are hardly creditable and that most of his trouble is his own doing.

Point was certainly conceived in the mold of such Shakespearean jesters as Touchstone and Feste (like them, he has a fitting name, "Point" suggesting both barbs of humor and a meaning behind the madness). But he is no wise man in fool's garb, and his two major actions in the opera—consenting to the Elsie-Fairfax wedding and plotting to fake the colonel's death—are anything but admirable.

Point's verse of "How Say You, Maiden" is in sharp contrast to Elsie's. She hastens to assure the Lieutenant that money as such is not her motivation for what she knows is a questionable arrangement, but Point provides a counterpoint of comic venality:

> Though as a general rule of life
> I don't allow my promised wife,
> 　　my lovely bride that is to be
> 　　to marry anyone but me,
> yet if the fee is promptly paid
> 　　and he in well-earned grave
> within the hour is duly laid,
> 　　objection I will waive!
> 　　Yes, objection I will waive!

Sullivan sets the last two lines in a toadying coo that emphasizes the contrast with Elsie's flowing expressions of principle.

Upon Fairfax's escape, Point displays an utter lack of sympathy for his lady-love's anguish: When Elsie turns to him with an appalled "What have I done! Oh, woe is me! / I am his wife, and he is free!" Point actually attacks her. His only concern is for his own interests:

> Oh, woe is *you?* Your anguish sink!
> Oh, woe is *me,* I rather think!
> Oh, woe is *me,* I rather think!
> Yes, woe is *me,* I rather think!
> 　　Whate'er betide
> 　　you are his bride,
> and I am left
> alone—bereft!
> 　　Yes, woe is *me,* I rather think!
> 　　Yes, woe is *me,* I rather think!

Elsie's situation is far worse than his, and she's entitled to expect sympathy from a partner, let alone a lover. But Point is entirely concerned with himself.

This self-centeredness mirrors Fairfax, a connection driven home by the next development. The Point-Shadbolt scheme to fake Fairfax's death is intended to allow Point to win Elsie—although she will, unknowingly, be committing the mortal sin (and legal crime) of bigamy.

This is essentially the same proposal that Fairfax (as "Leonard") almost simultaneously makes to Elsie:

Fairfax: A fig for this Fairfax! Be mine—he will never know—he dares not show himself; and if he dare, what art thou to him? Fly with me, Elsie—we will be married tomorrow, and thou shalt be the happiest wife in England!

The only difference is that, where Fairfax wants her to think she will be committing bigamy when she actually isn't, Point intends that she commit bigamy while thinking she isn't.

Elsie's response to Fairfax applies equally well to Point:

Elsie: Master Leonard! I am amazed! Is it thus that brave soldiers speak to poor girls? Oh! for shame, for shame! . . . Oh, sir, thy words terrify me—they are not honest—they are wicked words, and unworthy thy great and brave heart! Oh, shame upon thee! Shame upon thee!

Point's offense is worse than the colonel's. After all, even if she did as Fairfax suggests, Elsie wouldn't really be guilty of bigamy. The jester's plan requires that she should be.

Some have depicted Point's downfall as a tragedy of inarticulateness—arguing that, for all his vaunted glibness, he fumbles his true feelings when it counts. In reality, however, he's perfectly articulate with his true feelings—witness "Though as a general rule of life," "Yes, woe is me," the supremely self-pitying "A Private Buffoon Is a Light-Hearted Loon," and the despondent "When a jester is outwitted."

Point's appeal to Elsie fails for two simple reasons: First, he is at least as interested in himself as he is in her—he appeals to her by boasting of his youth, his looks, his wit, and so forth. His error lies in expecting her to find him as attractive as he does.

Ultimately this doesn't matter, however, because either way he is doomed to fail. In *The Yeomen of the Guard,* love owes nothing to words. Like Phoebe, Elsie has loved Fairfax since before they ever spoke—her attraction to him is evident in "'Tis Done, I Am a Bride," though she met him only moments before, and blindfolded.

If Point is just another self-centered egotist, lacking even Fairfax's bravery and charm, why isn't he another Bunthorne, a comically unpleasant lout whose final discomfiture leaves the audience laughing? Or another Wells, who like Point trades love for money and brings everyone to grief?

Simply because Point has one great redeeming factor: his love for Elsie. There is nothing in his reprise of "The Merryman and His Maid" to suggest artifice. It is self-pitying, but it's self-pity stripped of the cleverness that characterized Point's previous wallowing. It is a cry from the heart, and both Gilbert and Sullivan treat it as such.

Point has only this one redeeming point, but it is enough to make him real, and therefore pitiful (if not entirely sympathetic) in his downfall.

The opera's only truly sympathetic figures are Phoebe Meryll and her father.

In an opera in which practically everyone (Elsie excepted) are liars out for their own advantage, the Merylls pursue a noble cause—Fairfax's life. They may lie, but they do so out of determination that a man as brave as Fairfax should not perish unjustly. In short, they embody justice over duty.

This may seem an obvious choice, but under the shadow of the Tower it is a bold decision. Lieutenant Cholmondeley is a sympathetic figure, but he never considers rescuing his old friend; in fact, he does his best to apprehend him once he escapes—"bring him here alive or dead." Even Fairfax himself accepts his impending death with equanimity.

Only the Merylls rebel. And, of course, they suffer for it—arguably more than anyone else in the opera, even Point. Unlike the naive merryman and his maid, undone by circumstances they don't really understand, Phoebe and Meryll have consciously rebelled against the whole idea of the Tower—which makes it all the more tragic that, in the end, they must surrender themselves to Shadbolt and Carruthers, the two characters who embody everything the Tower stands for.

Phoebe is easily the opera's most likable character, if only because her actions are both believable and well intentioned. If the Victorians (like her dubious brother) might look askance at her outrageous flirting with her "brother" Fairfax, we (and Gilbert, clearly) see in it an expression of her liveliness, the buoyancy and hope that she alone brings to the opera. She brings a breath of fresh air to everything—in laughingly tormenting Wilfred, flirting with Fairfax, or cajoling her father, her naturalness is unfailingly winning.

Even in her errors, Phoebe is believable. Of all the opera's creaking plot contrivances, Elsie's revealing crucial information by talking in her sleep may be the most artificial; but the way Phoebe blurts out the truth to Wilfred in a frenzy, fresh from being spurned by Fairfax, feels absolutely natural. It's a mistake a real person would make.

That Phoebe is so real, and so really likable, makes it all the more appalling that she should be shackled to Wilfred. Shadbolt is truly the brute she calls him, a man for whom the erotic and the sadistic are closely intertwined. His love for Phoebe "racks him," "eats into his heart," and "turns his interior into boiling lead." His vision of married life involves "the prisoners stored away for the night," and his idea of humor is "the nice regulation of a thumbscrew."

(An early-draft song in which he explained that jealousy was like sitting on a red-hot coal or having his bones cracked on the rack, and followed by being jealous of the belt around her waist, the bird at her lip, or the cat she "fondles" on her lap [!] was fortunately cut.)[9]

The idea of Phoebe's buoyant freshness chained to this morbid, twisted jailkeeper is horrifying, and apparently Gilbert himself couldn't stand it.

He offers Phoebe's "We will be wed in a year—or two—or three, at the most. Is not that enough for thee?" as a hint that the resourceful girl may yet wriggle out of the match. In the opera's overall context it seems unlikely, but by this time any faint gleam of hope is welcome.

The same cannot be said for Sergeant Meryll's fate. Meryll is one of Gilbert's most appealing creations, a convincing father and old soldier who through the accumulation of detail becomes very real without any "big scenes." (His affectionate indulgence of Phoebe, for example, rings quite true.) His flaunting his duty to repay his debt to Fairfax is the antithesis of the grim impartiality that Carruthers admires so much.

If Meryll represents the opera's human side, Carruthers personifies its inhuman side—the Tower itself. Like Phoebe born and raised there, she represents a nightmare vision of what might lie ahead for the younger woman.

"I was born in the old keep, and I've grown gray in it, and, please God, I shall die and be buried in it," she says proudly, "and there's not a stone in its walls that is not as dear to me as my own right hand."

She and Meryll represent conflicting values, and in the end it is Carruthers who triumphs, "flushed with capture." The very humanity that led him to help Fairfax is Meryll's undoing.

It is the downfall of the Merylls, as much as Point's fate, that marks *The Yeomen of the Guard* as a tragedy. At the opera's end, its three worst characters (Carruthers, Shadbolt, and Fairfax) are the happiest, while three of its best (Phoebe, Meryll, and Point) are the unhappiest.

Even if Elsie's ending is construed happily, this is surely no bittersweet comedy. At best, it's a tragedy with comic undertones.

The source of that tragedy is, of course, love itself. Everything positive that is said in the opera about love proves untrue, and everything negative is borne out. Fairfax's grim imagery of marriage as a prison in "Free from His Fetters Grim" is exactly right for Phoebe and Meryll, while "though the altar be a tomb" perfectly sums up the Point-Elsie ending.

As in *Patience,* love in *The Yeomen of the Guard* is an arbitrary, elemental force that defies analysis, justification, or control. As Sergeant Meryll says, "What a helpless ninny is a lovesick man" (though, as its opening song suggests, the opera actually shows more lovesick women then men).

Patience expresses this view comically, however: The arbitrary force applies itself happily and, in particular, applies itself mutually and exclusively. Grosvenor really does love Patience and she him, and no one else truly loves either one. Their true love is the axis around which the various other "untrue loves" turn, from Bunthorne's self-centered hunger for Patience to the Ladies' trendy worship of Grosvenor and the Dragoons' "any wife will do" love for the Ladies.

Love is arbitrary, however, and *Patience* could easily have been a tragedy. We don't mind that Bunthorne doesn't get Patience, however, because he doesn't really love her, or that the Ladies don't get Grosvenor, because they didn't really love him. And the Ladies being stuck with the Dragoons is all right, because they themselves are as featherheaded as the Dragoons. But if the characters and their emotions were more believable, their losses would strike us as tragic.

The Yeomen of the Guard applies the same arbitrary force to essentially the same situation but produces a tragedy. The love of Fairfax and Elsie is at best indifferently mutual—she adores him, but he seems to care for little but her beauty. On the other hand, we do care that Point loses Elsie or that Phoebe loses Fairfax, because their loves, however one-sided, are genuine.

In a comic *Yeomen of the Guard,* Point would arbitrarily marry Phoebe and everything would end happily—but in this more realistic world love doesn't have the tidiness of comedy, and thus the arbitrary is tragic.

The point is not that *The Yeomen of the Guard* is almost a comedy or *Patience* almost a tragedy. Obviously, this is far from the case—they have different tones throughout.

But that the same basic idea can produce two stories so diverse in tone and impact speaks volumes for the creative evolution of Gilbert & Sullivan. From the farce of *Patience* through the mythic comedy of *Iolanthe,* then from the hope-tinged desperation of *Princess Ida* to the dark-shadowed *Ruddigore,* the two partners had been heading this way for a long time.

In many ways, *The Yeomen of the Guard* was the end of their journey together. It was not only the last time they were to consider the nature of love, but also the last time that who-marries-whom would be a significant plot issue. Nor was the intricate parallel-story-line technique ever to be used again—it would metamorphose into a strange "parallel opera" technique for *The Gondoliers* and then vanish entirely.

If, as both Gilbert and Sullivan later said, *The Yeomen of the Guard* was their favorite of their operas, it is understandable. At least since *The Sorcerer* they had been working toward the day when they would be able to write *The Yeomen of the Guard.* It had taken them 11 years and eight operas, but finally they had reached it.

The logical question was, where to go from here?

For Sullivan, the obvious next step was to grand opera. But in listening to *Ivanhoe,* which Sullivan began immediately after *The Yeomen of the Guard,* even a casual listener finds it thin by comparison.

The two operas, both drawing on historic English settings for ambiance and musical color, are clearly by the same man. Yet *The Yeomen of the Guard* has a vigor, a musical imagination, and an integrated coherence that *Ivanhoe* lacks. Sullivan saw *Ivanhoe* as the culmination of his career, a step above and beyond the Savoy, but now it seems clear that *The Yeomen of the Guard* was in fact that culmination.

Certainly *The Yeomen of the Guard* is a masterpiece for its composer. Its quality reaches a level of consistency previously approached only by *Iolanthe*. From its masterful overture, surely Sullivan's best, through its stirring finale, musical missteps are few and far between. Most critics awarded Sullivan the lion's share of the credit for the opera's success, to some extent deservedly so.

The composer brings to fruition many long-established techniques in his musical repertoire. He utilizes recurring themes deftly—the Tower theme from "When Our Gallant Norman Foes," for example, or his adaptation of the Act 1 funeral march into Act 2's "Night Has Spread Her Pall" to reestablish a properly gloomy mood. *The Yeomen of the Guard* also features several excellent "combination" numbers, as in "Tower Warders/ In the Autumn of Our Lives" or "Night Has Spread Her Pall/Warders Are We."

The score's real success, though, derives not from technical mastery but from its remarkable fusion of author and composer. *The Yeomen of the Guard* was by far the Gilbert story that most suited Sullivan's own inclinations, so already the librettist had done a great deal for Sullivan.

But he does much more, not even considering the oft-told story of Gilbert's providing the rhythm (and perhaps the melodic germ) for "The Merryman and His Maid." More impressive is the amazing variety of lyrical structures the librettist employs. Not only does Gilbert provide looser rhyme schemes, allowing room for "the music to speak for itself" (as Sullivan had once asked),[10] but he also creates some ingenious structures to inspire the composer.

There are dozens of examples to choose from, but two should suffice. Gilbert begins the Yeomen's opening chorus with three fairly conventional lines:

> In the autumn of our life,
>> here at rest in ample clover,
>> we rejoice in telling over . . .

This simple ABB opening implies a fourth line with an "-ife" rhyme, or possibly another "-over" rhyme, in a conventional ABBA or possibly ABBB–ACCC format. Instead, the verse continues:

> our tempestuous May and June.
>> In the evening of our day,
>> with the sun of life reclining . . .

By this point, there is no conventional expectation. The opening six lines rhyme ABBCDE, fitting no known rhyme scheme.

The effect is to give the composer plenty of leeway. Sullivan can set the lines without any marked structural sense—in this case, a massed semi-chorale with an appropriately churchlike tone.

Even when Gilbert finishes the verse with:

> we recall without repining
> all the heat of bygone noon.

its structure defies analysis, with an ABBC–DEEC scheme leaving the A and D lines ("life" and "day") unrhymed.

A second eight lines of chorus verse might clarify the structure, but instead Gilbert shifts to a 10-line solo with a slightly different scansion. As the soloist steps forward and the composer modulates to another key, the listening ear adjusts, writes off the preceding, confusingly structured passage, only to hear:

> This the autumn of our life,
>   this the evening of our day;
> weary we of battle strife,
>   weary we of mortal fray.

These are conventional alternating couplets in a quatrain, but the first line recapitulates the A line from the preceding verse and the second line the D line of that verse; then the third and fourth lines provide the long-withheld rhymes.

The scheme is in one sense intricate (overall, the 18-line structure is ABBCDEEC–ADADFGFGHH), but it is also simple, being so apparently loose that its structure doesn't distract a listener, as straight couplets might. When finally the song ends with a straight couplet ("Still would face a foreign foe/as in days of long ago"), it feels like "coming home"—a sense Sullivan reflects, exactly eight bars later, by modulating back to the original key.

The show sparkles with such lyrical ingenuity. "Here's a Man of Jollity," for example, could easily have been a tossed-off entry number for the chorus, and initially it looks like that—five four-line verses. After the first four lines ("jollity"/"jollify"/"quality"/"follify"), we recognize a standard ABAB. But then the next two are AABB, the fourth is AAAB, and the fifth returns to ABAB, an unexpected structural diversity.

Gilbert doesn't stop there, however. Instead of the overall structure ABAB–CCDD–EEFF–GGGH–IJIJ that the form implies, he brings back the B rhyme ("-ollify") as his I rhyme and makes his F rhyme ("-oh") into both his H and his J rhymes, producing a much more integrated ABAB–CDCD–EEFF–GGGF–BFBF.

But the final beauty of "Here's a Man of Jollity" doesn't emerge until after the song and a lengthy dialogue. After this, "The Merryman and His

Maid" begins . . . and the multiple "-oh" rhymes from the end of "Here's a Man" turn out to have set up the use of that syllable as a concluding tag throughout the song—"I have a song to sing, O!"

Such subtlety escapes most audiences' conscious notice. But it didn't escape Sullivan, who chose to link the two songs with orchestral underscoring beneath the dialogue to weave a coherent musical scene—something he had never done for an extended dialogue in any of the preceding operas.

These are only two examples of the remarkable intimacy between the two creators of *The Yeomen of the Guard.* They show not Gilbert's brilliance as a dramatist or Sullivan's as a composer but rather Gilbert's ability to think like a composer and Sullivan's to think like a dramatist. Throughout the operas one is struck by the way two artistic viewpoints seem to fuse into one, and nowhere more than in *The Yeomen of the Guard.*

The Yeomen of the Guard also finds Sullivan increasingly moving beyond simply setting Gilbert's words. He once described his work as "word-setting, I might almost say syllable-setting,"[11] and in some respects he had been right. By the time of *The Yeomen of the Guard,* however, he often uses Gilbert's words as the nucleus of a musical number, rather than its skeleton.

This is reflected in the opera's frequent use of "big endings." Again and again the composer creates elaborate codas, sometimes as long as the entire preceding song, in which the music steps to the fore.

The best example is "How Say You, Maiden?" Here Sullivan uses 13 bars to set a simple six-line chorus but then spins it into a striking 62-bar finish, with Point and the Lieutenant growling a syncopated "head over heels" beneath Elsie's soaring repetition of "Oh, temptation!" The extra 49 bars are built on only five words, yet they leave an indelible impression.

Sullivan also is quicker to alter Gilbert's work to enhance a scene's musical interest. "Alas! I Waver To and Fro" is clearly written as a simple two-verse song, but Sullivan boldly gives Meryll's verse an entirely different musical concept, so that the verse structure, so apparent on the page, essentially disappears on the stage.

The composer is not simply ignoring Gilbert, however: Sullivan's idea builds on a typically elegant structural tip—Phoebe's initial "Alas, I waver to and fro" goes rhymeless for the entire first verse, lending a looseness that is only marginally dispelled when the rhyme eventually appears, 11 lines later, as the first line of Meryll's verse.

Sometimes Sullivan does make free with Gilbert's work, however, as when he essentially scraps the entire metrical structure of "Tis Done, I Am a Bride."

Gilbert's lyric for the first verse is fairly conventional in structure:

Though tears and long-drawn sigh
   ill-fit a bride,

no sadder wife than I
 the whole world wide!

Ah me, ah me!
Yet wives there be
 who would consent to lose
  the very rose of youth,
   the flower of life,
  to be in honest truth
   a wedded wife,
 no matter whose!
Ah me! What profit we, O maids that sigh,
though gold should live, if wedded love must die?

Seeking a more propulsive, forward-driven design, Sullivan fragments this scheme. First he breaks up the verse—but not where the lyric naturally breaks, after "whole world wide." Instead he breaks after "Ah me, ah me," attaching that line to the first part and "Yet wives there be" to the second part, effectively destroying the rhymed couplet.

Next Sullivan attacks the line structure. Three lyric lines (ll. 6–8) become two musically identical lines, with the first line now breaking after "would consent" and the second after "rose of youth," effectively eliminating the "ah me/wives there be" and "to lose/no matter whose" rhymes by burying "there be" and "to lose" in the middle of lines.

Then he repeats the three-lines-into-two device on the next three lines, breaking after "to be"—which creates a "discovered rhyme" with "ah me" but buries the "flower of life/wedded wife" and "rose of youth/honest truth" rhymes.

Finally the composer destroys rhyme and rhythm in Gilbert's two-line couplet chorus by first repeating the words "though gold" to create a five-foot/six-foot couplet, then breaking two lines into four. By breaking the music at points different from where Gilbert has broken the words, Sullivan's final form makes Gilbert seem to be ending the song with four unmatched lines, two of which don't rhyme—"what profit we/gold should live."

When Sullivan is finished, the song has a much different form. Without adding or deleting any words, he has turned a strongly rhythmic, strongly rhymed song into virtual blank verse. The result is a powerful, "operatic" setting, but not at all what Gilbert had originally intended:

Gilbert's version:	*Sullivan's version:*
Though tears and long-drawn sigh	Though tears and long-drawn sigh
ill-fit a bride,	ill-fit a bride
no sadder wife than I	no sadder wife than I
the whole world wide!	the whole world wide,
	ah me, ah me.

Ah me, ah me!
Yet wives there be
who would consent to lose
the very rose of youth,
  the flower of life,
to be in honest truth
  a wedded wife,
no matter whose!
Ah me! What profit we, O maids
    that sigh,
though gold should live, if wedded
    love must die?

Yet wives there be who would consent
to lose the very rose of youth,
the flower of life, to be
in honest truth a wedded wife,
no matter whose,
no matter whose!

Ah me, what profit we
O maids that sigh,
though gold, though gold should live
    if wedded love must die?

It is a sign of his commitment to this uniquely demanding collaboration that Gilbert didn't kick up a fuss about such radical structural changes. He was perfectly willing to raise objections (he vetoed two versions of "Is Life a Boon?" before he was finally satisfied), but he was also willing to listen with an open mind, even after what he considered the mis-setting of *Ruddigore's* "ghost music."

Why, then, did the ambitious *Ivanhoe* prove so much less an artistic triumph than *The Yeomen of the Guard,* given its composer's recently demonstrated mastery?

It was, of course, the absence of Gilbert. Despite his topsy-turvy reputation, Gilbert gave Sullivan three things that *Ivanhoe* librettist Julian Sturgis could not—even though Gilbert himself had recommended Sturgis, calling him "the best serious librettist of the day."[12]

First, Sturgis lacked Gilbert's metrical ingenuity. The structural subtleties just discussed were far beyond Sturgis. (Of course, of all Gilbert's composers, only Sullivan proved to be equally attentive to such matters. If Sturgis didn't give Sullivan the kind of hints Gilbert did, Alfred Cellier, Osmond Carr, Edward German et al. didn't catch Gilbert's hints the way Sullivan did.)

Many of Sullivan's finest moments in *The Yeomen of the Guard* were inspired by Gilbert's cleverness—the radical reworking of "Tis Done, I Am a Bride" may have been inspired by a single altered triplet ("lose / youth / life / truth / wife / whose") and a single internal rhyme ("ah me/life to be"). *Ivanhoe* lacks such subtleties.

Second, Gilbert's libretti gave Sullivan potent theatrical situations to inspire similarly powerful music. Sullivan was every inch a man of the theater, quick to appreciate the sudden mood shift from the boisterous "To Thy Fraternal Care" to the ominous "The Prisoner Comes" or even envision the tremendous lift the audience would get from the sudden vigor of "Tell a Tale of Cock and Bull."

Ivanhoe's situations are drawn from Sir Walter Scott's novel, but where Gilbert reinvents *Maritana's* story and situations, Sturgis merely translates

Ivanhoe onto the stage. The result is empty melodrama, conventional situations that inspire conventional music.

Finally, Sturgis didn't inspire Sullivan's best work because he couldn't and wouldn't demand it. Sturgis wasn't Sullivan's partner, simply a (well-paid) hired hand. He cheerfully adjusted his work to fit Sullivan's needs, rarely defending his work and never rejecting anything of Sullivan's.

Ivanhoe shows the absence of Gilbert's prodding. Surely Gilbert benefited from Sullivan's prodding as well—his other collaborators were as fatally accommodating as Sullivan's—but the composer needed more prodding.

Gilbert was by nature a perfectionist, working doggedly and revising constantly. Sullivan was inherently a dilettante, by his own admission lazy and undisciplined. He waited as long as he could to begin anything and went through it as quickly as possible, always tempted by the easy road. It took Gilbert, despite and indeed because of how nettlesome Sullivan found him, to make Sullivan a great theatrical composer.

Sturgis's work on *Ivanhoe* isn't bad—it's merely uninspired and, worse, uninspiring. He apparently lacked Gilbert's talent (none of his works is performed today), but he also didn't have Sullivan's respect the way Gilbert did. Without that, the opera could be no more than a middling success—as, indeed, it was.

In retrospect, Sullivan was wrong in vowing to put forth his best artistic effort in *Ivanhoe.* He had already done exactly that, in *The Yeomen of the Guard.*

And Gilbert was wrong in recommending Sturgis. The best serious librettist of the day was actually Gilbert himself.

In 12 years of active collaboration, Gilbert and Sullivan had reinvented themselves, individually and collectively. *Thespis, Trial by Jury,* and even *The Sorcerer* had shown the talent of each man, but also a whole equal to no more than the sum of its parts.

In each ensuing opera, however, as the shows had grown more ambitious, the partners had grown closer, their techniques coming more into sync and their artistic interests growing more similar.

By the early 1880s, Gilbert & Sullivan actually was a creative force readily distinguishable from either Gilbert or Sullivan. The 1877 *The Sorcerer* reads like a Gilbert libretto for Frederic Clay in the 1870s and sounds like a Sullivan score for Burnand in the same era. But by 1882, *Iolanthe's* libretto could not have been written by Gilbert for any other composer, nor its score by Sullivan for any other librettist.

This was not merely a sign of their individual creative growth in the 1880s. The 1877 *The Sorcerer* also reads like an 1890s Gilbert libretto for Osmond Carr and sounds like an 1890s Sullivan score for Comyns Carr and Arthur Pinero. Within the partnership, each man exceeded his capabilities outside it, before or afterward. Gilbert & Sullivan were truly sui generis—not two of a kind but one of a kind.

The Yeomen of the Guard represents the end of that evolution, perhaps inevitably.

The closer the two came artistically, the more their contrasting personalities were bound to clash. The more ambitious their joint work, the more seriously they took it and the higher their standards. Even two soulmates would have chafed under these conditions (two Sullivans never would have finished anything, and two Gilberts would have killed each other years earlier).

Given this, it's remarkable that the two men had only one major quarrel in their first 17 years of collaboration, and no surprise that each of their next two shows was preceded by a volcanic quarrel.

Still, the upcoming "cipher quarrel" and "carpet quarrel" needn't have been fatal. Gilbert & Sullivan were fully capable of rising above personality conflicts—their greatest success, *The Mikado*, had followed the "lozenge quarrel," and their second-greatest was to follow the "cipher quarrel."

But matters were at once simpler and more complex. If not the end of a road, *The Yeomen of the Guard* was at least the furthest along it that either man wanted to go. It really was the culmination it seems to be—a masterly drawing-together of thematic ideas, dramatic and musical techniques, and collaborative interactions that had been being forged for a decade. After *The Yeomen of the Guard,* many of the things that had defined the Savoy operas neither could be nor needed to be done any more.

If the Gilbert & Sullivan collaboration was to continue, it needed to begin virtually anew. They would need new subject matters, new techniques, and new ways of working together. Whatever Gilbert & Sullivan opera had meant to this point, it would have to mean something else henceforth.

Sad to say, that new meaning was never to be found. There were three operas yet to come, including two of their finest, but all somehow lacked the one thing that previously had driven the collaboration—a sense of direction, of progression from one opera to the next. *The Gondoliers* was to be a sort of epilogue to the pre-*Yeomen of the Guard* collaboration, *Utopia, Limited* a pageant on Gilbert & Sullivan themes and *The Grand Duke* a self-referential exercise which was at once clever and a dead end.

In a real sense, with *The Yeomen of the Guard* the Gilbert & Sullivan collaboration went the way of Jack Point—to a death so powerful as to shake all who beheld it, yet not quite certainly a death at all.

Facing page: FIGURE 14.1. A *Punch* cartoon reflects the widespread view of *The Gondoliers*, with its themes of separation and reconciliation, as an allegory for the relationship between Gilbert and Sullivan. *Source:* Punch, *January 4, 1890. By permission of The British Library.*

14

The Gondoliers

By 1889 there were serious strains in the partnership between Gilbert and Sullivan, and *The Gondoliers* reflects those strains. Its quality remains superb, but both form and content reflect the fact of the growing disagreement between the partners.

By the time *The Gondoliers* was finished, the disagreement itself lay in the past, and Gilbert and Sullivan could exchange post-opening-night letters so complimentary as to border on flattery. The opera itself bubbles over with warmth and good feeling. But there are warning signs amid the roses, flaws masked by the brilliance of *The Gondoliers* that would seriously mar the team's remaining two operas, *Utopia, Limited* and *The Grand Duke.*

Thus *The Gondoliers* is both a masterpiece and a harbinger of problems to come.

Tonally, *The Gondoliers* is a radical step away from the seriousness of the team's later works, a growing darkness that had culminated in the grim starkness of *Ruddigore* and especially *The Yeomen of the Guard.* While the beauty of the operas had, if anything, grown richer, they had been suffused with an underlying, deeply serious coloration that gave them greater emotional depth.

In *The Gondoliers,* the tone is festive, even celebratory. Its romanticism is lush and welcoming, without the darker undertones that tinge *Iolanthe, Princess Ida,* or *The Yeomen of the Guard.* For the first time since *Patience,* matters of the heart take precedence over matters of life and death, and the tone is appropriately lighter, more youthful and frolicsome. When death is present at all—generally in the figure of the undertaker-like Don Alhambra—it is seen from far off, a dark shadow in the distance that makes the sunlight all the brighter.

This is the result of a thematic shift, of course. The earlier operas were deeper because of their "heavy" themes. The issues of mortality that drove *Iolanthe* or the generational violence of *Princess Ida* were by nature grim. The search for the meaning of love in *Patience* and *The Yeomen of the Guard* was, in its own way, even darker, shadowed (especially in the latter) by overtones of despair.

In these operas, the genius of Gilbert & Sullivan had been to counterbalance the seriousness of their subject matter with a human warmth and, in particular, a deft comic touch. Paradoxically, the contrast only enhanced the operas' emotional power.

But with *The Yeomen of the Guard,* they had come to a thematic dead end. Sullivan claimed to long for the scope and power of grand opera, but he didn't seem drawn to subject matter any darker than that of *Yeomen*—the lighter *Ivanhoe* was ample proof.

Similarly, while Gilbert also claimed that the darker, more operatic tone of *The Yeomen of the Guard* more suited his own sensibilities, his work belies those claims. In his non-Savoy works before, during, and after the collaboration, works in which he had all but complete freedom to express his own feelings, his treatments are almost always lighter, more ironic than tragic.

So, however Gilbert and Sullivan liked to posture as tragedians, the evidence suggests that *The Yeomen of the Guard* was the stopping point on an artistic road along which neither really wanted to continue.

The Yeomen of the Guard also closed many of the collaboration's central themes to date. The meaning-of-love theme, for example, had been falteringly explored in *The Sorcerer,* then developed more fully in the mature comedy of *Patience* and finally in the tragedy of *The Yeomen of the Guard.* Everything they had to say on the subject seemed to have been said.

Likewise, who-loves-who was never again a central issue in their operas. This is especially true of *The Gondoliers,* in which one couple is already married, while barely 20 minutes into the opera the other two are married off randomly—and apparently happily so. This arbitrariness stands as a virtual rebuttal to the previous operas' story-lines.

Similarly, the grand theme of head versus heart—the Victorian-style "Thou shalt not" versus the humanist "I must"—had been brought to full closure in *The Yeomen of the Guard.* After the spectacle of the warm, human characters of *Yeomen* (in particular, Sergeant Meryll and Phoebe) being broken on the wheel of duty, there was little more to be said on this subject, either.

The Gondoliers itself marks the final appearance of a theme that had been present to some degree in every opera from *The Sorcerer* through *The Yeomen of the Guard:* the idea that the present is burdened by the sins of the past—usually the sins of the parents—which must be set right before the younger generation can find happiness. The "Here Is a Case Unprecedented" scene, in which four young Italians and a young Spaniard try to sort out the assorted errors of Don Alhambra, the Duke and Duchess, and even old Baptisto Palmieri, encapsulates this theme. However, it never achieves the scope or impact it had in *Princess Ida* or *Ruddigore.*

In short, after *The Yeomen of the Guard* the central subject matter of the collaboration had been exhausted. The question was, would Gilbert & Sullivan find a new direction, and with it a new raison d'être for their collaboration?

In a real sense, the answer was no. The final three operas lack the driving power of the earlier works, and one senses in both authors a reluctance to commit themselves fully to the new, less focused works. Both men had good reasons to continue the collaboration—not least financial ones— but neither quite seemed to know where it was going.

The late operas are hardly themeless, but they lack the compelling thematic power that motivated the collaborators to their Herculean perfectionism—and, as a result, that perfectionism begins to slip. Errors and missed opportunities begin to pile up, as the two display an unwillingness to make the tough-minded editorial decisions that made their middle operas so flawless.

It is impossible to say what would have happened if events had gone differently. If the operas after *The Yeomen of the Guard* had been even darker, more resonant, and more elemental, would it have spurred Gilbert & Sullivan to even greater achievement? Or would they not have believed in their work enough to do it well? If they had found new themes to explore, would they have struck new veins of genius? Or did the 53-year-old Gilbert and the 47-year-old Sullivan simply lack the energy of 10 years earlier, or the willingness to challenge the expectations of their established audience?

In the end, it doesn't really matter. Gilbert & Sullivan wrote *The Gondoliers* and its successors because these were what they wanted to write at that time; to do otherwise, they would have had to be different people.

The fact is that *The Gondoliers* and *The Grand Duke* are, for all their flaws, brilliant pieces of theater; much of *Utopia, Limited* is on the same level. If they seem to glow less brightly than their predecessors, it is only because the team previously had set so high a standard.

The thematic element linking the final three operas is self-reference. After the breach between the partners that preceded *The Gondoliers* and the more serious one that followed it, their final three operas are to a considerable extent about themselves—about what it means to be a Gilbert & Sullivan opera and about the entire process of its creation.

Would the two have been moved to write *The Gondoliers,* an opera whose central theme is separation and reconciliation, if they hadn't quarreled and made up? Perhaps, but it surely gains from its resonances of their own situation. Consciously or unconsciously, they themselves increasingly become their own subjects.

As usual, Gilbert & Sullivan are writing about the issues that concern them most. And between 1889 and 1896 the issue that most concerned them was Gilbert & Sullivan—what the collaboration was, how it functioned, and even what it meant.

The concept of *The Gondoliers* as an allegory for Gilbert & Sullivan themselves—with Gilbert as Giuseppe, Sullivan as Marco, and perhaps Carte as the inquisitorial Don Alhambra—did not escape contemporary observers. A famous *Punch* cartoon of the day pictures Gilbert and Sullivan sitting squeezed into a single throne, a la Marco and Giuseppe. Gilbert brandishes a pen, Sullivan a conductor's baton (see figure 14.1).

Had the substance of the "cipher quarrel" been more widely known, the cartoonists would have found even more grist for their mill. Sullivan had announced that, in light of *The Yeomen of the Guard's* failure to match *The Mikado* in popularity, he would write no more comic operas. Instead he wanted Gilbert to write the libretto for a grand opera—which he defined as one "where the music is to be the first consideration—where words are to suggest music, not govern it."[1]

Moreover, he complained that at Gilbert's autocratic rehearsals he was not given his fair due as music director: "Except during the vocal rehearsals and the two orchestral rehearsals," he wrote to Carte, "I am a cipher in the theatre."[2]

Gilbert resented the suggestion that Sullivan had been forced to subvert himself. In fact, he responded, he himself had labored slavishly to meet Sullivan's requirements.

"You are an adept in your profession, and I am an adept in mine," he wrote to the composer. "If we meet, it must be as master and master—not as master and servant."[3]

Ultimately it was Carte who found a solution, by commissioning Sullivan simultaneously to write a grand opera and a new comic opera. Before long, both partners seemed to have forgotten their resentments. Gilbert was extravagant in his accommodations of the composer, and Sullivan returned the favor.

After opening night, Gilbert wrote to Sullivan: "I must thank you for the magnificent work you have put into the piece. It gives one the chance of shining right through the twentieth century with a reflected light."[4]

To which Sullivan replied, "Don't talk of reflected light. In such a perfect book as *The Gondoliers,* you shine with an individual brilliancy which no other writer can hope to attain."[5]

Future events, of course, were to prove both men accurate. It seems safe to say that they will shine right through the twenty-first century and beyond.

Thematically, *The Gondoliers* is an extended study of conflict, separation, and reconciliation.

Its putative subject matter, the parody of republicanism, is almost arbitrary. The parody is good for laughs, but only a small percentage of the opera treats it in any way. Indeed, when the authors had to pare the opera down to a manageable length, it was primarily the political satire that was cut.

Furthermore, the republicanism parody lacks focus. In *Thespis,* for example, Gilbert had shown the calamitous consequences of the actors' foolhardy ideas, and he would do likewise in *Utopia, Limited.* But *The Gondoliers* never shows any evidence that the gondolier/kings' republican approach has done Barataria any harm. We don't even have much sense that things will be any different under Luiz.

Quite probably they won't be—after all, his own experience has shown him that any drummer boy can be a king (Don Alhambra's sneering at the idea of a "Lord High Drummer Boy" is one of Gilbert's cleverer foreshadowings). At the least, it has hopefully engendered in Luiz a great deal of "patience for the presumption of persons in his plebeian position."

The most distinctive aspect of the opera is its dual structure, an extended metaphor for the Gilbert-Sullivan relationship—two self-contained stories whose interdependence mirrors that of author and composer.

The Gondoliers: or, The King of Barataria is virtually two operas stitched together, operating side by side with very little overlap. Earlier Savoy operas had woven together every aspect of their plots—for example, the Dragoons' pursuit of the Ladies is inescapably linked to Bunthorne's pursuit of Patience—but *The Gondoliers* sets up two story lines that only rarely intersect. The Duke of Plaza-Toro's incorporation of himself, for instance, has nothing whatever to do, either narratively or thematically, with the marital dilemmas of Marco and Giuseppe—they never learn of his incorporation, nor he of their multiple wives.

The two stories are not only almost entirely separate in terms of narrative, but also entirely different in tone. One is Italian, the other Spanish. One is Sullivanesque, reflecting the composer's structural demands, while the other is Gilbertian, much in the old manner. One is a new take on the Savoy style, while the other is firmly in the tradition of the earlier operas.

The Sullivanesque story is what might be called "The Gondoliers," a frothy, Italianate opera that uses Verdian pastiche to tell the story of two gondoliers who love their ladies, lose them, and win them again. It is predominantly musical, a strings-based show that opens with "List and Learn's" 20 minutes of uninterrupted music and follows with a second scene that leads off with "When a Merry Maiden Marries," and then after a brief dialogue sequence (introducing this story line's only Spanish character, Don Alhambra) finishes the act with 20 more minutes of consecutive music.

Its second act opens with "Of Happiness the Very Pith," and continues through six major musical numbers interrupted only briefly by dialogue, and then concludes its first scene with the big dance number "Dance a Cachuca." The second scene is very short, introducing the other three Spanish characters for some plot-related dialogue, three clever musical numbers, and then the big finale, a reprise of "Dance a Cachuca."

This story line is as skimpy on plot as it is on dialogue. By the end of the first number all the men and women have been paired off, which normally takes an entire opera. The only twist is the question "Which one is the king?" and it's resolved without any effort from the gondoliers themselves. In fact, the most characteristic dialogue line of "The Gondoliers" is an airy dismissal of the plot: "But never mind that—the question is, how shall we celebrate?"

Running parallel to the Sullivanesque half of the opera is the Gilbertian half, a Spanish story that might be called "The King of Barataria." Musically marked by trumpets and drums, it has a very short first act, opening with "From the Sunny Spanish Shore" to introduce the characters.

After a lengthy dialogue it offers a traditional self-introductory patter song, followed by a scene for the two parted lovers, whose "Oh, Bury, Bury" is a together-but-apart number in the tradition of *The Mikado's* "Were You Not to Ko-Ko Plighted" and *Ruddigore's* "I Know a Youth."

Its Act 1 finale, the typical philosophical ensemble "Try We Lifelong" (reminiscent of *Princess Ida's* "The World Is But a Broken Toy" or *The Mikado's* "See How the Fates"), leaves unanswered the pivotal questions of who is the king and if the young lovers will be reunited.

This story's Act 2 is also brief, opening with the song "With Ducal Pomp," interspersing three comic songs with extensive dialogue that serve to introduce four minor Italian characters, and segueing quickly to the grand finale, "Then Hail, O King."

Together, these amount essentially to two mini-operas fused together, linked only by the character of Don Alhambra and differing in matters of style, content, and tone. It is easy to imagine either being extended into a full-length work that would be more consistent, but the real ingenuity of *The Gondoliers* is the way it ties the two together without distorting the character of either.

Common to both halves is a cheerful fatalism—a sense that, while unpleasant things may lie ahead, the best we can do is enjoy the moment: "Away we go to an island fair, we know not where and we don't much care."

The same thought had been expressed grimly in *The Mikado* ("What though mortal joys be hollow? Pleasures come, if sorrows follow"), but in *The Gondoliers* it is more upbeat—it can't be helped, so why not have fun?

For the Spaniards, it is expressed as "Set aside the dull enigma, we shall guess it all too soon . . . then take life as it comes"; for the Italians, "fate in this has put his finger, let us bow to fate's decree . . . to the altar hurry we!" In both cases, the musical setting is buoyant—the order of the day is "reckless delight."

This merging of two disparate "operas" explains why *The Gondoliers* offers two romantic story lines (one with two heroes and two heroines), two comic baritones, and so forth—not to mention two consecutive finales.

This may in part reflect Gilbert's reported intention to create an opera with no stars—in reaction to the salary demands of the Savoy audience's established favorites such as Barrington and Bond—but that goal hardly mandated such an elaborate structure. He makes his point clearly enough by having his heroes choose the heroines randomly from the chorus.

I would suggest that the weaving-together of the Sullivanesque and Gilbertian story lines is intended to show not only that it can be done but that both are the richer for it.

The same point is made in the assigning of roles: Instead of the usual pairing of the high tenor with the lyrical soprano as "the pretty couple" and the baritone with the funny mezzo-soprano as "the funny couple,"

The Gondoliers pairs the high tenor Marco with the funny Gianetta to produce "the pretty, funny couple" and the baritone Giuseppe with the lyrical
Tessa to produce "the funny, pretty couple."

This differs from the casting switches in *Iolanthe* and *Ruddigore,* in which
tenors played the comic parts and basses or baritones the romantic leads.
Those changes were purely matters of vocal register, with the characters'
dramatic function remaining unchanged—baritone or not, the romantic
lead Robin was still paired with Rose, the lyrical soprano, as "the pretty
couple," as Strephon was with Phyllis. The switch in *The Gondoliers* is more
as if Phyllis had been paired with Lord Tolloller.

In *Iolanthe,* such a pairing would be ludicrous. In this case, however, the
result is to heighten the effectiveness of both through juxtaposition.
Marco and Tessa together might be cloying, Giuseppe and Gianetta irritating, but the pairing of opposites makes both couples more appealing—
just as was so often the case with the "funny" Gilbert and the "pretty"
Sullivan.

Matters of equality are also reflected in the opera's treatment of republicanism and in its characteristic "tradeoff" song form, in which one singer
finishes another's sentence. This ingenious device is used continuously in
The Gondoliers but rarely elsewhere in the Savoy operas, before or afterward.

"As One Individual" is the most famous example of this, of course, but
there are plenty of others: "After Sailing to This Island" gives Tessa and
Gianetta the same technique, as "With Ducal Pomp" does for the Duke
and Duchess. "In a Contemplative Fashion" varies the technique for comic
effect, with the singers arguing instead of agreeing with each other. In
the finale's "Speak, Woman, Speak" and "When Others Claimed Your
Dainty Hand," the whole cast uses the device. In the former, the eight-
line phrase beginning "speak, women, speak, / we're all attention" is divided line by line among eight singers, while in the latter Luiz, the Duke,
Casilda, and Duchess trade off a four-line verse.

Again, as often in the operas, the formal device has thematic implications, with the close collaboration of the characters reflecting that of Gilbert and Sullivan themselves.

The thematic point is driven home in the narrative structure of the opera,
which revolves around the axis of separation and reconciliation.

A remarkable number of the songs are about either separations ("From
the Sunny Spanish Shore," "Oh, Bury, Bury," "I Stole the Prince," "Kind
Sir, You Cannot Have the Heart," "Now, Marco, Dear," "Then Away We
Go," "Take a Pair of Sparkling Eyes," "In a Contemplative Fashion," "Here
Is a Case Unprecedented") or reconciliations ("When Alone Together,"
"When a Merry Maiden Marries," "Here We Are," "With Ducal Pomp,"
"On the Day When I Was Wedded," "Then Hail, O King," "Once More,
Gondolieri").

All these separations are ultimately resolved, however, to reflect Gilbert's "it must be as master and master." The "math problem" romantic entanglements boil down to the fact that two into one won't go—that just as Venice (at least in this version) holds exactly 24 gondolieri and exactly 24 contadine, making Casilda superfluous, so there is no room in her heart for both the drummer boy and the king. Remove the superfluous person—Casilda and "the king"—from both puzzles, and everything else falls into place.

And, of course, the "extra" person turns out to be imaginary: Casilda never was married to either gondolier, and the king and the drummer boy were always one and the same. The whole conflict proves to be pointless—probably Gilbert's view of the argument with Sullivan.

Until the end of the opera, the only element linking the two story lines is Don Alhambra, and his refrain "when everyone is somebody, than no one's anybody" has often been taken as the opera's "moral."

But Don Alhambra is not a hero, and his point of view is not Gilbert's. Immediately after "There Lived a King," we see an intriguing glimpse of an accommodation between Spaniards and Italians in "I Am a Courtier," as the gondoliers' beloved dancing forms a bridge between worlds ("that is the style of thing precisely").

And, of course, the drummer-boy-turned-king Luiz stands as evidence that a person can be somebody and nobody at the same time ("the characteristics of both conditions existing concurrently in the same individual"), or at least that every nobody may really be a somebody.

At first sight, the finale seems to hew to the "separate but equal" formulation. With two perfectly balanced finales, Gilbert reigns on his Baratarian-style throne ("the past is dead and you claim your own") while Sullivan rules in his musical Venice ("free from this quandary, contented are we").

More significant, however, the opera ends not on the Spanish pomp of "Then Hail, O King" nor the Italian raptures of "Once More Gondolieri." Instead it concludes with a sweeping transition into a rousing chorus of "Dance a Cachuca"—sung by the Italians in Barataria, and extolling the virtues of three dances and three wines . . . all of them from Spain.

There's even a final, implicit coda: Neither gondolier is the king, but they aren't brothers, either. One isn't really an Italian at all—he's Inez's son, a Spaniard. But we are never told which, because it really doesn't matter: From whatever lands they come, they are equals, friends, brothers.

In addition, *The Gondoliers* is another reflection of the Shakespearean influence on Gilbert & Sullivan (the composer's incidental music to *The Merchant of Venice*, composed 14 years earlier, strongly resembles his score for *The Gondoliers*).

The structure of the opera is Shakespearean, with scenes of nobles who are concerned with Great Matters (such as the plot) alternating with scenes of commoners who are concerned with earthier things (such as Marco and Giuseppe's tea or whether the queen would wear a feather). It even offers several instances ("Regular Royal Queen," "Then Hail, O King," "I Am a Courtier") of Shakespeare's frequent comic technique of commoners mimicking nobles, used to particularly good effect in *Henry IV*. And, just as Shakespeare enjoys having his nobles unknowingly imitate the commoners, so the mocking Act 1 chorus "Then Hail, O King" is transformed into a serious chorus for the Act 2 finale.

Like *The Gondoliers,* Shakespeare's comedies end with a message of unity. The nobles and commoners happily leave the forest together, each having learned something from the other. So Gilbert the conscious entertainer of the broad public and Sullivan the honored court composer end with the thought that much can be gained by combining the two.

In terms of technique, *The Gondoliers* shows ample evidence of both men's determination to make their partnership work—especially on Gilbert's side, where the supposed curmudgeon regularly goes out of his way to oblige Sullivan.

Obviously, *The Gondoliers* has far more music than any of the team's previous operas: Less than 10 minutes of the 90-minute first act is dialogue. Gilbert also obliges Sullivan (and his own inclinations) by making dance more important in *The Gondoliers* than in any previous show, by extension giving the music greater prominence.

Furthermore, he bends over backward to accommodate Sullivan's often-expressed dislike for eight-line, couplet-based songs. He forsakes the usual AABBCCDD or ABABCDCD rhyme schemes in favor of such intricate structures as the palindromic ABABBABA ("Thank You, Gallant Gondolieri") or ABAAABCDCCD ("I Stole the Prince"). He writes unusually short or long verses to allow Sullivan room to maneuver—from "Ah, Well-Beloved," a song actually shorter than its own recitative, to the 28-line verses of "Rising Early in the Morning."

He even changes line lengths in midsong. The 26-line verse of "On the Day When I Was Wedded" begins with two-foot lines—"on the day that I was wedded / to your admirable sire, / I acknowledge that I dreaded . . ." At of its 13th line, however, it shifts to one-foot lines—"to the thunder / of that Tartar / I knocked under"—only to change again, at its 25th line, to four-foot lines—"Giving him the very best and getting back the very worst / that is how I tried to train your great progenitor at first /."

Some of the show's most flamboyant, uplifting music comes not from Gilbert's unorthodox lyric forms—he even uses triplets (ABCABCDEF-DEF) for "Take a Pair of Sparkling Eyes"—but from Sullivan's continuing willingness (first displayed in *The Yeomen of the Guard*) to reshape the words.

He repeats lines or line fragments even more often than he had in *The Yeomen of the Guard,* uses nonverbal "tra la" choruses, and generally takes a looser approach to the lyrics. The torrential good humor of "The Merriest Fellows Are We," for example, draws 30 long lines of music from 10 short lines of lyrics.

Sullivan even discards three of Gilbert's words in "In a Contemplative Fashion," thereby "ruining" the rhythm and rhyme. Gilbert wrote Tessa's line as "If she married Messr. Marco, you're a spinster that is plain" (to rhyme with Gianetta's "doubt if her mother would know her again"), but Sullivan discards "that is plain," producing a line that is funnier but far less regular. (No objection from Gilbert has been recorded.)

Gilbert's willingness to accommodate Sullivan undoubtedly contributes to the infectious good spirits of the music. No other Gilbert & Sullivan show has so much simply happy music as *The Gondoliers*. There are moments of sadness, of course, but the tone is as cheerful as *The Yeomen of the Guard* was bleak.

Partly this good cheer reflects the story, but surely it also arises from the happiness of the composer—he and Gilbert were together again, he was at last writing his grand opera, and all was right in Sullivan's world.

In the rhapsodies of reconciliation, however, lay the seeds of failure. The partnership's success had been forged on the anvil of creative tension: Gilbert's stories, dialogue, and lyrics for the operas are better than anything he wrote because Sullivan constantly pushed him to fix weak spots, while Sullivan's music is more inspired because Gilbert would accept nothing less. As late as *The Yeomen of the Guard*, Gilbert's rejection of two separate settings of "Is Life a Boon?" had eventually produced the opera's most popular song.

In the wake of their reconciliation, both men went out of their way to be accommodating. Unfortunately, this led not only to a willingness to heed one another's advice but also to a reluctance to criticize—presumably in the hope of avoiding further conflict.

Each of their last three operas is longer than any of the preceding 11, reflecting this joint loss of editorial zeal. Rather than choosing between alternatives, Gilbert & Sullivan now tend to accept them both. This is fine for *The Gondoliers*, in which both alternatives are generally excellent, but it bodes ill for future works.

The earliest American editions of the Savoy operas represent their status two or three weeks before the London premieres, when the plates had to be shipped overseas. For the shows through *The Yeomen of the Guard*, these early editions reveal that substantial revisions of book, lyrics, and music were made up to the last minute—and, in almost every case, after opening night, with Gilbert and Sullivan meeting the following morning to reevaluate their work in light of the audience reaction.

As of *The Gondoliers*, however, the first American editions became largely the same as the first English editions. Fewer difficult-but-effective changes were being made, and the operas got longer and flabbier.

Gilbert & Sullivan had previously been ruthless in cutting even excellent material if it slowed the show (Gilbert nearly cut "A More Humane Mikado," for example). Extraneous dialogue, extra verses, even whole songs or scenes were scissored to tighten the pacing. But in the later operas they shied away from these tough decisions, making cuts only when sheer length forced them to.

Sullivan's reluctance to affront the temperamental Gilbert is particularly unfortunate, because it is Gilbert's slippage that is most apparent. The librettist still has his sharp eye and keen sense of humor, but he shows growing signs of lack of interest, even laziness.

Beginning with *The Gondoliers,* Gilbert is increasingly willing to invert syntax to find an easy rhyme, a practice he had largely abandoned in the mature operas. This produces complex, hard-to-follow lyrics such as "of happiness the very pith," "she of beauty was a model" or "though fate apart should rudely tear them." Nor do "bad" rhymes bother him—it's hard to believe that the younger Gilbert would have resorted to rhyming "shore" with "Duke of Plaza Tor'."

His previously unerring sense of rhythm also begins to desert him. The man who for *The Yeomen of the Guard* had written a note to Sullivan solely to suggest "down he dived" instead of the bumpier "down he jumped into the river" now produces "every*thing* is inter*est*ing, *tell* us, *tell* us all a*bout* it."

The line's rhythm works against the natural pronunciation of the words, making it harder for an actress to sing and an audience to comprehend. The insertion of two additional syllables would have achieved the natural rhythm of "really, *ev*erything is *in*teresting, *tell* us all a*bout* it." And Sullivan, previously quick to point out metrical awkwardness, remains silent.

Gilbert himself recognized that he was recycling plot elements for *The Gondoliers.* In a note to Sullivan, he wrote of a late song for Inez that "the situation became too much like the situation at the end of *Pinafore,* where Little Buttercup explains she has changed the children at birth"[6]—but he settles for cutting the song rather than revising the plot to make it fresher.

Gilbert also lets go of the watertight narrative structure that had become a hallmark of the mature Savoy operas. As early as *Patience,* the team had dropped out-of-context, virtuoso-showcase solos such as *The Sorcerer's* "For Love Alone" in favor of tightly contextualized songs such as *Patience's* "Love Is a Plaintive Song" or *The Yeomen of the Guard's* " 'Tis Done, I Am a Bride."

"Take a Pair of Sparkling Eyes" marks a regression. It has no specific relevance to the opera's story or to the character who sings it—it is not Marco's song of longing for Gianetta, any more than "The Nightingale" is Ralph's song about Josephine. Instead it is a generic love ballad, stopping the show dead so that the tenor can shine.

Sullivan's setting is, predictably, the most unimaginative moment in an otherwise ingenious score. And Gilbert's lyrics are among his most inane ever—in any previous opera, even his earliest, he probably would have shunned an image such as a hand "fringed with dainty fingerettes."

All in all, *The Gondoliers* shows a Gilbert whose interest is waning. He is more willing to avoid conflict by obliging Sullivan on some minor point than to risk it by being ambitious in his own work, and the result is an opera that works better moment-to-moment than it does in the big picture.

Like Sullivan, the librettist is still capable of excelling—as in, for instance, his deft portrayal of the bickering Duke and Duchess. But he excels in individual moments rather than over the course of the opera as a whole.

For example, Gilbert uses the opening number to establish imagery that links flowers and love, then develops it promisingly in the dead flowers of "Oh, Bury, Bury" and the transformational touch of "Merry Maiden's" "every flower is a rose." But unlike *Ruddigore*, in which a different flower imagery is woven consistently into the fabric of the opera, in *The Gondoliers* this imagery flickers and is gone by the second act.

The same is true of the light-and-darkness imagery, which is effective early only to drop out as the opera progresses, or the use of time imagery in such songs as "There Was a Time" (and its preceding dialogue) and "Try We Lifelong." Gilbert still can devise telling images, but he doesn't carry them far enough to make them unifying factors for the opera as a whole.

In *The Gondoliers,* this failing is covered by the brilliance and unity of Sullivan's score and by Gilbert's own unmistakable high spirits. But *The Gondoliers* has a feeling of afterthought, a sense of being an epilogue to the collaboration rather than a new step forward.

It prefigures more significant problems to come, in *Utopia, Limited* and *The Grand Duke.*

15

Utopia, Limited

Prior to *The Gondoliers,* Gilbert and Sullivan had disagreed regularly, but always on artistic matters. They were two very different personalities who approached their work from widely divergent perspectives, and it was natural that their best work arose from creative tension. It was all the more ironic, then, that the disagreement that ultimately sundered the team was not an artistic disagreement at all.

The so-called carpet quarrel, which escalated to a legal action filed by Gilbert against Carte and Sullivan's testimony on the producer's behalf, was only incidentally about the costs of new carpets for the Savoy Theatre and whether they could properly be deducted from the profits paid to Gilbert and to Sullivan.[1] The real issue was control: Who was ultimately in charge of the triumvirate that produced the operas?

Gilbert, himself a theater owner—in 1888 he had built the Garrick Theatre, which he owned for the remainder of his life—saw no great art to Carte's work. He felt that their success was due solely to the efforts of himself and Sullivan, and for years had implied in occasional jibes that he saw Carte as something of a parasite.

"I confess I don't feel very keen about Carte," he wrote to Sullivan in 1885. "He owes every penny he possesses to us. . . . When *we* manage the theatre for him he succeeds splendidly. When he manages for himself, he fails. Moreover, when he succeeds, he shows a disposition to kick away the ladder by which he has risen."[2]

Though Gilbert bears a reputation for being what modern slang would call a control freak, Sullivan was, in his own area, just as protective of his own prerogatives.

As author, lyricist, and director (and, at least occasionally, as costume designer, set designer, or choreographer), Gilbert ruled a wide range of domains. But as composer, orchestrator, music director, and (early in the run of a show) conductor, Sullivan similarly controlled far more than a musical theater or operatic composer customarily would, then or now.

Nor was Sullivan reluctant to wield his power. For all his "Mr. Nice Guy" reputation, his standards for performers were as demanding as Gilbert's. In describing Hugh Talbot, who originated the role of Frederic in *The Pirates of Penzance,* Sullivan wrote: "The tenor . . . is an idiot—vain and empty-headed. He very nearly upset the piece on the first night as he didn't know his words, and forgot his music."[3] (Talbot was subsequently replaced.)

Sullivan could also match Gilbert in apocalyptic threats when he felt that he was being slighted. During the run of *H. M. S. Pinafore,* he sent Carte a strong letter that said, in part,

> I regret to say that on my visit to the Theatre last Tuesday I found the Orchestra both in number and efficiency very different to what it was when I rehearsed the *Pinafore.*
>
> There seemed two second violins short and the whole band is of very indifferent quality. I beg to give you notice that if the deficiencies

are not supplied by Saturday and the efficiency of the orchestra in-
creased by engaging better players . . . I shall withdraw my music from
the theatre on Monday night.

You know perfectly well that what I say I mean.[4]

In assessing the "carpet quarrel," therefore, three points are central.

First, while Gilbert triggered the furor, and his combative temperament
prolonged it, he was not the only bullheaded member of the trio. Sullivan
and Carte could both be obstinate and in this case were.

Second, Gilbert's allegation that Carte was making improperly large
deductions for expenses before dividing the profits with his partners was
upheld in court. Carte, who was in the touchy position of renting his
theater to a partnership of which he himself was a member, was obliged
to make several thousand pounds in back payments to Gilbert—and, ironically, to Sullivan, though he had testified in Carte's favor.

Third and finally, the public perception that the quarrel was a great
deal of fuss over a comparatively small amount of money was entirely
accurate. The cost of the carpets in question amounted to approximately
150 pounds, and even the whole amount involved in the eventual settle-
ment paled before the amount that Gilbert and Sullivan had made from
their operas with Carte—which, as it came out during the trial, amounted
to more than 180,000 pounds between them.

So while Gilbert was apparently technically correct in his objections, it
was certainly penny-wise pound-foolish to disrupt the collaboration over
what totaled only a few thousand pounds. And though the two were to
reunite within two years' time—under a new financial arrangement under
which Carte and Sullivan were true partners while Gilbert worked on a
straight royalty basis—the collaboration was never the same.[5]

The final two operas, *Utopia, Limited* and *The Grand Duke,* would prove
as much.

The biggest problem with *Utopia, Limited* is not that Gilbert and Sullivan
are in disagreement. Rather, it is that they are so thoroughly in agreement—or, at any rate, keep their disagreements to themselves.

As had been the case when they began *The Gondoliers* after the "cipher
quarrel," the two men were delighted to be on good terms again. Gilbert
briefly joined Sullivan on a Riviera vacation to go over plans for the new
opera, bringing with him a story line that, after extensive revisions, Sullivan pronounced Gilbert's funniest ever.[6]

The music was written comparatively quickly, with hardly a word of
dissent from Gilbert, who for example called the Act 1 finale Sullivan's
best ever[7]—high praise indeed, given some of the previous examples in
the series.

This very congeniality was counterproductive, however. The collaboration had always been driven by candid criticism—each man would nit-pick
about even individual words or notes, reworking tirelessly until every lyric,

every tune, every speech seemed exactly right. Whole songs, scenes, and even characters could be altered or scrapped entirely, regardless of the time and effort already lavished on them, simply because they weren't up to the creators' exacting standards.

Now the situation was different. After nearly two years of conflict and another in which, though officially reconciled, they did not work together, neither man was in any mood to antagonize the other.

This lack of criticism did not mean that each found the other's work flawless; they merely refrained from rocking the boat. Gilbert's private opinions at the time can't be documented, but after Sullivan's death he wrote to Helen Carte saying that he planned substantial changes for a proposed series of revivals: "The alterations would probably be very material, especially in *Ruddigore, Utopia, Limited* and *The Grand Duke*."[8] (The revivals never took place.)

As for Sullivan, he simply dissociated himself from any problems with the final two operas. Where once he had served as virtual co-author of the plots for previous shows, dissecting characters, paring dialogues and rejecting lyrics without hesitation, now he went along with nearly anything that Gilbert wanted, as long as it didn't directly hamper the music.

In short, 1890s Gilbert & Sullivan is not 1880s Gilbert & Sullivan. The two men remain masters of their respective arts, but the distance between them is apparent even in both men's good-faith efforts to span that distance.

Works such as *Iolanthe* or *The Mikado* had seemed almost to emerge from one two-faceted mind, so in sync were their creators. *Utopia, Limited* and *The Grand Duke* reveal two separate minds at work. Again and again, music and lyrics don't quite fit, scenes drag, ideas appear and disappear, and mediocre efforts by librettist or composer are allowed to slip by unchallenged.

Compared with the middle operas, *Utopia, Limited* hardly counts as a collaboration, so disengaged were its creators. It resembles *Thespis* or *Trial by Jury,* operas for which Sullivan had basically set Gilbert's existing libretti without any say on his part. With *Utopia, Limited* and *The Grand Duke,* Sullivan is in certain respects once again a journeyman composer rather than a full partner in each opera as a whole. Neither man has the benefit of real input from the other, and the results prove only what intelligent observers had known all along: Gilbert & Sullivan was a good bit better than Gilbert or Sullivan.

The financial saga of *Utopia, Limited* embodied the partners' disengagement from true partnership. The "carpet quarrel" had begun with Gilbert's dismay that, as he wrote to Sullivan, "the preliminary expenses of the *Gondoliers* amounted to the stupendous sum of 4,500 pounds!!!"[9] Nonetheless, the lavish *Utopia, Limited* ran up preliminary expenses totaling 7,200 pounds, with hardly an eyebrow raised.[10]

In retrospect, Carte emphasized that it was *Utopia, Limited's* extravagant costs that, more than anything, caused it to run only a disappointing 245 performances—longer than *The Sorcerer*, to be sure, but nothing compared to *The Gondoliers'* 554. After *Utopia, Limited* closed, the producer wrote to Gilbert and Sullivan about their next work:

> I think that if the next production is to have a fair chance of being a successful commercial speculation, it is essential that the preliminary expenses should be something altogether different than those of *Utopia.*
>
> If the preliminary expenses of the next opera are reduced to, say, 2,000 pounds, and the salary list reduced to something like it was in the days of *Patience*, etc., we could afford after the first flash of crowded business in the opening month, to play for six months to an average of 150 pounds a month, and feel happy about it.[11]

But Carte's relations with Gilbert were so tenuous that he could not insist that due economy be observed, either with *Utopia, Limited* or its successor. *The Grand Duke* ended up costing nearly as much as *Utopia, Limited*, with a similarly large cast.

The greatest damage from Gilbert and Sullivan's excessive thoughtfulness toward each other is seen not in individual songs or characters but in the opera as a whole. Here Sullivan's impact had been greatest, and here his effective absence is most felt.

The team's best operas had worked on three separate levels—story, subject, and theme. As a whole, *Utopia, Limited* works on none. It has funny lines and nice tunes, but is almost nonfunctional as an opera.

Thespis (with which, as Jane W. Stedman points out, *Utopia, Limited* shares a plot structure, with a group of outsiders coming in and reordering the running of an established society)[12] had been purely a story opera, asking nothing more than "What happens next?" and taking its laughs where it found them. *Trial by Jury* had moved to the subject level, producing both a humorous narrative and a consistent satire of the passion for money that Gilbert felt drove Victorian society.

The Sorcerer and its successors had added a thematic level, but *Utopia, Limited* returns to the style of *Trial by Jury*. Its thematic level is so sketchy as to vanish entirely for long stretches, while its subject level languishes without *Trial's* razor-keen focus.

Even on the story level, *Utopia, Limited* falters. The love of Scaphio and Phantis for Princess Zara is a major plot thread in Act 1 but disappears completely by Act 2. Three of the Flowers of Progress—Captain Fitzbattleaxe, Lord Dramaleigh, and Mr. Goldbury—emerge as leading roles in the second act, while the other three all but vanish. Some apparently major plot elements dwindle (Tarara's threat to blow up the King), while others loom unexpectedly large (the *Palace Peeper*, which is introduced as a comic throwaway line but later becomes a crucial issue between Paramount and Lady Sophy). Throughout, the characters' personalities change at the drop of a hat.

In some cases, this incoherence arises from hasty cutting—an Act 2 continuation of the Scaphio/Zara/Phantis plot was cut in rehearsal.[13] In others it seems mere sloppiness—Gilbert is even more careless than he was in *The Gondoliers,* and Sullivan apparently doesn't care enough to dig in his heels and insist on improvement, as once he would have.

On a subject level, the scope of *Utopia, Limited's* wide-ranging satire of English society and its customs—and Gilbert's incompatibility with that scope—all but guarantee that it will be ineffective.

Gilbert was never a social satirist in the vein of Swift or Twain, because he didn't regard society as fatally flawed. The best satirists are radicals, opposed to nearly everything; Gilbert was a conservative, affectionately twitting the excesses of those (on either left or right) with whom he didn't really disagree too much.

His best satire, then, was localized. He could mock the Aesthetics without implying that there was anything bankrupt about a society that produced such people. He could parody republican ideals and aristocratic privilege alike while basically supporting the governmental system as he found it. Society as a whole was safe from his arrows.

Because of this misfit between subject and satirist, *Utopia, Limited* moves uncertainly between satire, parody, and mere spoof. Too often, Gilbert finds that he generally supports what he is supposedly mocking, leading to sequences that seem as if they ought to be funny but nevertheless aren't.

A prime example is the Drawing-Room scene, in which, under the influence of his English advisors, King Paramount adopts the rituals of Queen Victoria's drawing-rooms.

These strange quasi-ceremonies, more occasions for society ladies to be seen than for anything actually to happen, would have posed an inviting target for an antimonarchist who saw the royals as ludicrously glorified examples of ritualized mundanity. What could better suit a broad satire of Victorian England than an attack on Victoria herself, the quintessential symbol of the age?

But Gilbert fundamentally approved of both the age and its symbol, and as a result the Drawing-Room scene derails. The reviewers praised Gilbert's skill not in deflating the ritual of the Drawing-Room but rather in duplicating it. (No better evidence of this can be found than the fact that the Lord Chamberlain's office, which zealously prohibited any satiric treatment of the Queen or her family, found the scene unobjectionable.)

And indeed, Gilbert's stage directions are astonishingly detailed, specifying who enters in what order, who carries whose train, where everyone sits, and even how the guests' calling cards are conveyed to the king. Each actor's costume was painstakingly accurate, down to the king's military decorations (which drew a mild protest from the Prince of Wales, whose decorations had been exactly reproduced). Gilbert's staging-book diagrams for the scene have the precision of a military handbook. The entire scene is intricate, elaborate, excruciatingly accurate—and not at all funny.

Sullivan's music is a grand processional (one of several in the opera), but it has none of the tongue-in-cheek wit of *Iolanthe's* "Loudly Let the Trumpet Bray." It could, in fact, have been played with perfect decorum at an actual Drawing-Room.

In short, the Drawing-Room scene is nothing more than pageantry. Like much else in *Utopia, Limited,* it becomes what it supposedly mocks.

This scene is only the most extreme example of Gilbert's lack of satiric edge. His scattershot darts at English fashions, financial ethics, dressing-room mirrors, sanitary campaigns, political cartoons, and the like win some laughs, but they don't add up to anything. The whole is at best the sum of its parts, and often less.

The basic scenario of *Utopia, Limited* lends itself to satire. In fact, it vaguely echoes the island-hopping in *Gulliver's Travels* (1726). The trouble is, Gilbert doesn't have the attitude to create such satire. He doesn't think that England is fundamentally corrupt, as Swift does—to Gilbert, the country is merely filled with people who too easily get carried away.

Thus he routinely undercuts his own satire. For example, the delicious "Although of Native Maids the Cream" and "Bold-Faced Ranger" provide a satire of English womanhood that is almost worthy of Swift:

> English girls of well-bred notions
> shun all unrehearsed emotions.
>   English girls of highest class
>   practice them before the glass.

But Gilbert doesn't actually think that English girls are excessively prudish or artificial, nor that prudery or artifice are inherently bad. He is extremely fond of English girlhood, to tell the truth.

Thus his satiric bite is toothless. Lady Sophy, the embodiment of English stuffiness, doesn't meet with a comic downfall. Instead, she wins the man of her dreams, a "prudish paragon" of a king whose extreme propriety is presented as entirely admirable.

The trenchant satire of "Although of Native Maids the Cream" is utterly vanquished in Act 2, when Goldbury sings "A Bright and Beautiful English Girl":

> Her soul is as sweet as the ocean air,
> for prudery knows no haven there;

to find mock-modesty, please apply
to the conscious blush and the downcast eye.

Though this song might be read as a seduction by a calculating Goldbury, such a reading is not borne out by either words or music. By all indications Goldbury is sincere, and so are Gilbert & Sullivan.

But if so, what is the point? If English girls really are as Goldbury says they are, then the Utopians should indeed emulate them, and the whole point of the opera totters. Gilbert pins a bulls-eye on English girls but winds up putting them on a pedestal; he has a right to his opinion, of course, but it hardly makes for satiric bite.

In its own way, Goldbury's abrupt about-face is even more harmful to the satire. In Act 1 he is a cynical company promoter, boasting "It's shady, but it's sanctified by custom"; in Act 2, he emerges as a secondary romantic lead.

To function as a satire, the opera needs to argue (as it does for most of its first act) that Utopia is actually better than a corrupt, hypocritical England and that the Flowers of Progress are actually destroying the island by attempting to improve it. If England, like its girls, really is better than Utopia—and merely misrepresented by the prudish Lady Sophy and (in the early part of Act 2) the waggish Flowers—then the opera has nothing meaningful to say to the audience to whom it is addressed.

In short, if Goldbury is not an English serpent in a Utopian Eden, what is the point to him, or to the opera itself?

By late Act 2, when Goldbury sings "English Girl," the opera is seriously off course, but a satisfying ending could still salvage it.

In such structurally similar Gilbertian comedies as *The Wicked World* (1873) and *The Sorcerer*, the citizens come to their senses and cast out the corrupting outsiders. Eden drives off its serpents, and affairs are restored to their original complexion.

And indeed Gilbert provides his customary twist—the addition of government by party, which will transform the now-perfect Utopia into a mirror of England, gleefully imperfect and fully functional. But unlike those of previous operas, the ending of *Utopia, Limited* isn't thematically appropriate, fails to tie everything together, and provides no closure. It simply muddies the waters.

On a story level, the ending's topsy-turvy daffiness works to some extent. The lesson is that perfection (no war, no crime, no disease) is bad and that imperfection is the natural state of things. By forgetting government by party, Zara has accidentally created perfection, and only by restoring it can Utopia achieve true happiness. But on a subject level this ending makes no sense at all. Gilbert seems to argue that party politics is the only thing standing between England and paradise.

Now, Gilbert had long disliked party politics—as early as *H. M. S. Pinafore's* "When I Was a Lad" and *Iolanthe's* "When All Night Long," he had made comic hay out of the absurdities of political parties.

But *Utopia, Limited* has had nothing to do with party politics to this point. The ending upends the play, making it into a comprehensive attack on something that previously hasn't even been mentioned. This final twist drains meaning from everything that has passed before, leaving the whole opera unfocused and incoherent.

To succeed as a social satire, *Utopia, Limited* would have to attack England. And indeed the sheer effulgence of the Utopians' Anglophilia is a perfect vehicle for satire—a Voltaire or a Swift could have delivered a devastating indictment.

But to Gilbert, England really is vastly better than Utopia and, for all its minor flaws, about as good a society as can be imagined. He doesn't mine the full humor of his idea because, to all appearances, he himself doesn't see how humorous it is.

Ultimately, it may be that Gilbert & Sullivan couldn't really satirize English society because they were too much a part of it. As Gilbert had written to Sullivan five years earlier, "we are world-known, and as much an institution as Westminster Abbey."[14] The best satire has always been written by outsiders, and by 1893 both men were consummate insiders.

Satiric ineffectiveness is not a crippling failing, of course. The satiric aspects of *The Gondoliers* virtually evaporate over the course of the opera, as do those of *Iolanthe*, and neither opera is any worse for it. The thinness of the *Gondoliers* story and the incompleteness of its satire are more than compensated for by the opera's wit, its delightful characters, and its satisfying thematic coherence.

But *Utopia, Limited* is even less effective thematically than it is in terms of story and subject.

To the extent that *Utopia, Limited* has a thematic level, it is about truthfulness and the importance of avoiding masks. Goldbury captures its Socratean echoes most powerfully when he sings:

> Whatever you are—be that:
> > whatever you say—be true:
> > > straightforwardly act—
> > > be honest—in fact,
> > be nobody else but *you*.

This aversion to hypocrisy was not new to Gilbert. It was the central element in *The Mountebanks* (1892), his recently completed collaboration with Cellier, which had finally brought the lozenge plot to the stage. *The Palace of Truth* (1870) had used the story of a place where everyone unwittingly speaks the truth to argue that everybody is a hypocrite, while *Patience* had been among other things a wall-to-wall exposé of sham and pretense.

In Gilbert's works, hypocrisy is a means of distinguishing the bad characters from the good. Pooh-Bah, the Learned Judge, King Gama the self-proclaimed "philanthropist," the "aesthetic" Bunthorne, the "egalitarian" Sir Joseph Porter—all are scorned not so much for impurity as for pretending to purity.

To the extent that Gilbert holds a brief against English society as a whole, it is on the grounds of hypocrisy. *Utopia, Limited's* most successful socially satiric song, "Society Has Quite Forsaken All Its Wicked Courses," attacks precisely that point: King Paramount rejoices at the rooting-out of hypocrisy in Utopian society, noting that peerages no longer go to people who don't deserve them, rich people of doubtful character aren't seen at his Drawing-Rooms, and risqué stage costumes are as forbidden as suggestive language—in short, "no tolerance we show to undeserving rank or splendor, / for the higher his position is, the greater the offender."

In response the Flowers of Progress exclaim that England has also overcome all such hypocrisy, or at least is well on its way to doing so—which, of course, the English audience knows to be untrue. The Flowers reveal themselves (and the society they represent) to be doubly hypocritical, hypocrites even in denying their hypocrisy.

The same scorn for appearance-for-its-own-sake—and the same indication that England is run on such principles—is to be found in "Although of Native Maids the Cream," with its prudish assurance that "English girls are good as gold/ . . . demurely coy, divinely cold," and in "Bold-Faced Ranger," which applies to the rituals of English courtship exactly the sharp edge that is missing from the Drawing-Room scene.

Even the rapturous love duet "Sweet and Low" distinguishes between the shallowness of public raptures and the depth of true love's whispers. The whole idea that truth is paramount is summarized in "Bright and Beautiful English Girl" and the ensuing scene, celebrating truthfulness over everything else.

Taken together, these add up to a skeleton on which a satisfying thematic opera could have been built. Two problems, however, render that opera stillborn: first, too many scenes, songs, and characters that don't relate to this skeleton; second, an ending that brings no sense of thematic closure.

The power of the thematic level in Gilbert & Sullivan opera is precisely in its unifying aspect. No matter what may be going on at the surface of the opera, on what I have called its story level, the thematic level is being consistently developed.

As W. A. Darlington notes, all but one of the songs in the first act of *Patience* are about love.[15] Similar ratios apply to *Iolanthe's* study of mortality, *Ruddigore*'s morality tale, and the nature-of-love thematic inquiries in *The Sorcerer* and *The Yeomen of the Guard*.

The genius of Gilbert & Sullivan lies exactly in this knack—that they can write two love duets (*Iolanthe*'s "None Shall Part Us" and "If We're Weak Enough to Tarry") that function beautifully as self-contained songs but also constitute a related set of meditations on permanence and transience that relate integrally to the overall theme of mortality. In their best operas, virtually nothing works on only one level.

In *Utopia, Limited*, on the other hand, too much functions solely on one level. For example, "With Wily Brain upon the Spot" is a delightful song, but it has nothing to do, either musically or lyrically, with any other song in the show. The same is true of "A Tenor All Singers Above," "In Every Mental Lore," "First You're Born," the "Lifeguards" song and many others.

At best a quarter of the opera achieves anything like thematic unity. And since the test of a thematic structure is its comprehensiveness, it can fairly be said that *Utopia, Limited* has no linking thematic structure.

This is especially true in light of the ending. Gilbert's final lyric, after reciting a list of England's supposed virtues, concludes with a chorus that might have been a perfect union of satiric and thematic points, applying the appearance-versus-reality question to England herself:

> Such at least is the tale
> which is borne on the gale
> > from the island which dwells in the sea.
> Let us hope, for her sake,
> that she makes no mistake,
> > that she's all she professes to be!

Had the preceding opera revealed the blind spots in England's view of herself, this would have been a perfect summing-up. But since the plot resolution implies that England really is all that she professes to be, that effect is lost.

A fine cautionary finale is instead irrelevant (since apparently there is no mistake) and, accordingly, heavy-handed and preachy. The Utopians end up resolved not to be as they were but to become even more like England by adopting government by party; the lesson "Whatever you are, be that" is forgotten.

The various stories in the opera have failed to come together. They are, in fact, exactly that—different stories rather than different strands of the same story. The *Palace Peeper*, the Wise Men's pursuit of Zara, the Anglicization of Utopia, Sophy's quest for a mate—all are fundamentally unrelated and are resolved without recourse to one another. There is no central narrative to drive the thematic portion of the opera or to define the other stories in reference to it, and thus no powerful ending to tie it together.

Iolanthe's embracing death for the sake of those she loves serves as a magnificent capstone to the various story lines that make up *Iolanthe*. Patience's quest for the nature of love gives her opera an unshakable thematic center.

In *Utopia, Limited*, however—and it is significant that the less character-centered *Utopia* is the first opera since *H. M. S. Pinafore* not to be titled after people—there is no human story to center the opera. It offers no one to root for, nothing to hope for, nothing to feel for.

If *Utopia, Limited* lacks a fresh vision in its content, the same is true of its form. In terms of structure and technique, *Utopia* looks backward. *The Gondoliers* had in some respects been a coda to the preceding decade of masterworks, but *Utopia, Limited* is actually a step back along the path already taken.

In every previous opera, Gilbert & Sullivan had pushed the limits of both their individual arts and their genre. An attentive observer could deduce the operas' chronological order merely by studying their increasingly ambitious, increasingly accomplished style and substance. Such an observer would probably misassign *Utopia, Limited*, however, because it is in hardly any way a step beyond *The Gondoliers*, except perhaps in the scope of its social satire.

The evolution of Sullivan's music had been toward a more "operatic" style, with broader, more muscular orchestrations, more complex harmonies, and a deeper grounding of the music in the theatrical context of character and situation. He had moved from individual songs to musical scenes, lengthening the numbers and tying them more closely to one another—peaking in *The Gondoliers* with an ambitious, 90-minute first act that contained more than 80 minutes of music.

Conductor Raymond Osnato has suggested that Sullivan's less ambitious work on *Utopia, Limited* was motivated not by the "carpet quarrel" and its resolution but rather by the intervening production and failure of *Ivanhoe*.[16]

His first grand opera was to be the culmination of his development as an operatic composer, a step beyond *The Yeomen of the Guard* or *The Gondoliers*. When its success proved fleeting—it did run for 160 performances, unprecedented for a grand opera, but it had only infrequent revivals—Sullivan was greatly disappointed.

Going back to comic opera must have seemed a step backward, and perhaps the composer felt that one step back wasn't much different from 100 steps back and simply lost interest in musical theater.

In any event, the musical numbers in *Utopia, Limited* are generally shorter, with no effort to create coherent musical scenes. The Act 1 finale is long but, unlike the lengthy but coherent Act 1 finales of *Iolanthe* and *The Yeomen of the Guard*, it has no particular shape—it is a stringing-together of diverse songs rather than a thorough working-out of a consistent musical idea.

There are any number of individual gems—the swaggering "Make Way for the Wise Men," the witty "Although of Native Maids the Cream," the stirring (but too often repeated) "Life Guards" song, the ravishing duet "Sweet and Low," the intricate "With Wily Brain upon the Spot."

But they stand alone, neither developing previous ideas nor laying the groundwork for later numbers. *Utopia, Limited* is musically clever, at times even exuberant, but it is hardly the coherent score that Sullivan's previous works had been.

Most significant to the overall opera, Sullivan abandons his decade-long campaign for solid emotional story lines and a closer integration of music with plot and characters. Other than asking Gilbert to treat Lady Sophy more kindly (which the librettist readily agreed to do, though it weakened the comic purpose of the character), Sullivan more or less kept hands off the story. The result was an opera long on sarcasm and short on heart.

Gilbert's libretto is essentially cerebral, aimed at provoking laughter and social insight through satire rather than laughter and emotional involvement through situation comedy. It is the team's first significantly satiric opera since *Patience*, but whereas the social satire of *Patience* had been an overlay to a fundamentally resonant emotional story line, in *Utopia, Limited* the satire is the whole story. No one in *Utopia* could sing a song as deeply moving as "Love Is a Plaintive Song," because no one in the opera is human enough to suffer as Patience does.

Utopia, Limited's characters are sketchier than those of *Patience* and the problems they face are less meaningful. Their motivations are less consistent, as Gilbert regularly opts for easy laughs at the expense of character plausibility.

Paramount wants Utopia to be exactly like England, for example, except when Goldbury tells him that England isn't yet governed by the joint-stock principle, at which point Paramount endorses it anyway—"we will be before you."

The Flowers of Progress are sometimes truthful in describing England, sometimes blatant liars. Early in Act 2, as they boldly assure the king "we haven't any slummeries in England," they seem to be manipulative villains. Their turning the gullible king into the leader of a minstrel show seems downright cruel—though two of them nonetheless metamorphose into romantic leads shortly thereafter.

Fitzbattleaxe is a suave, confident hero in Act 1, canny enough to outmaneuver the two wisest men in Utopia. By the beginning of Act 2, however, he is a nervous, callow suitor singing "A Tenor All Singers Above" (afflicted by an insecurity that seems to have spared him for Act 1's seductive "Oh, Admirable Art"). Minutes later, of course, he is joining his colleagues in baldly lying to Paramount.

Each of these sequences works reasonably well as comedy, but at the expense of the whole. Because the laughs require the characters to behave inconsistently, the entire opera loses plausibility; ironically, its humor is less funny as a result.

The upshot is a show whose structural flaws, both musically and dramatically, make it less than the sum of its parts. Humor is allowed to supplant characterization and grand stage effects to replace real theatrical power. In either case, overall coherence is subverted to momentary effect.

On the level of technique, too, the absence of a central artistic vision is clear. Both Gilbert and Sullivan do excellent work on much, even most, of the opera. But both make elementary errors that they have not made since the beginning of their careers—precisely because their working relationship is now much as it was then.

Sullivan displays occasional awkwardness in suiting his music to his characters and a surprising lack of theatrical sensibility—both areas that had previously been among his greatest strengths.

The opening number, for instance, is on the whole lush and musically engaging. But Phylla's solo is set to a thumping, almost martial beat that doesn't match the serene lyric of "songs of birds" and "rippling play of waterway." Moreover, the song's musical rhythm doesn't quite fit the lyrics, requiring awkward stresses and the drawing-out of unaccented syllables.

Paramount's philosophical "First You're Born" is set as if it were a music-hall number, with a "ho ho ho ho ho ho ho" chorus that sounds almost like a drinking song. And, except for the verses for Captains. Fitzbattleaxe and Corcoran, the Flowers' introductory solos are neither melodically interesting nor in any way musically distinguished from one another.

There are many other instances of tunes that are tonally inconsistent with the lyrics or simply rhythmically conflicting. And because at this point both men value cooperation over quality, Gilbert doesn't complain about the weak setting, and Sullivan doesn't ask for different rhythms or for words that he would find more inspiring.

A low point in terms of theatrical effectiveness is the massive chorale "Eagle High." Musically this grand effort holds up well, at least by Victorian standards. But it brings the action, already dulled by the Drawing-Room scene, to a screeching halt.

Its most obvious antecedent is "Hail Poetry," the brief chorale in *The Pirates of Penzance*. But "Hail Poetry" is a mock chorale, burlesquing the penchant of cheap Victorian operas to pause in the middle of the action for a paean to some abstracted virtue. "Eagle High," on the other hand, is as earnest as "Hail Poetry" is tongue-in-cheek. Gilbert & Sullivan here actually become what they once mocked.

As a result, Sullivan's best work in *Utopia, Limited* is in the details. He catches the spirit of the arguing trio in "With Wily Brain upon the Spot" perfectly; introducing "Although of Native Maids the Cream," he sets the lines "How English and how pure" with a delightfully reverent tone; and he inserts a bit of hymn harmonization into the words "it needn't be a hymn one" in "Oh, Sweet Surprise."

"A Tenor All Singers Above" is a neat exercise in form following function, as Sullivan deftly employs each musical device that Gilbert's lyric mentions, while still making the song musically effective in its own right. "Society Has Quite Forsaken All Its Wicked Courses" utilizes close harmonies to capture the spirit of minstrel songs, along with orchestration that evokes banjos and even the use of actual tambourines.

And his melodic gift remains unimpaired, as does (when he sees fit) the new, broader harmonic repertoire displayed in his previous few operas. Both of the love duets ("Oh, Admirable Art" and "Sweet and Low") are ravishingly beautiful, and several of the ensembles are triumphs of pure music. "It's Understood, I Think, All Round" lets the composer play both harmonic and rhythmic games, juggling the Scaphio/Phantis patter and the Zara/Fitzbattleaxe duet to delightful effect.

But on a larger level there is little sense that the composer is giving his best effort. This is Sullivan the organ-grinder, an exceptionally skilled musician with a gift for melody and a flair for dance rhythms, filling in the blanks in the libretto Gilbert sends him. It is not Sullivan the musical-theater artist.

As for Gilbert, a common view of his work is expressed by Audrey Williamson: "Gilbert had run out of talent by *Utopia, Limited*."[17]

This is not strictly true. *Utopia, Limited* shows considerable talent but, as with Sullivan, it is a talent diffused, lacking the focus Gilbert had brought to the earlier operas.

Perhaps the most striking single element of the *Utopia, Limited* libretto is how often it refers to previous operas. If Sullivan's work is a stylistic glance back, Gilbert's is downright regressive in both form and content.

Two instances of this looking-back are obvious—the reintroduction of Captain Corcoran (and his "What, never?") and the reference to the Mikado of Japan as an authority on matters of punishment. These two allusions are virtually unique—except for an *H. M. S. Pinafore* reference (not a quote) in "I Am the Very Model of a Modern Major-General" 15 years before, Gilbert had alluded to the team's previous works only once, in the "What, never?" reprise cut from *The Pirates of Penzance* shortly after its New York opening, a cut that indicated confidence in *Pirates'* appeal in its own right as much as the use of a similar reprise in *Utopia, Limited*, suggests doubt.

Beyond these explicit citations, however, *Utopia, Limited* teems with line echoes and situation references so numerous as to defy mere coincidence. Every Savoy opera occasionally recalls previous ones—*Iolanthe's* "When I

Went to the Bar" evokes *Trial by Jury's* "When I, Good Friends, Was Called to the Bar," for example. But never before *Utopia, Limited* had there been so many obvious similarities.

The name Tarara, for example, was apparently a reference to the then-popular song, "Ta-Ra-Ra-Boom-De-Ay," but it also evokes both the Policemen's "Tarantara" *(The Pirates of Penzance)* and the Peers' "tantantara" *(Iolanthe).* The Public Exploder's determination to "accustom myself by degrees to the startling nature of my duties" by practicing with party "crackers" echoes Ko-Ko *(The Mikado)* and his intention to begin practicing executions on a guinea pig and work his way up to a Second Trombone. King Paramount's obsequious obedience to his subjects' whims reminds us of Marco and Giuseppe *(The Gondoliers),* while the line-finishing lyrics of Scaphio and Phantis in "In Every Mental Lore" suggests the frequent use of that device in *The Gondoliers,* especially in "As One Individual."

That Scaphio claims never to have loved is reminiscent of Patience, while his "accumulated fervor of 66 years" suggests Ruth's love that "has been accumulating 47 years" *(The Pirates of Penzance),* and his insistence that "All are opaque—opaque—opaque" reminds us of Bunthorne's "Oh, Hollow, Hollow, Hollow" *(Patience).* Phantis's line "you have placed me on the very pinnacle of human joy" recalls Aline *(The Sorcerer)* and her comment that a filter doesn't "place its possessor on the very pinnacle of earthly joy."

The discussion in "Bold-Faced Ranger" of tossing coins for a mate evokes a similar Mountararat/Tolloller dialogue in *Iolanthe,* while in the same song Gilbert reuses the rhyme "ladies / each a little bit afraid is" from "Comes a Train of Little Ladies" *(The Mikado).* Scaphio's comment that the king is "undoing by night all the despotic absurdities he's committed during the day" reminds one of Despard Murgatroyd *(Ruddigore),* while Paramount's "It's a quaint world" recalls Dick Deadeye *(H. M. S. Pinafore)* and his "It's a queer world." The humor-obsessed potentate Paramount suggests his correspondent, the similarly obsessed potentate the Mikado.

The English tutor Lady Sophy resembles the English tutor Lady Blanche *(Princess Ida),* while "Oh, Maiden Rich in Girton Lore" strongly resembles that opera's "Mighty Maiden with a Mission." The entrance of the Life Guards suggests "The Soldiers of Our Queen" *(Patience),* though the vocalized trumpet calls again suggest "Loudly Let the Trumpet Bray" *(Iolanthe),* while the "helmet hot and a tunic tight" suggests Arac's "This Helmet I Suppose" *(Princess Ida).*

The duet "Oh, Admirable Art," discussing what the lovers would do if only things were different, resembles both "Were You Not to Ko-Ko Plighted" *(The Mikado)* and "There Was a Time" *(The Gondoliers),* and Zara's "the army of the conqueror / in serried ranks assembles" recalls Nanki-Poo's "our warriors in serried ranks assembled" *(The Mikado),* especially since each is matched with a "tremble" rhyme.

This list of allusions gives only the most obvious ones from *Utopia, Limited*'s first act alone, but they should be enough to make the point clear: While a certain "family resemblance" is to be expected between any two Savoy operas, there are too many echoes, and they are too blatant, to be merely an accident.

The Gondoliers, with its theme of parting and reconciliation, had evoked the relationship of its creators. *Utopia, Limited* evokes the operas themselves, repeatedly waving a flag at the audience to make sure that they realize they're seeing a Gilbert & Sullivan opera.

One senses an insecurity on Gilbert's part, a need to remind the audience of the team's past successes. He could tell that things were not the same, and this awareness may have led him to create an opera that, instead of being as fresh and original as its predecessors, tried to evoke a sense of familiarity, a feeling of having seen the opera before.

It does not bode well for *Utopia, Limited* or any future operas. A librettist accustomed to moving forward is not only resting on his laurels but waving them for fresh acknowledgment from his audience.

More important, in looking so frequently to the past, Gilbert slights the present. The characters in *Utopia, Limited* remind us of memorable previous characters rather than being themselves memorable.

Utopia, Limited is the team's only opera since *Thespis* to produce no rich, colorful characters, great roles for great performers. This is traditionally laid to Gilbert's resentment of such departed stars as Richard Temple, George Grossmith, and Jessie Bond, leading to another attempt at an opera without stars (except for the enduring Rutland Barrington as Paramount and perhaps Rosina Brandram, a Savoy mainstay who never quite achieved popular stardom, as Lady Sophy). It's more likely, however, that he simply got caught up in other things—allusions to the past, grand ceremonials, diverse satiric ideas—and simply lost track of the need to create strong characters.

In any event, he apparently regretted this lack. The next opera, *The Grand Duke*, contributes several memorable characters to the repertoire, roles memorable because, instead of harkening back to previous favorites, they establish their own distinctiveness.

Utopia, Limited also continues the lyrical slackness that Gilbert had shown in *The Gondoliers*. He is more willing to force rhymes by distorting pronunciation—rhyming "island" with "my land," for example, or "university" with "her city." (Mere laziness would not seem to explain the rhyming of "please / ease / languages".)

More than ever, the librettist doesn't bother to shape sentences that rhyme naturally. Instead, he twists syntaxes mercilessly, producing hard-to-follow passages such as "If to refuse / the king decide, / the royal shoes / then woe betide!"

He even pulls words out of nowhere, words neither in character nor likely to be understood by the audience: "The earth is red and rosal," for example, may employ an actual word, but it manages to be both archaic and redundant. And when Zara addresses the Utopians as "South Pacific Island viviparians," it can only be to find a rhyme for "barbarians"—"viviparous" is a zoological term meaning "giving birth to live young" (as opposed to laying eggs) and, while the Utopians presumably do not lay eggs, it is difficult to believe that Zara would actually stress that fact.

Like any lyricist, Gilbert occasionally lapsed throughout his career, but now the lapses are more frequent and glaring. It may be that, if Sullivan had let him, he would have taken such easy outs all along, though I doubt it; but he certainly gets away with more in *Utopia, Limited* than in any previous opera, and neither his craftsmanship nor the opera benefits.

Throughout *Utopia, Limited*, both men mistake grandness of scale for theatricality. The opera rings with elaborate introductory processionals—in the first act alone there's "Make Way for the Wise Men" for Scaphio and Phantis, "Quaff the Nectar" for King Paramount, "How Fair, How Modest" for Nekaya and Kalyba, "Oh, Maiden Rich in Girton Lore" for Princess Zara and, essentially, the entire Act 1 finale for the Flowers of Progress.

Not that there's anything wrong with big processionals—there are four in *The Mikado*. But all of the earlier opera's are short, and each fills a different dramatic function: "Behold the Lord High Executioner" is brief and funny; "Comes a Train of Little Ladies" is brief and pretty; "With Aspect Stern" is brief and dramatic; and "Miya Sama" is brief and impressive.

The processions in *Utopia, Limited* are not brief. They let Sullivan show his musical resources and allow Gilbert to display not only lavish costumes but also what was apparently a real skill at creating beautiful stage tableaux. Victorian audiences enjoyed such effects, but—crowd-pleasers or not—every one of the *Utopia, Limited* processions stops the action dead.

None is funny, except perhaps for the final lines of "Maiden Rich in Girton Lore": "And teach us, please, / to speak with ease / all languages / alive and dead!" They tend to be impersonal, clichéd songs that establish no personality either for the chorus singing them or for the character being introduced. They merely dissipate whatever dramatic or comic momentum may have developed in the preceding scene.

The abundance of processions speaks to a key flaw of *Utopia, Limited:* Rather than developing the characters he has on stage, Gilbert is constantly ringing in a new set. No character is given the stage time of a Pooh-Bah, Sir Despard, Wilfred Shadbolt, or Don Alhambra to establish a memorable character. In the interest of novelty, scenic splendor, or a passing laugh, scene after scene passes with nothing really happening. There is more action in the Act 2 finale of *Princess Ida* than in the entire first act of *Utopia, Limited.*

Furthermore, Gilbert's libretto has a surprising number of sequences that are neither humorous nor dramatic—at best, they're preachy. "Eagle

High" is the most obvious example of earnestness replacing wit, but "A Bright and Beautiful English Girl" is so rhapsodic that it almost *must* be parodic, yet apparently isn't. "Oh, Admirable Art" and "Quaff the Nectar" might be funny if they tried, but they don't. And "First You're Born," shaped like a comic song, is arguably the most scathingly cynical, sardonically unfunny song Gilbert ever wrote.

As with Sullivan's contribution, Gilbert's libretto works best on a small scale. Though he never appears, the most amusing character in the opera may be "the celebrated English tenor, Mr. Wilkinson," who of course is actually a Utopian. In Utopia, apparently, seeming to be foreign born is as helpful to artistic reputation as it was (and is) in England, especially for Italian tenors. (Sullivan, who waged a long campaign on behalf of English musicians, must particularly have relished this bit.)

The opera's funniest story line is its only fully developed comic idea, the saga of the *Palace Peeper*. Here Gilbert, the one-time comic journalist, is as focused as he is elsewhere disjoint. His barbs at society journalism, editorial writing, and political cartooning surely reflect his own experience in these areas—and, like Paramount, he would surely find "A bad king but a very good subject" to be "a capital heading for next week's leading article." There is a good-natured tweaking here that is absent from much of the rest of the humor.

All in all, the greatest problem with *Utopia, Limited* is that it isn't what it professes to be—both a biting social satire and an old-fashioned Savoy opera. Gilbert & Sullivan try hard to evoke "the good old days" and then some. It isn't enough to recall Captain Corcoran and give him "three cheers and one cheer more," as in *H. M. S. Pinafore*—now it must be "three cheers more."

But, as Carte seems to have realized, for Gilbert & Sullivan less was more. The grandeur of *Utopia, Limited*, the complexity of its plot, the multiplicity of its characters, all aim to be bigger and better than ever but succeed only in being bigger.

Ultimately *Utopia, Limited*'s very extravagance works against it. Its length dissipates its impact. Its numerous story lines and characters prevent any one from being fully developed to comic or dramatic effect. Its lavish production values drain vitality from the script—more apparent now, perhaps, than in the elaborate 1893 production.

In general, *Utopia, Limited* lacks the cohesiveness that had made the mature operas great. It is less opera than pageant, an extravagant parade of Gilbert & Sullivan imagery. And under the changed circumstances of the collaboration, there was no one both willing and able to do anything about it.

In its fulsomeness, *Utopia, Limited* recalls the early-draft versions of *The Sorcerer, Iolanthe*, or *The Gondoliers*—but those drafts were mercilessly pared down by Gilbert & Sullivan until they were sharp and hard-edged. *Utopia*,

Limited is soft-edged, unformed, waiting for the unflinching revision that neither creator was by this time willing to undertake.

As it stands, it is more a collection of ideas for an opera than a finished opera.

From anyone else, such a product might have succeeded. But the standards Gilbert & Sullivan had set (and of which *Utopia, Limited* so often reminds the audience) created expectations so high that even they could meet the test only at their very best. Anything less, and the audience would feel—as critics and audiences for *Utopia, Limited* apparently did—that Gilbert & Sullivan had let them down.

In the end, perhaps the opera provides its own epitaph:

Though lofty aims catastrophe entail,
we'll gloriously succeed or nobly fail!

Facing page: FIGURE 16.1. Ilka von Palmay (right) as Julia Jellicoe in *The Grand Duke*, with Rutland Barrington (left) as Ludwig. The Hungarian singer's strong accent served as a vehicle for some the opera's most imaginative meta-theatrical humor. *Source: The V & A Picture Library.*

16

The Grand Duke

When Gilbert, in his famous 1907 speech at the Old Players Club,[1] acknowledged that he and Sullivan were "credited with one failure," the more knowledgeable among his audience must have been surprised to realize that he was speaking of *Ruddigore*, not *The Grand Duke.*

Today, that fact is even more striking. Since its revival in the 1920s, *Ruddigore* has been a part of the standard Gilbert & Sullivan repertoire. Owing in part to their relative unpopularity and in part to their considerable costs of production, *Utopia, Limited* was not revived by the Cartes until the 1970s, while *The Grand Duke* never was, and neither opera has ever been performed as frequently as its siblings.

It may be that Gilbert didn't think of *Utopia, Limited* as a failure. Its run of 245 performances was comparable to *Ruddigore's* 288, and it remained popular with audiences—it was closed primarily because its lavish production made it unprofitable even when it was still drawing substantial audiences.

But *The Grand Duke* is another story. If the two were credited with one failure, it would surely be this one. *The Grand Duke's* run of 123 performances, coupled with generally negative reviews and only brief popularity, easily qualified it as the team's least successful work after *Thespis.*

And nobody, not even Gilbert—who since the "carpet quarrel" had worked on a royalty basis, thus taking his payment directly from the gross receipts rather than sharing in the net profits—made any money from it.

Even at the time, neither creator thought much of it. Gilbert called it "an ugly, misshapen little brat" that he was glad to see the last of,[2] while in his diary Sullivan greeted the end of rehearsals with a heartfelt "Thank God" and noted his relief at the premiere: "Another week's rehearsal with W. S. G. and I should have gone raving mad. I had already ordered some straw for my hair."[3]

Criticism of *The Grand Duke* tended to agree that the music outshone the book: "There are still a number of excellent songs, but the dialogue seems to have lost much of its crispness," wrote *The Times,*[4] while *Stage Whispers* opined, "Mr. Gilbert has stood still, but Sir Arthur Sullivan has advanced."[5] *The Musical Standard* added, "Sir Arthur Sullivan has done better than his librettist."[6]

Criticism of the libretto focused on three main areas, each at least to some extent justified: its length, its complexity, and its flatness.

As to the length, its impact can hardly be denied. At close to three and a half hours, *The Grand Duke* is the longest of the operas, and its dialogue is often repetitive and almost always unduly convoluted.

As with *Utopia, Limited,* this opera never underwent the meticulous editing process of the earlier shows. Both men had been exhausted by their previous conflicts and were if anything overly solicitous of one another's feelings. This moderation had the unfortunate effect of causing each man to refrain from criticizing anything the other had done, even when criticism was called for.

In earlier years, Sullivan had scrutinized Gilbert's books carefully, almost as if he himself were the librettist. Whenever he spotted a weakness, he would insist that Gilbert rework it; in extreme cases, he had even rejected a book in its entirety until his concerns were addressed.

This made for a longer, more contentious writing process, but it produced better operas. Sullivan had a keen theatrical eye, and his suggestions almost invariably improved Gilbert's material.

On *The Grand Duke* Sullivan had as keen an eye as ever, but he held his tongue. Instead of voicing his objections to Gilbert, he confided them to his diary and in letters to friends. "Parts of it dragged a little—dialogue too redundant," he noted after the premiere.[7]

"Why reproach me?" he wrote in response to Burnand's criticism of the opera. "I didn't write the book!"[8]

But Burnand's complaint was a reasonable one. Not long before, it had not been unfair to credit Sullivan somewhat for the book and Gilbert somewhat for the music—each man had had an active voice in the other's work. By now, however, their working relationship had regressed almost to what it had been for *Thespis* or *Trial by Jury,* with each working in virtual isolation.

Thus *The Grand Duke* cries out for editing—not cutting, as is often done today, generally producing a show that is shorter but even less coherent or dramatically effective—but rewriting, compression, and consolidation. In short, the opera lacks the ruthless editorial shaping that had been applied to the earlier operas. Both men still had the talent and judgment to exact excellence, but neither wanted to rock the boat. Artistic achievement, long their ultimate goal, now took a second place to avoiding confrontation.

Its length aside, *The Grand Duke* is in most respects Gilbert's most incoherent libretto. Unlike *Utopia, Limited,* which began as a more-or-less coherent whole and was rendered incoherent by hasty cuts, *The Grand Duke* never did really add up.

Incoherence isn't the result of plot implausibility but rather of artistic inconsistency. *H. M. S. Pinafore* has a gaping plot hole in its famous age paradox, but it's deliberately absurd, parodying melodramatic convention with an intentionally artificial resolution. The same is true of *The Pirates of Penzance,* and both work admirably on the stage.

That is not the case with *The Grand Duke.* Its libretto wasn't intended to be illogical, but its series of implausibilities add up to, as W. A. Darlington says, a lack of "that indefinable air of plausibility which Gilbert, at his best, was able to infuse into the most unlikely situations."[9]

In part, this is because the plot mechanism itself creaks. A key event, such as Ludwig's persuading the Grand Duke to stage his own death, is made possible literally by the luck of the draw—Ludwig draws a higher card than Ernest. In *The Mikado,* similarly bizarre developments occur frequently, but they are done through characters negotiating, pleading, and arguing, offering a sound character basis for the superficially implausible ensuing developments.

The Grand Duke is built on an inherently weak plot framework. Most of the previous Gilbert & Sullivan operas rely on single preposterous elements—the witch's curse in *Ruddigore,* for example, or *The Yeomen of the Guard's* masked marriage—which are subsequently treated plausibly enough that each opera as a whole seems logical.

This is not the case with *The Grand Duke.* The implausibility of the statutory duel itself could be worked through, but it is joined by the infant engagement of Rudolph and the Princess of Monte Carlo, a conspiracy of actors, a good-humored detective, the invention of roulette, and so on.

To add to the unlikeliness of it all, as Alan Jefferson points out, the mechanism of the opera requires that all of the opera's key events, including the weddings of Ludwig and of Rudolph, the Princess's birthday, the expiration of the Statutory Duel law, and the overthrow of the Grand Duke, take place on the same day.[10] None has any relation to any other—they occur simultaneously simply because the plot won't work any other way.

Each of *The Grand Duke's* ludicrous elements is itself funny and can go over well in performance, but together they weave a web of implausibility that makes the opera as a whole seem trivial and gimmicky.

Finally, there is the question of character consistency.

The ending of *The Grand Duke* is Gilbert's least satisfactory in at least two regards. First, the plot is resolved through an oversight—the Notary's mistaken assumption about the rules of the statutory duel—and, second, the plot doesn't make sense according to the way the characters have been established.

Where in *Patience, Iolanthe,* or *Ruddigore* the "gimmick" is both funny and a manifestation of the evolution of the key character, in *The Grand Duke* it is purely a gimmick. And an arbitrary one at that, since it takes two coincidences—Ludwig happening to draw an ace against Ernest and then Ludwig and Rudolph likewise happening to use an ace in their staged duel—to make the mistake relevant. Had Ludwig drawn a 10 to Ernest's 9, the opera would presumably end unhappily.

This arbitrary gimmick is unfair to the audience as well. No clues have been planted to set it up, no logical conundrum posed for which the ending is a resolution. The whole opera has been a mistake, essentially, nothing more or less.

The ending still might work on stage, however, if it made sense from a character standpoint, either textually or emotionally. But it does not.

As anyone who has ever performed *The Grand Duke* can attest, audiences always root for Rudolph and the Baroness to end up together. They seem suited to each other, and the Princess is too sweet to be stuck with a grumpy old miser like Rudolph. When in the end Rudolph and the Princess are paired, it has none of the "rightness" of the pairing of Lady Jane and the Duke in *Patience* or of Ko-Ko and Katisha in *The Mikado*. In fact, it feels the way it would if Nanki-Poo were to wind up with Katisha.

The pairing-off of Ernest and Julia is even worse, because even on the plot's own terms it makes no sense. In accepting him she says that, now that he is no longer dead, "My objection falls to the ground." But in fact it doesn't at all: She didn't enjoy his being dead, but throughout the opera she's had one primary objection to marrying him—to wit, that she doesn't like him. She had been prepared to waive that objection to capture the plum role of Grand Duchess, but that motivation vanishes now that Ernest will never be the Grand Duke.

It seems, in short, as if Gilbert has tired of his own plot and grown too annoyed with its intricacies to work them out. He simply hacks the Gordian knot apart, pairs people off with slapdash disregard to their characters, and decrees it a happy ending.

No wonder audiences then and now have found it hard to accept.

All this granted, the excoriation of *The Grand Duke*'s book is to some extent unjustified. It is the result of unfair expectations: Its denouncers are judging it in comparison to the operas from *The Sorcerer* through *The Yeomen of the Guard*, character-driven, thematic works that form the heart of the Savoy canon.

By those standards, *The Grand Duke* is unquestionably an abject failure. Moreover, it is all but incomprehensible—Gilbert does things that simply don't make sense, and discerning the unifying theme is impossible. Theatrical imagery, game imagery, death imagery—all blur together in an apparently arbitrary mess.

But *The Grand Duke* was written in 1896, not 1886. It is Gilbert's third attempt to find a new path after *The Yeomen of the Guard* and, like *The Gondoliers* and *Utopia, Limited*, it is both more original and less effective than the pre-1889 operas.

In fact, it is less effective precisely because it is more original: While it does reflect longstanding interests of the author, it is a type of work that Gilbert & Sullivan hadn't attempted previously, and they simply aren't as good at it as they had become at their canonic operas.

In this respect, this opera's best antecedent is the rather lame *Sorcerer*, a first fling at a new approach to comic opera that they themselves didn't yet fully understand. The difference is that, where *The Sorcerer* set their feet on a rewarding path to future triumphs, *The Grand Duke* had no successors. We will never know where it might have led had the collaboration lasted into later years.

The Gondoliers had been an allegory, a reflection on the process of the Gilbert & Sullivan collaboration, while *Utopia, Limited* had been in large part a pageant, a celebration of the renewal of the collaboration.

Both works were based in self-reference, but self-reference is an inherently limited form—one self-referential work is clever, but 10 would be egomaniacal. To truly move beyond *The Yeomen of the Guard*, a new approach was needed. And, while *The Grand Duke* has certain self-referential aspects, it also breaks new ground and explores a theatrical genre familiar to Gilbert but (with one partial exception) new to his collaboration with Sullivan—a genre known as metatheater.

The Grand Duke is at its heart more about form than about content—or, to be more precise, it uses form as its content, and vice versa.

The actual plot content of *The Grand Duke* is rather trifling. The entire opera is a buildup to the brief scene in which Ludwig finds himself surrounded by four brides, all either married to him or engaged to be. Certain other aspects of the statutory duel are mined for humor—notably the idea of Ernest being legally "dead"—but its primary goal is to reach the four-brides scene, and thereafter the opera is resolved so hurriedly that audiences generally are left a bit bewildered.

Unfortunately, that scene isn't so hilarious as to justify three hours spent getting there. Yet there is no strong thematic thrust to the opera, nor any other serious plot elements to bolster it. No wonder, then, that people who came hoping for a new *Iolanthe* were disappointed. They had come for theater and instead received metatheater.

Speaking broadly, metatheater is theater that is about theater—about the act of the play itself. It breaks down the hypothetical fourth wall separating the audience from the actors, and rejects suspension of disbelief in favor of blurring the line between art and reality.

Modern authors have made it virtually a cliché (the classic of the genre is Luigi Pirandello's 1921 play *Six Characters in Search of an Author)*, but in Gilbert's day it was a relatively new idea and certainly not one appreciated by mainstream audiences.

Gilbert had used metatheater many times before. Indeed, he was almost certainly the Victorian era's leading practitioner of this dramatic form.

In his 1870 operetta, *Our Island Home,* presented at Thomas German Reed's Royal Gallery of Illustration, Reed, his wife, and two other members of his company appeared as themselves, supposedly marooned on a desert island while touring with Gilbert's previous Reed show, *Ages Ago.*

Obviously, the fact of the actors playing themselves as actors in a play by Gilbert kept the audience well aware that this was itself a play by Gilbert. But the author didn't stop at that. The actor Arthur Cecil, famous for his sunny disposition, was portrayed as an arrogant prima donna—eliciting humor that was based solely on the contrast between the personalities of the character and of the actor who was playing him, and thus working only as long as the audience did *not* accept Cecil as the character he was playing.

In a final stab at the audience's suspension of disbelief, the only character not playing himself was a pirate named Captain Bang. Eventually Captain Bang is unmasked as . . . Alfred Reed, the real-life son of Mr. and Mrs. Reed (accounts differ as to whether the junior Reed actually played the role himself).[11]

Nor was *Our Island Home* Gilbert's only venture into metatheatrical issues. While not metatheatrical itself, his 1871 play *A Sensation Novel* is about metaliterature: A novelist faces a rebellion by his own characters, who insist on his rewriting the book according to their directions. (The saintly heroine actually detests the hero and is in love with the evil baronet, and so forth.)

Jane W. Stedman offers another example, Gilbert's play *The Blue-Legged Lady* (1874). In this curtain-raiser about the rehearsal of a play, she writes, "[m]embers of the cast played themselves, stepping in and out of character; in fact, most reviewers believed that the anonymous author was W. J. Hill, who acted that role in the play."[12]

Most notably, of course, *The Mikado* uses metatheatrical elements to lighten its grim story line. From the actors' repeated acknowledgments of the theatricality of their undertaking (the chorus's opening address to the audience, for example) to the frequent debunkings of the Japanese setting ("but Japanese don't use pocket handkerchiefs"), *The Mikado* breaks through the fourth wall repeatedly. Its signature attitude is a not-very-subtle wink to the audience, assuring them that everything is in good fun.

The Mikado had gone only so far, however. It was more restrained than *Our Island Home* in that the metatheatrical elements were generic, rather than specific—the point to Sullivan's setting the opening of "Behold the Lord High Executioner" to the tune of "He's a Fine Old English Gentleman" was that Ko-Ko and his chorus were really English, not that they were George Grossmith and the Savoy chorus.

And while it broke through the fourth wall repeatedly, it did so purely for comic relief, and it never toppled the wall completely. The audience was still kept at a distance from the events onstage.

With *The Grand Duke,* Gilbert makes his longstanding penchant for meta-theater the centerpiece of the opera. What previously had been used mainly as comic relief (as in Despard Murgatroyd's comment "This particularly rapid, unintelligible patter isn't generally heard, and if it is it doesn't matter" in *Ruddigore*) here becomes central. Compared to *The Grand Duke,* even the metatheatrics of *The Mikado* are restrained.

It's almost as if Gilbert, knowing that this would be his last opera, felt free to play.[13] (He would write one more, *Fallen Fairies*—written in 1909, 14 years after *The Grand Duke*—but in 1896 he apparently had no idea of doing so.) Compared to the meticulousness of the earlier Savoy operas, there is a loose sense of fun about *The Grand Duke* that manifests itself most significantly in its metatheatrics.

The most obvious metatheatrical touch is the casting of actors as actors. Ludwig, Lisa, Ernest, Julia, and the entire chorus appear as actors, as do the Monte Carlan actors who appear as the Prince's Six Supernumeraries in Act 2. And while they do not wear their own names, it is clear that the characters they play are modeled on the actors themselves with varying degrees of subtlety.

Gilbert uses Barrington's considerable girth as a subject for jokes at Ludwig's expense, for example. And when Ludwig moves from his humble post as lead comedian to succeed Ernest as producer ("manager," in British terminology) of the company, it recalls Barrington's ill-fated resignation from the Savoy after *Ruddigore* to attempt to become a manager/star in his own right.

Ernest, on the other hand, seems to be a self-parody on Gilbert's part— a dictatorial director, smitten with his leading lady (most likely Gilbert originally had his protégé Nancy McIntosh in mind for the role) and convinced that he knows best about everything, including how the country should be run. Of all his songs, few speak for Gilbert more than this one:

> The man who can rule a theatrical crew,
> each member a genius—and some of them two—
> > and manage to humor them early and late
> > can govern this tuppenny state!

The most obvious case of self-referentiality involves the role of Julia, played by Ilka Von Palmay, who, by all accounts, had an impressive voice— as well as an impressive Hungarian accent. As such, she would automatically seem out of place in a company whose membership was defiantly English (though it says something about the decline of the Savoy that the last two Gilbert & Sullivan sopranos were both foreigners).

Gilbert literally structures the entire opera to address this problem— but does it in a fashion that is typically (for *The Grand Duke*) offbeat. The obvious answer would have been to set the play in England or some English-speaking country, with Palmay cast as the only foreigner in the piece. Instead Gilbert flips the idea, setting the entire opera in Germany and casting Palmay as the only *English* person in the mix.

This sets up some remarkable metatheatrical mindbenders. One of the most universally understood theatrical conventions is the tacit understanding that, for example, Hamlet and his friends speak in Danish. The authorial "translation" into English is accepted without question by even the most skeptical audience, no more to be questioned than why the walls of Gertrude's bedchamber are open on the side facing the audience.

This suspension of disbelief is shattered, however, where Julia is concerned. When she exclaims "Ach, what a crackjaw language this German is!" or Ernest mentions that Julia's dramatic ability "is so overwhelming that our audiences forgive even her strong English accent," the audience is simultaneously drawn into the play (because they have the same difficulty in comprehending Palmay that the play's characters have with Julia) and pulled away from it (because the device, by calling attention to the actress, distracts from the character she is playing).

Again, the entrance of a nobleman accompanied by a chorus of aristocrats was nothing new to Gilbert & Sullivan—*Iolanthe* provides the most obvious example (though the Lord Chancellor is not technically an aristocrat), but the previous two operas *(The Gondoliers* and *Utopia, Limited)* had offered similar processions.

And, in every case, the aristocrats look not like actual noblemen of the period in which their operas are set but rather like stage aristocrats. The audience accepts them at face value, however, since the acceptance of an actor as his character is another age-old convention of the stage.

Such is the case initially with the arrival of the Prince and his entourage. They enter, and the audience on one level notices that they are actors wearing stage costumes but on another level disregards that fact. The entire effect happens unconsciously, without the audience ever deliberately suspending its disbelief—the conventions of theater are so strong that it's not necessary.

All the more disconcerting, then—and funny in a way uncharacteristic of the previous Savoy operas—to have the Prince announce that, in fact, they are wearing "costumes that we've hired by the day/from a very well-known costumier." The disorienting effect is all the stronger when the aristocrats are revealed to be actors "engaged from the Theatre Monaco."

The humor here comes from recognition—not of the fact that these really are actors (which of course the audience knew all along) but of the ease with which the theatrical illusion took us in. In a sense, the laugh is on ourselves and how gullible we become when we look at a stage.

The ironies are many. If an actual nobleman—say, one of Sullivan's titled friends—entered, the audience might be disappointed at his everyday dress and demeanor. By "not looking like a nobleman," he'd fail not at being a nobleman but at creating a stage effect of being one—in other words, he'd fail to resemble the many past actors who have looked not like real noblemen but like the stage convention that communicates "nobleman."

The Monte Carlo chorus, on the other hand, does look like stage noblemen—in short, like actors who are supposed to be noblemen. By the conventions of opera, the audience readily accepts them as noblemen—only to have Gilbert pull the rug out from under them.

A particularly intricate example of this metatheatrical gamesplaying—and one especially likely to confuse or disconcert a Victorian audience—comes during Act 1.

Despite being set in the town of Speisesaal, *The Grand Duke* never actually introduces the people of that town. The chorus plays touring actors, and none of the local commoners are seen, save perhaps the Notary. The rest of the population is conveniently absent throughout.

Again, the audience isn't troubled. It's an unvoiced but universally accepted tradition, no more to be wondered at than why random passersby don't interrupt Rose Maybud's chat with Robin Oakapple or why, of all the scores of sailors presumably aboard the *Pinafore,* the only ones who respond to Ralph's call for help are the handful we've already seen. That's the way things are done—we don't ask where the other people are, and the playwright usually doesn't tell us.

Thus it's odd when the characters themselves raise the question of where everybody else is—first the Baroness, implicitly, and then Ludwig, explicitly. Even more offbeat is Rudolph's answer: that the townspeople are, in fact, sitting just offstage, watching the proceedings through opera glasses.

Most modern audiences for *The Grand Duke* don't use opera glasses, of course; but the Savoy audience did, and they must have been taken aback to find that they themselves had become characters in the play. (Presumably Rudolph gestured to the audience at the appropriate point.)

Adding an especially sharp twist is the tightfisted Rudolph's side note that "the sale of opera glasses . . . is a Grand Ducal monopoly." At the Savoy, of course, the sale of opera glasses was reserved to Richard D'Oyly Carte, whose financial practices Gilbert had questioned on several previous occasions!

An unusually intricate example of metatheater comes in "About a Century Since," the Notary's song explaining the idea of the statutory duel. In the second verse he sings:

> But each a card shall draw,
>> and he who draws the lowest
>>> shall, so 'twas said,
>>> be henceforth dead,
>> in fact, a legal 'ghoest.'

So far there is nothing unusual about the song. "Ghoest" is, of course, a forced rhyme—but by this stage in his career Gilbert had lost the meticulousness that had once characterized his verse.

What is unique, however, is the next three lines, in which the Notary himself acknowledges that fact:

> (When exigence of rhyme compels,
>> orthography forgoes her spells
> and 'ghost' is written 'ghoest.')

Once again a basic convention of theater is being flouted. "Exigence of rhyme" applies only to lyricists, not to their characters—though characters speak in prose and sing in rhyme, they do so unconsciously, with only the audience aware of the difference.

In this case, however, the Notary not only is aware of it but actually criticizes Gilbert's weak rhyming, noting that it requires a forced misspelling—"orthography" means "spelling"—to make it work. He actually functions here as a "foil," a metatheatrical character whose criticism of the work itself is intended to disarm an audience's criticism of the author. (A contemporary parallel occurs in Oscar Wilde's *The Importance of Being Earnest* [1899], in which a particularly unlikely plot twist leads Lady Bracknell to observe, "I need hardly tell you that, in families of high position, strange coincidences are not supposed to occur.")[14]

The Notary's "orthography" line of course sets up a labored pun on the double meaning of "spells," which in turn produces a metatheatrical aside from the other four singers:

> With what an emphasis he dwells
> upon 'orthography' and 'spells'!
That kind of fun's the lowest.

So after the Notary has criticized Gilbert's forced rhymes, the ensemble rebukes him for his resort to forced puns!

This is an exceptionally rich passage, with several levels of self-referential humor. But it is also an intricate one—even today, with audiences who are more used to such conceits, it usually passes by before the audience has time to think it through and appreciate its humor.

There are, of course, numerous other aspects of the play that are metatheatrical. Many of its scenes are rehearsals for future scenes (some of which occur, some of which don't). There's a constant awareness not only of theatricality as such but of theatrical convention: Ludwig is not merely an actor but a leading comedian (as, of course, was Barrington, who played him), Lisa, as Julia cuttingly reminds her, is a soubrette, not a leading lady, and so forth.

The metatheatricality is what Gilbert relishes about *The Grand Duke*. He's much less interested in its putative plot, which, as Wolfson points out, was cobbled together from works by others, including a newspaper article on "legal death" sent him by an admirer; a short story—uncredited, it first appeared in *Blackwood's Magazine* in 1853—entitled, "The Duke's Dilemma" (1853), about a poor duke who hires actors to play courtiers and so on, to impress his rich fiancee; and *The Prima Donna*, an 1888 comic opera by H. B. Farnie, Alfred Murray, and Tito Mattei that was based on "The Duke's Dilemma."[15] Promising aspects of the statutory-duel concept, such as Ludwig's style of running a theatrical company, are left entirely unexplored.

But however much Gilbert may have enjoyed metatheater, and however much it may have been in the vein of the Victorians' renowned taste for games, *The Grand Duke* was unlikely to appeal to the audiences of its day.

This is only in part because it abandons the character comedy and thematic drama that had become the Gilbert & Sullivan style. It also requires a modern frame of mind to appreciate metatheater.

Instead of allowing an audience to initially work out the "ground rules" of the fictive world of the play (Titipu, for example) and then slip into passivity while the author does all the work, metatheater asks an audience to work. By dancing along the barrier between fact and fiction, it demands a greater alertness. It takes more effort to "get" the joke about the opera glasses than to appreciate the humor of Pooh-Bah or the "often/orphan" dialogue.

To say that *The Grand Duke* is an exercise in metatheater is not to posit that Gilbert was a precursor of Pirandello or the modern theater of Tom Stoppard or Michael Frayn, nor is it to make a case for *The Grand Duke* as an unappreciated masterwork.

Our Island Home and *A Sensation Novel* were each bolder in concept than *The Grand Duke,* for one thing. They didn't deign to dress up their metatheatrical content in the attire of conventional comic opera—they were what they were, and thus they remain more satisfactory works than *The Grand Duke.*

Nor did English metatheater begin with Gilbert. English pantomime, because of the stringent constraints of its plot and characters, had always displayed a metatheatrical undercurrent, and Gilbert was a devotee of pantomime. Music-hall performers and musical-comedy actors would often break through the fourth wall, albeit usually only for lame in-joke asides to the audience.

These strands of metatheater were already in place before Gilbert began to write, and they run through him to everything from Frayn's *Noises Off* (1982) to the fourth-wall–bending comedy of Monty Python.

The Grand Duke might have been stronger, however, if Gilbert & Sullivan had not been so tied to the genre they had created. Ironically, the team that had begun its career by lacerating stale operatic conventions ended by flailing at the new conventions they themselves had created.

Julia Jellicoe's Act 2 solo, "Broken Every Promise Plighted," is an excellent example of this convention-bound struggle. In form, it's a strong dramatic aria for a female character in the depths of despair, akin to Princess Ida's "I Built upon a Rock" or Katisha's "Alone, and Yet Alive" *(The Mikado).*

However, the *Princess Ida* number draws its power from what we've already seen of the character and her situation. It develops imagery established previously in the opera and draws an audience closer to an initially unsympathetic character.

Julia's song does nothing of the kind, because she is not a sympathetic character. She has been played entirely comically to this point—indeed, her earlier, flamboyantly theatrical solo ("Now, Julia, Come") is the comic high point of act 2—and her sudden conversion into an allegedly realistic character is even more jarring than the comparable shift with Katisha.

As a result the song, however musically powerful, makes no impact and feels interminably long. It seems to be exactly what it is—a "big" number for the soprano, inserted because . . . well, because the long-since-established Gilbert & Sullivan conventions require a "big" number as the story reaches a crisis point.

The same applies to the constant choral entrances and exits in elaborate processions. These suit the genre traditions that Gilbert & Sullivan have established and give Gilbert an opportunity to practice his widely admired stagecraft, but they bleach interest from the story, distancing the audience from the plot and from the metatheatrical humor that might have driven the opera.

The trouble is not that the Gilbert & Sullivan formula has grown stale—audiences flocked to revivals before and after *The Grand Duke*, proving themselves still much in the mood for the "old" Gilbert & Sullivan. Nor is it that Gilbert & Sullivan themselves had lost the knack for clever lyrics, memorable characters, witty dialogue, and captivating music. *The Grand Duke* contains ample examples of all four.

Ultimately, the trouble is the combination of two underlying weaknesses. Either might have been overcome, but together they spelled doom for *The Grand Duke* and for the collaboration as a whole.

First, the great thematic cycle had ended with *The Yeomen of the Guard*, and both men were groping for an artistic raison d'êfetre for their continued collaboration. Money alone could only get them to embrace the idea of writing together—what to write about was a puzzle for which neither man had a ready solution.

This was no different from their situation after *Trial by Jury*, however. Had they been younger, both physically and emotionally, they might have embarked on something new after *The Yeomen of the Guard*, not one-shot experiments but a sustained campaign to create something original and important. The self-reference of *The Gondoliers* and *Utopia, Limited* was by its nature a dead end, and *The Grand Duke's* metatheater at best pointed the way to a new style for the collaboration, not a new subject matter.

That Gilbert & Sullivan were indeed no longer young was the second crippling factor. Granted, both men were still under 60 and, though in poor health at the time of *The Grand Duke*, might reasonably have expected to be productive for years to come. (As indeed they were—Gilbert was to write four more plays and Sullivan three operas and a major ballet.)

But emotionally, as individuals and especially as a team, Gilbert and Sullivan were tired. They lacked the boldness to be truly creative, as well as the inclination to face the conflicts that creativity had always brought them.

Sullivan's music for *The Grand Duke* is a perfect example of this, combining some of his most charming work—the Menotti-esque "Strange the

Views Some People Hold," the Offenbachian "Won't It Be a Pretty Wedding," and the sweeping "As Before You We Defile"—with pedestrian oompah-pah patter songs that are less inspired than anything he'd done in 25 years with Gilbert.

In Gilbert, the same laziness prevails. When playing with his metatheatrics he's fresh and interesting—"Now, Julia, Come" is masterful—but at other times he simply seems in a rush to get things done. Rhymes like "tallow/yellow/swallow" and "chooses/shoeses" find him shockingly indiscriminate.

Writing Gilbert & Sullivan opera had never been easy, however effortless the works seemed to be onstage. The working papers of the two men are filled with creative ferment as they argue over form and content, constantly rethinking the "good enough" to make it great. By 1896, frayed by the carpet quarrel and advancing age, neither man had the guts for it.

That fact, which was apparent to both, underlies the final remarkable aspect of *The Grand Duke:* its similarities to *Thespis,* the first Gilbert & Sullivan collaboration.

In this respect, *The Grand Duke* returns to the self-reference that had informed *The Gondoliers* and *Utopia, Limited.* If those works had been in part about writing Gilbert & Sullivan opera and about being Gilbert & Sullivan opera, respectively, *The Grand Duke* is to a lesser (but still notable) degree about being the final Gilbert & Sullivan opera.

That this was to be the pair's final collaboration had been no secret since its genesis. Gilbert intended to retire and had made no bones about that intention. Nor did Sullivan attempt to talk him out of it. As early as March 1894, the composer asked Gilbert for suggestions as to future collaborators for operas at the Savoy.

"One librettist is as good as another, if not better moreover," Gilbert wrote to Sullivan on 1 April 1994.[16] "This is the last libretto I shall ever write & it matters nothing to me who is to succeed me."

Sullivan's inquiry wasn't absurd—Gilbert had suggested Sturgis for *Ivanhoe,* after all—but his helpfulness with *Ivanhoe* had reflected his desire to entice Sullivan into *The Gondoliers,* and this time he had no such reason to care.

Given the creators' awareness of the ending of their collaboration, *The Grand Duke's* resonances with *Thespis* are remarkable.

Just as *Thespis* had depicted a troupe of actors interrupting the wedding of two of its members to take control of the world, so *The Grand Duke* shows a troupe of actors interrupting the wedding of two of its members to take control of the country.

Had *Thespis* not been, by 1896, at best a fading memory even to its immediate participants, certain elements of the press would doubtless have chided Gilbert for unoriginality, just as they had over *Ruddigore* and

The Yeomen of the Guard. But Gilbert and Sullivan themselves must have recognized the *Thespis* connections. To both, surely, it represented the closing of a circle, bringing their collaboration back to where it had started.

This idea of circularity is mirrored in the opera itself. It is not unusual for a Gilbert & Sullivan opera to end with a reprise—indeed, of their 14 works, only *Utopia, Limited* ends with an original tune. Only one, however, returns to its opening number for its finale, and that one is *The Grand Duke.* Just as the story of *The Grand Duke* brings the Gilbert & Sullivan collaboration full circle, so the reprise of "Happy Couples, Lightly Treading" brings the opera itself full circle.

It is an apt summation for the collaboration. As a celebration of couplehood, it evokes the successes of the collaboration; but in its evocation of the early, less creative *Thespis* it reflects the regression of the partnership from the intimate closeness of *The Yeomen of the Guard* to the studied civility of *The Grand Duke.*

The Grand Duke was not quite the end for Gilbert and Sullivan. The two men continued to meet occasionally, primarily at the opening nights of revivals at the Savoy—revivals whose success demonstrated that prime Gilbert & Sullivan remained as popular as ever.

But the failure of *The Grand Duke*—unequivocal and thoroughgoing—demonstrated that the days of *Iolanthe, The Mikado,* and *The Yeomen of the Guard* lay behind them. Audiences were no more enthusiastic for *The Grand Duke* than its collaborators had been in creating it.

When it was withdrawn and replaced with a far more popular revival of *The Mikado,* it was as if Carte and audiences alike were telling Gilbert & Sullivan what both men already knew: Their collaboration was brilliant, but it was in the past.

It was time to stop.

17

Gilbert after Sullivan, Sullivan after Gilbert

With occasional intervals for rest and refreshment, the Gilbert & Sullivan collaboration had lasted almost exactly 25 years. After *The Grand Duke,* it came to an end.

There might have been at least one more Savoy opera: In 1898 or 1899, Gilbert submitted his libretto for *Fallen Fairies* to Sullivan.[1] The composer passed on it, however, and it was rejected by composers as diverse as Elgar, Massanet, and Messager before finally being accepted by Edward German in 1909.

Despite what in retrospect appears to have been an artistic dead end, in a way it's strange that the collaboration ended when it did. *Utopia, Limited* and *The Grand Duke* had not lived up to financial expectations, but many longstanding conflicts seemed to have been resolved.

FIGURE 17.2. Arthur Sullivan in 1899, a year before his death. Though plagued by kidney disease and other ailments, the composer continued to work productively until almost the day of his death. *Source: The Pierpont Morgan Library, Gilbert and Sullivan Collection.*

For example, Sullivan had apparently gotten his desire to write grand opera out of his system. After *Ivanhoe,* he never seriously looked in that direction again. (He is rumored to have said of *Ivanhoe,* "A cobbler should stick to his last," but the reliability of the quote is questionable.)[2] Instead, after *The Grand Duke* he wrote three more operas for Carte and the Savoy, though none ran even as long as *Utopia, Limited.* As if to stress Sullivan's new flexibility, the first of these operas, *The Beauty Stone,* involved exactly the sort of magical talisman he had always objected to in Gilbert's plots—in this case, a gem that made its possessor fabulously beautiful.

The simmering financial issues that had erupted as the "carpet quarrel" were also now resolved. The new royalty arrangement under which Gilbert had written *Utopia, Limited* and *The Grand Duke* seems to have worked well—there were no serious disagreements between Gilbert and Carte, at any rate, though Gilbert's lack of profit participation may have made the librettist more agreeable to the lavishness of *Utopia* in particular.

If there were fewer financial and artistic grounds for dispute, why did the partnership end? Simply, both men had less zeal for their work. Both were financially secure beyond even Sullivan's capacity to gamble away his wealth.

More important, both had steered their careers steadily toward the serious (Gilbert to *The Yeomen of the Guard,* which he and Sullivan both called their best joint work, and Sullivan beyond it to *Ivanhoe*) and been disappointed with the public response. Their later works, together and apart, display a sense of listlessness. They still contain excellent work, but it seems to have taken more of an effort than it once had.

Their collaboration had always been draining for both men. Neither ever trusted another collaborator with the kind of artistic veto they had given each other. In Basil Hood, librettist of his final two operas, Sullivan found a comparative novice who let the composer be the guiding hand; Gilbert's final works were either straight plays (no collaborator needed) or operas with younger composers such as his erstwhile star Grossmith, Alfred Cellier, Osmond Carr, or German—men who, like Hood, let the senior partner rule unchallenged.

The "carpet quarrel" and its legal entanglements had left their mark, but well before then both men had found working together harder than working with anyone else. They pushed each other, and their differing artistic inclinations and equally high standards forced each to excel himself, often against his own first inclination. With less money to be made and less need of it, and with the artistic fire of both men burning lower, the path of least resistance led away from the collaboration.

In retrospect, it's less surprising that Gilbert & Sullivan wrote nothing more after 1896 than that they worked together for as long as they did. Theatrical history offers no comparable example of such independently successful artists collaborating for so long. Each man brought his own star to the partnership; that it lasted so long is little short of miraculous.

By the time *The Grand Duke* premiered in 1896, Sullivan had barely four years to live. His always precarious health was in steady decline, and in photographs from these years he looks tired, gaunt and rapidly graying, older than his actual 50-plus years.

Nevertheless, as always, poor health didn't impede Sullivan's musical productivity. Though his largest-scale works were behind him—he talked of future grand operas, oratorios, and even a second symphony but never actually embarked on them—he worked steadily. The years 1896–1900 saw five major works in as many years, his most productive period since the mid-1880s.

Unfortunately, they were not his most successful. *Utopia Limited*'s total of 245 performances was less than half that run up by *The Gondoliers,* and *The Grand Duke*'s 123 only half that of *Utopia.* When *The Beauty Stone* followed with only 50 performances, it seemed as if Sullivan's operatic vein might be entirely tapped out.

By 1898, he had composed six operas in the 1890s, including *Ivanhoe, Haddon Hall* (written with Sydney Grundy during the rift with Gilbert), and *The Chieftain,* the revamped version of the 1867 Sullivan-Burnand opera *The Contrabandista.* None had been a success, at least not by the usual Savoy standards.

However, *The Beauty Stone* was to prove the nadir of Sullivan's career. In many respects, this 1898 opera was his worst. It was all the more disappointing in that he had placed considerable hopes in it.

Billed not as a comic opera but as "a romantic musical drama," *The Beauty Stone* united Sullivan with Arthur Wing Pinero, the top serious dramatist of the late Victorian era. The lyrics were by J. Comyns Carr, likewise a respected dramatist, for whose *King Arthur* (1895) Sullivan had composed incidental music. The dramatic story had resonances of *Faust,* with an evocative period setting and plenty of operatic flavor. Sullivan was excited. He told an interviewer.

> I am most anxious that the public should understand that the forthcoming Savoy piece is an entirely new departure. It is a serious, earnest romantic drama. I don't mean to say there is no humor in the piece, but there are no comic songs or numbers in the acceptation of the term. I insist that this piece is an absolute novelty. Here you have a strong plot and dialogue written by Mr. Arthur Pinero, surely the most brilliant dramatist of our day in London—and lyrics by Mr. Comyns Carr, a man of poetical feeling. I have only to add that I have tried to do my share of the work with the most scrupulous and exacting care.[3]

Sullivan's comments seem to embody his hope for emancipation from Gilbert, who he had always felt tried too hard to be funny when humor wasn't called for. Now he thought he had what he had been seeking—grand opera, perhaps, under a different name.

In the event, however, the opera must have made him long for Gilbert—if not for the authoritarian director then at least for the meticulous lyricist whom he had occasionally taken for granted.

In an 1880 letter to his mother, Sullivan had noted, almost offhandedly, that the libretto for *The Pirates of Penzance* was "beautifully written for music, as is all Gilbert does."[4] Now, as early as seven months before the premiere of *The Beauty Stone,* he was already noting to his diary that Pinero and Carr were both "gifted and brilliant men, with *no* experience in writing for music."[5]

In his biography of Sullivan, Arthur Jacobs notes that the composer found both men "unhelpful and inflexible when he wanted alterations in order to improve the musical construction."[6] Sullivan even suggested that they had taken advantage of Carte in negotiating financial terms.

If he was to argue with his collaborators over money and matters of dramatic construction, Sullivan must have thought, he might as well be doing it with Gilbert, who at least appreciated the musical needs of his operas.

Given this background, it's not surprising that *The Beauty Stone* was a crashing failure. Its 50-performance run was the shortest Sullivan had ever had. The critics lambasted Pinero and Carr, but Sullivan did not escape criticism.

"I do not feel inclined seriously to discuss the music, which practically only illustrates the lighter side of the 'romantic drama' with any measure of success," wrote *The Musical Standard.*[7] "To say that is equal to saying that Sir Arthur's share is somewhat of a failure, and I am afraid that must be the verdict."

To a modern ear, *The Beauty Stone* is rather a mess. Its faux-medieval dialogue almost defies comprehension, while the cliché-riddled lyrics are so awkwardly distorted in syntax, rhyme, and rhythm that one can readily understand Sullivan's dismay.

Just as damaging is the self-defeating dramatic structure. In place of Gilbert's two uninterrupted acts, two sets at most and (until the final operas) relatively small casts of characters, *The Beauty Stone* offers three acts with seven scenes in five different sets (surely leading to some long midact pauses) and a cast of 21 principals.

Sullivan's music never overcomes the lyrics, which are so lacking in rhythm as to make virtually everything sound like recitative, singularly lacking in propulsive momentum. Only the Devil's comic "It Ever Comes Back to Me" and a stirring march that closes the Act 2 finale show Sullivan at his best. Otherwise he largely relies on orchestral touches for musical interest—it is one of his best-orchestrated shows.

Sullivan was a generous and discreet man, always ready with a good word and cautious with a bad one. He never made any public comment on *The Beauty Stone* or his experiences with it. But when his "authorized biography" was written by Arthur Lawrence in 1900, Sullivan sat for several interviews, and reviewed and approved the resulting text. It therefore represents the closest the composer ever came to an autobiography, and Lawrence's view of *The Beauty Stone* is uniquely scathing:

> The central motive of this musical drama was a delightful one, and I think that some of the music in this work is among the best that Sir Arthur has written. Undoubtedly the piece suffered much by the tender way in which the superabundant dialogue was treated. There is such a superfluity of words that the dramatic significance of the play is often lost sight of; but I think it will be admitted that wherever the composer has been given a chance he has made excellent use of it. . . . It may not be too much to hope that one day *The Beauty Stone* may be revived, with about half the libretto ruthlessly cut away.[8]

The experience might easily have soured Sullivan on opera, especially given that the previous year had seen his only success of the decade, *Victoria and Merrie England,* a ballet celebrating the Queen's diamond jubilee. It was Sullivan's second ballet and his first since 1864; it ran for six months and was remarkably lucrative (since there was no lyricist to share the proceeds).

Still, 1900 saw him back at the Savoy for *The Rose of Persia,* with a libretto by Basil Hood, a retired army captain. This "new comic opera" doesn't show Sullivan at his best, and he probably undertook it primarily out of friendship for Carte, who had met with little success aside from Gilbert & Sullivan revivals.

Sullivan enjoyed working with Hood far more than with Pinero and Carr. He found the exotic Persian setting engaging, and Hood's combination of Gilbertian influences and respectful deference to the composer probably struck Sullivan as the best of two worlds.

All the same, he wasn't optimistic about the opera's chances. In negotiating the contract terms with the Cartes, he wrote to them:

> I feel instinctively—superstitiously if you like—that the luck has gone from the theatre for a time at least. It was built for a specific purpose and its raison d'etre is now over; every kind of combination has been tried and failed. Do you think it encouraging to devote months again to work which I feel, however good it may be, will have no other result than the works which have preceded it since 1890?[9]

One can almost feel his astonishment in his diary entry for the opera's opening night, November 24, 1899: "First performance of *The Rose of Persia* at Savoy Theatre. I conducted as usual. Hideously nervous as usual—great reception as usual—great house as usual—excellent performance as usual—everything as usual—except that the piece is really a great success I think, which is unusual lately."[10]

By *Mikado* standards, the 213 performances of *The Rose of Persia* was no great success. But the opera was popular and profitable to all concerned, and Sullivan's relief was palpable.

Today, the opera seems a bit thin. Hood emulates Gilbert with a fair degree of stylistic success but without any of the substance Gilbert brought to the collaboration. *The Rose of Persia* is a lighthearted story that has nothing to say but says it well. Hood's lyrics are smooth and conventional, while the dramatic construction is in the approved Gilbertian mode—two acts, two sets, all smoothly managed.

Sullivan's music is reminiscent of *The Grand Duke,* with some added chromaticism to evoke the Middle Eastern setting. The biggest hit was the drinking song "I Care Not If the Cup I Hold," which is still a rousing number, but there are several other high points, including "From Morning Prayer the Popular Sultan Comes," another fine march; "The Vigilant Vizier," a spooky ensemble with a distinct Oriental flavor; and a catchy dance number, "If a Sudden Stroke of Fate." The opera has a great deal of music for female ensembles, much of it outstanding.

Generally, however, the score is only adequate. If he had foreseen how many people would eventually hear it, Sullivan might have put more into it, but as his diary entry reveals, its success caught him rather by surprise.

A second Sullivan-Hood opera seemed a natural, but it wasn't to be: *The Emerald Isle* was left unfinished at Sullivan's death in November 1900. The remaining third of the music, mostly from the second act, was finished by Edward German, and the opera was presented at the Savoy in 1901, to a respectable reception.

Hood's libretto is perhaps a bit stronger than his work on *The Rose of Persia.* The story is only modestly more substantial, but the lyrics are wittier and even more Gilbertian. There is even a song that makes fun of an aging contralto and another that offers some cutting social satire, "The Age in Which We Live."

By the time we learn that the hero and heroine first met at the ages of two and one, a la Prince Hilarion and Princess Ida, it is clear that Hood is unabashedly mimicking Gilbert; if there is little gold left in the vein, Hood certainly captures his predecessor's stylistic flavor to good advantage.

The most distinctive aspect of *The Emerald Isle* is Sullivan's music, however. Himself of Irish descent, he had always loved Ireland (his first symphony was known as "the Irish"), and the setting for *The Emerald Isle* clearly inspired him. In the Irish jigs and ballads, and especially in the sequences inspired by Irish myth, Sullivan produces some of his best music. "On the Heights of Glenlaun" is hauntingly beautiful, and the eerie siren song "Come Away" stands up well against the supernatural music from *Iolanthe* or *Ruddigore.*

In all, *The Emerald Isle* is easily Sullivan's best score since *The Grand Duke*, perhaps even since *The Gondoliers*. Inspired by the subject matter and heartened by the unexpected success of *The Rose of Persia*, the composer seems reinvigorated. It's unfortunate that he didn't live to complete it.

The end of the collaboration did not end either the Gilbert/Sullivan relationship or their works. In the years between *The Grand Duke* and Sullivan's death, they met occasionally and corresponded periodically, generally cordially.

Gilbert's last letter to his former partner, written on the eve of his departure to Egypt on his doctor's orders, was prompted by Sullivan's being too ill to attend the opening night of a *Patience* revival. Its warmth is noteworthy—oddly enough, only after the "carpet quarrel" did Gilbert begin to write to Sullivan with any personal openness, as if seeking to prove his own humanity.

> My dear Sullivan,
>   I would be glad to come up to town to see you before I go, but unfortunately in my present enfeebled condition a carriage journey to London involves my lying down a couple of hours before I am fit for anything, besides stopping all night in town. The railway journey is still more fatiguing. I have lost sixty pounds in weight, and my arms and legs are of the consistency of cotton-wool. I sincerely hope to find you all right again on my return, and the new opera running merrily.
>
> Yours very truly,
> W. S. Gilbert
>
> P.S. The old opera woke up splendidly.

Gilbert did indeed find *The Emerald Isle* running when he returned, but Sullivan had died mere weeks after the letter was written. Word did not reach Egypt in time for Gilbert to attend the funeral.

Unlike Sullivan, who if anything was more professionally active after the collaboration than during it, Gilbert moved into semiretirement after *The Grand Duke*. He produced only four works in the 15 years until his death: *The Fortune-Hunter*, an 1897 drama; *The Fairy's Dilemma*, a comedy produced in 1904; *Fallen Fairies*, a 1909 opera with music by German; and *The Hooligan*, a short one-act drama produced in 1911.

Instead, Gilbert became something of a curator of his own legacy, revisiting and often revising many of his previous works. Most of his new works were similarly retrospective—*Fallen Fairies* was an adaptation of his 1873 play *The Wicked World*, while an unkind critic wrote of *The Fairy's Dilemma* that it might have worked better in verse than in prose and added: "Verse is not the only thing that it ought to have been written in; it ought also to have been written in the '70s."[11]

By this time, though he lived vigorously in the present—new passions for photography and automobiles were augmented when his decades-old gout vanished (perhaps due to a changed diet), allowing him to resume his life as an energetic tennis player and swimmer in the 1900s—Gilbert's artistic vision was focused increasingly on the past.

In 1898 he returned to *The Bab Ballads*, preparing a new edition with minor revisions, generally improving them. However, he noted in his introduction: "I have always felt that many of the original illustrations to *The Bab Ballads* erred gravely in the direction of unnecessary extravagance. This defect I have endeavored to correct through the medium of the 200 new drawings which I have designed for this volume. I am afraid I cannot claim for them any other recommendation."[12]

Most modern readers have preferred the original illustrations, feeling that their extravagance is exactly what recommends them.

In 1908, Gilbert wrote prose versions of *H. M. S. Pinafore* and *The Mikado* for illustrated editions (the latter was not published until 1921). From 1902 through 1911, he oversaw new versions of his three volumes of *Original Plays*, as well as a new fourth volume encompassing *The Grand Duke*, his later plays, and miscellaneous works not previously collected (among them *Thespis*—but he died before revising and correcting the text, leaving it enigmatic to the end).

Most of all, though, Gilbert shaped his legacy through the revivals of Gilbert & Sullivan at the Savoy. He directed the various 1890s revivals that preceded and followed *Utopia Limited, The Grand Duke*, and Carte's various other new operas by Sullivan and other composers.

After Carte's death in 1901, the Savoy was leased to various tenants, and the operas were seen only infrequently in London, though the touring company continued, under the aegis of Carte's widow, to bring Gilbert & Sullivan to the provinces.

Once she had become accustomed to running the company on her own, however, Helen Carte reclaimed the Savoy. From 1906 to 1909, she presented revivals of *The Yeomen of the Guard, The Gondoliers, Patience, Iolanthe, The Mikado, H. M. S. Pinafore*, and *The Pirates of Penzance*. Gilbert returned to stage the operas, with occasional revisions (for example, an updated "Little List" for Ko-Ko that included "the scorching motorist" and "the red-hot Socialist").

These revivals were great successes and helped bring Gilbert recognition as a living legend, if not a currently brilliant playwright. He was knighted by Edward VII in 1907.

Amid all this retrospective activity, Gilbert's new plays got relatively little attention, even from him.

The Fortune-Hunter was his last full-length drama. It is one of his more engaging serious works, with a pronounced international flavor: The principal roles include an English gentleman, an earthy American woman wedded to an elderly English duke, an Australian heiress, and the title character, a French adventurer in quest of a wealthy wife.

In content, *The Fortune-Hunter* reflects Gilbert's preoccupation, especially in his straight plays, with the question of redemption. There are virtually no out-and-out villains in the Savoy operas, but a disproportionate number of Gilbert's plays feature villains whose better natures ultimately come to the surface, usually inspired by a woman's sacrifice. The theme appears in *Randall's Thumb* (1871), *Brantinghame Hall* (1888), and, in a comic version, *The Fairy's Dilemma* (1904). *The Fortune-Hunter* is his strongest treatment of the theme, and its unflinching seriousness makes it his best.

Unfortunately, the play remains overwrought and melodramatic in many of its scenes, and exceptionally verbose. Tightly plotted and often very witty, its dialogue is more naturalistic than that in Gilbert's earlier plays, but every act, every scene, even every speech seems to go on longer than it needs to. It was a modest success at best.

The Fairy's Dilemma was perhaps most notable for being Gilbert's only play to be staged at the Garrick, the theater he himself had built in 1889.

To a modern reader, the play has a certain charm. Like *Utopia, Limited* and *The Grand Duke*, it starts out with an engaging idea—a fairy who, through ineptness and a passion for trashy novels, ensnarls the lives of four innocent mortals. Particularly punished is Sir Trevor Mauleverer, a kindly baronet whom she mistakenly assumes to be a villain because "Why, aren't all baronets bad?"[13]

As a plot, this is certainly a promising idea, and Gilbert finds some real humor in it. For fans of the Savoy operas, there are obvious resonances with *Ruddigore* in the not-so-wicked baronet; *The Sorcerer* in the nervous clergyman whose love is misdirected through supernatural intervention; and of course *Iolanthe* in the fairy herself. (There is even a subtle tip of the cap to Sullivan, as the Reverend Aloysius Parfitt is initially discovered playing "The Lost Chord" on a harmonium.)

But the dialogue is exceptionally wordy, far beyond the razor-honed cleanness of the best Savoy operas. In particular, Act 1 staggers under long expositions in which, for the audience's benefit, characters tell one another things they all already know.

And the plot runs out of steam too soon, leading Gilbert to devote the final two acts to an entirely different central comic concept: The fairy stages a pantomime transformation scene, changing the characters into the classical pantomime figures—Harlequin, Pantaloon, and so on. Since all are ridiculously badly suited for their new roles, it's an amusing (and Bab-like) idea; but it comes out of nowhere and is never really developed.

The Fairy's Dilemma is like an early draft of a funny play. It needed the canny eye of a Sullivan to point out weak dialogues, recycled comic ideas, lapses in pacing, and the like. Without a collaborator to prod him, Gilbert seems lazy and self-indulgent. He takes the easy path too often, and the play suffers for it.

Fallen Fairies is by far the most substantial of Gilbert's later works. It was intended as the first in a series of operas adapted from his plays of the 1870s, with *The Palace of Truth* planned to follow. And while it is not Gilbert at his best, it has much in common with the Savoy operas, especially the middle series of *Patience, Iolanthe,* and *Princess Ida.* Of all the works Gilbert or Sullivan wrote after their collaboration, *Fallen Fairies* is clearly the best.

Based on Gilbert's *Wicked World* (1873), the opera tells of a group of fairies who, intending to reform the world, transport two mortal men to Fairyland. They hope that exposure to the fairies' purity will reform the mortals.

Instead, the mortals corrupt the perfect world of Fairyland. Soon after their arrival jealous rivalries erupt, and by the time they depart the Fairy Queen has been deposed and the fairies are at one another's throats.

As one fairy sums up the ending, "Heaven be praised, / these mortal men have gone to their own earth / and taken with them the bad influence / that spread like an infection through our ranks."[14] Fortunately, with the departure of the men the fairies regain their senses and peace is restored.

The obvious parallel is, of course, to *Iolanthe.* These are the same type of fairies, creatures who are at once powerful and innocent, versed in fairy lore but mystified by mortal doings and, particularly, the power of love. Once love insinuates itself, whether in the person of the Lord Chancellor or the two knights, it undercuts the foundations of the whole fairy system. There are even two fairies in *Fallen Fairies* named Leila and Fleta.

Yet, reflecting its earlier source more than its later date, *Fallen Fairies* is less mature than *Iolanthe.* The earlier opera's resonance rises from its realization that knowledge cannot be unlearned—the fairy system really is doomed the moment a fairy falls in love. If the contagion's spread is more explicit in *Fallen Fairies,* that opera's ending makes it less powerful.

Despite its title, *Fallen Fairies* doesn't let its fairies fall; instead of growing up, moving on, and embracing love and mortality as the *Iolanthe* fairies do, these later fairies are able to retreat back to innocence and childhood.

Besides *Iolanthe, Fallen Fairies* also suggests *Patience.* Like that opera, it is a search for the meaning of love, with the fairies collectively taking Patience's role as the questing innocent. There are numerous songs about the nature of love, ranging from the ecstatic mysticism of "With All the Misery" (in which love is "the sweet enchantment in his breast" that makes mortals bear all the other burdens of life) to the cynical manipulation of "When a Knight Loves Lady" (in which the caddish Sir Ethais preaches that men are ever faithful, and only women are ever untrue) and the strident denunciation of "The Warrior Girt in Shining Might" (in which "Love's the source of every ill! / Compounded with unholy skill, / it proves, disguise it as you will, / a gilded but a poisoned pill!").

However, the fairies' quest for knowledge is never fully realized, because (unlike *Patience)* it has no counterbalance to the evil seducers. Sir Ethais and Sir Phyllon fill the Bunthorne role, but there is no Grosvenor to embody true love. *Fallen Fairies* reaches the stage of *Patience's* "Love Is a Plaintive Song" but never moves beyond it. The image of love as contagion is the final one; the opera is pathological rather than resonant, a dissection of a disease rather than a look at human nature.

Fallen Fairies is also reminiscent of *Princess Ida*. It is the most woman-centered opera Gilbert ever wrote—it has no male chorus and only three male characters—and the political battle for Queen Selene's crown recalls the power plays between Ida and Blanche.

More notably, however, it resembles *Princess Ida* in structure—in particular, it has the same faults. *The Princess* (1870) and *The Wicked World* were written only three years apart, while Gilbert's skills were still emerging. While *The Wicked World* is a considerably better play, its dialogue is still well below the standard of the mature Savoy operas—and, as with *Princess Ida*, Gilbert simply transfers huge blocks of dialogue from the early play into the later opera. The result is that the dialogue (like that of *Princess Ida* all blank verse) is far inferior to the lyrics.

And perhaps because Gilbert was older and less motivated or perhaps because German wasn't as demanding as Sullivan, the cut-and-paste work of *Fallen Fairies* is substantially inferior to that of *Princess Ida*. Most of the songs are preceded by dialogue that essentially says everything that's in the song, occasionally almost word for word. Gilbert hasn't pruned the revised script of unnecessary repetitions, and it slows the show.

Overall, *Fallen Fairies* stands as a seriously flawed work that might easily have been better. Still, it is the best work of Gilbert's last 15 years.

Unfortunately, it was hamstrung by Gilbert's longstanding support for Nancy McIntosh, the American soprano who was his adopted daughter.[15] Gilbert had shoehorned her into *Utopia, Limited* as Princess Zara, and he insisted on her appearing in *Fallen Fairies* as Queen Selene.

How good or bad McIntosh may have been we can never know. For the record, at least, Sullivan and German both endorsed her, though she was notably absent from the cast of *The Grand Duke*. But it is certain that the financial backers of *Fallen Fairies* disliked her. So did C. H. Workman, who had made a name for himself in the Grossmith roles in the 1906–1909 Savoy revivals and was producing *Fallen Fairies* as well as playing its main comic role.

Whatever the details, within two weeks of the opera's December 15 opening at the Savoy, McIntosh had been fired. Gilbert threatened legal action but found that under the terms of the production contract Workman was indeed entitled to fire her if he chose. Author and producer then skirmished in the courts for several weeks; this cannot have helped the opera, which closed at the end of January.

Among the casualties of the affair must be reckoned a series of Gilbert & Sullivan revivals that Workman had planned to follow *Fallen Fairies*, including revised versions of *Ruddigore*, *Utopia, Limited*, and *The Grand Duke*. He remained interested in obtaining the performance rights, but Gilbert was still incensed and flatly refused Workman's overtures.

As to *The Hooligan*, it is unique among Gilbert's works. Running a scant 15 minutes, it was billed as "A Character Study" and takes place in the cell of a condemned man minutes before his scheduled execution.

Hyperrealistic and deadly serious—its sparse humor is black indeed, as in a running gag about preventing prisoner suicide—it brings out the social and economic pressures that have brought a poor, sick, and mentally slow man to death row. (Its Dickensian edge is reminiscent of, but far sharper than, the socially conscious "Fold Your Flapping Wings," cut from *Iolanthe*, in which Strephon meditates that only an accident of birth separates him from the violence and squalor of the streets.)[16]

The Hooligan's twist ending is anything but Gilbertian in its savage irony—at the moment he is reprieved, the prisoner falls dead of a heart attack.

Gilbert had been fascinated by the highly publicized case of Crippen, a doctor who had butchered his wife and fled the country with his secretary, only to be arrested at sea through the use of a new invention, radio. Gilbert visited Pentonville Prison several times to assure the authenticity of his details, even bringing his star, James Welch, to the condemned cell to get its feeling.

The Hooligan was a great success, surprising the critics as much as it does modern readers. Gilbert probably would not have pursued this new line of drama—it was outside his normal inclinations, and he himself probably saw it as a fluke. He had, after all, repeatedly announced his retirement from play-writing and had not had a solid hit since 1889.

In any event, he was not to have the chance to follow it up. *The Hooligan* premiered on February 27, 1911, and on May 29 Gilbert was dead, stricken by a heart attack while rescuing a young woman who was floundering in the lake on his estate.

There was a strange symmetry to the final years of Gilbert and of Sullivan. They lived to see their works become both classics and out of style, as their old works were embraced by a public that dismissed their new ones. And each found a strange final moment in the sun, Sullivan with *The Rose of Persia* and Gilbert with *The Hooligan*, unexpected but surely welcome.

Their age had definitely passed. The musical world into which they had been born had changed irrevocably and was to change even further: In 1837, the year after Gilbert's birth, Verdi began writing his first opera; in

1909, two years before Gilbert's death, Schoenberg wrote *Ewartung*, his first atonal opera.

Gilbert and Sullivan had come together at the perfect moment, producing their best works in a relatively small window of opportunity that was distinctly theirs. They were not only of their age but embodiments of it, at least at its best. Lytton Strachey, the piquant chronicler of the Victorian Age, predicted that the Gilbert & Sullivan operas would be "the most permanent and lasting achievement of the Victorian Age."[17]

And so indeed they have. Of all Britain's artistic creations during the great age of Queen Victoria, only Dickens's novels have rivaled the Savoy operas for staying power. If the first half of the old queen's reign now looks like the Age of Dickens, the second half is surely the Age of Gilbert & Sullivan.

The only question was what their legacy was to be. Would Gilbert & Sullivan linger as a symbol of an era, recognized but outmoded and unloved, as the melodramas of the previous generation had become symbols of a bygone age? Or, like Shakespeare's, would their works truly live on into future generations?

Facing page: FIGURE 18.1. Kevin Kline (left center, in flowing sleeves), as the Pirate King, threatens Tony Azito (right center), as the Sergeant of Police, in the 1983 film version of *The Pirates of Penzance*. As the presence of a poster for *H. M. S. Pinafore* at upstage center suggests, this production—based closely on an earlier Broadway revival with an almost identical cast—was not entirely traditional. However, the listing of a "G. Rutland" as Sir Joseph Porter is presumably a salute to George Grossmith and Rutland Barrington, stars of the original production of *H. M. S. Pinafore. Source: Copyright 1983 Universal Pictures.*

18

Legacy

The most remarkable thing about Gilbert & Sullivan's legacy was how quickly and how sharply it divided into two streams, one of which proved astoundingly rich while the other dried up almost immediately.

Every creative person or team leaves two forms of legacy: their surviving works and their influence on subsequent generations of artists. Dickens, for example, lives on not only in the fact that people still read *David Copperfield* but also in hundreds of later writers who to this day are influenced by his work.

By the time of Gilbert's death in 1911 the operas themselves showed every sign of fading into musical/theatrical history, only to have a stunning revival in later decades that has ultimately made them the world's most popular body of musical-theater works and left them second only to Shakespeare in the history of English-language theater.

Strangely, however, the widespread popularity of the operas has produced only indirect artistic influence. The genre that Gilbert & Sullivan created virtually died with them, and musical theater took an entirely new direction in the twentieth century. For all their success, Gilbert and Sullivan died artistically, as well as literally, childless.

The story of the Gilbert & Sullivan operas in the twentieth century is inextricably linked with that of the D'Oyly Carte Opera Company.

With Carte's son Rupert at the helm, the company's return to London in the 1920s and to America in the 1930s was the driving force behind the Gilbert & Sullivan revival that has continued to the present day. Whatever the verdict on its artistic value, no one can deny that it was the Carte company that ensured that the operas would be accessible to later generations and evolve from contemporary successes into enduring classics.

The artistic legacy of the D'Oyly Carte was defined by two related concepts: tradition and exclusivity. Self-conscious guardians of the "authentic" Gilbert & Sullivan tradition, Rupert D'Oyly Carte and, later, his daughter Bridget saw their family enterprise as a delicate combination of a business, a museum, and a crusade. This attitude came to be shared with the company's generations of fans, as the word "Savoyard" gradually came to mean not primarily those who performed the operas but those who venerated them.

This attitude was made possible by the company's dual exclusivity: It performed nothing but Gilbert & Sullivan, ensuring that its identity would be inescapably tied to the operas; and it held the exclusive British copyright for professional performance of the operas, ensuring that their identity would be tied to the company.

Neither was an unmixed blessing. The concept of "tradition," in particular, would prove both a blessing and a bane to the D'Oyly Carte, while the company's exclusivity ironically both strengthened and weakened it.

The D'Oyly Carte claim to "the tradition" was always deceptive. Doing "Gilbert & Sullivan the way it was meant to be done" was widely understood to mean "as it had originally been done," but that claim was honored more in the breach than in the observance.

As I have previously noted, for example, when the company revived *Princess Ida* and *Ruddigore* for the first time, in the 1920s under the management of the younger Carte, substantial cuts were made, so that the operas of the 1920s were significantly different than they had been in the 1880s.

There was nothing wrong with this per se. Gilbert had declared his intention to make substantial revisions to *Ruddigore, Utopia, Limited,* and *The Grand Duke* for 1900s revivals that were never realized. But, coupled with a series of elaborate redesigns of sets and costumes (often striking but most of them far removed from the obsessive literalness that had characterized Gilbert's designs), these changes radically undercut the claim of true authenticity.

Instead the burden of "the tradition" fell most heavily on performers and directors. The stage "business" was sanctified and mandated, so that Henry Lytton was forced to fill Grossmith's shoes, Martyn Green to fill Lytton's, and so forth. The D'Oyly Carte essentially had no stage directors but only a series of stage managers following in the obsessive footsteps of Gilbert himself.

Ironically, the stage business didn't stagnate—Green's memoirs describe the evolution of many of his personal bits of business[1]—but rather accreted: Green added his own bits to what he had received from Lytton and passed it all on to Peter Pratt, and thence down the line.

The result was a performance tradition that was increasingly actor oriented and encrusted with business that Gilbert himself most likely would have detested. Green used a series of gradually enlarging fans for a famous (though difficult to concisely describe)[2] bit of business as Ko-Ko, for example, and got big laughs—but the bit would almost certainly have drawn an acerbic note from Gilbert, as similar interpolations by Rutland Barrington often did.

Indeed, the distinctive quality of the D'Oyly Carte productions, despite their talented performers and their splendid mountings (at least in London—on tour the standards often lagged considerably), was the lack of an overseeing eye focused on the text—the music and words that were supposedly the core of the company's appeal.

With "directors" who were forbidden to rethink the overall presentation of any given opera, who were generally excluded from production design, and who weren't allowed to add or delete any major elements of staging, the D'Oyly Carte was automatically forced to the sidelines of the theatrical history of England. Whatever new spirits blew through English theater, they would not penetrate the walls of Castle Carte.

The same was true in the musical realm. Only one conductor of stature led the company in the twentieth century—Malcolm Sargent, later Sir Malcolm. His tenure with the D'Oyly Carte was marred by controversy over his insistence on taking musical tempos that audiences and performers considered "wrong."

The irony was that Sargent had gleaned those tempos from Sullivan's own metronome markings on the manuscript scores. Over the years prior to his arrival in 1926, the musical treatment of the operas (like their theatrical performance) had subtly shifted from the original approach, but by now it was the "new" tempos that were "the tradition," even in the face of Sullivan's own markings.

As for a conductor taking different tempos simply because his or her musical inclinations suggested a different interpretation—well, that would have been unthinkable. Conductors, like performers and directors, were expected to work within a narrow range of interpretive expression, a range defined by "the tradition."

Such constraints would have mattered little had not the D'Oyly Carte enjoyed exclusivity within Britain. After all, "historical" productions of Shakespeare contribute to our appreciation of his plays, as "original instruments" performances of Bach do for his works—but in large part because other performance traditions exist side by side.

This was not the case with D'Oyly Carte, which until the 1961 expiration of Gilbert's copyright owned sole British rights to the operas. And indeed, by then the D'Oyly Carte interpretation of Gilbert & Sullivan had become "the" interpretation to such an extent that, even after the copyright expired, it was some years before independent producers, directors, and performers ventured new approaches to the operas.

The full consequences of "the tradition"—both within the Carte company and within the generations of fans who helped sanctify "the tradition"—will never be fully understood, because we can never know for certain what might have been.

What can be confidently said, however, is that the combination of "the tradition" and D'Oyly Carte exclusivity kept several generations of performers, conductors and directors from bringing their gifts to Gilbert & Sullivan.

We will never know what Noel Coward might have brought to the role of Sir Joseph Porter, for example, or how Charles Laughton might have played Wilfred Shadbolt. Julie Andrews never sang Josephine or Mabel. Sir Thomas Beecham never conducted *The Yeomen of the Guard*.

The lifeblood of Shakespeare has been his attractiveness to the most talented theatrical people of each succeeding age. Every great actor, actress, designer, or director sooner or later itches to measure him/herself by the standards of Shakespeare. A lot of terrible Shakespeare is done, of course, but many brilliant productions are done as well, providing insights into the plays that no single approach could offer.

For most of the twentieth century, however, Gilbert & Sullivan was deprived of that richness. The D'Oyly Carte provided a brilliant showcase, with smooth, professional productions featuring several generations of performers who earned the admiration of fans the world over, but it show-cased only one vision of the operas.

We can appreciate the many benefits of the D'Oyly Carte approach, but we can only speculate on what was lost.

Ultimately, however, the fall of the D'Oyly Carte came about for reasons unconnected with "the tradition" or even the widespread fear that its loss of exclusivity in 1961 would mean its end.

In the event, the expiration of the copyright had little impact. There were other productions, notably by the Glyndebourne Opera, but they didn't detract from the D'Oyly Carte. It continued doing what it did best, and while the generation of fans bred on the 1920s and 1930s D'Oyly Carte productions complained that the newer singers weren't up to their predecessors, the company didn't suffer unduly from the loss of its exclusivity.

When the end finally came, it resulted from financial stresses unconnected with the operas per se. In the 1950s, 1960s, and 1970s, the D'Oyly Carte had become recognized as a uniquely valuable national institution, on a par with museums, libraries, and the like. This merit was recognized in the title conferred on Dame Bridget D'Oyly Carte, granddaughter of the company's founder, and in general acclaim for the company as a national treasure.

Complacent in this status, however, the company had gradually lost the shrewd business management that had always been the Carte family's trademark. As early as the 1950s, longtime patter-baritone Green was complaining in his memoirs that its inept publicity—whether from ignorance or from a principled refusal to baldly promote itself—was causing it to play to half-empty houses on tour.[3]

By the late 1970s and early 1980s, it became apparent that a company that had thrived for more than a century as a profit machine, making its founders extraordinarily wealthy, had forgotten how to stage Gilbert & Sullivan and make money.

Despite outcries for public support—which, during the reign of Conservative Prime Minister Margaret Thatcher, fell largely on deaf ears—and a variety of suggestions on how to rescue it, the D'Oyly Carte's financial crisis proved terminal. It staged its final performance on February 27, 1983.

A successor company, using the same name and funded in part by Dame Bridget's estate, was founded a few years later. However, it has no meaningful continuity with the original company—it performs non–Gilbert & Sullivan works, bases itself in cities other than London, and has few if any performers or staffers in common with the original D'Oyly Carte.

Some had predicted that the demise of the D'Oyly Carte would mean a loss of interest in Gilbert & Sullivan worldwide, but there has been little sign of such decline.

A variety of high-profile productions by directors such as Wilford Leach (whose *Pirates of Penzance* enjoyed an extended Broadway run in the 1980s) and Peter Sellars (who staged *The Mikado* in Chicago and has long spoken of staging *The Gondoliers*) testifies to the operas' enduring appeal to top professional directors and performers. Meanwhile, productions by companies such as the English National Opera and the New York City Opera have proven the financial and artistic viability of high-quality professional productions.

In recent years, a British television series—*The Compleat Gilbert and Sullivan* (which, despite its title, omitted *Utopia, Limited* and *The Grand Duke*)—and a steady stream of new recordings by various companies and orchestras, as well as compact-disc reissues of classic D'Oyly Carte recordings, have attested to the continuing popularity of the operas, as has an ongoing barrage of books on the subject.

Most impressive of all, perhaps, are the more than 200 companies worldwide performing primarily or exclusively the works of Gilbert & Sullivan, a phenomenon matched only by Shakespeare. Both professionals and amateurs, tens of thousands of people perform in the operas every year, before audiences in the millions.

Clearly, the works of Gilbert & Sullivan are more than a passing fad. More than a century after the final Savoy opera closed, long after the deaths of virtually everyone who knew Gilbert or Sullivan and even after the demise of the D'Oyly Carte Opera Company, the operas are more widely popular than they ever have been and show no signs of fading in popular esteem.

Another century from now—or two or three, for that matter—it seems likely that people will still be debating the reasons for their enduring appeal.

They will not, however, be tracing the ancestral descent of the Savoy operas. Given the immense success of the operas, then and now, it is all the more surprising that, in terms of theater history, they represent an evolutionary dead end.

It is the nature of the arts that one success breeds others, if only in the form of imitations aiming to cash in on its success. Shakespeare continues to influence playwrights centuries after his death. Picasso, Hemingway, Hitchcock, Rodgers & Hammerstein, Stephen Sondheim, and Philip Glass all shine atop "family trees" of artistic influence that in many cases span generations.

Yet Gilbert & Sullivan, who stood astride their respective worlds like twin colossi and whose works have earned millions upon millions of dollars for generations of producers and performers, have left behind them theatrical and musical worlds in which their lasting success seems an anomaly, disconnected from the stream of artistic history before or since.

In part, this disconnection came about because the logical order of succession was thwarted by the deaths of several people who, working in the Gilbert & Sullivan tradition, might have been their most obvious successors.

Alfred Cellier and Frederic Clay, both friends of Sullivan and collaborators with Gilbert, died unexpectedly young. Cellier, whose *Dorothy* was a bigger hit than *The Mikado* and ran for more than 900 performances, died in 1891; Clay was felled by a stroke in 1883 and died five years later without fully regaining his capacities.

The man most likely to succeed to the light-opera crown was Edward German, who clearly aspired to do so. As early as 1888 he had worked with Gilbert, composing a song for a revival of *Broken Hearts* (1875). He completed Sullivan's final opera and composed Gilbert's final one, clearly seeing himself as Sullivan's heir.

He was a deft composer in his own right—describing his music for *Fallen Fairies*, Gilbert spoke admiringly of "its high technical qualities, its fund of delicate melody & its great variety."[4] After *The Emerald Isle* German joined with its librettist, Basil Hood, to compose two more operas for the Savoy.

One of these, the still-engaging *Merrie England* (1902), stands as the final flowering of the minimal Gilbert & Sullivan legacy, but its successor, *A Princess of Kensington* (1903), was not a success. The two wrote a more serious opera, *Tom Jones*, in 1907, but did not work together again.

German & Hood might have been as long-running a team as Gilbert & Sullivan, if less inspired. But though German lived until 1936, he was disillusioned with opera and did not work in the genre after *Fallen Fairies*, limiting himself to orchestral and chamber music; Hood died in 1917.

With their retirement from the field, and with the death in 1901 of Richard D'Oyly Carte, the direct "line of descent" was snuffed out. Helen Lenoir Carte continued to operate the company but commissioned few original works, none of which were successful.

There would be Gilbert & Sullivan imitators—such as Noel Gay (d. 1954), whose highly Gilbert & Sullivanian musical comedy *Me and My Girl* had a surprisingly successful revival on Broadway in the 1980s, complete with a ghostly-portraits-come-to-life scene—but no Gilbert & Sullivan inheritors.

In another sense, the lack of a Gilbert & Sullivan legacy is the result of historical circumstance. Gilbert died on the eve of World War I, which not only cost England the lives of many of its next generation of artists but also ushered in the first wave of modernism, erasing much of the previous artistic tradition in many genres.

Gilbert & Sullivan are not the only artists of their generation to have left few obvious descendants. The influence of the poets of the Victorian tradition has largely vanished. The great painters of the age, such as Sergeant or Millais, are similarly without obvious legacy.

Playwrights such as Barrie, Pinero, and Boucicault had little influence on the 1920s and beyond. Thackeray, Trollope, and Gissing have had scant impact on twentieth-century literature.

The twin blows of the Great War and modernism hit England hard. There are few English artists, painters, novelists or playwrights among the great moderns—the interwar years were overall artistically stagnant ones in England; the dominant figures were aging prewar holdovers (such as Shaw), American expatriates (such as T. S. Eliot), or determinedly frivolous diversionaries (such as Coward or P. G. Wodehouse). It was not until the 1950s that England again took a leading role in the arts.

But Gilbert & Sullivan are unlike most other premoderns in that, while their influence has been marginal, their works have not. Plenty of individuals appreciate Thackeray or Tennyson, enjoy Millais's paintings or even read Pinero, but none of these works have remained popular with the general public.

Gilbert & Sullivan, on the other hand, retain their vitality. Each year there are more productions of *The Grand Duke*, the least successful of the Savoy operas, than of all Pinero's 50-plus plays put together. A young playwright inclined to take after Boucicault may never even encounter his work, whereas nearly every English-speaking person sooner or later runs into a Gilbert & Sullivan show, if only accidentally.

So it cannot easily be said that modernism has taken Gilbert & Sullivan's legacy off the table. The works are there still, readily accessible to any young artist open to their influence.

Why, then, has that influence been so limited?

In part, that influence was inhibited by "the tradition," as embodied in the D'Oyly Carte Opera Company.

Because of the D'Oyly Carte's emphasis on tradition, its bedrock appeal, from the 1920s on, was to older audiences and their families, not to cutting-edge artists. Well into the 1950s, a mainstay of the D'Oyly Carte audience was people who remembered the original productions they had seen as children; in later years it was the children of those 1920s–1950s audiences, to whom Gilbert & Sullivan represented family, stability, and predictability.

Because there were no bold new productions to shake up the status quo and cause younger artists to see new aspects of Gilbert & Sullivan on which they could draw, "the tradition" had the effect of causing new generations of artists and audiences alike to define themselves against Gilbert & Sullivan rather than in light of them. "The tradition" was, however, only one aspect of a general tendency to misunderstand Gilbert & Sullivan, to focus on their form rather than their content.

This was embodied in the gradually narrowing reputation of Gilbert & Sullivan as creators of patter songs. When one spoke of "a Gilbert & Sullivan sort of song" in the 1880s, it might be a patter song, a ballad, a chorus, or one of Sullivan's beloved intricate ensemble numbers. By the 1920s, however, it would definitely have been a patter song.

The very way D'Oyly Carte fans defined the company's chronology reveals this change: It was the "Lytton years" yielding to the "Green years," not the "Fancourt Years" leading to the "Adams years." Darrell Fancourt and Donald Adams were beloved performers, but it was the patter man who defined an era, a production, or a recording.

This was counter to the spirit of the original productions—*Trial by Jury* and *The Gondoliers* had succeeded despite the absence of Grossmith or any comparable star as patter man. Moreover, this attitude tended to pigeonhole Gilbert & Sullivan by reference to something that they did well, perhaps even uniquely well, but that was hardly the only thing they did well. In particular, the emphasis on patter led to a focus on the sound of words and the cleverness of individual lines rather than the shaping of character and theme that was the real genius of the Gilbert & Sullivan style.

Thus, the artists in whose work the influence of Gilbert & Sullivan is most easily found are generally the lyricists of the American musical theater, with its tradition of light verse.

For example, E. Y. "Yip" Harburg (1896–1981)—lyricist of the film *The Wizard of Oz* (1939) and the play *Finian's Rainbow* (1947)—offered a recollection of a 1910 encounter during his school days that is at once gratifying and disturbing to those familiar with the operas. Harburg told authors Bernard Rosenberg and Ernest Goldstein in *Creators and Disturbers* (1982):

> Perhaps my first great literary idol was W. S. Gilbert. I adored his light verse. One day at school I pulled out a book of his 'Bab Ballads' and other poems, and the kid sitting next to me showed great and excited interest. His name was Ira Gershwin. We always sat side by side—he was 'G,' I was 'H.'
>
> Ira took a look at the book and said, "Do you know that a lot of this is set to music?" I was incredulous. "There's music to it?" "Sure is. I'll show you."[5]

In a way, this anecdote testifies to Gilbert's influence—after all, Harburg and especially Gershwin (1896–1964) were to write some of the most popular musical-theater and musical-film lyrics of the next three decades, and they clearly knew Gilbert's work intimately.

On the other hand, it also shows a superficial understanding of the operas. To think of Gilbert & Sullivan as "Bab Ballads" set to music is to see them shallowly.

A similar point of view is conveyed by Stephen Sondheim (b. 1930), the lyricist of *Gypsy* (1959) and lyricist/composer of *A Little Night Music* (1972), *Sweeney Todd* (1979), and *Sunday in the Park with George* (1984):

> I don't know Gilbert and Sullivan's work very well. I've probably heard each of the operettas once and seen a couple of them once.
> Moreover, I don't much like them, heretical though that opinion may be. I find Gilbert's lyrics fussy and self-conscious to an irritating degree, and Sullivan's music rather dull.
> So I'm afraid to report that their work hasn't influenced my own at all, the one exception being the parody of their work in the British Admiral's section of "Please Hello" in *Pacific Overtures*. . . . In fact, in my own show-off way, I put in a series of hidden inner rhymes in that little section to out-Gilbert Gilbert.[6] (ex.18.1)

Like Harburg and Gershwin, Sondheim relates to Gilbert's lyrics in isolation from their theatrical context. (Ironically, his complaint against Gilbert is one many critics have made against him!)

Most musical-theater authors and lyricists acknowledge at least some influence from Gilbert. Wodehouse, who as Jerome Kern's lyricist for *Leave It to Jane* (1917), *Oh, Lady, Lady* (1919), and other shows had a considerable influence on 1920s Broadway, grew up in the same area where Gilbert spent his last years, and recorded his recollections of children's parties hosted by Gilbert at his estate, Grim's Dyke.

Similarly, Noel Coward (1899–1973) was indoctrinated with Gilbert & Sullivan virtually from birth. According to his biographer, Philip Hoare,

> Coward noted that he was "born into a generation that still took light music seriously. The lyrics and melodies of Gilbert & Sullivan"— which he later professed to dislike, and yet which appeared to be a discernible influence on his work—were "hummed and strummed into my consciousness at an early age . . . By the time I was 4 years old, 'Take a Pair of Sparkling Eyes,' 'Titwillow,' 'We're Very Wide Awake, the Moon and I,' and 'I Have a Song to Sing, O' had been fairly inculcated into my bloodstream."[7]

The young Cole Porter (1891–1964) made no secret of the extent to which his work, especially his early work, was inspired by Gilbert & Sullivan. In a 1955 newspaper article, the lyricist/composer of *Anything Goes* (1934) and *Kiss Me Kate* (1948) wrote: "I'm becoming less and less interested in tricky rhymes. I think I used to go overboard on them. In Yale I was rhyme crazy. That was due to the fact that I was Gilbert and Sullivan crazy. They had a big influence on my life."[8]

Adolph Green (b. 1915), who with his partner Betty Comden wrote the screenplays for *On the Town* (1949) and *Singin' in the Rain* (1952), as well as the books for the Broadway hits *On the Twentieth Century* (1978) and *The Will Rogers Follies* (1991), reports that his acquaintance with Gilbert & Sullivan goes back to a production of *The Mikado* which he saw at Public School 39 in the Bronx when he was 10.

"I got to be an instant fan," he says, "hearing it and loving it. I have quite a few of their recordings, and I've seen practically all of them on-stage. My favorites are *The Mikado* and *Iolanthe*—just gorgeous in every way."

As for their impact on his own work, Green can't cite specifics but feels confident that the operas affected both his lyrics and his book-writing.

"I don't see how it could help but have an influence," he says. "They had a way of attacking pomposity, false social standards and phony balo-ney, but doing it with sheer fun—the nonsense, the humor. That was their mastery—the music and words were so lyrical at the time, and still fun. Lyrical, sharp and brilliant."[9]

Alan Jay Lerner (1918–1986)—author/lyricist of *My Fair Lady* (1956), *Gigi* (1958), and *Camelot* (1960)—proves his own devotion, if perhaps also his tendency to exaggerate, by writing that "Gilbert was the Adam of mod-ern lyric writing. P. G. Wodehouse, Lorenz Hart, Cole Porter, Ira Gersh-win, Oscar Hammerstein and their contemporaries and descendants all owe their lyrical, genetic beginning to W. S. Gilbert."[10]

Direct examples of Gilbert & Sullivan's influence on musical theater are rarer, but two examples are provided by Sheldon Harnick (b. 1924), lyr-icist of the Pulitzer Prize–winning *Fiorello!* (1959) and *Fiddler on the Roof* (1964), two of the most popular shows of Broadway's 1950s/1960s "Golden Age."

Harnick recalls growing up with the operas but says he really appreci-ated them for the first time as a teen-age violinist in the orchestra at Chicago's Goodman Theater. .

> I remember that I found the production delightful and, in particular, I remember being bowled over by the patter song. I had been collab-orating with a high-school friend, writing song parodies and some original material . . . so I was becoming aware of the art (and the problems) of lyric-writing. And what I heard during the rehearsals and performances at the Goodman Theater made me sit up and take notice. . . .
>
> The first things I responded to in Gilbert's lyrics were his mastery of rapid-fire lyrics and his way with a comic line. Then, as I matured, I began to appreciate his many other virtues. And somewhere along the line I also began to appreciate Sullivan's art-istry.

18.1. Stephen Sondheim's "Please, Hello," from *Pacific Overtures*, uses parodies of nineteenth-century national music styles to depict the arrival of various outsiders to Japan, including a British admiral who sings a Gilbert and Sullivan parody. "Please, Hello." Music and lyrics by Stephen Sondheim. © 1975 Rilting Music, Inc. (ASCAP). All rights on behalf of Rilting Music, Inc. (ASCAP) administered by WB Music Corp. All rights reserved. Used by permission. Warner Bros. Publications U.S. Inc., Miami, FL 33014.

an-chored rath-er near to shore, It's noth-ing but a met-a-phor That acts as a pre-ven-ta-tive.

As to his own work, Harnick says,

> I think the overall influence exerted on me by Gilbert's work was a heightened awareness of the *craft* of writing lyrics: the sharpness and inventiveness of the language, the strongly marked rhythmic schemes and the play of wit. I don't mean to suggest that I learned those things through conscious study; I imagine, rather, that I absorbed them through repeatedly hearing (and sometimes singing) the lyrics.

Looking back over his own work, Harnick thinks of instances from his two most popular shows, both of which he wrote with composer Jerry Bock (b. 1928):

> When Jerry Bock and I wrote "Little Tin Box" for the show *Fiorello!* we had the chorus (in this case, half a dozen hack politicians) deliberately echo the words of the soloist, a device we deliberately borrowed from Gilbert & Sullivan for humorous effect.
>
> And in *Fiddler on the Roof,* in the number "Tevye's Dream," we sneakily inserted a line which was our own private bow to Gilbert & Sullivan, musically and lyrically. It occurs just before a nightmare-version of a character named Fruma-Sarah enters. (I never realized until this minute that Fruma-Sarah is a close kin to Katisha!) Anyway, just before she enters, the chorus looks offstage, sees her approaching and sings (in what I intended to be true Gilbertian diction [ex.18.2]):

> What woman is this
> by righteous anger shaken?

"Those are just two examples," Harnick concludes, "but I'm reasonably sure that, if I searched, I'd find examples of the Gilbert & Sullivan influence scattered here and there throughout my entire catalogue."[11]

He adds that it gave him great pleasure when the Bock & Harnick musical *She Loves Me* (1963) opened in London—at the Savoy Theatre.

Bock, on the other hand, sees little influence of Gilbert or Sullivan on his own work, though he recalls that he played Bunthorne in a summer-

18.2. The Jerry Bock/Sheldon Harnick musical *Fiddler on the Roof* includes, in the song "Tevye's Dream," a passage that—according to lyricist Harnick—was specifically intended to evoke Gilbert & Sullivan, presumably through its inverted diction and the use of an echoing chorus. Portions of the music from "Tevye's Dream," from *Fiddler on the Roof,* © 1962, renewed 1994 by Mayerling Productions Ltd. and Jerry Bock Enterprises.

camp production at 15 or 16 and, the next year, participated in a "swing" version of *Iolanthe* at the camp.

> It was called *Hot-olanthe*, which will give you an idea of what it was like!
> It was Gilbert that I admired, that really took me to Sullivan. But Sullivan seems to be more stylistically out of date than Gilbert. Gilbert & Sullivan weren't any real influence on my work, I don't think.[12]

Like Bock, most musical-theater composers are less likely to point to Sullivan as an influence than are lyricists to look to Gilbert. The most notable exception is John Kander (b. 1927), composer of such Broadway hits as *Cabaret* (1966), *Chicago* (1975), and *Kiss of the Spider-Woman* (1990).

> I grew up with the complete recordings after 1927. I've known them intimately all my life, since I was a child. I saw most of them done by the Oberlin College Gilbert & Sullivan Players, and of course I saw the D'Oyly Carte on tour whenever they came to New York. . . .
> It's astounding how much the satire still works, and how original the operas are. About 95 percent of all musical theater is adaptations—Gilbert is the great exception to that.[13]

Kander's music has a jazzy, dark tone that is very different from Sullivan's, but he still sees the Victorian composer as a substantial presence in his own work.

> His major influence probably has to do with word-setting. He was extremely meticulous in seeing that every word could be heard by reflecting the natural rhythm of the lyrics in his music. There's a great reciprocity between his music and Gilbert's words.
> The natural setting of words is very important to me, and I'm sure that comes from Sullivan.

(Completing the inversion of the standard pattern, Kander's partner Fred Ebb (b. 1936) writes: "I know very little about Gilbert and Sullivan," though he adds: "Of course, I admire those lyrics tremendously and hope that my work will someday be as proficient.")[14]

Stephen Schwartz (b. 1948), composer/lyricist of *Godspell* (1971), *Pippin* (1972), and the film *Prince of Egypt* (1999), recalls his parents taking him to D'Oyly Carte performances of *H. M. S. Pinafore* and *The Pirates of Penzance* as a child during the 1950s—though, he notes,

> by then they were getting pretty old and tired, and I preferred the local troupes. I also remember seeing a television production of *Mikado* with Groucho Marx in the cast. I can't admit to being a huge

aficionado, but I was certainly familiar with the music, at least of those three works. I think my own work was in fact somewhat influenced, particularly in my earlier writing and primarily lyrically. The most obvious example is the song 'War Is a Science' (from *Pippin*), which is a deliberate Gilbert and Sullivan pastiche" (ex.18.3).

"Beyond that, of course," Schwartz concludes, "all musical-theater writers are inheritors of the Gilbert and Sullivan tradition."[15]

Frank Wildhorn (b. 1959), composer of *Jekyll and Hyde* (1996) and *The Scarlet Pimpernel* (1997), reports that Gilbert and Sullivan not only influenced his work but were responsible for his attraction to the theater.

Gilbert and Sullivan were the great "pop" songwriters of their day. They took many of the musical vocabularies of their time and used them in imaginative ways by thinking "outside the box." They were melodic and accessible to the public, who adored them.

When I was in college [at the University of Southern California], I was in the chorus of *H. M. S. Pinafore*—my first theatrical experience. They are heroes![16]

Tom Jones (b. 1928), librettist of *The Fantasticks* (1960) and other shows, recalls his childhood days in West Texas during the 1930s and 1940s.

We had no direct connection with theater or cultural events of any sort. When I was a freshman in high school, an uncle of mine gave me an album of records which featured Nelson Eddy (of all people) singing the patter songs of Gilbert & Sullivan.

I was enchanted. The wit, the verbal dexterity, the ebullience of the music—all of these things somehow managed to get through to my uneducated ear . . . I quickly learned most of the songs, and amused myself by singing "Am I Alone?" and "John Wellington Wells" and others from *Pinafore* and *Pirates* and, most particularly, *The Mikado*.

"Am I Alone?" was the most appropriate because I was alone and I had no one among my family or friends with whom I felt I could share this enthusiasm.

As a freshman at the University of Texas, Jones writes, he wrote and performed an *H. M. S. Pinafore* parody at the annual Curtain Club banquet, which led to a series of "send-ups and sketches" over the rest of his college years.

"And these sketches, which began with my send-up of *Pinafore*, were the only writing I did during my undergraduate years. (I was majoring in directing.)"

18.3. Composer/lyricist Stephen Schwartz calls his song "War Is Science," from *Pippin*, "a deliberate Gilbert & Sullivan pastiche." Its use of patter rhythms suggests Gilbert, while the song closes with a joint chorus with the men and women singing out of sync with one another, a favorite Sullivan device. Reprinted by permission.

That experience, he adds, led to his writing several college musical shows during graduate school, which began his collaboration with composer Harvey Schmidt (b. 1929), with whom he wrote *The Fantasticks, I Do! I Do!* (1966), and other shows.

"As to the specific influence of G & S (and especially G) on my/our later work," Jones says, "it may be found most clearly in the two fathers'

if the fates feel friv - o - lous and all our plans they smoth - er   well, sup -

[Charles]

pose this war does shriv - el us, there'll al - ways be an - oth - er! And then,   and then,   and

[Soft Shoe 4]   [Men]

gen - tle - men, and then,   And then the

songs in *The Fantasticks*. Both 'Never Say No' and, most particularly, 'Plant a Radish' are in the patter-song tradition."[17]

Perhaps the theatrical artist most unlikely to be a Gilbert & Sullivan fan apparently was, incidentally. James Knowlson's 1996 biography describes Samuel Beckett (1906–89), the future author of *Waiting for Godot* (1952) and *Endgame* (1957), as a Gilbert & Sullivan expert.

(Pantomime) and the Gilbert & Sullivan productions by the visiting D'Oyly Carte Opera Company were Beckett's first introductions to the theater. Beckett used to play Sullivan's music on the piano at home; a friend recalled that "he sang irreverent, ribald Beckett librretti in substitute for Gilbert's words." The same friend remembered that the Becketts had a set of gramophone recordings of the D'Oyly Carte operas that they would play whenever rain interfered with the tennis at Cooldrinagh.

His interest in music and verse at the time [1921] led him to have the reputation of being "almost word perfect over the whole range of Gilbert & Sullivan operas."[18]

Knowlson makes no claim, however, for a Gilbert & Sullivan influence on Beckett's plays!

Even rock 'n' roll has seen its share of Gilbert & Sullivan influences, as unlikely as that may seem. Rocker Todd Rundgren probably confounded his fans when he recorded "The Nightmare Song" from *Iolanthe*,[19] while singer/songwriter Billy Joel told a master-class audience that the pattery piano accompaniment for his song "Angry Young Man" (1975) was inspired by "I Am the Very Model of a Modern Major-General."[20]

Most notable in these instances of Gilbert & Sullivan's continuing influence is that with few exceptions their view of the Savoy masters is a narrow one, focusing on their gifts as songwriters.

Nonetheless, Gilbert & Sullivan were preeminently crafters of shows, not writers of songs. Of the hundreds of songs they wrote together, only one ("The Distant Shore," 1874) was written fully independent of dramatic character and context. The common perception of their work has emphasized Gilbert's most gimmicky lyrics and, on the whole, Sullivan's least interesting music, completely out of the context for which these songs were created.

For example, it is possible to appreciate the Lord Chancellor's "Nightmare Song" from *Iolanthe* as a succession of cleverly phrased, tripping lyrics (as Gershwin probably did) or to see it as obsessively gimmicky (as Sondheim apparently does). But to do either overlooks the fugal leitmotif Sullivan weaves through his accompaniment, a leitmotif that is used for the Chancellor's act 1 entrances as well and, in fact, is one of a number of character signatures used throughout the opera.

To focus on the cleverness of the individual lyrics is most likely to miss the intricate circle imagery that ties the song together and that is mirrored in its orchestration. And to see the song independent of the character who sings it is to miss the fact that its nightmare visions are not arbitrary fantasies but rather psychologically appropriate fears for this particular character in this particular situation.

The result of this misfocus on patter lyrics over the rest of the Savoy equation is that Gilbert & Sullivan are imitated (or parodied) more often than they are emulated, which in turn twists what they represent as artists into virtual unrecognizability. However much Gershwin admired Gilbert, for example, he specialized in slangy not-quite-rhymes ("I'd go to Hell for ya / or even Philadelphia") that would probably have appalled the generally meticulous Gilbert.

Meanwhile, the creative minds most likely to benefit from the influence of Gilbert and Sullivan—those dedicated to serious, character-oriented, and thematically driven musical theater—close themselves to it and busy themselves reinventing a wheel on which the Savoy operas have already rolled to immortality.

There are some exceptions to this generalization. Sir Timothy Rice (b. 1944), librettist for *Jesus Christ Superstar* (1971) and *Evita* (1979) as well as lyricist for the phenomenally successful stage and film productions of *The Lion King* (1994 on film, 1998 on Broadway), reports that he is not only an aficionado of the Savoy operas but also is particularly impressed by Gilbert's books.

"I saw quite a few of the operas as a child," Rice said. "I had a master at school who was quite keen on it, and since then I've seen most of the operas. It's one of those things I'm always wishing I saw more often, actually."

As an author and lyricist, Rice says, he always appreciated the fact that Gilbert was accorded equal stature with his composer—not often the case in traditional opera or in much of contemporary musical theater.

> I always liked the idea of a partnership in which the lyrics were considered equal or even superior to the music [laughing]. And of course Gilbert wrote both book and lyrics. Constructing the stories is as important as writing the actual lyrics—the plot outlines, comic in most cases, are a very strong part of the operas.
>
> Shows that are writer driven are always better, and there's an old saying that, in musical theater, the three most important things are the book, the book and the book.

Rice doesn't see the influence of Gilbert & Sullivan as "noticeably specific" in his own work, however. He says the standards they set, as well as the degree of control they exercised over their own work, are more significant to him.

"They kept tabs on everything," he said, "and that must be a reason for their success. In musicals today producers and directors tend to want to interfere in things they ought not to."[21]

Tom Jones, too, remains intrigued by a side of Gilbert & Sullivan's work that has nothing to do with patter songs.

> What I would like to do, but haven't done yet, is explore the more structural side of the G & S shows—the blatant theatricality which allows them to explore form in a bold, presentational, nonrealistic way. We are, in our time and for most of this century, so influenced by the middle-European operetta (not the comic operetta) that there is a great effort to hide the basic theatricality and to present characters and situations (and sets) as "realistic." This has been particularly true since [Rodgers and Hammerstein].
>
> But I am convinced that audiences can accept (and welcome) occasional different approaches which allow the structure to be as "artificial" as the great Gilbert and Sullivan masterworks.

Rice and Jones are in the minority, however: While many lyricists list the Savoy operas as among their influences—usually an early one soon outgrown—few contemporary authors of musical theater cite Gilbert & Sullivan as relevant to their work.

Thus Gilbert and Sullivan's legacy leaves them in an appropriately paradoxical position: Their works are universally known and all but universally misunderstood. The people who love their operas don't necessarily understand why they do, and the people who dislike them do so for reasons that aren't necessarily so.

If there is any comfort to be found in this appealingly awkward paradox, it is that it will probably unravel as time progresses. The Gilbert & Sullivan operas are what they are, but the full shape of the Gilbert & Sullivan legacy won't be known for decades, even centuries to come.

After all, a century after their composition, Shakespeare's plays were appreciated primarily as great vehicles for actors and as sources for poetic epigrams. More than half were virtually unknown, while most of the rest were performed only in drastically truncated or rewritten (or both) versions. The underlying thematic power of the plays—while still exerting its influence—was all but ignored.

As the years passed, however, the power of Shakespeare's plays became more, not less, apparent. Superficialities have dropped away, and the universal appeal of the plays has grown with time.

Since it's my assertion that the core appeal of the Gilbert & Sullivan operas lies in exactly the same underlying thematic power, I feel little hesitation in concluding that the real legacy of Gilbert & Sullivan is only beginning to be felt.

Time will winnow the folly, I feel, and make more apparent the grain or two of truth among the chaff.

Appendix A: The Stories of the Savoy Operas

Thespis; or, The Gods Grown Old (1871)

The opera is set on Mount Olympus, where the Greek gods, old and worn out, are wondering why no one worships them any more or even seems to care about them.

They are interrupted by the arrival of a theatrical company, on a picnic excursion to celebrate the wedding of two of its members. Sparkeion and Nicemis, the bridal couple, arrive first and sing a love duet, "Here Far Away from All the World." The other actors arrive, singing a chorus of "Climbing Over Rocky Mountain," and settle down for a picnic.

Some commotions ensue within the company, but its manager, Thespis, quiets them. He explains that it's his philosophy to be distant from his actors, and he sings them a song, "I Once Knew a Chap," about the dangers of being too congenial with one's inferiors.

The gods appear, but the actors are not much frightened—they play gods themselves—and Thespis advises the gods that they are out of touch and need to freshen themselves up. This they decide to do, journeying to the mortal world to find out what's changed in their absence. Meanwhile, Thespis and his company are left behind to rule as the gods in their stead.

The second act finds that the actors have made a mess of things. Apollo is played by an actor married to the actress playing Diana, so the sun shines all night while he is with her; Tipseion, a reformed drunkard now a teetotaler, has been cast as Dionysus, and the grapes all now give ginger beer; a peace-loving Mars has abolished battles; and so on.

The gods reappear and oust the mortals, punishing them with a hideous curse: Henceforth, instead of being comedians, they will all be "eminent tragedians, whom no one ever goes to see."

Trial by Jury (1875)

Before the opera, which is set in the London Court of the Exchequer, the engagement of Edwin and Angelina has ended unhappily, and she has sued him for breach of promise of marriage.

As the opera begins, the usher quiets an unruly crowd and, in "Now, Jurymen, Hear My Advice," instructs the jury to be objective—and to favor Angelina's side. Edwin arrives and, in "When First My Old, Old Love I Knew," explains that he simply changed his mind—which the jurymen can understand, since they reveal similar incidents in their own past in their "Oh, I Was Like That When a Lad."

The Judge enters and, in "When I, Good Friends, Was Called to the Bar," recalls that he made his way by first wooing "a rich attorney's elderly, ugly daughter" and then jilting her once he was rich.

Angelina arrives to the tune of "Comes the Blushing Flower," and the Judge and jury are immediately smitten with her. Her counsel denounces Edwin in "With a Sense of Deep Emotion," and Edwin in turn sings "Oh, Gentlemen, Listen, I Pray," claiming that to change is natural, even in matters of the heart.

After the Judge has admitted that they face "A Nice Dilemma," Angelina throws herself on Edwin, proclaiming "I Love Him, I Love Him." He responds with "I Smoke Like a Furnace," painting himself as so unpleasant that she's better off without him.

The jury is baffled, but the Judge resolves the matter by deciding to marry Angelina himself. All rejoice at this happy resolution of the case, and with a chorus of "Oh, Joy Unbounded" the opera comes to an end.

The Sorcerer (1877)

Before the opera, which is set on Sir Marmaduke Pointdextre's estate outside the small village of Ploverleigh, Sir Marmaduke's son Alexis has been engaged to Aline, daughter of the wealthy Lady Sangazure, with whom Sir Marmaduke was once in love.

As Act 1 begins, the chorus has gathered for a breakfast as preparations are being made for the formal signing of the marriage contract. They sing "Ring Forth Ye Bells" and depart, as the young Constance appears.

Despite the best efforts of her mother, Mrs. Partlet, Constance is distraught over her love for the vicar, Dr. Daly, as she sings in "When He Is Here." Daly appears, singing "Time Was When Love and I Were Well-Acquainted" and bemoaning his loveless life, but he doesn't catch the broad hints that Mrs. Partlet throws his way on Constance's behalf.

The women leave as Alexis and Sir Marmaduke arrive for the signing of the contract, followed by the choruses—singing a lusty "With Heart and with Voice." Aline enters and sings a song of joy, "Happy Young Heart." Meanwhile Sir Marmaduke and Lady Sangazure catch one another's eye and sing the graceful "Welcome Joy"—whose decorous platitudes are interrupted by passionate interior monologues declaring their love for each other. An elderly Notary appears and, singing "All Is Prepared," officiates at the signing of the marriage contract.

All but Alexis and Aline withdraw, and Alexis expresses his opinion that only love makes life worth living in "For Love Alone." He then reveals to her that he has hired a sorcerer, John Wellington Wells, to introduce a love potion into the tea at the upcoming village banquet. Wells appears, sings his introductory "My Name Is John Wellington Wells" and, despite Aline's qualms, carries out a demonic incantation and puts the potion into the teapot.

Chorusing "Now to the Banquet We Press," the villagers arrive. All drink the tea, and all but Alexis, Aline, and Wells fall into a deep sleep.

Act 2 returns to the same scene, that night, as Wells, Alexis, and Aline reappear to sing " 'Tis Twelve, I Think." They then watch as the villagers slowly awaken and madly fall in love with one another.

But Wells, dismayed to see rich and poor alike asleep together, has had Lady Sangazure, Sir Marmaduke, Dr. Daly, and the Notary carried to their homes. Alexis and Aline initially appreciate his delicacy, but it turns out to have been a mistake.

Constance appears and, in "Dear Friends, Take Pity on My Lot," declares her love for the aged Notary. Nevertheless, Alexis is pleased and asks Aline to take the potion as well, to ensure their love. She refuses, saying that her love is already irrevocable. He denounces her, singing "It Is Not Love."

Sir Marmaduke arrives not with Lady Sangazure but with the lowly Mrs. Partlet, and in "She Will Tend Him" they plan their future of married bliss.

Wells appears, troubled by what he has seen; Lady Sangazure appears and, to his dismay, falls madly in love with him. They sing "The Family Vault," with Wells trying to avoid an increasingly affectionate Sangazure, and ultimately both leave.

Aline reenters, having decided to drink the potion. She does so, singing "Alexis, Doubt Me Not." But it is Dr. Daly whom she first meets, and the two fall madly in love, singing "Oh, Joyous Boon."

Alexis appears and denounces both, and then appeals to Wells for help. The sorcerer says the only way to break the charm is for either himself or Alexis to yield up his life to the demon Ahrimanes. The company agrees that it should be Wells, and he is swallowed up through a trap door; the spell is broken, and all pair off properly and repair to the mansion for another feast, singing "Now to the Banquet We Press."

H. M. S. Pinafore; or, The Lass That Loved a Sailor
(1878)

Before the opera, which is set aboard *H. M. S. Pinafore* as it rides at anchor in Portsmouth, the humble sailor Ralph Rackstraw has fallen in love with

Josephine, his captain's daughter. Alas, she is engaged to Sir Joseph Porter, the first lord of the admiralty.

As the opera begins, the sailors are discovered singing "We Sail the Ocean Blue." Little Buttercup, a bumboat woman (or barge-borne saleswoman), sings her famous "I'm Called Little Buttercup" while selling trinkets to the crew, except for the lovesick Ralph and the malevolent Dick Deadeye.

The Captain appears, and in "I Am the Captain of the Pinafore" explains his policies of lenience and especially of no bad language. "What, never?" the sailors ask. "Well, hardly ever," he replies. They leave, and Josephine appears, sadly singing "Sorry Her Lot," and confides to her father that she can't love Sir Joseph because she loves another—a common sailor aboard the ship. But she promises to repress that love forever.

Sir Joseph arrives, accompanied by his entourage of sisters, cousins, and aunts, and introduces himself with "I Am the Monarch of the Sea." He recounts the story of his ascent to power in "When I Was a Lad," explains his egalitarian principles ("a British sailor is any man's equal, excepting mine") and then retires to the Captain's cabin.

Inspired by "A British Tar Is a Soaring Soul," an inspirational song composed by Sir Joseph, Ralph finally approaches Josephine, but in "Refrain, Audacious Tar" she spurns him.

He prepares to commit suicide. At the last moment, however, Josephine reappears and admits that she loves him; aided by the crew and Sir Joseph's sisters, cousins, and aunts, the couple plots an elopement after dark, and then, ignoring the warnings of the sinister Deadeye, celebrate with "Let's Give Three Cheers for the Sailor's Bride."

The second act finds the Captain, distraught over Josephine's reluctance to marry Sir Joseph and his own attraction to Buttercup, singing "Fair Moon, to Thee I Sing."

Buttercup appears and hints of a dark secret in "Things Are Seldom What They Seem," but the Captain doesn't understand her. Sir Joseph appears, miffed at Josephine's rejection; she then appears, torn by conflicting emotions about her imminent elopement, and sings "The Hours Creep On Apace." Sir Joseph approaches her once more, and she seems to consent—though it's Ralph she really plans to marry. They celebrate with the rousing "Never Mind the Why and Wherefore."

The Captain's joy is shattered when Deadeye appears and, in "Kind Captain, I've Important Information," reveals the planned elopement. The elopers appear, singing "Carefully on Tiptoe Stealing," and the Captain confronts them. He's about to flog Ralph when the Bos'n stops him, reminding the captain that "He Is an Englishman."

Thwarted, the Captain says "Damme"—just as the prudish Sir Joseph enters. He sends the Captain to his cabin but is horrified when he hears of the elopement. Ralph is sent to the brig, and all seems lost until Buttercup finally reveals her darkest secret in "A Many Years Ago": Long ago she was a nursemaid and accidentally switched two babies, one of whom grew up to be Ralph and the other the Captain.

On learning this, the two men switch places. Sir Joseph no longer wants to marry the daughter of a common sailor, so she marries Ralph; the Captain is now sufficiently working-class to marry Buttercup, and Sir Joseph consoles himself with his cousin Hebe. The opera ends with a chorus of "Oh Joy, Oh Rapture" as all three couples head for the altar.

The Pirates of Penzance; or, The Slave of Duty (1879)

Before the opera, which takes place in 1877 on the coast of Cornwall, England, Frederic has been accidentally apprenticed to a band of pirates—Ruth, his nursemaid, was told to apprentice him to a "pilot" and misunderstood. Remorseful, she has joined the pirates as a maid-of-all-work to look after him.

As Act 1 begins, the pirates are singing "Pour, Oh, Pour the Pirate Sherry," celebrating Frederic's 21st birthday and his release from his indentures. He bids farewell to the pirates—a sorry lot who never succeed because they are too tenderhearted, as Frederic tells them, particularly because they will never molest an orphan. Frederic invites them to return to civilization with him, but the Pirate King declares in "Oh, Better Far to Live and Die" that piracy is the most honest, because the least hypocritical, of all human endeavors.

The pirates leave, and Frederic is about to depart when Ruth (who is in love with him) implores him to take her with him; she is the only woman he has ever seen, and she has told him she is beautiful, so he agrees. Just then, however, he hears the voices of young women—glimpsing them, he realizes that Ruth has lied, and he spurns her.

The girls arrive, singing "Climbing Over Rocky Mountain," and prove to be the wards of Major-General Stanley, out for a seaside picnic. Frederic appeals to them in "Oh, Is There Not One Maiden Here," but despite his beauty they reject him because of his shady past—except for Mabel, who falls in love with him at first sight and rebukes her sisters in "Poor Wandering One." Frederic and Mabel retire upstage, and her sisters pretend to talk about the weather—in "How Beautifully Blue the Sky"—while actually listening carefully.

The pirates return and seize the girls and are about to carry them off— "Here's a First-Rate Opportunity to Get Married with Impunity"—when the Major-General appears and confronts them. He introduces himself with "I Am the Very Model of a Modern Major-General" and then (falsely) claims to be an orphan. The softhearted pirates are touched and let him and his daughters go.

Act 2 takes place on the Major-General's estate, where the duty-driven Frederic is preparing to lead a band of policemen against the pirates. The

Major-General is disconsolate over his lie—"Oh, Dry the Glistening Tear," his daughters comfort him—but hopes that Frederic's arresting the pirates will ease his guilt.

The police appear, and in "When the Foeman Bares His Steel" reveal themselves to be timid souls who can stoke their courage only by singing "Tarantara." After several false starts, they set off in search of the pirates.

The Pirate King and Ruth appear, and in "A Most Ingenious Paradox" show Frederic his original apprenticeship papers, which stipulate that he is a pirate until his twenty-first birthday—and Frederic was born on February 29 and so is technically only 5¼ years old. He feels duty bound to rejoin them and to reveal to them the Major-General's deception, leading the Pirate King to resolve, in "Away, Away," to get revenge by killing the Major-General and his daughters.

The King and Ruth storm away angrily, leaving Frederic to bid a tearful farewell to Mabel in "Ah, Leave Me Not to Pine." Awed by his sense of duty but determined to do her own, Mabel summons the policemen and sets them against Frederic as well. The nonplused Sergeant muses that "A Policeman's Lot Is Not a Happy One," especially if by nature he's a gentle, nonviolent sort.

Just then the pirates are heard approaching, singing "Come, Friends, Who Plow the Sea." The policemen quickly hide, and the pirates arrive—but on hearing the Major-General approach, they too hide. The insomniac Major-General sings a poetic "Sighing Softly to the River," but the mood is broken when the pirates burst forth and seize him.

The police confront them but are overpowered—until the Sergeant appeals to the pirates to surrender "in Queen Victoria's name." The pirates do, because, as the Pirate King says, "with all our faults we love our queen."

They are about to be dragged off to jail when Ruth reveals that they are all noblemen who have gone wrong. This is a different story: The Major-General frees them, and (as they propose to return to civilized society) gives each of them one of his wards to marry. Frederic is reunited with Mabel, and all ends happily with a reprise of "Poor Wandering One."

Patience; or, Bunthorne's Bride (1881)

Before the opera, which is set in 1880s England, the 35th Dragoon Guards have left their native town for maneuvers, leaving behind their sweethearts, who have in the meantime fallen in love with an aesthetic poet, Reginald Bunthorne.

As the opera begins, the lovelorn ladies are discovered singing "Twenty Lovesick Maidens We" outside Bunthorne's castle. They are distraught because Bunthorne is in love with Patience, the village milkmaid—and the only woman in town who doesn't love him. She is mystified by the ladies' misery and declares that "I Cannot Tell What This Love May Be."

The dragoons return, to the swaggering "The Soldiers of Our Queen," and Colonel Calverley provides his recipe for "A Heavy Dragoon." Among his company is the Duke of Dunstable, who in an effort to escape luxury and deference has signed on as a lieutenant.

The ladies reappear, singing "In a Doleful Train" as they escort Bunthorne in. He appears to be lost in his poetry but is actually basking in the attention. The dragoons are appalled by the women's snubbing them and over their chorus sing "Now, Is Not This Ridiculous?" Bunthorne reads his poem, which bores the dragoons but enraptures the ladies—except for Patience, who doesn't understand it. Bunthorne and the ladies exit, and the Colonel rues the apparent loss of glamour for the military uniform in "When I First Put This Uniform On."

Bunthorne reenters and, in "If You're Anxious for to Shine," reveals that his aestheticism is mere pretense to attract admiration. Patience appears, and he attempts to seduce her, but she rejects him and he exits. Mystified by love, she asks Lady Angela what it means, and Angela tells her that love is self-sacrifice. Patience recalls in "Long Years Ago" that she did once love—an infant boy who loved her just as much until they were separated.

Suddenly a stranger arrives—the wandering poet Archibald Grosvenor, who woos Patience in "Prithee, Pretty Maiden." Patience is delighted to recognize him as the boy she loved as a baby, and he returns her love—only to be rejected when she realizes that because he is perfection (as he readily admits) she cannot love him, since love is self-sacrifice. They sadly part.

Meanwhile, Bunthorne is about to put himself up as a lottery prize when Patience interrupts and claims him as her own—explaining that since "True Love Must Single-Hearted Be" and love is sacrifice, what could be nobler than loving the detestable Bunthorne? The spurned ladies return briefly to the dragoons for the lyrical "I Hear the Soft Note," only to be drawn to Grosvenor when he appears. The act ends with Grosvenor besieged by the ladies and with Patience, Bunthorne, and the dragoons all consumed by jealousy, as the dragoons reprise "Now, Is Not This Ridiculous?"

In Act 2, all the ladies but the aging Jane have deserted Bunthorne. She explains that though she may be aging—"Silvered Is the Raven Hair"—she's still canny enough to win Bunthorne.

Grosvenor enters, followed by the lovesick ladies singing "Turn, O Turn in This Direction." He reads them some of his verse—mere nursery rhymes—and sings them "The Magnet and the Churn" to argue that their love is as hopeless as his for Patience.

Bunthorne appears with Patience and Jane. The miserable Patience now thinks she knows what love is—"Love Is a Plaintive Song"—and Bunthorne is jealous of her love for Grosvenor. In "So Go to Him and Say to Him," he and Jane resolve to force Grosvenor to give up aestheticism.

Meanwhile, the Colonel, the Major, and the Duke have decided to become aesthetes themselves—"It's Clear That Medieval Art Alone Retains Its Zest"—in an attempt to beat Grosvenor at his own game. They're awkward, but it's enough to captivate the ladies Angela and Saphir, and they celebrate with the festive "If Saphir I Choose to Marry."

Bunthorne threatens Grosvenor into renouncing aestheticism, and they sing "When I Go Out of Door," Grosvenor rejoicing in his new normality and Bunthorne in his regained aestheticism. But Bunthorne is celebrating too soon—it turns out that the ladies have also renounced aestheticism, figuring (as Angela puts it) that "if Archibald the All-Right chooses to discard aestheticism, then aestheticism ought to be discarded."

The ladies flock to Grosvenor as before, but Patience declares that, as he is no longer an aesthetic poet, she can now love him. The two pair off, as do the dragoons and the ladies, leaving Bunthorne with Jane—until she captures the Duke in the final "After Much Debate Internal," leaving Bunthorne ironically without a bride.

Iolanthe; or, The Peer and the Peri (1882)

Before the opera, whose first act is set in the English countryside, the fairy Iolanthe has married a mortal and given birth to a son, Strephon. Though it is death for a fairy to marry a mortal, the Fairy Queen has instead commuted her death sentence to exile; she has lived at the bottom of a nearby stream, watching her son grow up.

As the opera begins, the fairies are dancing and singing "Tripping Hither, Tripping Thither," but they still miss Iolanthe terribly, even after 20 years. They implore the Queen to pardon Iolanthe, which she does in "Iolanthe! From Thy Dark Exile." Iolanthe reveals that Strephon is now 25 and is a fairy only down to the waist—his legs are mortal. He is in love with Phyllis, ward of the Lord Chancellor of England. Strephon arrives, caroling "Good Morrow, Good Mother," and reveals that the Chancellor has rejected his appeal.

The Queen promises Strephon her support, and the fairies depart just as Phyllis arrives, caroling "Good Morrow, Good Lover." She and Strephon sing a love duet, "None Shall Part Us from Each Other," and leave together.

The entire House of Lords, in formal robes and coronets, arrive, singing "Loudly Let the Trumpet Bray." The Lord Chancellor follows them, and in his "The Law Is the True Embodiment" reveals that he is in love with one of his wards—who turns out to be Phyllis. But he feels that, as her guardian, it wouldn't be right to marry her.

Phyllis appears, and in "Of All the Young Ladies I Know" the peers offer her their love; but in "Nay, Tempt Me Not" she refuses them, saying that only low-born people can truly love. Lord Tolloller responds with "Blue Blood," insisting that "hearts just as pure and fair / may beat in Belgrave Square / as in the lowly air / of Seven Dials." Phyllis reveals that she loves another, and Strephon appears, singing "A Shepherd I." Spurned, the peers exit in a huff, followed by Phyllis.

Strephon appeals once more to the Chancellor, who once again rejects him, explaining in "When I Went to the Bar as a Very Young Man" that he can't afford to let emotion cloud his judgment.

Distraught over the standoff, Strephon is comforted by his mother in "When Darkly Looms the Day"—but they are seen by the peers and Phyllis, who won't believe that the 17-year-old girl he is embracing is really his mother. In "For Riches and Rank I Do Not Long" she spurns him and pledges herself to either Lord Mountararat or Lord Tolloller—she doesn't care which.

Strephon calls on the fairies for support, and they challenge the peers in "Go Away, Madam." The Queen promises to send Strephon into Parliament and undo all of the Lords' traditional privileges—"Henceforth, Strephon, Cast Away"—and the act ends with the peers and the fairies defying each other in "Young Strephon Is the Kind of Lout."

Act 2, set at night outside the Houses of Parliament, finds Private Willis, a sentry, musing about politics in "When All Night Long a Chap Remains."

The fairies and peers appear and, in "Strephon's a Member of Parliament," reveal that with the fairies' aid Strephon can now pass any law he likes, including a bill to make the peerage open to competitive examination. Lord Mountararat insists in "When Britain Really Ruled the Waves" that a dull, inactive peerage is best, and the peers stalk out—leaving behind the unhappy fairies, who have fallen in love with them. The Queen rebukes them in "Oh, Foolish Fay," saying that however strong love may be (and she herself is powerfully drawn to Willis), fairy law must be stronger.

Mountararat and Tolloller enter and come to the verge of a duel before they decide to waive their mutual claim to Phyllis—"In Friendship's Name." The Chancellor appears, unable to sleep and singing "The Nightmare Song." Anxious to marry Phyllis off, the two peers sing "If You Go In," urging the Chancellor to award her to himself, which he eventually agrees to consider doing.

Meanwhile, Strephon has reunited with Phyllis after revealing his secret. They sing "If We're Weak Enough to Tarry" and ask Iolanthe to intercede with the Chancellor. When she does so, in "He Loves," he reveals that he intends to marry Phyllis himself; she in turn reveals herself as his long-lost wife and Strephon as his son.

In so doing she incurs death, and the Queen is about to execute her when the fairies reveal that they have all married peers. To save her from having to execute the entire band, the Chancellor helps her to revise the law so that each fairy shall die who does *not* marry a mortal. Strephon and Phyllis are engaged, as are the Queen and Willis, and in "Soon As

We May, Off and Away" all the mortals are transformed into fairies and fly off to live happily ever after in Fairyland.

Princess Ida; or, Castle Adamant (1884)

Before the beginning of the opera, which is set in an undefined time period, Princess Ida of Hungary has been married in infancy to Hilarion, son of King Hildebrand, ruler of a neighboring country and the enemy of Ida's father, King Gama of Hungary. She is supposed to be turned over to Hilarion on her 21st birthday, but in the meantime she has run away from home and established a women's university, of which she is principal.

In the opera's first act, Hildebrand's courtiers are discovered awaiting King Gama—"Search throughout the Panorama." Hildebrand appears and, in "Now Hearken to My Strict Command," threatens to kill Gama if he doesn't bring Ida to marry Hilarion. Meanwhile, Hilarion idly ponders the mathematical implications of having married a woman half his age— one to his two—in "Ida Was a Twelve-month Old."

Gama's dense but muscular sons, Arac, Guron and Scynthius, arrive and introduce themselves with "We Are Warriors Three." Gama appears and sings "If You Give Me Your Attention, I Will Tell You What I Am" to introduce himself. He tells Hildebrand that Ida has run away from home to found her college. In "Perhaps If You Address the Lady," he convinces Hilarion to pursue her there, though Hildebrand warns that Gama and his sons will remain as hostages for Hilarion's safety. Hilarion and two courtiers, Cyril and Florian, plan to seduce Ida and her women in "Expressive Glances Shall Be Our Lances." The Warriors Three complain at their treatment in "For a Month to Dwell in a Dungeon Cell," and the act ends as Hilarion sets forth.

In the second act, set at Ida's university, the students are discovered receiving a lecture from Lady Psyche, second in command at the college, and singing "Toward the Empyrean Heights." The formidable Lady Blanche, third in command, arrives to announce the day's punishments, all of which have to do with thinking about men—even chessmen are prohibited at the college.

Ida appears to a chorus of "Mighty Maiden with a Mission," offers a prayer to Minerva in "Oh, Goddess Wise," and greets new students with a lecture on the implacability of their mission—they will conquer the world or be destroyed.

Later, Hilarion, Cyril, and Florian make a stealthy entrance—"Gently, Gently"—and mock the university in "They Intend to Send a Wire to the Moon." Finding a set of women's robes, they disguise themselves as women, singing "I Am a Maiden," and when Ida appears they pledge themselves as students. She preaches to them her cynical philosophy in "The World Is But a Broken Toy," then leaves.

Psyche appears and turns out to be Florian's sister. She explains the college's principles in "The Lady and the Ape" and is dismayed when they are overheard by the young Melissa, Blanche's daughter. Melissa, smitten with Florian, promises not to reveal the secret, and all celebrate in "The Woman of the Wisest Wit."

Blanche enters and catches sight of the men. Blanche, who is plotting Ida's downfall, is persuaded to remain silent as the luncheon bell rings.

At lunch Cyril gets drunk and makes a spectacle of himself, singing a ribald song, "Would You Know the Kind of Maid?" Infuriated, Hilarion hits Cyril, inadvertently revealing himself. In the ensuing confusion Ida falls into a river, from which Hilarion rescues her. The women plead with Ida to pardon him because he saved her, but Hilarion declares his love for her and, in "Whom Thou Hast Chained," urges her to kill him if she cannot love him.

Ida is torn, but before she can decide the castle is attacked by Hildebrand's forces—"Walls and Fences Scaling." The two sides battle to a standstill, and in "Some Years Ago, No Doubt You Know" Hildebrand demands Ida's surrender, which she refuses. He threatens to execute Ida's father and brothers if she doesn't surrender, to which Ida responds by threatening to execute Hilarion, Cyril, and Florian. Hildebrand gives Ida a day to think it over, and the act ends with the two armies howling "Defiance!" at one another.

The third act finds Ida in desperate straits. Despite their resolve of "Death to the Invader," her army of women is no match for Hildebrand's troops, as shown in Melissa's "Please You, Do Not Hurt Us." Despairing, Ida sings the sorrowful "I Built upon a Rock."

King Gama arrives, distraught—as he sings in "Oh, Don't the Days Seem Lank and Long"—at how well Hildebrand is treating him. He bears a message: Hildebrand proposes that the issue be decided by a battle between her three brothers and Hilarion, Cyril, and Florian.

The armies arrive—"When Anger Spreads His Wing"—and Arac decides that his armor is more trouble than it's worth in "This Helmet, I Suppose." The battle takes place, and the apparently outmatched Hilarion nevertheless wins.

Ida surrenders and offers herself to the victor, but Hilarion surprises her by refusing to take her as a prize, and instead appeals for her love. She accepts him (and, more tentatively, Psyche and Melissa accept Cyril and Florian), and the opera ends on a note of hope with a final song, "With Joy Abiding."

The Mikado; or, The Town of Titipu (1885)

Before the opera, which is set in Titipu, Japan, the Mikado of Japan has decreed flirting a capital crime. To evade the law, the townspeople of Titipu have appointed Ko-Ko lord high executioner. Ko-Ko, a cheap tailor, is himself already under sentence of death for flirting. All the officers of state have resigned in disgust except one—Pooh-Bah, a young aristocrat who now holds all of their former offices.

As the opera begins, the male chorus is discovered singing "If You Want to Know Who We Are." Nanki-Poo arrives and introduces himself with "A Wandering Minstrel I." He is seeking Ko-Ko's ward Yum-Yum, with whom he is in love—she had been engaged to Ko-Ko, but he thinks Ko-Ko has been beheaded. In "Our Great Mikado," Pish-Tush explains Ko-Ko's rise to lord high executioner, and in "Young Man Despair" Pooh-Bah reveals that Ko-Ko and Yum-Yum are to be married that very afternoon.

To the chorus "Behold the Lord High Executioner," Ko-Ko appears, and in "I've Got a Little List" explains the many people he's prepared to execute if it ever comes to that. Yum-Yum and her sisters, Pitti-Sing and Peep-Bo, are escorted in to the chorus "Comes a Train of Little Ladies" and introduce themselves with "Three Little Maids from School."

Left alone briefly, Nanki-Poo and Yum-Yum dream of the happiness they might have "Were You Not to Ko-Ko Plighted." Nanki-Poo reveals that he is actually the son of the Mikado, forced to flee in disguise to escape the attentions of the elderly Katisha.

Meanwhile, Ko-Ko is alarmed by the arrival of a letter from the Mikado demanding an immediate execution. Ko-Ko himself is next on the list, but in "I Am So Proud" he, Pooh-Bah, and Pish-Tush explain why each can't be executed. Ko-Ko is desperate when Nanki-Poo appears, bent on suicide. He and Ko-Ko make a deal: Nanki-Poo agrees to allow himself to be beheaded in a month—if Ko-Ko will let him marry Yum-Yum meanwhile. Ko-Ko agrees.

The chorus arrives "With Aspect Stern and Gloomy Stride," but Ko-Ko reveals the deal, which delights everyone and leads to a chorus, "The Threatened Cloud Has Passed Away." All celebrate the engagement, despite the sudden appearance of Katisha, who tries to reveal Nanki-Poo's secret but is drowned out by the celebrating chorus. She leaves, vowing to go to the Mikado himself.

The second act finds the wedding preparations underway in "Braid the Raven Hair." Yum-Yum muses on her own beauty in "The Sun, Whose Rays Are All Ablaze," and all are depressed by Nanki-Poo's impending execution in "Brightly Dawns Our Wedding Day."

Ko-Ko appears, having learned that, if Nanki-Poo is beheaded, his wife is required by law to be buried alive. Under the circumstances Yum-Yum declines to be married, and a despairing Nanki-Poo demands to be beheaded at once. Instead, the tenderhearted Ko-Ko resolves to swear a false affidavit (witnessed by Pooh-Bah and Pitti-Sing) that he has executed Nanki-Poo. His presumed death will allow him to marry Yum-Yum and leave Japan forever.

The chorus "Miya-Sama" is heard, and the Mikado appears with Katisha. After he has explained his novel principle to "Let the Punishment Fit the Crime," Ko-Ko gives him the affidavit, and he, Pooh-Bah and Pitti-Sing provide an elaborate description of the death scene in "The Criminal Cried."

The Mikado is actually looking for his lost son, however, and the affidavit leads to Ko-Ko, Pitti-Sing, and Pooh-Bah being condemned to death. They appeal to Nanki-Poo and Yum-Yum, but the couple aren't willing to condemn themselves by revealing the deception. The only way out: If someone—Ko-Ko, for example—would marry Katisha, Nanki-Poo says, existence would be as welcome as "The Flowers That Bloom in the Spring."

Katisha appears, disconsolately singing "Alone, and Yet Alive." Ko-Ko woos her with the story of a lovelorn bird, "Titwillow," and the two become engaged, singing "There Is Beauty in the Bellow of the Blast."

The Mikado returns for the executions, and Katisha (having married Ko-Ko offstage, with Pooh-Bah officiating) pleads for their lives—only to be infuriated when Nanki-Poo appears, alive and married to Yum-Yum. The Mikado is initially angry at the deception, but Ko-Ko talks him around, and all ends happily with a chorus of "For He's Gone and Married Yum-Yum."

Ruddigore; or, The Witch's Curse (1887)

Many years before the opera, which is set in and around the English fishing village of Rederring during the early 1800s, the first baronet of Ruddigore burned a witch at the stake. In revenge, she cursed him and his line to commit a crime a day or die horribly. The curse has shadowed each generation up to the beginning of the opera.

As the first act begins, a chorus of professional bridesmaids is singing "Fair Is Rose," hoping to induce her to marry. Dame Hannah Trusty, her guardian, tells them it is useless. They ask her if she would marry, but she reveals that her true love—Sir Roderick Murgatroyd, the bad baronet of Ruddigore—died 10 years before. She tells them the saga of the curse in "Sir Rupert Murgatroyd."

Rose appears, and in "If Somebody There Chanced to Be" we learn that she is so particular about etiquette that she will probably never marry—only one man in town, the young farmer Robin Oakapple, would measure up to her standards, and he is too shy to speak.

Robin enters, and in "I Know a Youth" he and Rose hint obliquely of their love for each other, but he is too shy and she too proper to actually speak. Robin's servant, Old Adam Goodheart, comes to tell him that his foster brother, the sailor Richard Dauntless, has returned from years at sea. We learn that Robin has a dark secret: He is really Sir Ruthven Murgatroyd, rightful baronet of Ruddigore, but fled his home years before, leaving his brother Despard to inherit the title and the curse.

Richard arrives, escorted by a chorus of admiring women. He sings "I Shipped, D'Ye See," the tale of his courageous nonbattle at sea (with their small coastal vessel confronted by a mighty French frigate, the English

sailors decided to be merciful and fled ignominiously) and dances a vigorous hornpipe. Robin reveals his modesty to Richard in "My Boy, You
May Take It from Me" and convinces Richard to speak to Rose on his
behalf.

But when Richard sees Rose he is smitten with her and woos and wins
her for himself—"The Battle's Roar Is Over." Roused to action by Richard's treachery, in "In Sailing o'er Life's Ocean Wide" Robin convinces
her to take him instead.

Mad Margaret, a local lunatic, appears and sings a pathetic "To a Garden Full of Posies," revealing that it was a broken heart that drove her
mad. Rose returns, and we learn that it is Sir Despard who jilted Margaret.

Sir Despard arrives with his band of ruffians, and in "Oh, Why Am I
Moody and Sad?" reveals that his conscience pains him for his crimes.
Richard appears and reveals Robin's secret, and in "You Understand?" the
two plot to disrupt Robin's approaching wedding.

The town assembles for the wedding, singing the lovely "When the Buds
Are Blossoming," but Despard appears and denounces Robin. Rose is
forced to spurn Robin; the reformed Despard resolves to marry his jilted
sweetheart, Mad Margaret, while Rose agrees to marry Richard because
he is "the only one that's left." The chorus "Oh, Happy the Lily" is disrupted by Robin's return as the evil baronet.

In the second act, set a week later in the picture gallery of Castle Ruddigore, Robin and Adam revel in their evil in "I Once Was as Meek as a
Newborn Lamb," though Robin has been utilizing technicalities to avoid
actually doing anything wrong.

Richard and Rose appear, singing "Happily Coupled Are We," to seek
Robin's consent for their marriage, which he reluctantly gives in the song
"In Bygone Days."

The stage darkens, and in "Painted Emblems of a Race" the portraits
of Robin's dead ancestors come to life. His late uncle, Sir Roderick, sings
"Ghost's High Noon" and then threatens Robin with hideous torture unless he agrees to a real life of crime. After being tortured briefly, Robin
agrees. The ghosts vanish, and he sings the frantic song "Henceforth All
the Crimes That I Find in the Times" and sends Adam out to carry off a
maiden.

Despard and Margaret, now reformed—as they sing in "I Once Was a
Very Abandoned Person"—arrive to urge Robin to reform, even though
it means death, and he resolves to do so in the delirious "Matter Matter
Matter" trio.

But before he can do so, Old Adam returns with the maiden. It is the
belligerent Dame Hannah, who so frightens Robin that he calls Roderick
for help. The two former lovers are miraculously reunited, and they sing
the touching "There Grew a Little Flower."

Their fleeting happiness is made permanent, however, when Robin realizes that because refusing to commit a daily crime is suicide, and suicide

is itself a crime, none of the baronets need ever have died at all. Roderick comes back to life to marry Hannah, Rose agrees to marry Robin, Richard consoles himself with the bridesmaid Zorah, and all end in a jubilant reprise of "Oh, Happy the Lily."

The Yeomen of the Guard; or,
The Merryman and His Maid (1888)

Before the opera, which is set at the Tower of London during the reign of Henry VIII, Colonel Fairfax has been condemned to death on charges of sorcery trumped up by an evil kinsman hoping to usurp the colonel's inheritance.

As the first act begins, Phoebe Meryll is discovered at a spinning wheel, singing the sad "When Maiden Loves" over the imminent death of Fairfax, with whom she is in love. Her unpleasant suitor, the jailer Wilfred Shadbolt, approaches her, but she rebuffs him.

The Yeomen enter, singing "In the Autumn of Our Lives," and the grim Dame Carruthers rebukes Phoebe for her sorrow in "When Our Gallant Norman Foes," a testimony to the Tower's tradition of relentless impersonality.

Phoebe's father, Sergeant Meryll, consoles her and reveals a desperate plan: In an effort to save Fairfax, who once saved Meryll's life in battle, they will steal the key to his cell, free him, and have him disguise himself as her brother, Leonard Meryll, who is expected to return to the Tower after years at war. The three Merylls vow their best effort in "Alas, I Waver To and Fro."

Fairfax is brought in by guards. He attempts to comfort Phoebe with his philosophical "Is Life a Boon?" to no avail. He then secretly asks the master of the Tower, his old friend Lieutenant. Cholmondeley, for a final favor: In an effort to thwart his kinsman, he wants to be secretly married to an anonymous woman, and asks the Lieutenant to find one before his execution, only an hour off. The Lieutenant reluctantly agrees.

The chorus returns, excited by the arrival of Jack Point and Elsie Maynard, two strolling players. They perform "The Merryman and His Maid," a song about a jester in love with a merrymaid who in turn is in love with a lord, and are then approached by the Lieutenant. He asks Elsie to marry Fairfax for a hundred gold crowns; Elsie needs the money for her ailing mother, but Point (who is in love with Elsie) consents only reluctantly, in "How Say You, Maiden?"

Elsie is taken off to Fairfax's cell, while Point angles for a job as the Lieutenant's jester by singing "I've Wisdom from the East and from the West."

Elsie returns, married and distraught, and sings " 'Tis Done, I Am a Bride." She leaves, and Shadbolt appears. Phoebe seeks him out and flirts with him, singing "Were I Thy Bride," while purloining his keys and slipping them to her father, who rescues Fairfax.

Disguised as Leonard, Fairfax is introduced to the other Yeomen in "Oh, Sergeant Meryll, Is It True?" He is uncomfortable accepting praise meant for Leonard but relishes the chance to flirt with his affectionate "sister," Phoebe.

All gather for the execution of Fairfax—"The Prisoner Comes to Meet His Doom"—and are astounded when his escape is reported. The Lieutenant offers a huge reward for his capture, dead or alive, and the act ends as Elsie faints in horror.

The second act begins the next night. Fairfax has not been found, to the dismay of all—"Night Has Spread Her Pall Once More." Point, who is frustrated by Elsie's marriage, and Shadbolt, who is in disgrace for allowing Fairfax's escape, agree to a hoax: Wilfred will fire a gun and claim to have spotted the fleeing Fairfax and shot him dead as he swam the river, and Point will back his story. In return, Point will teach Shadbolt how to be a jester. Point sings "A Private Buffoon," and the two celebrate their plan in "Tell a Tale of Cock and Bull."

Fairfax, still as "Leonard Meryll," appears and rues his hasty marriage in "Free from His Fetters Grim." Meryll, Dame Carruthers, and her niece Kate enter, and Fairfax learns from Kate's report of Elsie talking in her sleep that Elsie is his anonymous bride. The four ponder the strange turn of events in "Strange Adventure."

Smitten by Elsie, Fairfax "tests her principles" by imploring her to flee with him and forget that she ever married Fairfax. She is appalled, but just then a shot rings out. Shadbolt and Point tell their story in "Like a Ghost His Vigil Keeping," and Shadbolt becomes a hero.

Point then attempts to woo the "widowed" Elsie for himself, but Fairfax (under the guise of teaching him how to woo in "A Man Who Would Woo a Fair Maid") wins her for himself. Phoebe and Point are both distraught in "When a Wooer Goes a-Wooing," and the former, frustrated at being jilted by Fairfax, lets slip "Leonard's" secret to Shadbolt.

As a result, she is forced to agree to marry him to ensure his silence; when she tells her father this, they are overheard by the sinister Dame Carruthers, and Sergeant Meryll must marry her to buy her silence—prompting a duet, "Rapture, Rapture," which is more joyous for her than for him.

The wedding of Elsie and "Leonard" begins with "Comes the Pretty Young Bride" but is disrupted by news that Fairfax's pardon has been received and that he still lives. Elsie is horrified but has no choice but to submit to her husband—and is delighted when it turns out to be "Leonard" after all. Point appears, heartbroken, and sings a tragic reprise of "The Merryman and His Maid," but he can only temporarily delay the celebration. Fairfax and Elsie embrace as Point "falls insensible at their feet."

The Gondoliers; or, The King of Barataria (1889)

Before the opera, which is set in Venice in 1750, the King of Barataria has been slain in an uprising, and his infant son has been spirited to safety in secret. Twenty years later the revolution is finally repressed, and a search begins for the long-lost king.

The first act finds the maidens of Venice lacing flowers and singing "List and Learn" as they await two handsome gondoliers, the brothers Marco and Giuseppe, who are about to choose wives. The other gondoliers are told they must wait their turn, which Antonio says they don't mind, "For the Merriest Fellows Are We."

Marco and Giuseppe arrive, with an Italian-language greeting—"Buon Giorno, Signorine"—and a song, "We're Called Gondolieri." They reveal that, since all the girls are lovely, they've decided to choose at random, and they pick Gianetta and Tessa from the chorus in a game of blind man's bluff. The four head off to get married, to the strains of "Thank You, Gallant Gondolieri."

An approaching drum is heard: It is the noble but impoverished Duke of Plaza-Toro, arriving with his wife, his daughter Casilda, and a single servant, the drummer boy Luiz. Entering queasily to "From the Sunny Spanish Shore," the Duke then explains his history of (somewhat craven) leadership in "In Enterprise of Martial Kind" and informs Casilda that as a baby she was secretly wed to the long-lost King of Barataria. They then exit in quest of Don Alhambra, the Grand Inquisitor of Venice, who long ago stole the infant king.

Luiz and Casilda fly to one another's arms, revealing in "Oh, Rapture!" that they are secretly in love. But as she is married to another, they sadly realize that their love must be a thing of the past, in "There Was a Time."

The Duke and Duchess return with the Grand Inquisitor, who in "I Stole the Prince" reveals that the king was raised by a gondolier as his son and is either Marco or Giuseppe—but he won't know which until the baby's nursemaid (Luiz's mother, as it happens) is brought to identify him. Casilda is dismayed to learn that she's married to an unknown husband, and Don Alhambra and her parents try to console her in "Try We Lifelong."

The two gondoliers and their wives return, newly married, as Tessa sings "When a Merry Maiden Marries." Don Alhambra tells them that one is the king, which delights them and spurs their festive "Then One of Us Shall Be a Queen." They are less pleased to hear that, for the nonce, they can't bring their wives. So the celebration of "For Everyone Who Feels Inclined"—and the comic "As One Individual"—is shadowed by the parting of "Now, Marco Dear, My Wishes Hear." As the curtain falls, the two gondoliers set off for Barataria to the strains of "Away We Go to an Island Fair."

Act 2 finds them in Barataria, ruling as very odd kings, since their democratic principles keep them from ruling as such—instead, they do all the work while their putative servants relax and sing "Of Happiness the Very Pith." Giuseppe details their frantically busy days of menial work in "Rising Early in the Morning," while Marco dreams of his absent wife in "Take a Pair of Sparkling Eyes."

Suddenly a burst of music—"Here We Are at the Risk of Our Lives"—heralds the arrival of the women, including their wives. All are delighted and resolve to have a banquet and a ball—"Dance a Cachuca."

Don Alhambra appears, dismayed at the democratic court. He sings "There Lived a King," telling the story of an egalitarian monarch undone by his own principles. He then reveals to the two kings that one of them is an unintentional bigamist, leading the four Italians to try to straighten out matters "In a Contemplative Fashion."

The Duke and Duchess arrive with great fanfare—he has incorporated himself as the Duke of Plaza-Toro Ltd., and is now very rich, as they explain in "Small Titles and Orders." After the Duke attempts to teach the gondoliers proper etiquette in "I Am a Courtier," Marco, Giuseppe, Casilda, Tessa, and Gianetta try in vain to sort out their relationships in "Here Is a Case Unprecedented."

Just in time the nursemaid Inez is produced and reveals that the real king is . . . her supposed son, Luiz. He takes the throne with Casilda at his side to the strains of "Then Hail, O King," while Marco and Giuseppe, "Once More Gondolieri," return happily to Venice after one final reprise of "Dance a Cachuca."

Utopia, Limited; or, The Flowers of Progress (1893)

Before the opera, which is set on the South Pacific island paradise of Utopia, King Paramount has sent his daughter, Princess Zara, to college in England, where the Anglophilic king hopes she will learn how Utopia can be remodeled along English lines.

As Act 1 begins, the people of Utopia are relaxing in a garden, singing "In Lazy Languor, Motionless." Calynx arrives with word of Zara's imminent arrival, which pleases everyone except for Tarara, the Lord High Exploder. His sole job is to blow up the king if he succumbs to tyranny, as directed by the two wise men, Scaphio and Phantis. But though the local newspaper, the *Palace Peeper*, is full of outrageous acts committed by King Paramount, Scaphio and Phantis refuse to act.

A chorus singing "O Make Way for the Wise Men" ushers in Scaphio and Phantis, who introduce themselves with "In Every Mental Lore." Phantis is sick with love for Zara, and Scaphio promises him that they will force the king—under threat of having Tarara explode him—to plight her to Phantis. They celebrate with a song, "Let All Your Doubts Take Wing."

Another chorus—"Quaff the Nectar, Cull the Roses"—introduces King Paramount, who sings "A King of Autocratic Power We" and then introduces his two daughters. Nekaya and Kalyba have been brought up by a strict English governess, Lady Sophy, as models of English girlhood, as they explain in "Although of Native Maids the Cream." Under Sophy's direction, they then act out an allegedly typical case of English courtship in "Bold-Faced Ranger."

All exit but Paramount and the wise men, who proceed to bully him. It emerges that none of the stories in the *Palace Peeper* is true—most have in fact been written by the king himself, under the wise men's compulsion. Paramount, who prides himself on his sense of humor, sings "First You're Born," expressing his belief that all life is a joke.

He is less amused when Lady Sophy, with whom he is in love, confronts him with the *Peeper* and demands that he have the author arrested and slain. Unable to tell her why he can't, he joins her in a sad duet, "Subjected to Your Heavenly Gaze."

Zara returns, heralded by a chorus singing "O Maiden, Rich in Girton Lore." She is escorted by six soldiers of the First Life Guards, led by Captain Fitzbattleaxe, with whom she has fallen in love.

Scaphio and Phantis approach, but upon seeing Zara Scaphio also falls in love with her. They argue, and Fitzbattleaxe deftly proposes that, until the timid wise men can get up their courage to duel, he hold the princess in trust for the eventual winner. All four agree to this arrangement in "It's Understood, I Think, All Round," which after the wise men's exit segues into the love duet "Oh, Admirable Art."

At Zara's request, Paramount assembles the people. She has brought back six Englishmen to help reform Utopia: Captain Fitzbattleaxe; Sir Bailey Barre, an attorney; Lord Dramaleigh, a theatrical censor; Mr. Goldbury, a company promoter (we'd say a financier); Mr. Blushington, a city councilman; and Captain Sir Edward Corcoran, who turns out to be the former captain of the *H. M. S. Pinafore.*

After each has been introduced, the so-called Flowers of Progress resolve to restructure Utopia entirely, beginning with Mr. Goldbury's vow to float it as a limited company, which (as he explains in "Some Seven Men Form an Association") is essentially a means to avoid risking one's own money in launching a company. It sounds shady to Paramount; but on the assurance that England is heading that way he agrees that it shall be done, and the act ends with general rejoicing.

The second act, set in the throne room, finds Fitzbattleaxe battling shyness in an effort to serenade Zara in "A Tenor, All Singers Above." She reassures him, and they sing the love duet "Sweet and Low."

King Paramount plans to host a drawing-room reception a la Queen Victoria, but the humorously inclined Englishmen have instead modeled it on the Christy Minstrels. In "Society Has Quite Forsaken All Her Wicked Courses," he explains that everything has been made perfect in Utopia—

morality, health, peace, and cleanliness prevail everywhere, even in the arts ("literary merit meets with proper recognition"). The Drawing-Room is a great success, ending with a vast chorale, "Eagle High."

Meanwhile, the wise men are infuriated at the way the Flowers have usurped their power. They threaten the king, but he tells them that, now that Utopia is not a kingdom but a limited company, they can do nothing but file a complaint with the board of directors. Defied, Scaphio, Phantis, and the similarly sidelined Tarara devise a secret scheme "With Wily Brain upon the Spot."

Goldbury and Lord Dramaleigh flirt with Nekaya and Kalyba, urging them to be less prim and proper—Goldbury's "A Bright and Beautiful English Girl" convinces them, and all four dance wildly to "Oh, Sweet Surprise."

Lady Sophy enters, and in "When but a Maid of 15 Year" reveals that she loves Paramount but will marry only a perfectly moral man—which she knows him not to be, based on the *Peeper*. Overhearing her, Paramount confronts her and, finally free of the wise men's threat, reveals the truth about the *Peeper*. They fall into each other's arms, singing "Oh, the Rapture Unrestrained."

At this point a mob assembles, led by the wise men and complaining that the general peace and prosperity has thrown lawyers, doctors, and even soldiers out of work. Sir Bailey comes up with the answer, however: Government by party can foil any good idea—just introduce it, and everything will be as chaotic as it is in England.

The king agrees, the wise men are thwarted, and all end rejoicing in "Such, at Least, Is the Tale," a hymn to England with a cautionary conclusion: "Let us hope, for her sake, / that she makes no mistake, / that she's all she professes to be!"

The Grand Duke; or, The Statutory Duel (1896)

Before the opera, which is set in the tiny German principality of Pfennig Halbpfennig, Ernest Dummkopf's troop of strolling players has planned an uprising against the Grand Duke, using the confusion of the Duke's wedding day to make their move.

The opera opens on the day of the wedding of the comedian Ludwig and the soubrette Lisa, which happens to be the day before the Grand Duke's wedding. The actors are discovered singing "Won't It Be a Pretty Wedding," but the Notary finds on arriving that the ceremony has been canceled, since the Duke's upcoming wedding has monopolized all the town's clergy.

He mentions the conspiracy, but in "By the Mystic Regulation of Our Dark Association" Ludwig insists that first they exchange the secret recognition signal, which involves eating a sausage roll. All express doubt about Ernest's qualifications to become Grand Duke, as the plot calls for, but in "Were I a King" he assures them that a man who can run a theatrical company can run a country with ease.

Ernest is in love with Julia Jellicoe, the company's exotic English leading lady, and is delighted to find that, though she despises him, she intends to marry him because she is professionally entitled to the role of Grand Duchess. In "How Would I Play This Part?" they dream of their future (sham) bliss.

The chorus rushes back in, horrified to learn that Ludwig has accidentally revealed the plot to the Duke's detective, as he explains in "Ten Minutes Since I Met a Chap." Fortunately, the Notary recalls an ancient law that will help them: As he explains in "About a Century Since," 100 years ago, to cut down on deaths by dueling, a previous Grand Duke decreed that duels be henceforth fought by cutting cards, with the loser becoming legally dead while the winner assumes all his rights and obligations.

The law is due to expire the next day, so the Notary suggests that Ludwig and Ernest fight a statutory duel, with the winner going to the Grand Duke and turning evidence against the loser, blaming everything on him. He will be pardoned, while the loser will be conveniently dead—until the next day, when the law expires and everything will be as it was.

In "Strange the Views Some People" hold, all agree that this is a much better method of dueling. In "Now Take a Card," the two duel and Ludwig wins (ace over king).

The Grand Duke Rudolph now enters, to the chorus "The Good Grand Duke of Pfennig Halbpfennig," and, in "A Pattern to Professors of Monarchical Autonomy," reveals himself to be extraordinarily cheap. His fiancee, the similarly cheap Baroness Von Krakenfeldt, appears, and after he has reassured her about a report that he was engaged in infancy to the Princess of Monte Carlo (the deal is void unless she arrives by the next day, and her debt-ridden father, the Prince, is trapped within his own palace) the two sing "As o'er Our Pennyroll We Sing," dreaming of their future penny-pinching bliss.

Rudolph reads the detective's report and is horrified, collapsing in despair for "When You Find You're a Broken-Down Critter." Ludwig appears and "nobly" suggests that they fight a statutory duel, rigged so that Ludwig wins (ace over king). He will then become Grand Duke and be the target of the plot, and when the act expires the next day, Rudolph can safely come to life again.

To the tune of "Big Bombs, Small Bombs, Great Guns and Little Ones" they stage the duel, and Ludwig becomes Grand Duke—apparently for only a day. However, in "A Monarch Who Boasts Intellectual Graces" he renews the law for another hundred years—though he is a bit discomfited to find that, having inherited Ernest's obligations, he is now obliged to marry Julia.

Still, all rejoice with "This Will Be a Jolly Court" as the act ends.

The second act finds Ludwig and Julia newly married and the chorus saluting them in "As before You We Defile." Ludwig explains in "At the Outset I May Mention" that, since the company happens to have the costumes, their court will be designed along classical Greek lines.

Left alone, Ludwig finds that marriage to Julia will be much different from marriage to Lisa, as in "Now Julia, Come" she explains her melodramatic view of the role, including the crazed murder of a presumed rival. Ludwig is nonplused but is distracted by the return of the chorus, fleeing the just-arrived Baroness. Learning of the situation, she insists on her own rights under the law, demanding that Ludwig marry her, which he reluctantly sets off to do.

Julia is left behind to sing her despairing yet resolved "Tomorrow" aria—only to be horrified at the arrival of the "dead" Ernest. They sing the mock ghost-scene duet, "If the Light of Love's Lingering Ember."

The wedding party returns, and the Baroness sings "Come, Bumpers, Aye, Ever So Many," rejoicing in finally feeling free to live generously, since it's Ludwig who's paying for it.

At this point a Herald arrives, announcing "The Prince of Monte Carlo." The Prince enters, accompanied by the Princess and six actors he has hired to play noblemen for the occasion. In "The Roulette Song," he explains his marvelous new invention, which has solved his financial problems permanently. He then presents his daughter and demands that Ludwig, as heir to Ernest's obligations, marry her as well.

With four wives, Ludwig is on the verge of distraction, when the Notary appears, with the "dead" Ernest and Rudolph, to reveal that he had overlooked one point of the law: The ace counts as the lowest card, not the highest. So instead of Ernest and Rudolph being dead, Ludwig is dead—but just then the law expires.

Ludwig, restored to life, returns to Lisa; Ernest marries Julia, Rudolph marries the Princess of Monte Carlo and the baroness—well, that isn't really resolved. But all exit merrily, reprising the opening number, "Won't It Be a Pretty Wedding?"

Appendix B:
Revisions to *Ruddigore*

Gilbert & Sullivan made seven substantial changes to the Act 2 text of *Ruddigore* following its opening night.[1]

1. A second verse was deleted from the Act 2 Robin-Adam duet, "I Once Was as Meek as a New-born Lamb":

> *Robin:* "My face is the index to my mind,
>   all venom and spleen and gall—
> or, properly speaking,
> it soon will be reeking
>   with venom and spleen and gall!
>
> *Adam:* My name from Adam Goodheart you'll find
>   I've changed to Gideon Crawle!
> For a bad Bart's steward
> whose heart is much too hard,
>   is always Gideon Crawle!
>
> *Both:* How providential when you find
> the face an index to the mind,
>   and evil men compelled to call
>   themselves by names like Gideon Crawle!

Along with this cut, all references to "Gideon Crawle" were changed to "Old Adam"—except for one, immediately after the ghost scene, which remained to puzzle generations of audiences.

2. The dialogue after the Robin-Adam duet was trimmed, deleting the following:

> *Adam:* . . . the confidential adviser to the greatest villain unhung! It's a dreadful position for a good old man.

335

Robin: Very likely, but don't be gratuitously offensive, Gideon Crawle.

Adam: Sir, I am the ready instrument of your abominable misdeeds because I have sworn to obey you in all things, but I have *not* sworn to allow deliberate and systematic villainy to pass unreproved. If you insist upon it I will swear that too, but I have not sworn it yet.

Robin: Come, Gideon, I haven't done anything very bad, so far.

Adam: No. Owing to a series of evasions which, as a blameless character, I must denounce as contemptible, you have, so far, nothing serious on your conscience. But that can't last, and the sooner you yield to your destiny the better. Now, sir, to business. What crime do you propose to commit today?

3. A patter song immediately following the ghost scene was cut and replaced by the current patter song, "Henceforth All the Crimes That I Find in the *Times.*"

This change was suggested by Gilbert, who wrote to Sullivan the day after the opening, "I can't help thinking that the 2nd Act would be greatly improved if the recitation before Grossmith's song were omitted, and the song reset to an air that would admit of his singing it desperately—almost in a passion—the torrent of which would take him off the stage at the end."[2]

As it worked out, the new song, "Henceforth All the Crimes," retains the original recitative, but its social commentary is sharper than the original song, which ran as follows.

For thirty-five years I've been sober and wary—
my favorite tipple came straight from a dairy—
I kept guinea-pigs and a Belgian canary—
      a squirrel, white mice and a small black-and-tan.
I played on the flute and I drank lemon-squashes—
I wore chamois leather, thick boots, and macintoshes,
and things that will someday be known as galoshes,
      the type of a highly respectable man!

For the rest of my life I abandon propriety—
visit the haunts of Bohemian society,
wax-works, and other resorts of impiety,
      placed by a moralist under a ban.
My ways must be those of a regular satyr,
at carryings-on I must be a first-rater—
go night after night to a wicked theayter—
      it's hard on a highly respectable man!

Well, the man who has spent the first half of his tether
on all the bad deeds you can bracket together,
then goes and repents—in his cap it's a feather—
    society pets him as much as it can.
It's a comfort to think, if I now go a cropper,
I shan't, on the whole, have done more that's improper
than he who was once an abandoned tip-topper,
    but now is a highly respectable man!

Besides making Robin's commentary more political, the omission of the original song unintentionally made Robin's age ambiguous—here it's clearly 35.

Many would applaud the change, however, simply to be rid of the awkward "satyr/first-rater/theater" rhyme, just as the earlier cut spared the world "a bad bart's steward/whose heart is much too hard".

4. Among several less important cuts, a key bit of dialogue was eliminated from the Despard-Margaret-Robin scene. Originally, the sequence went:

Despard: . . . My brother—I call you brother still, despite your horrible profligacy—we have come to urge you to abandon the evil courses to which you have committed yourself, and at any cost to become a pure and blameless ratepayer.

Robin: That's all very well, but you seem to forget that on the day I reform I perish in excruciating torment.

Despard: Oh, better that than pursue a course of life-long villainy. Oh, seek refuge in death, I implore you!

Margaret: Why not die? Others have died and no one has cared. You will not be missed.

Despard: True—you could die so well!

Robin: You didn't seem to be of this opinion when *you* were a bad baronet.

Despard: No, because *I* had no good brother at my elbow to check *me* when about to go wrong.

Robin: A home-thrust indeed! [Aloud] But I've done no wrong yet.

Besides providing a delightful sample of Margaret's less than ideal bedside manner, this brings out Despard's resentment over Robin's having betrayed him by running away (which Robin himself clearly feels guilty about). It also shows Robin being urged to his death—both elements subsequently reinforced in the "Matter Matter Matter" trio but more pointed here.

5. A brief monologue for Robin following the "Matter" trio was also eliminated:

> Yes, my mind is made up. I don't know what crimes I may not have committed by deputy, but since I've been the worst baronet that ever lived, my life has been practically blameless. Today I will commit no crime and consequently, tonight I perish!

Again, by eliminating the phrase "and consequently tonight I perish," the cut postpones introduction of the idea that by committing no crime Robin is committing suicide. This in turn causes the eventual ending, which uses that idea to resolve the plot, to seem more abrupt and arbitrary than it originally did.

6. A long dialogue between Sir Roderick and Dame Hannah was cut, occurring after "There Grew a Little Flower." In it, the two discussed whether she could become a ghost's wife or merely his widow. It was cut partly for length and partly because some viewers found it in bad taste— "It is a grisly idea," one wrote to *The St. James Gazette*, "it is not funny; and it is in doubtful taste." (It later reappeared, somewhat revised, in *The Grand Duke;* since there the death was only a legal fiction, it was deemed funnier and less offensive.)

7. Finally, two changes were made for practical considerations.

The picture-frame mechanism, which has bedeviled Gilbert & Sullivan troupes ever since, was no more cooperative at the Savoy. The *Times* reviewer noted:

> The stage management was not here equal to Savoy level. A set of very ugly daubs . . . pulled up as you might a patent iron shutter to reveal a figure in the recess behind, can hardly be called a good example of modern stage contrivance, especially when, as on Saturday night, one of these blinds or shutters comes down at an odd moment, while another refuses to move in time.[3]

Given these problems and more critical carping about tastelessness, Gilbert & Sullivan decided not to have all the ancestors revive at the end, leaving the frame trick as a one-time effect. They also eliminated Roderick's re-entrance through a balky trapdoor. Undoubtedly, both were wise decisions.

Notes

1. Gilbert before Sullivan

1. This anecdote is retold in numerous sources, including Michael Hardwick, *The Drake Guide to Gilbert and Sullivan* (Drake, New York, 1973), p. 11. All of these stem from Gilbert, however, and the story might be apocryphal.

2. Quoted in Percy M. Young, *Sir Arthur Sullivan* (Norton, New York, 1971), p. 63. He would later occasionally make this complaint of Sullivan's work for their joint operas.

3. Quoted in Caryl Brahms, *Gilbert and Sullivan: Lost Chords and Discords* (Little, Brown, Boston, 1975), p. 141. Contrast with his opinions on Arthur Pinero and Comyns Carr, discussed in chapter 17.

4. In W. S. Gilbert, *Gilbert before Sullivan*, Jane W. Stedman, ed. (University of Chicago Press, Chicago, 1967), p. 50. Stedman's discussion of Victorian theater, here and in her Gilbert biography, is most enlightening.

5. A step back that apparently embarrassed Gilbert—when, a decade later, he published *The Princess* in his *Original Plays*, he deleted nine of the play's original 13 songs.

6. Quoted in Leslie Baily, *The Gilbert and Sullivan Book* (Coward-McCann, New York, 1952, rev. 1957), p. 13.

7. Quoted in William Archer, *Real Conversations* (Folcroft Library Editions, London, 1904), p. 114.

8. Quoted in John Bush Jones, ed., *W. S. Gilbert: A Century of Scholarship and Commentary* (New York University Press, New York, 1970), p. 8. His penchant for legal actions, especially in his later years, was no help.

9. In Hesketh Pearson, *Gilbert: His Life and Strife* (Harper, New York, 1957), p. 49.

2. Sullivan before Gilbert

1. According to Young, *Sir Arthur Sullivan*, p. 12. It does not survive.

2. Quoted in Baily, *Gilbert and Sullivan Book*, p. 59.

3. Quoted in David Eden, *Gilbert & Sullivan: The Creative Conflict* (Fairleigh Dickinson University Press, Rutherford, NJ, 1986), p. 188.

4. According to Stedman, *Gilbert before Sullivan*, p. 80. It's a pity it didn't work out—*Our Island Home* is a much more effective work than *Thespis*.

3. Thespis

1. In *Thespis: A Gilbert & Sullivan Enigma* (Dillin's University Bookshop, London, 1964). His argument is based primarily on inconsistencies in the script (which are certainly numerous) and on review quotations of material that does not appear in the script, which seems to me more likely to reflect performers' ad libs.

2. Quoted in Reginald Allen, *The First Night Gilbert and Sullivan* (Heritage Press, New York 1958), p. 6.

3. In the *Daily Telegraph,* quoted in Allen, *First Night Gilbert and Sullivan,* p. 5.

4. It's unpublished—I am grateful to the late Jerry March for sharing his copy with me.

5. Quoted in Jane W. Stedman, *W. S. Gilbert: A Classic Victorian and His Theatre* (Oxford University Press, New York, 1996), p. 94.

4. Trial by Jury

1. Cited in Stedman, *Classic Victorian,* p. 121. It certainly seems an odd pairing to a modern ear.

5. The Sorcerer

1. This affair is well discussed in Stedman, *Classic Victorian,* pp. 200–201. Basically, Gilbert couldn't tolerate Russell's star persona, especially her lateness for rehearsals.

2. Quoted in Arthur Jacobs, *Arthur Sullivan: A Victorian Musician* (Oxford University Press, New York, 1984), p. 111. Sullivan was a great cultural nationalist, especially in his conducting work, in which he took great pride in hiring English musicians and playing English music, neither of which was previously fashionable.

3. Described in detail in Allen, *First Night Gilbert and Sullivan,* pp. 70–71.

4. Quoted in Jacobs, *Arthur Sullivan,* p. 115.

5. From his prologue to *Gretchen* (1879), quoted in William Archer, *English Dramatists of Today* (1882), excerpted in Jones, *W. S. Gilbert,* p. 25.

6. This interesting fact is touched on briefly in Stedman, *Classic Victorian,* p. 154.

7. Max Keith Sutton, *W. S. Gilbert* (G. K. Hall, Boston, 1975).

6. H. M. S. Pinafore

1. As recounted in Jacobs, *Arthur Sullivan,* p. 160.

2. This story is possibly apocryphal, as Sullivan first told it in a speech at a banquet, but it's to be found in Arthur Lawrence, *Sir Arthur Sullivan: Life Story, Letters and Reminiscences* (Herbert S. Stone, Chicago 1899), p. 166–68.

3. Quoted in Stedman, *Classic Victorian,* p. 248.

4. Bond's assertion is in *The Life and Reminiscences of Jessie Bond* (John

Lane The Bodley Head, London, 1930), but a letter from Sullivan to Carte, quoted in Young, *Sir Arthur Sullivan*, p. 111, seems to convincingly debunk her account.

5. Described in Grossmith's memoir, *A Society Clown: Reminiscences*, quoted in Leslie Ayre, *The Gilbert & Sullivan Companion* (Dodd, Mead, New York, 1972), p. 141.

6. In *St. James Magazine*, 1881, reprinted in Jones, *W. S. Gilbert*, p. 45.

7. Quoted in Jacobs, *Arthur Sullivan*, p. 117.

8. Mentioned in Geoffrey Smith, *The Savoy Operas* (Universe Books, New York, 1985), p. 48. This again may be apocryphal—"Pinafore" seems so right for the baby-obsessed Gilbert.

9. At any rate, it doesn't appear in the first American vocal score of the opera (which, as always, reflects the show as it stood two weeks or so prior to opening); see Gilbert & Sullivan, *H. M. S. Pinafore* (Oliver Ditson, Philadelphia, n.d.—circa 1878).

10. For example, in a scathing review of *H. M. S. Pinafore*, *Figaro* wrote: "The fact that three of the five directors [of the Comedy Opera Company] are in some way or another connected with the firm of music publishers who publish the burlesque will explain the presence in the score of so many shop ballads, to be sung by a company whose strong point is certainly not vocal." Quoted in Allen, *First Night Gilbert and Sullivan*, p. 78.

11. In his preface to *Poems and Plays by W. S. Gilbert* (Random House, New York, 1932).

12. Quoted in Herbert Sullivan and Newman Flower, *Sir Arthur Sullivan: His Life, Letters and Diaries* (Cassell, London, 1927), p. 99.

7. The Pirates of Penzance

1. Quoted in Baily, *Gilbert and Sullivan Book*, p. 176.

2. Sullivan's diary offers a wonderful picture of the chaos of these days. The best excerpted version is in Jacobs, *Arthur Sullivan*, pp. 130–133.

3. Quoted in Baily, *Gilbert and Sullivan Book*, p. 190.

4. Quoted in Baily, *Gilbert and Sullivan Book*, pp. 182–83.

5. Quoted in Allen, *First Night Gilbert and Sullivan*, p. 109.

6. Quoted in Allen, *First Night Gilbert and Sullivan*, pp. 101–2.

7. Quoted from *The Poetical Works of Tennyson*, G. Robert Stange, ed. (Houghton Mifflin, Boston, 1974), pp. 226–27.

8. This insightful discussion may be found in Sutton, *W. S. Gilbert*, p. 100.

9. Quoted in Ian Bradley, *The Annotated Gilbert & Sullivan*, vol. 1 (Penguin Books, New York, 1982), p. 158.

10. Quoted in Baily, *Gilbert and Sullivan Book*, p. 190.

8. Patience

1. Described in Jacobs, *Arthur Sullivan*, p. 162. Carte's reaction to what must have been an expensive and time-consuming last-minute request is not recorded.

2. In *St. James Magazine*, 1881, reprinted in Jones, *W. S. Gilbert*, p. 46.

3. For a fuller account of this commentary, see Pearson, *Gilbert,* p. 244.

4. W. A. Darlington, *The World of Gilbert and Sullivan* (Crowell, New York, 1950).

5. Quoted in Allen, *First Night Gilbert and Sullivan,* p. 140.

6. In Allen, *First Night Gilbert and Sullivan,* p. 141.

7. Quoted in John Wolfson, *Final Curtain: The Last Gilbert and Sullivan Operas* (Chappell, London, 1976).

8. Described in François Cellier and Cunningham Bridgeman, *Gilbert and Sullivan and Their Operas* (Benjamin Blom, Bronx, 1970).

9. Bradley, *Annotated Gilbert and Sullivan,* vol. 2 (Penguin Books, New York, 1984), p. 124.

10. Cited in Bradley, *Annotated Gilbert and Sullivan,* vol. 2, p. 126. *Maritana* is, of course, also the most significant source for *The Yeomen of the Guard.*

11. Quoted in Allen, *First Night Gilbert and Sullivan,* p. 141.

12. I am indebted for this useful term to Charles Hayter, *Gilbert and Sullivan* (Macmillan, London, 1987), p. 5.

13. Quoted in Jacobs, *Arthur Sullivan,* p. 282.

14. In a letter quoted in Stedman, *Classic Victorian,* p. 248.

9. Iolanthe

1. Both men discussed these ideas at length in several works. See, for example, Carl Gustav Jung, *Symbols of Transformation* (1912) and Bruno Bettelheim, *The Uses of Enchantment: The Meaning and Importance of Fairy Tales* (Knopf, New York, 1976).

2. James M. Barrie, *Peter Pan* (originally *Peter and Wendy*) (Bantam Books, New York, 1985), p. 165. Barrie begins his final tale with "And then one night came the tragedy. It was the spring of the year. . . ."

10. Princess Ida

1. *Asimov's Annotated Gilbert & Sullivan* (Doubleday, New York, 1988), p. 428.

2. Bradley, *Annotated Gilbert and Sullivan,* vol. 2, p. 211.

3. I include in the "unfunny 20" "Search throughout the Panorama," "Now, Hearken to My Strict Command," "From the Distant Panorama," "Perhaps If You Address the Lady," "Expressive Glances," "Toward the Empyrean Heights," "Mighty Maiden with a Mission," "Oh, Goddess Wise," "Come, Mighty Must," "The World Is but a Broken Toy," "The Woman of the Wisest Wit," "Oh Joy, Our Chief Is Saved," "Whom Thou Hast Chained," "Walls and Fences Scaling," "Some Years Ago," "To Yield at Once," "I Built upon a Rock," "When Anger Spreads His Wing," "This Is Our Duty Plain," and "With Joy Abiding."

4. See "The Princess," in *The Poetical Works of Tennyson,* G. Robert Stange, ed. Incidentally, fans of *The Mikado* should find an interesting allusion in the description of Ida as "the Lucius Junius Brutus of her kind."

5. Smith, *Savoy Operas,* p. 122.

6. Cellier and Bridgeman, *Gilbert and Sullivan and Their Operas.*

7. William Shakespeare, *1 Henry IV,* I.3.60–61.

8. The pairs of characters are, respectively, from *Richard III* and *Much Ado about Nothing.*

11. The Mikado

1. Jacobs, *Arthur Sullivan,* p. 189.

2. Jacobs, *Arthur Sullivan,* p. 191.

3. Jacobs, *Arthur Sullivan,* p. 194.

4. Asimov, *Annotated Gilbert and Sullivan,* p. 430.

5. Sutton, *W. S. Gilbert.*

6. Described in an interview with *The New York Herald,* quoted in Baily, *Gilbert and Sullivan Book,* pp. 269–70.

12. Ruddigore

1. At the Old Players Club, on the occasion of his knighthood; quoted in Baily, *Gilbert and Sullivan Book,* p. 414.

2. Quoted in Allen, *First Night Gilbert and Sullivan,* p. 276.

3. Quoted in Pearson, *Gilbert,* p. 250.

4. Quoted in Jacobs, *Arthur Sullivan,* p. 249.

5. Quoted in Allen, *First Night Gilbert and Sullivan,* p. 271.

6. Quoted in Allen, *First Night Gilbert and Sullivan,* p. 274.

7. Ibid.

8. Quoted in Baily, *Gilbert and Sullivan Book,* p. 278.

9. Quoted in Christopher Hibbert, *Gilbert & Sullivan and Their Victorian World* (American Heritage, New York, 1976), p. 200.

10. Quoted in Bradley, *Annotated Gilbert and Sullivan,* vol. 2, p. 348.

11. Quoted in Bradley, *Annotated Gilbert and Sullivan,* p. 346.

12. Stephanie M. Muntone, conversation with the author, 1994.

13. Further details are in Frank Ledlie Moore, *Crowell's Handbook of Gilbert and Sullivan* (Crowell, New York, 1962), p. 87.

13. The Yeomen of the Guard

1. Quoted in Allen, *First Night Gilbert and Sullivan,* p. 312.

2. Quoted in Allen, *First Night Gilbert and Sullivan,* p. 307.

3. Quoted in Allen, *First Night Gilbert and Sullivan,* p. 312.

4. Quoted in Bradley, *Annotated Gilbert and Sullivan,* vol. 2, p. 413.

5. The excised verses are reproduced in Bradley, *Annotated Gilbert and Sullivan,* vol. 2, p. 460.

6. Lytton's claim is discussed in Bradley, *Annotated Gilbert and Sullivan,* vol. 2, p. 514.

7. Allen's severe judgment of Lytton's claim may be found in *First Night Gilbert and Sullivan,* p. 342.

8. Gordon's recollection is quoted in Bradley, *Annotated Gilbert and Sullivan,* vol. 2, p. 514.

9. The excised lyric is reproduced in Bradley, *Annotated Gilbert and Sullivan,* vol. 2, p. 418. Sullivan apparently never set it.

10. In an 1884 letter to Gilbert, quoted in Jacobs, *Arthur Sullivan,* p. 189.

11. Ibid.

12. In a letter of February 20, 1889, quoted in Jacobs, *Arthur Sullivan,* p. 282.

14. The Gondoliers

1. Quoted in Baily, *Gilbert and Sullivan Book,* p. 328.

2. Quoted in Baily, *Gilbert and Sullivan Book,* p. 329.

3. Ibid.

4. Quoted in Baily, *Gilbert and Sullivan Book,* p. 344.

5. Ibid.

6. Quoted in Bradley, *Annotated Gilbert and Sullivan,* vol. 1, p. 460.

15. Utopia, Limited

1. The best narrative is in Stedman, *Classic Victorian,* pp. 269–277.

2. Quoted in Jacobs, *Arthur Sullivan,* p. 215.

3. In a letter to his mother, quoted in Smith, *Savoy Operas,* p. 71. Sullivan wasn't the only one who felt this way—the opening-night critics variously described Talbot as the "weak spot in the cast," said that he "had unfortunately not thought it necessary to commit his lines," called him "shamefully ignorant of his lines," noted his "groping after his cue in a most vague manner," said that he "did inexcusable mischief," and characterized him as "loathsome and disgusting"—all quotes from Allen, *First Night,* p. 106.

4. Quoted in Jacobs, *Arthur Sullivan,* p. 126. Jacobs suggests that the letter may have been aimed more at Carte's penny-pinching partners than at Carte, to whom it was actually sent.

5. Described in Stedman, *Classic Victorian,* pp. 288–89.

6. According to Gilbert, anyway, in a letter to his wife, quoted in Pearson, *Gilbert,* p. 169.

7. According to Wolfson, *Final Curtain,* p. 31.

8. As before, this can be found in Pearson, *Gilbert,* p. 250.

9. Pearson, *Gilbert,* p. 137.

10. According to Carte, as cited in Sullivan and Flower, *Sir Arthur Sullivan,* p. 231. Gilbert acknowledged the desirability of saving some money on *Utopia* but then proceeded to itemize all the things he wanted to keep—with the end result that the cost remained much the same.

11. Ibid.

12. In Stedman, *Classic Victorian,* p. 290.

13. Wolfson, *Final Curtain,* has interesting material on this and other cuts throughout. The opera would certainly have been more coherent, if no more listenable, at its original length of close to four hours.

14. As before, quoted in Stedman, *Classic Victorian,* p. 248.

15. As before, in Darlington, *World of Gilbert and Sullivan,* p. 82.

16. Conversation with the author, 1995. Mr. Osnato is, among other things, the longtime music director of the Gilbert and Sullivan Light Opera Company of Long Island.

17. In Audrey Williamson, *Gilbert & Sullivan Opera: A New Assessment* (Marion Boyers, London, 1953/1982).

16. The Grand Duke

1. Quoted in Baily, *Gilbert and Sullivan Book,* p. 414.
2. Quoted in Stedman, *Classic Victorian,* p. 309.
3. Quoted in Jacobs, *Arthur Sullivan,* p. 367.
4. Quoted in Brahms, *Lost Chords and Discords,* p. 232.
5. Ibid.
6. Ibid.
7. Quoted in Allen, p. 172.
8. Quoted in Jacobs, *Arthur Sullivan,* p. 367. Burnand, who as the author of *Cox and Box* had always felt as though he should be in Gilbert's place, was always quick to criticize Gilbert and had done so in this instance.
9. Darlington, *World of Gilbert and Sullivan,* pp. 161–162, has a nice summary of this whole aspect of the show.
10. In Alan Jefferson, *The Complete Gilbert and Sullivan Opera Guide* (Facts on File, New York, 1984), p. 320.
11. Stedman, *Classic Victorian,* pp. 80, offers an intriguing description of the offbeat play, which may be found in Gilbert, *Gilbert before Sullivan,* Stedman, ed.
12. Stedman, *Classic Victorian,* p. 122. As far as I can determine, the play has not been published.
13. See hereafter.
14. In *The Norton Anthology of English Literature,* vol. 2 (Norton, New York, 1979), p. 1728. The play has several lines that echo Gilbert's work, especially *Engaged.*
15. In Wolfson, *Final Curtain,* pp. 68–70.
16. Quoted in Young, *Sir Arthur Sullivan,* p. 199.

17. Gilbert after Sullivan, Sullivan after Gilbert

1. According to Pearson, *Gilbert,* p. 248. Isaac Goldberg, *The Story of Gilbert and Sullivan* (Simon and Schuster, New York, 1928), p. 292, says that it was actually submitted to Sullivan in 1882 as a possible successor for *Iolanthe,* but I have been unable to find any source to confirm this.
2. Supposedly said to the American composer Reginald De Koven and recounted in a biography of De Koven, so the chain of attribution is tenuous at best. Quoted in Gervase Hughes, *The Music of Arthur Sullivan* (St. Martin's Press, New York, 1960), p. 24.
3. In an 1898 interview with *The Daily Mail.* While this was an interview aimed at promoting the show, Sullivan is unusually fervent, even eloquent

in describing the upcoming opera, and seems to be speaking from the heart.

4. Quoted in Baily, *Gilbert and Sullivan Book*, p. 190.

5. Quoted in Jacobs, *Arthur Sullivan*, p. 379.

6. Ibid.

7. Quoted in Jacobs, *Arthur Sullivan*, p. 380.

8. Expressed in Lawrence, *Sir Arthur Sullivan*, pp. 197–199.

9. Quoted in Jacobs, *Arthur Sullivan*, p. 388.

10. Quoted in Jacobs, *Arthur Sullivan*, p. 391.

11. It was Max Beerbohm, supposedly a friend of Gilbert, writing in *The Saturday Review* and quoted in Pearson, *Gilbert*, pp. 225–26.

12. Quoted in W. S. Gilbert, *The Bab Ballads*, James Ellis, ed. (Harvard University Press, Cambridge, 1970), p. 28.

13. W. S. Gilbert, *Original Plays*, 4 series (Chatto & Windus, London, 1922), p. 5. The play occupies pp. 1–42.

14. Gilbert, *Original Plays*, p. 233. The play occupies pp. 187–234.

15. Stedman, *Classic Victorian*, is the best source on the personal and professional relationships between Gilbert and McIntosh. As far as can be determined, despite occasional snide comments from contemporaries, the relationship seems to have had neither romantic nor sexual components.

16. The lyrics to the excised song, which was set by Sullivan and which survives in the original American score for the opera, may be found in Bradley, *Annotated Gilbert and Sullivan*, vol. 1, pp. 240–42. It is probably the most socially aware song Gilbert ever wrote and was probably cut specifically because its acerbic tone clashed with the rest of *Iolanthe*.

17. Quoted in Maurice Baring, "Gilbert and Sullivan," in *Lost Lectures: or The Fruits of Experience* (Knopf, New York, 1932).

18. Legacy

1. Martyn Green, *Here's a How-de-do: My Life in Gilbert and Sullivan* (Norton, New York, 1952). Green's performance-centered view of the operas is a very useful corrective to the usual academic/biographic approach, which focuses (as this book does) primarily on the texts.

2. See the description in Green, *How-de-do*, pp. 127–28.

3. This illuminating, highly prophetic discussion may be found in Green, *How-de-do*, pp. 223–24. He is discussing specifically the D'Oyly Carte tour of America in 1948/49.

4. Admittedly, in a letter to the composer himself, of October 24, 1909, which may have been less than candid. It may be seen at the Pierpont Morgan Library in New York.

5. Quoted in Bernard Rosenberg and Ernest Goldstein, *Creators and Disturbers*, as excerpted in the spring 1994 issue of the City College of New York alumni magazine, *Alumnus*. Thanks to the late Jerry March for bringing it to my attention.

6. Stephen Sondheim to author, April 25, 1995.

7. In Philip Hoare, *Noel Coward: A Biography* (Simon & Schuster, New York, 1995).

8. "Cole Porter Talks of His Musicals," *The New York Herald Tribune*, February 20, 1955, quoted in William McBrian, *Cole Porter: A Biography* (Knopf, New York, 1998), p. 363.

9. Telephone conversation, May 1999.

10. In Alan Jay Lerner, *The American Musical Theater: A Celebration* (McGraw-Hill, New York, 1986), p. 26.

11. Sheldon Harnick to author, May 16, 1999.

12. Telephone conversation, May 1999.

13. Telephone conversation, March 1999.

14. Fred Ebb to author, April 11, 1999.

15. Stephen Schwartz to author, June 28, 1999.

16. Telephone conversation, June 1999.

17. Tom Jones to author, July 29, 1999.

18. James Knowlson, *Damned to Fame: The Life of Samuel Beckett* (Simon and Schuster, New York, 1996), p. 59.

19. As "Lord Chancellor's Nightmare Song," on his album *Todd* (1975).

20. March 13, 2000, at SUNY/Stony Brook, cited in Letta Tayler, "Piano Man Does Stand-up," *Newsday*, March 15, 2000. The song "Angry Young Man" is on the album *Turnstile* (1975).

21. Telephone conversation, May 1999.

Appendix B. Revisions to Ruddigore

1. As reflected in Allen, *First Night*, pp. 271–305.

2. Quoted in Allen, *First Night*, p. 304. Post-opening changes in the operas were common, but the writing of a new number was extremely rare. Other than the post–New York revisions of *The Pirates of Penzance*, which is a special case, and the finale of *Utopia, Limited*, such changes were almost invariably cuts.

3. Quoted in Allen, *First Night*, p. 274.

Bibliography

Allen, Reginald
   The First Night Gilbert and Sullivan (The Heritage Press, New York,
      1958)

An indispensable reference source. Allen has done admirable research,
both in the D'Oyly Carte files and in apparently every review of any Gilbert
& Sullivan first night ever published.

He presents the libretti of the operas as each appeared on its opening
night, complete with songs cut later and dialogue subsequently revised
(subsequent research has revealed some errors, but in general he's reliable). He prefaces each opera with a discussion of the opening night itself,
largely through quotations from the reviews of the day, which are often
fascinating. A short section after each play describes the major changes
that were made.

The format could be improved—it's hard to pick out the passages that
were subsequently altered (notes or differentiations in type would help).
But Allen's text stands as a unique and valuable reference, and can be
recommended to anyone who can find a copy—especially if it still has the
facsimiles of the original programs, included in the same slipcover in the
original package.

Allen, Reginald
   Sir Arthur Sullivan (Pierpont Morgan Library, New York, 1975)

The hardbound catalogue for the Gilbert and Sullivan Centenary exhibit
at the Morgan Library in 1975, this is an intriguing listing of the many
items that made up the exhibition. Unfortunately, most of the items are
merely referred to, with tantalizing extracts at best. Some are pictured, in
the book's best feature, but many more are not, alas.

This is a handy guide for a scholar, especially one contemplating a visit
to the Morgan; but, while it contains a number of nuggets interesting to
the general reader, it isn't intended to please such a reader and seldom
does.

Archer, William
   Real Conversations (Folcroft Library Editions, London, 1904)

Of interest because one of the 12 interviews herein is a famous 1901 conversation with Gilbert. It's a fascinating colloquy, with Gilbert waxing nostalgic for the old-time theater and offering trenchant commentary on the contemporary stage. A few quotes from this interview are standard references, but there is more to be gleaned here, including Gilbert's canny encomium to Sullivan's music and especially the power of its orchestration.

   Gilbert did very few interviews, and this is his best—required reading for anyone who wants to understand the librettist.

   Incidentally, many of the other interviews are fascinating reading even now, including talks with the famous—playwright Arthur Wing Pinero, novelist Thomas Hardy, and the Irish painter/writer George Moore—and the obscure but fascinating; the interview with the Scottish university professor David Masson may be the best in the volume, other than the Gilbert conversation.

Asimov, Isaac
   Asimov's Annotated Gilbert and Sullivan (Doubleday, New York, 1988)

The weakest annotated Gilbert & Sullivan available and the most expensive; essentially a vanity production in which Doubleday indulged its star science-fiction writer.

   Asimov was a Gilbert & Sullivan fan, not an expert. The best thing about the book is his enthusiasm for the works, especially in performance. His ceaseless self-promoting is hardly as welcome. He primarily aims to provide definitions and push his own preferences—he seldom ventures into analysis, and when he does he's completely off base. His reading of *Princess Ida*, for example, is wrong from beginning to end. His glossings are also often mistaken—he draws on nothing except the *Encyclopedia Britannica* and his own memory, and thus frequently repeats misinformation with blithe unawareness.

   For an annotated Gilbert & Sullivan, Ian Bradley's version is infinitely preferable.

Ayre, Leslie
   The Gilbert and Sullivan Companion (Dodd, Mead, New York, 1972)

A good-natured but hardly essential book in glossary format, including (1) lengthy plot summaries of the operas, including nearly all the lyrics; (2) annotations of obscure references; (3) character and song-title listings; and (4) brief biographies of, seemingly, every D'Oyly Carte principal ever.

All this is welcome, of course, and only a plethora of typos gets in the way. But the fact is, most of this is available elsewhere—the annotations in more useful format in Bradley, the plot summaries in the libretti themselves. Song listings and D'Oyly Carte biographies are more in the "who needs them?" category, interesting though a few of the biographies are—most simply give location of birth, education, and roles played.

There are a few fresh anecdotes here, but overall it's a handsomely prepared work of synthesis that isn't really necessary to an appreciation of Gilbert & Sullivan.

Baily, Leslie
The Gilbert and Sullivan Book (Coward-McCann, New York, 1952, (rev. 1957)

Even after decades, the definitive joint biography, often mined by subsequent biographers but never matched.

Baily doesn't analyze, and his usually graceful style occasionally gets a bit faux-Victorian in its floridity. And his ceaseless boosting of Richard D'Oyly Carte makes it a virtual authorized biography. (Bridget D'Oyly Carte gave him rare access to the company's files, and he clearly returns the favor.)

But he tells a story running from 1836 to 1957 with admirable attention to detail and a clear love of the operas. Particularly engaging are the recollections of many people who had performed in or seen the original productions; these people, elderly when the book was written and soon thereafter deceased, give a particularly human feel to the whole project.

A must-read for anyone who really wants to know about Gilbert & Sullivan.

Baily, Leslie
Gilbert and Sullivan: Their Lives and Times (Viking Press, New York, 1974; published in Britain as *Gilbert and Sullivan and Their World,* Thames & Hudson, London, 1973)

A 118-page book that promises on its cover "with 143 illustrations," chances are, will be like this—a thin work beefed up to book length with lavish use of illustrations and wide margins (at least one-third of every page is margin).

Yet it works. The familiar story is well told and goes down smoothly. And the illustrations are remarkably interesting and attractively presented. Surprisingly few are familiar—the classic shots are here, but also fresh ones of Gilbert and Sullivan, some rare production shots from the original shows, and some very welcome extras, such as shots of the various theaters, and the homes of Gilbert and Sullivan and other items, lending a real sense of the Victorian world in which they flourished.

This is not an essential book by any means but is a genial one that is fast, enjoyable reading and does indeed offer a few new glimpses into the world of Gilbert & Sullivan.

Baring, Maurice
"Gilbert and Sullivan," in *Lost Lectures: or The Fruits of Experience* (Knopf, New York, 1932)

A warm, appreciative lecture, originally delivered in 1922, that has some properly appreciative things to say about the Savoy operas and their creators. Most interesting, however, as a snapshot of the state of public appreciation at a crucial point in Gilbert & Sullivan history, immediately following Rupert D'Oyly Carte's Prince's Theatre revivals in 1920. The famous quotation from Lytton Strachey, predicting that "the most permanent and enduring achievement of the Victorian age would be . . . the operas of Gilbert & Sullivan" is from this lecture.

Bell, Diana
The Complete Gilbert and Sullivan (Wellfleet Press, Secaucus, NJ, 1989)

Yet another handsomely produced volume on Gilbert & Sullivan that is undone by the author's lack of real knowledge of the operas. Bell is best at the beginning, in her knowledgeable summary of the pre-Savoy Victorian theater, and at the end, in an informative timeline.

In between, however, she reveals a shocking unfamiliarity with the operas. Plots are misinterpreted, song titles are wrong ("Love Is a Plaintive Thing"?), quotes are either misquoted or misinterpreted, and so on. Bell also accepts all her sources unquestioningly, citing pure speculation as undoubted fact.

This may be the best looking book on Gilbert & Sullivan ever, particularly with its large-scale renderings of Gilbert's drawings, but it is second only to Michael Ffinch as the most flawed Gilbert & Sullivan book ever.

Benford, Harry
The Gilbert and Sullivan Lexicon (Richards Rosen Press, New York, 1978)

A meticulously researched dictionary of Gilbert & Sullivan terms, defined with clarity, terseness, wit, and a clear love for the operas. The format is a bit awkward (definitions are grouped by show and in show order, as in an annotated text without the text, rather than alphabetically, as in a dictionary), and there are a few errors. Geoffrey Shovelton's amateurish cartoons are a big minus, proving the former D'Oyly Carte tenor to be more a tenor than the "master cartoonist" that the front copy claims.

In all, though, this is a useful work. Benford has checked nearly every relevant source and doesn't hesitate to include alternate opinions while still expressing his own ideas. Even an expert can learn a few things from his work.

Bond, Jessie
  The Life and Reminiscences of Jessie Bond (John Lane The Bodley Head, London, 1930)

The memoirs of the original Hebe, Edith, Angela, Iolanthe, Melissa, Pitti-Sing, Mad Margaret, Phoebe, and Gianetta make for engaging reading for any Savoyard.

Bond's book is a testimonial to herself—her talents as a singer and actor and, especially, her beauty and popularity. Around the edges, however, an interesting backstage story emerges, along with some engaging anecdotes.

Written 35–55 years after the events, when she was 77, Bond's version (written with Ethel MacGeorge) is not entirely reliable but always interesting—for example, her portraits of a demanding but courteous Gilbert and a sarcastic, grudge-nursing Sullivan and her strange recounting of how the role of Hebe became so small.

But anyone who loves Gilbert & Sullivan will be interested in this unique memoir by "One Who Was There."

Bradley, Ian
  The Annotated Gilbert and Sullivan
  (Vol. 1, Penguin Books, New York, 1982—*H. M. S. Pinafore, The Pirates of Penzance, Iolanthe, The Mikado, The Gondoliers*)
  (Vol. 2, Penguin Books, New York, 1984—*Trial by Jury, The Sorcerer, Patience, Princess Ida, Ruddigore, The Yeomen of the Guard*)
  (Collected version, Penguin Books, New York, 1996—adds *Utopia, Limited* and *The Grand Duke*)

Easily the best annotated Gilbert & Sullivan currently available (though volume 2 is hard to find). Bradley combines Reginald Allen's work in *The First Night Gilbert and Sullivan* with his own research into the operas' creation, then adds thorough, informative glossing (including some neat musical commentary) to produce a work that can surprise and intrigue even the most knowledgeable reader.

Annotators usually miss the forest for the trees, and Bradley is no exception. His strength is line-by-line reading, his weaknesses overall thematic content and dramatic structure. (He is almost unique in having read Tennyson's "The Princess," for example, but misses the point of its contrasts with *Princess Ida.*)

But all in all, this is an exceptional book. The collected version is an essential for any Gilbert & Sullivan lover's bookshelf.

Brahms, Caryl
    Gilbert and Sullivan: Lost Chords and Discords (Little, Brown, Boston,
    1975)

A profoundly irritating book. Brahms's initially welcome breeziness wears
thin quickly, especially her penchant for parenthetical observations: "(Oh,
Sir Arthur!)." Anything fresh or clever is repeated to the point of becoming obnoxious.

Brahms's focus on personality conflicts distorts her story, and the der-
ivation of her material is dubious. Often she cribs directly from other
authors (in her preface, she admits she "helped herself copiously"); other
assertions are so unfamiliar and unattributed as to suggest outright invention. For example, she cites—without attribution—Victorian rumors that
Sullivan was gay (and the duke of Edinburgh among his lovers), a claim
that flies in the face of plentiful existing evidence.

All in all, a book almost without merit. All its good stuff comes from
other readily available sources, and its initially refreshing tone quickly
wears thin.

Cellier, François, and Cunningham Bridgeman
    Gilbert and Sullivan and Their Operas (Benjamin Blom, Bronx, 1970)

This memoir by two longtime Sullivan intimates amounts to virtual hagi-
ography. Apparently Gilbert and Sullivan disagreed only once in 25 years,
and that briefly. Their personal quirks are blithely sanitized, and seldom
is heard a discouraging word.

For all of that, this is often intriguing reading. Cellier, in particular, was
there, and has intriguing anecdotes about everybody of importance in the
Gilbert & Sullivan story.

The minimal analysis of the operas appeals mainly for its Victorian viewpoint, which will surprise modern readers (Bridgeman raves about *Utopia,
Limited,* for example.) Alas, these Sullivan loyalists give the music a free
ride—only Gilbert is occasionally knocked, most notably in Bridgeman's
remarkable attack on *The Grand Duke).*

All in all, an interesting book. Would that its high-flown Victorian style
(sometimes amusing, often leaden) had been cleaner, simpler, and a
great deal more candid.

Darlington, W. A.
    The World of Gilbert and Sullivan (Crowell, New York, 1950)

Darlington aims to explicate the world in which the operas were written,
and in general provides welcome context. His summary of the social implications of *H. M. S. Pinafore,* for example, is excellent, providing crucial
frame-of-reference information.

But the book is also frustrating because Darlington so often misses the
real point of the operas. He notes that almost every song in *Patience* is

about love, not art; but never rethinks his preconception that the show is about art.

Darlington is also a rabid Gilbert partisan, atypically depicting Sullivan as grasping and difficult, comparing him to an ambitious, pushing wife to Gilbert's practical, harassed husband. This bias taints some of the artistic commentary, as do a number of major errors and omissions.

Nevertheless, this is well worth reading for its insights into the social context of the Savoy operas.

Dunhill, Thomas F.
Sullivan's Comic Operas (Edward Arnold, London, 1928)

A rather disappointing book despite a strong beginning and ending, it seems to be a rebuttal, of sorts, to a disparaging view of Sullivan in Ernest Walker's *History of Music in England,* and begins with a vigorous rebuttal of Walker; the final chapter, "Recognition," is a fine summary that energetically defends Sullivan against his critics.

Otherwise, the promised analysis of Sullivan's music from a musician's point of view falls apart. It's really more of an appreciation than an analysis, acknowledging flaws as well as strengths but offering only rudimentary commentary. Dunhill runs through the operas song by song, with no room for more than a brief judgment with little or no supporting evidence.

A Savoyard may appreciate this strong statement from a musical fan of Sullivan; the more critical reader, however, will find better grist in the later works of Gervase Hughes and Percy Young.

Eden, David
Gilbert and Sullivan: The Creative Conflict (Fairleigh Dickinson University Press, Rutherford, NJ, 1986)

At heart not as unorthodox and groundbreaking as its author would like us to believe; essentially a pro-Sullivan brief, stressing Gilbert's artistic limitations and trying personality (Eden convincingly paints him as, at times, a roaring, infantile megalomaniac) and Sullivan's artistic talent and forbearing personality.

The picture of Gilbert is unfortunately wrecked by excessive psychological speculation, generally on the thinnest possible evidence. The sexual theorizing and speculative readings of carefully chosen Bab Ballads and opera elements as autobiographical are at times laughably thin and never very plausible.

It's a pity, because distorting the works to fit an intriguing but forced thesis undercuts Eden's legitimately interesting ideas on the operas. Hopefully, he'll someday write another Gilbert & Sullivan book focusing more on the art and less on the artists.

Ffinch, Michael
  Gilbert and Sullivan (Weidenfeld and Nicolson, London, 1993)

The worst book I've read on Gilbert & Sullivan.

Ffinch seems to know or care little about the operas—there are literally hundreds of errors in the lengthy summaries of the operas that make up half the book, ranging from trivia to major plot misunderstandings, characters and songs misidentified, and so on. The remaining half of the book is cribbed, often without acknowledgment, from previous biographies, especially Sullivan-Flower on Sullivan and Dark-Grey on Gilbert.

For himself, Ffinch has virtually nothing to say, and what little he says is either demonstrably wrong or undocumented speculation.

Any lover of Gilbert & Sullivan should avoid this book for anything but some easy laughs.

Fischler, Alan
  "Gilbert and Donizetti," *The Opera Quarterly*, 2:1 (1994), pp. 29–42

A moderately interesting journal article pointing out supposed influences of Donizetti's operas (especially *L'Elisir D'Amore* and *Don Pascale*) on Gilbert. Best on Gilbert's early burlesques of Donizetti in *Dulcamara* and *La Vivandiere*, weaker on the Savoy operas, where the author generally mistakes both librettists' common use of old ideas for direct influence of one on the other.

However, he offers a convincing explication of a double-Donizetti influence on the otherwise perplexing "Sighing Softly to the River" from *The Pirates of Penzance*.

Fitzgerald, Percy
  The Savoy Opera and the Savoyards (Chatto and Windus, London, 1894)

A fascinating book; the only major work on the operas written during their composition—in this case, while *Utopia, Limited* was still running at the Savoy.

Fitzgerald is painstakingly careful to stay on the good side of Gilbert and Carte, so there's no dark side here (the "carpet quarrel" is brushed off as a private affair, while the title *Ruddygore* is attributed to "a printer's mistake"). And he relies on his own memory, so there are occasional errors, as well as the complete omission of *Thespis* (which he didn't see).

Still, his commentary is surprisingly insightful, particularly on the operas' evolution over time; and his contemporary yet relatively objective viewpoint is almost unique. Reading this book gives one an unmatched sense of actually being there, listening to an informed, educated critic writing well of operas he clearly admires. An essential book for any student of the operas.

Geis, Darlene
The Gilbert and Sullivan Operas (Abrams, New York, 1983)

This profusely illustrated companion book to the PBS television series "The Compleat Gilbert and Sullivan" has both the strengths and weaknesses of the series. Most of the photos are from the series and generally steer away from its occasional untraditional eccentricities; there are also some fresh historical pictures, making the book visually intriguing.

But Geis doesn't know much about Gilbert & Sullivan. Her material is straight from other sources and is occasionally misunderstood at that. She sometimes confuses production decisions by the PBS directors with textual elements of the operas themselves, and her plot summaries are sometimes bewildering, stressing minutiae and skipping over important points.

Not a particularly useful book for novice or expert.

Gilbert, W. S.
Authentic Libretti of the Gilbert and Sullivan Operas (Bass, New York, 1934)

This edition, released in conjunction with the highly successful American tour of the D'Oyly Carte Opera Company and featuring a puffy foreword by Frederick Hobbs, the company manager, is hardly what a modern reader would call "authentic."

It is a collection of individually published libretti bound into a single volume; it completely omits *Thespis, The Sorcerer, Utopia, Limited,* and *The Grand Duke,* and reflects occasional cuts (for example, *Ruddigore*'s "Henceforth All the Crimes") to reflect D'Oyly Carte's performance practice at the time. So it's more authentic D'Oyly Carte than authentic Gilbert & Sullivan.

In any event, there are many better, later editions to choose from.

Gilbert, W. S.
The Bab Ballads, with which are included Songs of a Savoyard (Macmillan, London, 1904–60)

A handsome edition of the *Ballads,* this is generally an attractive, engaging presentation of some of the best comic verse in the English language.

Two caveats: Gilbert's "Songs of a Savoyard" lyrics are generally out of place, though they do offer some interesting later variations on the forms in the operas, and the excerpts from *The Mountebanks* and *His Excellency* are hard to find elsewhere. And Gilbert's "new" drawings, replacing many of the original Bab drawings because he felt those "erred gravely in the direction of unnecessary extravagance," are charming—but not nearly as much as the "extravagant" ones they replace.

All in all, however, and despite the absence of James Ellis's scholarly insights, this is a fine edition and well worth having.

Gilbert, W. S.
>   *The Bab Ballads,* James Ellis, ed. (Harvard University Press, Cambridge, 1970)

No one should need a scholarly reason to read *The Bab Ballads,* which would be required reading even if their author had never written a single opera. Ellis's edition provides excellent printing, good paper, and a roomy design that gives each poem and illustration room to breathe; his helpful introduction and discreet, informative notes are exactly what's called for.

There really isn't that much in the *Ballads* for students of the operas, except for an occasional line echo or possible source for a story line. But they're such fun that everyone should read them for the sheer pleasure of their delightful rhythms, offbeat humor, and eccentric illustrations.

Gilbert, W. S.
>   *The Best Known Works of W. S. Gilbert* (Halcyon House, Garden City, NY, 1932)

Utterly unnecessary—libretti to *H. M. S. Pinafore, The Pirates of Penzance,* and *The Mikado,* plus 19 Bab Ballads, all with a plethora of Gilbert illustrations (some in the libretti actually from marginally similar Babs).

Nothing wrong with this book, but it's not at all needed, if it ever was.

Gilbert, W. S.
>   *Complete Operas* (with a preface by Deems Taylor) (Dorset Press, 1932)

A reasonably competent but otherwise unremarkable edition, from the same plates as the Modern Library edition, illustrated with Gilbert's "Songs of a Savoyard" drawings.

Taylor's preface, lifted from an edition of Gilbert's plays, is resolutely biased in Gilbert's favor and offers a fairly conventional tour through the familiar biographical territory. The essay is interesting for its 1930s perspective *(Fidelio* and *The Magic Flute* are listed as works that have never been part of the conventional operatic repertoire) but is marred both by lack of access to later scholarly work and by several gratuitous errors.

Gilbert, W. S.
>   *Gilbert before Sullivan,* Jane W. Stedman, ed. (University of Chicago Press, Chicago, 1967)

Stedman's collection of Gilbert's six short operas for Thomas German Reed's Royal Gallery of Illustration is essential reading for those interested in Gilbert's development as a dramatist.

A thoughtful introduction convincingly establishes the Reed shows as key antecedents of the Savoy operas—not only in providing ideas but also in developing Gilbert's talent for original rhythms, his familiarity with repertory-company writing, and his reliance on solid writing to make up for the Royal Gallery's lack of chorus, orchestra, or stage machinery.

Of the plays themselves, *A Sensation Novel* is the best and *Our Island Home* perhaps the funniest—both are ancestors of *The Grand Duke* in their use of metatheatrical elements. The vaunted *Ages Ago* isn't much (nor much like *Ruddigore*), while *Happy Arcadia* seems flat and underdeveloped. *No Cards* and *Eyes and No Eyes* are essentially tossed-off whimsies.

Gilbert, W. S.
  Lost Bab Ballads, Townley Searle, ed. (Putnam, London, 1932)

Seriously flawed and superseded by Ellis's edition of the ballads. Searle's scholarship is shady—Ellis notes that he cribs from the works of others and that, of the 16 poems he supposedly uncovered, four were by other people and three were actually opera lyrics from 20 years after the *Ballads* were written.

In any event, Searle's own illustrations aren't a patch on Gilbert's, and why he chose to discard Gilbert's drawings for his own amateurish sketches is unclear. He also omits any illustration at all for the ending of "A. and B.; or, the Sensation Twins," which ends with a cue for an illustration.

This outdated book's only real interest is that it includes the rare lyric "The Ballad of Jim-Jams," written for *The Mountebanks* and never set, but revised two years later for *The Grand Duke* as "When You Find You're a Broken-Down Critter." (Searle seems not to have picked up on this, however.)

Gilbert, W. S.
  The Lost Stories of W. S. Gilbert, Peter Haining, ed. (Robson Books, London, 1982)

This collection of miscellaneous short stories (one of which, the delightful "Poisoned Postage Stamp," is apparently not by Gilbert) is entertaining and informative, revealing a prose style surprisingly reminiscent of Mark Twain and more accessible to modern readers than anything else Gilbert wrote.

The most intriguing, of course, is "An Elixir of Love," the source for *The Sorcerer*. Its similarities and differences are interesting, though not particularly shocking or revelatory.

Haining's introduction is incoherent at times, making comments about the stories that seem to make no sense at all—as in describing "Diamonds," a simple romantic melodrama with comic touches, as a horror story or calling the anti-heroic "Jones' Victoria Cross" an example of Gilbert's romanticizing of the military. Nor does he seem to understand much about the operas.

But the stories themselves remain interesting and, often, very funny indeed.

Gilbert, W. S.
  The Mikado (Godfrey Cave, London, 1928)

The libretto, illustrated with watercolors by W. Russell Flint and pen-and-ink drawings by Charles E. Brock.

A couple of Flint's eight watercolors are modestly appealing, but his compositional sense is strange and his choice of scenes to illustrate truly bizarre—"Here, Nanki-Poo, I've good news for you"?

Brock's black-and-white drawings are more effective, particularly his fat, smug Pooh-Bah (vaguely reminiscent of Leo Sheffield in the role), but aren't as good as his drawings for *The Yeomen of the Guard* in the same series.

Gilbert, W. S.
  The Mikado, Philip Smith, ed. (Dover, New York, 1992)

A printing of the libretto, illustrated with woodcuts from the *Songs of a Savoyard* series and with a minimal editorial note. Not worth any particular attention.

Gilbert, W. S.
  Original Plays, 4th series (Chatto & Windus, London, 1922)

Thespis and *The Grand Duke* bookend Gilbert's final collection of his plays, including his final works as well as various previously uncollected works. The book includes *The Gentleman in Black* (1870), *Randall's Thumb* (1871), *Creatures of Impulse* (1871), *Thespis* (1871), *Brantinghame Hall* (1888), *Haste to the Wedding* (1892), *His Excellency* (1894), *The Grand Duke* (1896), *The Fortune-Hunter* (1897), *The Fairy's Dilemma* (1904), *Fallen Fairies* (1909), *The Hooligan* (1911), and the magazine playlet *Trying a Dramatist*.

Most of these don't play very well today—besides *The Grand Duke*, only the whimsical, very Gilbertian *Gentleman in Black*, the melodramatic but affecting *Fortune-Hunter*, and the intriguing *Fallen Fairies* (perhaps the best play in the volume) have much of interest, and even these seem dated in their diction and melodramatic plotting. Still, this is an essential collection to understanding Gilbert the playwright.

Gilbert, W. S.
  Plays by W. S. Gilbert, George Rowell, ed. (Cambridge University Press, Cambridge, England, 1982)

Four plays—*The Palace of Truth, Sweethearts, Engaged,* and *Rosencrantz and Guildenstern*—plus one operetta *(Princess Toto)* make up this intriguing sampling of Gilbert's non-Sullivan plays.

Engaged and *The Palace of Truth* come off best, the former for its sparkling wit (there are several scenes reminiscent of the later works *The Mi-*

kado, The Gondoliers, and even *The Importance of Being Earnest)*, the latter for its interesting concept. *Sweethearts* is agreeably short and sometimes effective but a bit cloyingly sentimental; *Rosencrantz and Guildenstern* is a clever riff on *Hamlet*.

Princess Toto, which might be expected to be the best, since its author is best known for his comic opera, is instead shallow, implausible, and without lyrical sparkle.

A valuable collection for any fan of Gilbert, offering some interesting insights into his later operatic work. Rowell's introductory material is informative and admirably focused.

Gilbert, W. S.
Poems and Plays by W. S. Gilbert (Random House, New York, 1932)

A mildly interesting collection of the Savoy libretti, the *Bab Ballads*, and three other Gilbert works—*The Palace of Truth, The Mountebanks*, and *His Excellency*. The Savoy libretti and the Babs are amply available elsewhere, but this is a good collection because of the other three plays, especially the two late operettas, which are hard to find elsewhere.

Also interesting is Deems Taylor's lengthy preface, printed as well in *The Best Known Works of W. S. Gilbert*.

Gilbert, W. S.
Poems of W. S. Gilbert, William Cole, ed. (Crowell, New York, 1976)

An entirely superfluous edition inferior to Ellis's edition of the *Bab Ballads* on nearly every score.

About the only advantage is the inclusion of some of Gilbert's *Songs of a Savoyard* and their drawings, but of course Gilbert's own edition is more complete in this regard. Cole's introduction is perfunctory and sloppy on the facts, while his notes are merely perfunctory; his page layouts are far worse than Ellis's, with the end of one poem and the beginning of the next crammed onto the same small page. And his selection of 50 or so poems and song lyrics is subjective at best.

Quite dispensable.

Gilbert, W. S.
The Princess (Samuel French, London, 1870?)

Gilbert's play offers interesting insights into *Princess Ida*, including dialogue cut from the opera or assigned to different characters, the original scene structure, and so forth.

There are a few major differences—Arac, Guron, and Scynthius throw the final battle, for example, and Ida releases Hilarion in return for his saving her life—that make the play more like the poem than the opera, but in general the play and opera are close in everything but tone (a good bit softer in the play).

This book also offers a look at Victorian theater before Gilbert & Sullivan, and shows what pioneers both were—*The Princess* has songs that set new lyrics to tunes from popular operas of the day, and all the young men's roles (Hilarion, Cyril, Florian, Arac, Guron, and Scynthius) were originally played by women.

Gilbert, W. S.
  The Yeomen of the Guard (Godfrey Cave, London, 1929)

The libretto of *Yeomen* is handsomely presented, with illustrations by W. Russell Flint and Charles E. Brock.

Both illustrators are very much in the style of the 1920s, but while Flint's eight watercolor plates are stiff, poorly composed, and uninteresting, Brock's numerous pen-and-ink drawings evoke the opera nicely, especially in his eye for character—a hulking Wilfred Shadbolt stands out most.

A nice gift for a Savoyard, though hardly essential.

Gilbert, W. S., and Arthur Sullivan
  H. M. S. Pinafore, vocal score (Oliver Ditson, Philadelphia, n.d.–circa 1878)

This early American edition of the opera, most likely a pirated one, represents *H. M. S. Pinafore* more or less as it was presented on the night of the London opening.

The differences are minor but interesting—most notably, of course, a recitative running from Sir Joseph's "Here, take her sir" through the end of the finale. Ralph's language is also a good bit less flowery—either this comic element succeeded and Gilbert elaborated on it for later editions or the annotator couldn't keep up with the more elaborate dialogue and only approximated it.

There are numerous other changes, mostly reflecting apparent actor ad libs or second thoughts by Gilbert himself, which were then incorporated into later editions.

Not, perhaps, essential, but still intriguing reading for anyone who knows *H. M. S. Pinafore* well.

Godwin, A. H.
  Gilbert & Sullivan: A Critical Appreciation of the Savoy Operas (Kennikat Press, Port Washington, NY, 1926; reprint, 1969)

More a collection of essays by an obvious devotee of the operas than a book about them, this is a welcome take on the operas themselves instead of the usual biography/history. Godwin's 1926 viewpoint also makes for some interesting juxtapositions (Gilbert & Sullivan acting compared to silent-film acting, for example).

Unfortunately, Godwin doesn't really know much about the operas—the book is riddled with misquotes and mistakes about plot and characters—and he has several pet theories that just don't hold water. (Despite textual evidence to the contrary, he insists that Jack Point is in his 40s, for example.) Moreover, he devotes absurd amounts of space to chapters on "The Six Best Lyrics" and "The Six Best Airs" and other purely subjective topics.

Overall, this is occasionally interesting but generally frustrating, the opinions of a loving but not particularly thoughtful fan.

Goldberg, Isaac
The Story of Gilbert and Sullivan (Simon and Schuster, New York, 1928)

Easily the best written book on Gilbert & Sullivan ever—after more than 70 years, still one of the best available.

Besides his witty but not self-indulgent, learned but not pedantic style, Goldberg's greatest virtue is his sense of balance. He writes of the Gilbert-Sullivan conflicts but neither overstates nor downplays them; he has his own ideas about the operas, and presents them well, but doesn't let his book degenerate into an argument for them; he discusses what Gilbert and Sullivan each brought to the collaboration, as artists and as men, but doesn't get involved in assigning blame or credit to either man over the other.

Basically biographical, this book nevertheless includes some very pithy commentary on the operas. At 550-plus pages, it looks long—but it's so well written that one hates to see it end.

Green, Martyn
Here's a How-de-do: My Life in Gilbert and Sullivan (Norton, New York, 1952)

Green isn't interested in writing a modern autobiography—he tells us how he met his wife but never mentions her first name, mentions "my mother and sisters" about halfway through without revealing their names, and cites his brother only in a photo caption. He says at the beginning that many people have asked why he and 26 others have resigned from the D'Oyly Carte company, but says that he won't discuss it here—and indeed essentially doesn't.

So there's no scandalous stuff, nor anything personal. But Green's perspective as a working actor—not a museum-keeper or an altar votary—is interesting and in its own way revealing. His complaints about the way the Carte company is organized and, in particular, about its ignorance about and scorn of modern publicity are telling, even 30 years before the company's eventual dissolution.

And Green's writing style is delightful—witty, understated, and reminiscent of his contemporary P. G. Wodehouse.

Green, Martyn
  Martyn Green's Treasury of Gilbert and Sullivan (Simon & Schuster, New
  York, 1961)

To Green, of course, D'Oyly Carte is Gilbert & Sullivan, and vice versa. His annotated book reflects not Gilbert & Sullivan as such but rather as interpreted in the canonically approved versions.

Nevertheless, it's a lot of fun, though short—*Thespis, Utopia, Limited,* and *The Grand Duke* are omitted, and Green's brief introductions and seemingly random annotations are fleshed out with sheet music for more than a hundred favorite songs and many of Lucille Corcos's not-very-attractive illustrations drawn from Deems Taylor's *Treasury.* Green's notes focus primarily on his own scenes, with plenty of backstage anecdotes and personal opinions; he also provides some of the usual glossings of unfamiliar terms.

It's a fresh look at D'Oyly Carte, showing clearly how performer-driven the company was by the 1930s and 1940s. Green's tone is light and consistently amusing, much as one imagines his performances were. In all, this is hardly a necessity for the serious student, but it's a welcome diversion.

Halton, Frederick J.
  The Gilbert and Sullivan Operas: A Concordance (Bass, New York, 1935)

Of at least seven books written primarily to elucidate obscure Savoy-opera references, this is the first and the least useful.

Instead of using an annotated-text or dictionary format, Halton goes through each opera, selecting some phrases and disregarding others. An alphabetical index at the end lets one look up particular words but demands two lookings-up per word.

Halton's work is highly dated—besides some very sexist commentary, he uses "niggers" as a commonplace word. Most damaging, his information is often simply wrong, whether through bad proofreading (Ovid's *Metamorphoses* are described as "mythic stories about transportation"), misquoting ("for yam I should get toko" becomes "for jam"), or simple misinformation ("pops of Sillery" he takes to refer not to Sillery champagne being uncorked but rather an obscure Scottish poet named Sillery).

An outdated book; get ye to Ian Bradley for the right stuff.

Hardwick, Michael
  The Drake Guide to Gilbert and Sullivan(Drake, New York, 1973)

A reference work for nonexperts, aimed at the nonfan who is about to attend one of the operas. There are seven parts—a biographical introductory essay; an index of Gilbert & Sullivan characters; plot summaries, with very brief introductions and a collection of excerpted quotes from songs and some lyrics; an index of songs, by first line; a glossary of obscure terms; a discography; and a bibliography.

Unfortunately, most of the sections are badly organized. The character index would be most helpful grouped by show, as would the glossary; both are instead arranged alphabetically. The first-line index should be alphabetical but instead is grouped by show. Only the glossary contains anything fresh or particularly interesting.

Overall, most potential readers will probably turn to Leslie Ayre, *The Gilbert & Sullivan Companion,* a better-organized entry in the same field.

Hayter, Charles
Gilbert and Sullivan (Macmillan, London, 1987)

Hayter is an expert in Victorian theater, and his knowledge of the world in which Gilbert (and, to a lesser extent, Sullivan) moved and how it influenced their works gives his book freshness. His textual criticism is often fresh and convincing, treating story and subject well, though offering little on a thematic level.

But Hayter doesn't know the operas that well. Unfortunately, he is most familiar with the popular but atypical *The Mikado,* which he misguidedly treats as an exemplar of the team's work. He treats only six of the operas in depth, disposing of the others in a paragraph or two; to *The Grand Duke* he allots only a single mention, in a list of "other works."

This cripples an otherwise interesting commentary. Apparently he didn't want to bother studying the operas he didn't already know, and the result is a hit-and-miss book, with revealing insights marred by inaccurate generalizations and flat-out errors.

Hibbert, Christopher
Gilbert & Sullivan and Their Victorian World (American Heritage, New
  York, 1976)

Nothing new here, but the familiar story is smoothly told, with lavish illustrations that are also familiar, but still interesting. Best on the Victorian context for the operas, especially on theater before Gilbert & Sullivan; there is also some interesting American information, especially on early productions.

Hardly essential reading for the Gilbert & Sullivan initiate, and the biographical information is often erroneous.

Hughes, Gervase
The Music of Arthur Sullivan (St. Martin's Press, New York, 1960)

Probably the best book written to date on Sullivan's music. Eschewing biographical/historical detail and resisting the temptation to stray into anecdote, plot summary, or extensive quotation, Hughes brings a musician's eye to Sullivan's works themselves—primarily the Savoy operas, but also his 10 other operas, his symphony, his oratorios, instrumental music, incidental music, and so on.

He clearly knows the music well and isn't afraid to be either critical or enthusiastic, with either position well defended. Instead of proceeding chronologically, he provides separate studies of Sullivan's melodic skills, orchestration, harmonization, and the like, and every section has intriguing insights.

The reader with a thorough musical background will get the most out of this occasionally jargony book, but even the general reader who knows the operas can benefit from reading it.

Jacobs, Arthur
  Arthur Sullivan: A Victorian Musician (Oxford University Press, New York, 1984)

Easily the best biography of Sullivan available. Drawing on uncensored excerpts from Sullivan's diaries and letters (previously bowdlerized in the biography by Herbert Sullivan and Newman Flower), Jacobs places the composer squarely in the context of Victorian music.

By painting a thoroughly convincing picture of Sullivan the man (complete with his flaws, including discreet womanizing and indiscreet gambling) before he even reaches the famous collaboration, Jacobs makes sure that, though the central part of his story is often told, he provides a fresh angle on it.

This is pure biography—what criticism or analysis of the works there is comes primarily in excerpts from contemporary reviews—but as a portrait of the man who wrote the music it is invaluable, far more thorough and well rounded than any previous entry in this category.

Jefferson, Alan
  The Complete Gilbert & Sullivan Opera Guide (Facts on File, New York, 1984)

Jefferson's book of the librettos, along with plot synopses and brief analytic/critical introductions to each opera, is full of absurd opinions, misunderstood facts, and blatant errors. He sees cribbing in virtually every Sullivan tune, sees homosexuality everywhere (in Bunthorne, for example, or in Lord Tolloller, inexplicably described as "traditionally played in falsetto"), and so on and on and on. The libretti themselves are handled in a slapdash manner, and even photo captions are sometimes incorrect.

Here and there Jefferson does have some interesting ideas. His overarching thesis attributing the operas' success to "their deep-rooted foundation on folk tradition" is overstated but interesting, and he has occasional fresh insights into the music and even the characters.

But the sea of errors swamps all else. Overall, the only reason to read this book is for comic relief.

Jones, John Bush, ed.
   W. S. Gilbert: A Century of Scholarship and Commentary (New York University Press, New York, 1970)

A collection of essays from the sublime to the ridiculous. Among the sublime are two early, distinctly unawed reviews of *The Bab Ballads* ("the dreariest and dullest fun we ever met with"); Max Beerbohm's loving appreciation of the ballads; William Archer's still-intriguing 1881 look at Gilbert's plays and early operas; G. K. Chesterton and Isaac Goldberg on Gilbert, each with a splendidly engaging writing style; and Jane W. Stedman and Jones himself with modestly interesting looks at sources for *Patience.*

As for the ridiculous, Herbert Weisinger's essay "The Twisted Cue," considering Gilbert & Sullivan as Christian allegory, stands out. Charles E. Lauterbach devotes a whole essay to how much Gilbert got paid, per inch and per word, by *Fun.* Jones also reprints his own absurdly specialized bibliographical essay on *The Grand Duke.*

Overall, an interesting roundup of diverse opinions on Gilbert. Perhaps Jones will add a Sullivan counterpart sometime.

Lerner, Alan Jay
   The Musical Theatre: A Celebration (McGraw-Hill, New York, 1986)

Only one chapter here on Gilbert & Sullivan, and Lerner obviously is no expert (though he died shortly after completing the book and probably didn't proof it). For example, he asserts that *Princess Ida's* lyrics are in blank verse, he's never heard of *Thespis*, he believes that Sullivan sat in the audience on opening nights, and he thinks that D'Oyly Carte had an American company.

But the chapter is worth reading, if only for the star Broadway lyricist's testimony that "Gilbert was the Adam of modern lyric writing. P. G. Wodehouse, Lorenz Hart, Cole Porter, Ira Gershwin, Oscar Hammerstein and their contemporaries and descendants all owe their lyrical, genetic beginning to W. S. Gilbert."

Unsurprisingly, as a lyricist Lerner also asserts that "[a]lthough one cannot underestimate the grace, skill and melodic invention of Arthur Sullivan, there is no doubt that Gilbert was the driving force."

Lubin, L. B.
   Gilbert without Sullivan (Viking Press, New York, 1981)

The libretti for *H. M. S. Pinafore, The Pirates of Penzance, The Mikado,* and *The Gondoliers* are illustrated by L. B. Lubin in this handsome edition.

Lubin is better at lavish fabrics, intricate furniture, and especially painstakingly rendered flowers than he is with people; his figures rarely suggest the richness of Gilbert's characters, and his choice of subjects is idiosyncratic in the extreme.

Still, this is an attractive book, though of no scholarly importance whatever.

MacLeod, Charlotte
The Plain Old Man (Avon Books, New York, 1985)

A run-of-the-mill murder mystery whose only appeal is its setting in and around an amateur production of *The Sorcerer*.

There are some fairly heavy-handed Gilbert & Sullivan references, but the author is either sloppy or simply uninformed on Gilbert & Sullivan: Several details of the *Sorcerer* plot are wrong, and Mrs. Partlet mysteriously becomes "Dame Partlett" throughout.

There's no suspense to the book and no wit, and the characters aren't especially interesting.

Mander, Raymond, and Joe Mitchenson
A Picture History of Gilbert and Sullivan (Vista Books, London, 1962)

As its title suggests, a book of photos (and a few drawings, posters, and programs) from Savoyard history. All are in black-and-white, which is a pity; one misses the color in Wilson and Lloyd's *Gilbert & Sullivan: The Official D'Oyly Carte Picture History*, and thus the stage pictures are a bit disappointing.

Where Mander and Mitchenson excel, however, is in their selection of non-D'Oyly Carte photos. There are some fresh pictures of Gilbert and Sullivan themselves and many rare shots from their other, non–Gilbert & Sullivan works. A potpourri of non–D'Oyly Carte Gilbert & Sullivan productions, travesties, and parodies is a particular pleasure.

At 160 pages this is a light work, and its presentation is anything but lavish. Still, a good selection of pictures—and generally informative captions—make it worthwhile for the Gilbert & Sullivan fan.

Marriott, J. W., ed.
Great Modern British Plays (George G. Harrap, London, 1928)

Of interest primarily for Gilbert's *Pygmalion and Galatea*, hard to find elsewhere.

Probably the best of Gilbert's verse plays, it offers some fairly good poetry and some interesting philosophical discourse. But the blank-verse format and the very old-fashioned view of women are serious drawbacks—this is interesting to read but stacks up as a good play whose time has nonetheless passed.

The book's other plays, most of them neither great nor modern any more, also include Robertson's *Caste*, which clearly influenced Gilbert in many ways (there are two lines obviously echoed in *The Mikado* and *The Gondoliers*), and *Trelawney of the "Wells,"* by Arthur Wing Pinero, Sullivan's collaborator on the ill-starred *The Beauty Stone*. To judge by the thoroughly engaging *Trelawney*, Pinero was a far better playwright than *The Beauty Stone* would suggest.

McBrien, William
  Cole Porter: A Biography (Knopf, New York, 1998)

An odd book with some strange emphases—Porter's homosexuality is mentioned for the first time (offhandedly) on page 96 of a 400-page book—but it is generally a convincing portrait of a man who was more charming than likable, as well as being arguably the best songwriter since Gilbert & Sullivan.

Porter's early Gilbert & Sullivan influences are made clear, as well as his later move toward other genres, especially Latin music. And even late in his life, we learn, Porter frequently attended D'Oyly Carte performances.

Most of us would probably not agree with Ring Lardner, however, who in reviewing *The Gay Divorce* (1932) wrote that in a single couplet—"Night and day, under the hide of me, / there's an, oh, such a hungry yearning burning inside of me"—"Mr. Porter not only makes a monkey of his contemporaries but shows up Gilbert as a seventh-rate Gertrude Stein."

Moore, Frank Ledlie
  Crowell's Handbook of Gilbert and Sullivan (Crowell, New York, 1962)

A fairly good reference work, consisting of opera summaries (including production information, original cast, song lists, plot summary, and historical notes); capsule bios of Gilbert, Sullivan, and Carte; a listing of all the original creators of G & S roles; a G & S timeline; indexes of G & S characters, song titles, and famous lines; and a selection of the famous songs (including some music, plus the complete lyrics); and a bibliography.

Moore writes well, and his concept is good—the timeline is particularly interesting, while the indexes are useful (though unconventionally alphabetized, using "The" as the first word for a great many songs).

Unfortunately, he is sloppy, committing numerous minor but noticeable errors—a serious failing in a reference work. Still, he has some interesting, fresh points, and his work is worth reading, as long as one has the background to catch his errors.

Olsen, David C., ed.
  The Best of Gilbert & Sullivan (CPP/Belwin, Miami, FL, n.d.)

A songbook with a total of 54 songs from *H. M. S. Pinafore*, *The Pirates of Penzance*, *The Mikado*, and *The Gondoliers*. The arrangements are simplified, with all harmonies omitted; the words appear to be accurate. Much better versions are available in the Green/Taylor *Treasury*.

Orel, Harold, ed.
>*Gilbert & Sullivan: Interviews and Recollections* (University of Iowa Press, Iowa City, 1994)

This collection of 40 original-source periodical articles and book extracts is essential to a serious student of Gilbert & Sullivan.

Orel's notes are haphazard and often incorrect, but his selection of materials, ranging from widely known sources such as Arthur Lawrence, Gilbert's biographical essay for *The Theatre*, William Archer, and Cellier-Bridgeman through rarer materials such as the autobiographies of Rutland Barrington, Henry Lytton, and John Hollingshead to real rarities such as Nellie Melba, the earl of Dunraven, and C. V. Stanford, is invaluable.

Together, these "real people" contemporaries of Gilbert and Sullivan offer a unique view of these iconic figures as real men doing the real work of producing real entertainments that turned out, to everyone's surprise, to be enduring classics.

Pearson, Hesketh
>*Gilbert: His Life and Strife* (Harper, New York, 1957)

Pearson uses Gilbert's diaries and letters to paint a convincing picture of an angry man who nevertheless had a pronounced warm streak, especially for young women and for anyone in need of help. It's a persuasive picture, convincingly attributed to Gilbert's troubled family background.

Pearson tells his story tersely and with a suitable theatricality. His 269-page book seems barely 100 pages long, so briskly does it move; yet he isn't afraid to linger on important details, such as the relationship between Gilbert's parents.

Finally, Pearson is writing a biography of Gilbert and knows it. His subject is born on the second page of his narrative and dies on the final page. There's little on Sullivan or on the operas themselves—and what there is is usually misguided—but he delivers what he aims for: A sturdy, unspeculative biography that remains an effective portrait of a fascinating man.

Rees, Terence
>*Thespis: A Gilbert & Sullivan Enigma* (Dillin's University Bookshop, London, 1964)

An agreeably short (100 pages plus the *Thespis* libretto), focused book. Rees thoroughly explores all the original sources—letters, press reports, reviews, memoirs—and reports his findings in writing that is crisp and to the point, yet very readable.

Rees reconstructs the circumstances of *Thespis* admirably and argues convincingly that the surviving *Thespis* libretto differs substantially from the performed version. (Ironically, Gilbert was editing proofs of a collected edition of his plays when he died; had he lived even a few more days, he probably would have corrected *Thespis*, resolving many problematic aspects of the text.)

There may be more to be said about the content of *Thespis*, but it seems impossible that (barring the unearthing of the original score) any subsequent work will have anything significantly new to offer as to its history. This is a very good book, essential for anyone interested in *Thespis*.

Searle, Ronald
  Dick Deadeye (Harcourt Brace Jovanovich, New York, 1975)

This book of drawings from the animated film *Dick Deadeye, or Duty Done* is far from essential for any Gilbert & Sullivan student but entertaining nevertheless.

Searle's drawings are delightful, detailed yet never cluttered (particularly a busty Little Buttercup and a thoroughly sinister J. W. Wells), while his bawdy versions of Gilbert & Sullivan characters reveal both a love for the Savoy operas and a healthy freedom from veneration.

The whole thing has a loopy incoherence that makes it great fun.

Smith, Geoffrey
  The Savoy Operas (Universe Books, New York, 1985)

Smith does surprisingly well in "giving each opera an affectionate dusting-off to show how, freed from preconceptions, it actually works as entertainment." Himself a musician, he has much insightful musical commentary throughout.

He is less consistent on the words. On-the-mark commentary on *The Mikado* follows misreading of *Iolanthe* and *Princess Ida* prompted by the very preconceptions he scorns. He reads *The Gondoliers* cannily but all-but-completely misreads *The Yeomen of the Guard*. And he neither knows nor cares anything about *Thespis*, *Utopia, Limited*, or *The Grand Duke*.

Smith is better on lyrics than on characters or themes. He handles satire well—his summary of the treatment of aestheticism in *Patience* is perfect—but rarely sees further. Still, that he even acknowledges the operas' thematic element is refreshing.

Despite weak spots, Smith's work is excellent—a step forward that, one hopes, will inspire others to move further.

Stedman, Jane W.
  W. S. Gilbert: A Classic Victorian and His Theatre (Oxford University
  Press, New York, 1996)

Easily the definitive biography of Gilbert, making a fine companion for Jacobs on Sullivan.

Stedman's meticulous research casually demolishes apocryphal stories, accepted generalizations, and easy categorizations. Even when she has nothing substantially new to report (on the "carpet quarrel," for example), Stedman can be relied on for the telling detail or an illuminating alternative viewpoint.

The book is strongest on Gilbert's early work (reflecting Stedman's own expertise) and on his final years (reflecting her invaluable contacts with people who knew Gilbert first- or secondhand in the 1900s). As its title suggests, the book also draws masterfully on Stedman's encyclopedic knowledge of the Victorian theater to put Gilbert in his native setting, a setting largely unfamiliar to previous writers.

A most insightful, illuminating work.

Stone, Michael Shawn, and W. S. Gilbert & Arthur Sullivan
    Thespis (Unpublished)

This reconstructed *Thespis* is better at identifying problems than solving them. Like Rees, Stone deems the existing libretto a rough draft; thus he feels free to rewrite it whole hog, cutting or rearranging lines and whole scenes, interpolating dialogue from other Gilbert & Sullivan operas, and writing his own new material.

The script's cut-and-paste nature is glaringly obvious, and Stone's footnoted justifications are unintentionally hilarious. While I haven't seen the score, it must be similarly haphazard, consisting of stitched-together passages from various Sullivan tunes, often four or five to a song. Sullivan's music was extremely site specific, and this approach seems fatally flawed.

On the other hand, Stone has a good sense of *Thespis* as a theatrical work, and his offbeat solutions at least help point out cruxes in the play; a few even seem effective. (His editing of the dialogue, however unjustified, certainly improves it overall.)

Sullivan, Herbert, and Newman Flower
    Sir Arthur Sullivan: His Life, Letters and Diaries
    (Cassell, London, 1927)

Entirely superseded by the Arthur Jacobs biography, this is a fine example of the hagiographic school of biography prevalent earlier in the century.

This Sullivan, as presented by his nephew and an illustrious and prolific but conventional biographer, has no warts at all—he hardly gambles, "resigns himself to celibacy" at an early age (his relationship with Fannie Ronalds, who is mentioned only three times in the book, is described only as "frequently misunderstood"), and so on.

For all that, it's smoothly written and many of the letters and diary entries are of interest. Still, Jacobs convincingly demonstrates that these entries have been highly censored, and there are frequent errors; those interested in fully understanding Sullivan in his own right should turn to Jacobs.

Sutton, Max Keith
   W. S. Gilbert (G. K. Hall, Boston, 1975)

An indispensable source on Gilbert in pre-Sullivan days, Sutton is one of the rare authors to acknowledge the thematic aspect of the Savoy operas.

Unfortunately, his writing is often overly academic and assumes familiarity with writers from Aristophanes to the Victorians; it's a slow read, though often rewarding.

And Sutton's attempt to make what I call the head-versus-heart dilemma ("the individual versus the law," to him) into the operas' sole theme distorts his analysis. He is strongest where this thematic element is heavy—*The Mikado*, especially, and *The Pirates of Penzance*. He is on the right track with *Iolanthe* and *Ruddigore* but loses his way through misemphasis. On some others, he's way off the mark.

But a must read, especially for his efforts to link Gilbert's early plays and later works—thematically, instead of a simplistic "This Bab ballad foreshadows this opera."

Taylor, Deems, ed.
   A Treasury of Gilbert and Sullivan (Simon and Schuster, New York, 1941)

A standard treasury of the more popular Gilbert & Sullivan tunes, with oversimplified and transposed piano arrangements. Taylor's brief introductions to the operas are often factually wrong, and the magazine-illustration, 1940s-style cartoons by Lucille Corcos haven't worn well.

Martyn Green's Treasury of Gilbert and Sullivan is generally better, offering the same illustrations and musical arrangements (skillfully done by Albert Sirmay), and with commentary that's more recent, more knowledgeable, and more engagingly written.

Tennyson, Alfred
   "The Princess," in *The Poetical Works of Tennyson*, G. Robert Stange, ed.
   (Houghton Mifflin, Boston, 1974)

Obviously, this poem is the single most essential text for anyone seeking to understand *Princess Ida*. Otherwise, while it may have been popular and even good for its day, it's difficult to get through now, owing to its artificial language and stilted meter.

Still, Tennyson has much of interest to say in his own right, and the poem repays the necessary effort. And it provides the ground on which Gilbert shaped *Princess Ida*, offering a beacon to guide readers to an understanding of that all-too-misunderstood opera.

Thane, Adele
   Gilbert and Sullivan Operas Adapted for Half-Hour Performance (Plays,
      Boston, 1976)

Of no scholarly significance, this is a collection of half-hour versions of
eight of the operas, aimed at school performances.

Some aspects of the adaptations are quite clever—Thane has a knack
for compressing portions of two or more verses into a single verse that
works. Others are achingly bad, as one would expect from so quixotic an
enterprise—the insertion of spoken dialogue into *Trial by Jury* or the
choice to have Jack Point simply "exit" at the end of *The Yeomen of the
Guard* stand out.

And Sullivan is trashed throughout, with portions of verses left to stand
alone or fused awkwardly onto other portions of other verses; all harmonies are omitted, and the music is without even piano accompaniment.

Half-hour Gilbert & Sullivan operas are hardly necessary; if they must
exist, though, these are as good as any other.

Williamson, Audrey
   Gilbert & Sullivan Opera: A New Assessment (Marion Boyers, London,
      1953/1982)

Despite a number of flaws, this is the single best book on the operas
themselves yet to appear.

Williamson has little thematic concept of the operas, but she illuminates
the techniques of storytelling and songwriting with a keen eye and profuse
examples. She is almost uniquely iconoclastic, criticizing Saint Gilbert and
Saint Sullivan whenever necessary. Though she never really understands
the operas themselves, she does provide numerous worthwhile insights.

Supposedly revised in 1982, the book still contains detailed critiques of
the D'Oyly Carte productions of the operas as they stood in 1953, which
gets tiring quickly. And, as with most writers, Williamson has a hard time
distinguishing the Gilbert & Sullivan operas from their D'Oyly Carte productions.

Still, 40-plus years later, this remains essential for anyone interested in
a more-than-superficial understanding of the operas.

Wilson, Robin, and Frederic Lloyd
   Gilbert & Sullivan: The Official D'Oyly Carte Picture History (Knopf, New
      York, 1984)

This is a "picture history" with the emphasis on the "picture," not the
"history." Fan Wilson and longtime D'Oyly Carte general manager Lloyd
aren't interested in a balanced appraisal of D'Oyly Carte and its legacy in
the history of Gilbert & Sullivan. Controversy is sugar coated, seldom even
alluded to, and never detailed or evaluated.

Instead, we have 107-plus years' worth of pictures. Most are black-and-white production photos of various artists in their roles and are very interesting as documentation of costume designs and (to some extent) long-gone performers' interpretations of classic roles. The few color pictures, mostly of sets and of costume designs, are even more interesting.

Hardly worth the name "history," this book should still be interesting to anyone who loves Gilbert & Sullivan; to anyone who loved D'Oyly Carte, it should be downright fascinating.

Wolfson, John
  Final Curtain: The Last Gilbert and Sullivan Operas (Chappell, London, 1976)

This study of *Utopia, Limited* and *The Grand Duke* mixes interesting information and absurd interpretations. Wolfson presents the original rehearsal scripts and traces the various revisions (and how they affected the final versions) to fascinating effect.

On the other hand, his conclusions are laughable. He sees both operas as attacks on English society and on Sullivan in particular. His evidence is sometimes wrong (his idea that Julia Jellico is a parody of Queen Victoria stems primarily from the mistaken notion that the queen spoke with a strong German accent) and sometimes merely silly (he takes every mention of Ireland as a snub to Sullivan, for example).

Fortunately, the texts are included in full, and one can check them out without reading Wolfson's whimsical interpretations unless one feels the urge for a vexed chuckle.

Young, Percy M.
  Sir Arthur Sullivan (Norton, New York, 1971)

Falling somewhere between Arthur Jacobs's definitive biography and Gervase Hughes's meticulous musicological study, Young's book combines elements of both books without quite matching either. His biographical material has been superseded by that of Jacobs, while his musical analysis has less depth than that of Hughes.

Still, this is a smooth and workmanlike book, offering a good introduction for the musically literate beginner. It is, however, marred by an inexplicable lapse into pop psychology on literally the last page. Here, in quick succession, we "learn" without evidence that Sullivan was "strongly homo-erotic, as instanced in his relationship with Grove" and that this was "in large part, no doubt, due to his particular and long dependence on his brother."

Add to these inane suggestions the assertion that the famously open-handed Sullivan had an obsessive fear of poverty, and Young's previously impressive work is noticeably diminished.

Index

The following codes indicate operas and plays: *FF = Fallen Fairies, FotR = Fiddler on the Roof, G = The Gondoliers, GD = The Grand Duke, H = Hamlet, HMS = H. M. S. Pinafore, I = Iolanthe, IoBE = The Importance of Being Earnest, M = The Mikado, P = Patience, PI = Princess Ida, PoP = The Pirates of Penzance, OIH = Our Island Home, R = Ruddigore, S = The Sorcerer, T = Thespis, TBJ = Trial by Jury, U = Utopia Limited, WW = The Wicked World, Y = The Yeomen of the Guard.*